Cultural Contingencies

Cultural Contingencies

BEHAVIOR ANALYTIC PERSPECTIVES ON CULTURAL PRACTICES

Edited by
P. A. Lamal

PRAEGER

Westport, Connecticut
London

Library of Congress Cataloging-in-Publication Data

Cultural contingencies : behavior analytic perspectives on cultural
    practices / edited by P.A. Lamal.
        p.   cm.
    Includes bibliographical references and index.
    ISBN 0–275–95776–4 (alk. paper)
    1. Social psychology.   2. Behavioral assessment.   3. Social
interaction.   4. Human behavior.   I. Lamal, Peter A.
    HM251.C945   1997
    302—dc21   97–1919

British Library Cataloguing in Publication Data is available.

Library of Congress Catalog Card Number: 97–1919
ISBN: 0–275–95776–4

First published in 1997

Praeger Publishers, 88 Post Road West, Westport, CT 06881
An imprint of Greenwood Publishing Group, Inc.

Printed in the United States of America

The paper used in this book complies with the
Permanent Paper Standard issued by the National
Information Standards Organization (Z39.48–1984).

10 9 8 7 6 5 4 3 2 1

To the Memory of My Parents
Isabel Conway Lamal and Andre Lamal

Contents

Preface

The 1990s have seen renewed interest in a behavior analytic approach to societies and cultural practices. Books on the subject have been published and a number of relevant articles have appeared. Convention presentations have been devoted to the topic. The behavioral analysis of cultural practices continues to mature and evolve. This book is a contribution to the ongoing development of this area.

This book eschews chapters devoted to consideration of behavior analytic concepts and principles in the abstract; many other books and articles already provide the reader with excellent outlines and explanations of those concepts and principles. In contrast, the contents of this book are wholly devoted to consideration of particular cultural practices, across three countries. The first four chapters are concerned with cultural practices having to do with individual and public health, Chapters 7–9 are concerned with contingencies that affect families. Other chapters (5, 6, 10, 11, and 12) address a variety of cultural practices. At first glance it may appear that the reader is presented with a potpourri, but that is not, in a fundamental sense, true. What gives these diverse chapters coherence is their shared foundation in a behavior analytic approach to the description and interpretation of cultural practices.

I thank Paul Foos, Chairman of the Psychology Department of the University of North Carolina at Charlotte, for his support; I also thank the department's staff. Special thanks goes to George Windholz for help with indexing.

Cultural Contingencies

1

Preventive Medicine and Cultural Contingencies: A Natural Experiment

MELBOURNE F. HOVELL, DENNIS R. WAHLGREN, AND STERGIOS RUSSOS

Preventive medicine is a subspecialty of medicine, analogous to surgery. Physicians and other clinicians are obligated by professional standards and cultural norms to screen for potential disease and injury, and to provide services that will prevent or mitigate the severity of impending disease or injury. These services are to be provided in addition to curative care, usually in the context of curative care medical visits. All physicians, even highly specialized surgeons, are expected by peers and patients to provide some level of preventive and primary care services. However, the extent to which clinical medicine physicians provide preventive services appears limited (Hovell, Kaplan, & Hovell, 1991).

The concern about failure to provide critical preventive medicine services is illustrated by the Centers for Disease Control and Prevention (CDC) funded program for increasing childhood immunization (e.g., Infant Immunization Initiative: County of San Diego Department of Health Services, 1992). This program contains a number of features, including school record reviews, but most interestingly, it includes direct prompts to private physicians to check medical histories and provide immunizations for those children not yet immunized. This program would not be needed if clinicians were already achieving the accepted standards of medical care. This failure demonstrates the need for interventions that can establish and sustain both primary and preventive services.

The practice of medicine in the United States is undergoing major changes. The political controversies surrounding Hillary Clinton and the Clinton administration in their attempt to establish a major revision in medical care financing was but a dramatic step in an ongoing process which is changing medical care. The ultimate form to be taken by medical care services in this country is yet to be determined. However, some of the factors responsible for change are apparent and some of these will be discussed as they apply to both curative and preventive medicine. Some of the changes are in response to advances in science and technology, some are due to changes in the causes of disease, some are due to ongoing trends in costs of care, and some are due to changes in the broader culture within which the practice of medicine takes place.

The superimposition of "managed care" on traditional curative medicine and the recent addition of responsibility to prevent disease and promote well-being are interacting to radically change the practice of medicine. Perhaps not since the advent of readily available antibiotics and vaccines has there been as great an "in vivo experiment" in medical care. Managed care is reputedly aimed at reducing costs of medical care, a relatively new constraint on the practice of medicine, including preventive medicine (O'Connor & Lanning, 1992). Preventive medicine has evolved in the last 25 years to the point of a recognized specialty, and prevention has become an important goal of all medical care. This change probably came about, in part, due to reductions in infectious diseases and the recognition that lifestyles are associated with chronic disease. The combination of trends in the development of managed care, or cost containment, and the concurrent trends toward expansion of preventive medicine services represent the outcomes to date of a profound and ongoing experiment in the practice of medicine, which has now reached the point of dramatic effects—both beneficial and damaging.

This chapter will extend our previous review (Hovell et al., 1991) of factors responsible for preventive medicine services. This extension will be both theoretically interpretive and based on empirical evidence from our own work as well as the literature. It will emphasize the probable role of changes in disease etiology in relation to medical technology, the influence of reimbursement and social consequences on clinicians' practices, and the likely effects of managed care on prevention procedures. This review will be founded on our interpretation of operant learning and its extensions to cultural influences (Lamal, 1991; Skinner, 1953). Principles derived from this model will be employed to help explain why the practice of preventive medicine has come about, why it is not practiced at a higher rate, as well as how to increase the rate at which it is practiced.

THEORETICAL BACKGROUND

Behavioral-Ecological Model

We have employed an extension of the operant learning model of individual behavior, with liberal adoption of the concept of metacontingencies (Glenn, 1988). Our model is an expansion of an operant explanation of behavior which emphasizes application within multiple social systems (Willems, 1974). This model presumes that an individual's behavior is selected as a function of consequences (response/consequence contingencies). The model presumes that contingencies of reinforcement and punishment may be viewed on a continuum from the simple to complex schedules, with contingencies applicable to an individual to those affecting whole communities. Glenn (1988) defined a meta-contingency as a functional relation between a cultural practice and the outcome it produces. The outcome selects for sets of interlocking behavioral contingencies affecting the behavior of the group's members. Because most such interlocking contingencies are social (i.e., provided by other people), the metacontingency selects for patterns of behavior across individuals in a group. We have operationally defined metacontingencies as social contingencies of reinforcement that affect a large segment of the population or subpopulations, where many individuals (members of a particular culture) who provide consequences for others' behavior are not necessarily working in collusion with one another; the strength of the metacontingency can be defined, in part, by the probability/rate of an individual encountering social consequences. We assume that metacontingencies are probabilistic and that any given individual may vary in his/her likelihood of encountering contingent consequences. The probability that an individual will acquire behavior consistent with the cultural practice is directly related to the frequency with which the person encounters the contingency. High-density metacontingencies are pervasive across individuals within a defined group (e.g., students at a school, licensed drivers, employees of a company, Californians, members of a particular ethnicity, etc.). Metacontingencies include such concrete systems as laws, and incarceration or financial penalties for violations, or government/business policies that stipulate behavior-consequence contingencies that apply to employees. Corporate policies regarding dress codes may illustrate such a small-scale metacontingency: most or every individual member of a corporate organization will encounter the contingency, will encounter it several times from several sources, and act to perpetuate it by informing new members. This leads to common dress styles.

Engineering Metacontingencies

The Behavioral-Ecological Model presumes that metacontingencies can be engineered. This is illustrated by governmental laws and policies. Although it is hard to define the origin of a series of interlocking contingencies, reference to the California initiative system, by which voters can pass policy laws, provides some examples. One of these is the 1988 California Proposition 99 initiative (Tobacco Tax and Health Promotion Initiative), which resulted in a tax on cigarettes from which 20% of the revenue had to be spent on antitobacco interventions. About seven years later, the social climate in California regarding cigarette use is now remarkably and increasingly negative. While antismoking educational campaigns may have had only minimal *direct* effects on tobacco use, these campaigns have shaped among the nonsmoking public a critical response to smoking: the probability that a smoker will encounter a nonsmoker who actively avoids him/her, or who asks the smoker to refrain, is now much higher. The combination of increased price of cigarettes and negative social sanctions is almost certainly responsible for the dramatic decrease in prevalence rates among adult smokers, a nearly threefold greater decrease than experienced in the rest of the country (Pierce et al., 1994). The initiative illustrates engineered social contingencies now affecting smokers almost everywhere in the state, even the United States. President Clinton's proposal to require the Food and Drug Administration (FDA) to regulate tobacco as an addictive drug, and to set policies restricting tobacco advertising to decrease adolescent use of tobacco, is partially attributable to the change in social acceptance of tobacco. The effects of FDA regulation are yet to be determined, but can be expected to influence public opinion substantially, which may, in turn, affect tobacco use. Regulatory effects are already evident in the decision of at least one major department store chain to cease carrying tobacco products (Feder, 1996).

Legal, policy-based, and social metacontingencies are operating to influence physicians' practice of preventive and curative medicine. We next examine several metacontingencies which may have played a role in the development of modern preventive medicine, and which may contribute to its decline or rise to further importance. The sources of control of the practice of preventive medicine will be examined in the history of preventive medicine and the biology of disease, interlocking social contingencies between physicians and patients, financial and business-based contingencies (e.g., managed care), and politically and professionally imposed contingencies.

HISTORY OF PREVENTIVE MEDICINE

Germ Theory

Traditional medicine has been based on "Germ Theory," proposed by Louis Pasteur in 1861, since the discovery of microorganisms and drug "treatments." This model presumes that an invading organism causes illness. The illness can be cured by killing the organism. Since the discovery of antibiotics, the use of drugs has been the treatment of choice. Indeed, next to surgery, pharmacotherapy is synonymous with medicine—witness the use of the phrase "Take your medicine." The relative effectiveness and ease of administration of antibiotics provides a highly reinforcing consequence for the prescription of drugs. The institutionalization of curative drug treatment in medicine may be conceptualized as a metacontingency supporting medical care behavior that competes with or is incompatible with preventive services.

Germ theory led to the development of preventive medicine. Infectious diseases can be prevented by blocking exposure to the infectious agent: quarantine remains an important control procedure even today. For instance, communicable disease units within hospitals are isolated by space and technology from all other areas of the hospital in order to prevent the transmission of disease from infected to uninfected patients. Prevention also can be achieved with the artificial production of natural immunity to infectious agents. The use of vaccines, live or attenuated forms of infectious organisms, can be administered to healthy individuals in order to elicit development of antibodies and other changes in the immune system, enabling it to attack the live infectious organism if the individual is later exposed. The Salk vaccine for polio is a classic example. Although use of vaccines may require patients to attend a medical clinic, little lifestyle practice need be changed to effect prevention. The ease of use and effectiveness of these drugs could add to the support of simple ''magic bullet'' cure or preventive services. As drug treatments have become nearly synonymous with the practice of medicine, so has the use of vaccines become synonymous with preventive medicine. Unfortunately, the germ theory has proved less useful for some infectious agents for which drug therapy is limited or for which vaccines are not developed (e.g., AIDS), and for diseases that are caused by processes other than infectious agents.

Shift from Acute to Chronic Disease

Since the early part of the twentieth century, the rate of illness and death from infectious disease has fallen. This change, while possibly due to improved medical care and the use of antibiotics, was very likely due to improved sewer systems, sanitized water, and improved nutrition of the population. Regardless of the cause, the decrease in infectious disease and concurrent increase in life expectancy led to increased focus on chronic diseases. Chronic disease is now responsible for most deaths and increasing levels of disability in developed nations (U.S. Department of Health and Human Services [U.S. DHHS], 1995). Coronary disease is one of the most notable chronic diseases and remains the number-one killer in the United States. Chronic diseases tend to be caused by a combination of one's genes, lifestyle, and environmental factors, with little contribution from infectious organisms. Traditional medicine has not been as effective for chronic as for infectious diseases; dramatic cures of the kind achieved by antibiotic therapy are not attained. Medicine has continued to rely on that part of the repertoire that has been most richly reinforced, drug treatments, but with less complete reversal of disease. This attenuated effectiveness may result in leaner schedules of intermittent reinforcement. This shift toward leaner schedules can be expected to increase resistance to extinction (i.e., sustain drug use as a treatment choice); it may also increase variability in treatment choices, some of which may be more effective (and possibly reinforcing) than drug treatment. These experiences may lead to discovery of alternatives to ineffective drug treatment, and discrimination regarding effective versus ineffective treatments.

Shift to Behavioral Risk Factor Treatments

Increased research into the etiology of chronic diseases has led to a recognition of the substantial influence of behavior and lifestyle. Specialists in preventive medicine now recognize the need for changing lifestyle practices as well as treating medically the signs and symptoms of chronic disease. Screening for risk conditions is standard practice, especially for adult patients. However, the prescriptions provided in the face of identified risks tend to emphasize traditional medicine. Physicians may casually advise patients to exercise or eat a lower-calorie diet, and to lower cholesterol and high blood pressure. However, most practitioners emphasize prescription medications known to lower biological precursors of disease, such as elevated cholesterol. This appears to be a subtle generalization from standard curative care—the use of antibiotic drugs to treat infectious disease—to the use of drugs for changing chronic conditions. Unfortunately, the use of medication for long-term control of risk factors brings risk in its own right; drug treatment of elevated cholesterol or other risk conditions can be toxic, may not lower the level of cholesterol enough to reduce risk of disease, and may not be safe to sustain for all patients.

As these drug treatments have proven to be relatively weak preventive agents, preventive medicine practitioners have added recommendations for changes in lifestyle practices and medical interventions to assist in lifestyle change, such as the prescription of nicotine gum or transdermal patches to aid smokers in quitting. Even where behavior change has been the target for preventive medicine, emphasis has been directed to drug-based interventions to aid behavior change efforts. Advice to change behavior remains at the level provided by a friend, which can yield changes in a small proportion of patients (possibly achieving an important public health benefit) but which fails to approximate the clinical effects often attained from antibiotics.

Limited Ability to Change Behavior—A Metacontingency

Unfortunately, the addition of lifestyle change to the preventive medicine agenda has not been followed by the provision of training to medical students in principles of behavior and procedures of behavior change; nor has it provided clinicians with the best context, access, or basis for sustaining behavior change. For instance, physicians interested in increasing patients' rate of exercise cannot observe exercise in a clinic setting, cannot observe exercise while the patient is presenting with an illness, and cannot provide prompts to initiate, or consequences for, exercising. In short, physicians cannot directly shape the behavior. The physician or other clinician is generally limited to advice or possibly contingency management procedures, if trained to understand them. With few tools and unfavorable conditions for changing behavior, physicians are at risk of failing in their attempts. Failed attempts by physicians to change patient behavior are likely to extinguish future attempts. When initial attempts to modify patient behavior fail across several individual physicians, and this is replicated at several institutions, the practice, the training of the practice, and the support of professional organizations are likely to extinguish. This may represent an extinction metacontingency.

Ineffectiveness of Medication and Reliance on Lifestyle Changes

Preventive medicine recently has been extended to the prevention of infectious diseases for which curative medicine is no longer effective. The classic example of an infectious disease for which physicians have had to emphasize recommended changes in lifestyle is AIDS. Caused by a retrovirus similar to that which causes the common cold, science has not yet produced a reliable means of drug treatment or an effective vaccine for AIDS. Physicians are left with palliative care for the ill and recommendations for reduction in risk practices for both uninfected as well as infected patients.

Evolution of Infectious Organisms and Their Dynamic Interaction with Medicine and Public Health

This change in the practice of medicine is profound, as it applies not just to AIDS, but to many diseases for which traditional medical care is no longer reliable. As microorganisms evolve, new strains are proving insensitive to antibiotic and antiviral drugs, and even to the chlorine used to ensure the safety of drinking water (Garrett, 1994; Tenover, 1995; Vess et al., 1993; Wu & Jiang, 1992). The drug resistant microorganism responsible for tuberculosis is an example. Antibiotics have been widely used only since World War II, and evolutionary changes in microorganisms are only now far enough along for us to detect drug resistant strains, and to recognize that this evolution is a natural and unavoidable process. Microorganisms are undergoing constant genetic change, with selection of those organisms most capable of surviving in today's world. Surviving in the context of antibiotics is part of this ecology. The degree to which drug resistant strains of microorganisms will cause disease and death cannot be predicted with certainty; however, this should not be interpreted as a minor problem. The potential for renewed infectious disease epidemics other than AIDS is substantial. The implications are profound. To control infectious diseases as we have in the last 50 years will require accelerating pharmaceutical and biomedical bench science in order to discover new medications that can destroy new infectious agents without damaging patients. This may require discoveries faster than we can make them. Rapid increases in drug resistant disease will require more historical approaches to control and prevention of disease.

Historically, such approaches have involved preventing people from coming in contact with the infectious agent. What makes this a profound change in medicine and preventive medicine is that effective means of preventing exposure often require substantive changes in lifestyle practices. AIDS, again, serves as a classic example. To avoid exposure to HIV, injected drug use must be avoided, or sterile equipment used; sexual intercourse must be avoided, or condoms employed. To prevent infections as well as chronic diseases (or precursor conditions), clinicians must change patients' behavior. Reducing the incidence of colds, for instance, may be achieved by teaching people not to touch their face, mouth, nose, or eyes (Corley et al., 1987).

However, the frequency with which physicians promote these types of preventive activities is likely to oscillate between behavior change efforts and drug treatment, depending on the relative ease and success of each type of treatment. The success of drug treatments or vaccines will oscillate over time as organisms evolve and drug resistant strains arise. One of the most important metacontingencies affecting medicine, which evokes lifestyle-directed preventive medicine services, is the natural oscillation between use of pharmaceutical agents to kill infectious organisms and the evolution of organisms that are drug resistant. Changes in the nature of illnesses, and physicians' ability to prevent or cure them by traditional means, will lead physicians to increase (or decrease) their attempts at behavior change. The practitioner's varying emphasis on drug versus behavior change interventions will depend, in part, on social contingencies as well.

SOCIAL CONTINGENCIES AFFECTING MEDICINE

Audience Control

One of the more powerful and least-studied metacontingencies likely to be responsible for the type and style of delivery of medical services stems from patients' requests and feedback. Patients request or demand services and outcomes, and provide varying types of feedback once services are delivered. The nature and opportunity for discussion and even debate between a physician and patient change importantly with the addition of lifestyle changes as part of the advice provided by the physician.

Historically, physicians have been viewed as experts: professionals whose rare knowledge and skill should be solicited by patients and followed blindly in order to effect cures. This cultural contingency is most likely to be sustained where patients do not understand the pathophysiology or the treatment provided. They only understand that the treatment often works or works better than the alternatives. Taking an antibiotic is simply taking a pill from the patient's perspective. Taking pills has worked and worked very quickly in the modern history of medicine. Further, the patient has a history of receiving a drug treatment from most physicians seen and for most disorders, and is constantly barraged with media promotion of drug treatments. Even the first recommendation from peers is to try an over-the-counter drug or see a physician for a prescription medication. This experience has taught the patient that physicians are expert and their treatments, especially drug treatments, work fast. Hence, the evolution of the "magic bullet."

Patients Have Learned that Immediate Cure Is Possible

Under these conditions, patients do not question physicians very much and they tend to follow simple instructions to take a medication for limited periods.

Most medications prescribed have been so powerful that even relatively great deviations in adherence to the prescription on the patient's part have not compromised effectiveness. Taking an antibiotic for three to four days may result in cessation of almost all symptoms and the patient may recover completely even if he/she does not complete the prescribed two-week regimen. This represents a cultural learning history where patients ask for and expect simple and effective treatment. Patients also ask for and expect magic bullets for chronic disease and for many newly developing infectious diseases, which the physician cannot reliably supply.

Patient Reactions to Behavior Change Prescriptions

When clinicians advise behavior change to prevent disease, patients are usually being asked to change well-established lifestyles for which long histories of ongoing reinforcement can be assumed. Simply being asked to give up these reinforcers can be expected to elicit anxiety and countercontrol, and result in limited attempts to change. A patient's history of failure to change diet or other lifestyles can result in loss of confidence about the practitioner's expertise. Future contacts may involve greater patient demand for a quick cure—a pill that will enable fast weight loss—without giving up the reinforcers now attained from eating high-calorie diets, and without giving up substantial leisure time on the couch.

As physicians continue to discuss behavior change objectives, the patient may become an equal or even greater "expert" in the conversation. No longer is the issue seemingly complex or mysterious as it is with pathophysiology. All adults are as expert about behavior as the physician. This change in the relationship can be expected to diminish the physician's "authority," or stimulus control effects and, for experienced patients with a history of advice to alter behavior and repeated attempts that failed, simply prescribing change may not even result in trying, let alone sustained behavior change.

The Power of Feedback

We have recently completed a clinical trial designed to decrease the number of adolescents who begin smoking tobacco. The study required clinicians (orthodontists and their staffs) to provide adolescents with "prescriptions" and counseling that described negative consequences of tobacco use and to formally ask them never to start. The rates of prescription delivery were recorded and a number of possible determinants of prescribing practices were explored. The most powerful correlates of prescribing rates were: praise or positive statements from patients, models (other staff providing prescriptions), and the use of a tracking system that enabled the orthodontist and staff to know who was and was not provided a prescription (Russos et al., in press).

These results suggest that the orthodontists and clinical staffs who tracked the delivery of prescriptions and who received positive feedback from the youth were more likely to provide the target number of prescriptions than those who did not. Praise is a well-recognized potential reinforcer and it is no surprise that positive feedback from patients could contribute to practitioners' frequency of preventive medicine practices.

We replicated this analysis but limited it to counseling provided only by the orthodontist (Russos et al., 1995). This showed that an average of 25.0% of the orthodontists in the experimental condition provided counseling to avoid to-bacco, while only 3.2% did so among controls. This suggests that the interven-tion markedly increased counseling levels among these doctors, but left substantial room for even greater increases. This analysis also demonstrated that counseling youth to never start smoking was associated with receiving praise from patients, praise from staff, and praise from parents (Russos et al., 1995). Again, the "audience control" was apparent, where the audience included the patient, the patient's parent(s), and other staff. However, in some ways, the association between prescription provision and tracking of outcome by the cli-nician is even more important.

Tracking, Discriminating Success, and the Public Health Perspective

Physicians may not assess the proportion of patients who change and they may not track the patients asked to change. Simple tracking systems might provide a source of reinforcing feedback regarding the achievement of an ex-plicit or implicit goal for service delivery. This seems to have been the case in our study.

As described elsewhere (Hovell et al., 1991; Hovell et al., 1986), the public health perspective defines successful treatment or prevention in terms of changes in populations rather than individuals. This perspective could be very important for physicians to identify successful preventive medicine interventions.

Clinicians are reinforced by immediate cures when treating patients. They are concerned with curing *every* patient. This standard sets the physicians up for failure, especially when treating or trying to prevent chronic disease. When using interventions of limited power or which cannot be delivered completely for all patients, only a small fraction of those who receive care will benefit. These few "successes" may not be discriminated as satisfactory medical care on the part of the practitioner. When the clinician advises 100 smokers to quit and 10 do so, the professional standards (i.e., professional audience feedback) may con-sider this a failure. However, from a public health perspective, this may be considered a substantial success.

The population perspective treats the whole population as the client of con-cern, not the individual. If five to seven smokers quit for unknown reasons and this rate can be increased to ten by simply asking smokers to quit, a substantial public health intervention has been demonstrated. The difference between ten and five quits represents a 100% improvement relative to usual treatment. If even two or three of these patients avoid heart attacks or cancer, and this is achieved for the thousands of smokers who are so advised by their physicians, thousands of lives could be saved. Unfortunately, this public health or population perspective is not recognized by most clinicians, is not discriminated, and cannot function as a reinforcer for preventive services.

Formal training in preventive medicine can improve practitioners' understanding of public health success and may begin to change the culture of specialists in preventive medicine such that feedback regarding population rates and relative success could enter into new metacontingencies. This requires changes in concepts as well as changes in formal data collection, summary, and feedback; population-relative rates for rare events cannot be discriminated one patient at a time.

FINANCIAL CONTINGENCIES

Differential Pay and the Effect of Relatively Small Payments

Unfortunately, clinicians are busy and have limited time for collecting, summarizing, and reviewing population data. To add these tasks to the normal routine of practice requires compensation. Preventive services and tasks, such as data analyses, compete with curative care and rarely generate the same level of financial remuneration.

A number of studies suggest that financial contingencies affect the nature and rate of medical service provided (Donelan et al., 1996; Morrow, Gooding, & Clark, 1995; Saver & Pirzada, 1995). Our recent study of tobacco use prevention provided a partial demonstration of the potential of even relatively small financial reinforcement. Orthodontists in the experimental group were provided with training, instructions to establish an antitobacco office environment, and were paid $0.50 per prescription delivered to adolescent patients. Almost all of the offices in the experimental group established an antitobacco environment, while none did so among controls (Hovell et al., in press). Similarly, the orthodontists in the experimental condition personally counseled over 25% of their targeted patients, while orthodontists in the control group counseled less than 4% of their target youth (Russos et al., 1995). These results demonstrate that, in the context of brief training and in the context of annual incomes in excess of $200,000 per year, a $0.50 per prescription incentive seemed to be reinforcing.

Although few studies provide direct comparison of differing rates of reimbursement or the differential effects of financial versus social contingencies, it is likely that monetary reinforcement, even when provided on a salary or other time basis, is more powerful than nonmonetary contingencies. These findings in concert with theory suggest that financial reinforcement will make preventive services most reliable. Unfortunately, there exists no policy or legal system for ensuring monetary reimbursement for preventive services. The advance of man-

aged care further complicates the financial contingencies and provision of primary care and preventive services.

MANAGED CARE

Systems of Cost Containment and Rationing

The rapid rise of managed care may well be the most important natural experiment in metacontingencies in the twentieth century. Managed care is characterized by prepaid, coordinated medical care. The predominant types of
managed care in the United States are health maintenance organizations (HMOs)
and independent practice associations (IPAs), or preferred provider organizations
(PPOs). The Federal HMO Act describes three elements of an HMO: an organized system for providing medical care or assuring medical care in a geographic
area, an agreed-upon set of basic and supplemental health maintenance and
treatment services, and a voluntarily enrolled group of people. An HMO system
may consist of a provider group, hospital, medical center, or network of these
in which providers are contracted or directly salaried by the HMO. In contrast,
IPA physicians maintain their independent practices with both fee-for-service
(FFS) and IPA patients. Generally, in managed care membership, patients or
their employers pay a fixed fee noncontingent on the amount or type of service
needed. Most plans have no deductibles, require small or no copayments, and
do not require filing claims for reimbursement. Preventive and wellness care are
usually included with the membership. Coverage for preexisting conditions varies, as does coverage for prescription drugs, drug addiction rehabilitation, mental
health, and dental care services. Medical care received outside the managed care
system is often not reimbursed. The critical component of managed care systems
is the use of primary care physicians as coordinators of all medical services,
and as gatekeepers whose approval is required in most cases for access to care
by specialists.

Cost Containment

The United States spends approximately 13% of its Gross National Product
(GNP) on medical and health care (Bore, 1992; Hanks, 1992). This is far greater
than other Western nations (e.g., Japan = 6% [Mori, 1995]; France = 8%, the
highest in Europe [Triomphe, 1993]) and it is usually referred to as an unrea-
sonable expense. This is especially true in light of less-than-favorable rates of
some current morbidity indicators, such as underweight births and teen pregnancy rates. The conclusion is that we pay more for medicine and get less in
return than other developed nations. One of the foundations for the growth of
health promotion and preventive medicine is the promise of possible cost savings. The rationale assumes that the costs of preventing disease or injury will
offset the greater costs of treating serious illness, if not prevented. The growth

of managed care also is cost driven, but ironically, managed care has yet to fully embrace preventive medicine.

Where Does the Buck Stop?

Perhaps more importantly, with 13% of the GNP going to medical care services, the economic profits to be achieved in those services are substantial. The profits to be achieved in managed care systems are also considerable. As an indicator of the profitability of managed care business, medical alliances are now one of the fastest growing industries in the United States. Profits from medical care services, however, are likely to be directed to very different recipients under traditional fee-for-service and managed care systems. Traditionally, profits were realized by physicians and other nursing service employees. With the increase in HMOs, PPOs, and large insurance companies entering the managed care business, profits are now directed toward white-collar executives and stockholders of companies no longer directed by physicians.

This shift in who receives the profits changes the nature of the contingencies operating to influence the kind, quality, and amount of care to be delivered. For instance, HMOs and other companies responsible for delivering medical services must limit services in order to maximize short-term profit from prepaid contracts. Complex or time-consuming preventive services, even the taking of a medical history, risk exhausting short-term profits. Paradoxically, preventive services may be less likely under managed care systems.

Employee Benefits

The cost to businesses for providing employees with mandatory health insurance is climbing. Historically, the cost of medical care has been borne to a great extent by the worker. Now that business and industry are required by law to provide health insurance programs for their employees (and in order to remain competitive in attracting prospective employees), rising costs have become a serious concern. Industry's traditional response to increasing costs of overhead, including employee benefits and health insurance, is to suppress the cost per unit of purchase. Managed care systems offer employers "composite billing rates," which provide a discounted cost by pooling both high- and low-risk employees in a large group to be provided medical care services and contracting with providers for discount services.

These contracts are typically of two forms. First, an insurance carrier might inform its contracted practitioners that to receive compensation the practitioner must lower rates for a typical exam from $50 to $35. To continue to obtain income from insured patients the practitioner must agree to lowered compensation. The practitioner then must see additional patients or lower his/her overhead to sustain income. Second, insurance companies may contract with providers on a prepaid capitation basis. In these contracts a flat fee is paid in advance and at substantially lower rates than typically charged for contracted services. Providers must see fewer patients, prevent them from needing care, or lower overhead to sustain historical income. In either of these two contexts, provision of preventive services may increase overhead and function as a response cost.

Profit and Loss Ratios

As industry increasingly buys its medical care from one of a limited number of provider groups at discounted prices, a number of consequences are likely. Some providers will go bankrupt. Those that continue to provide service will be more efficient; but efficiency is measured presently only in terms of profit and loss ratios. The quality and nature of the medical care delivered are not assessed or are only minimally considered. Almost invariably, medical care providers who sustain contracts for discounted services will achieve a positive profit-to-loss ratio by cutting services—by rationing medical care.

Generally, managed care systems profit by receiving a lump sum of money per patient regardless of services used and by paying medical providers on a salary rather than a fee-for-service basis. Managed care systems contributed to decreasing the rate of growth in physicians' pay between 1989 and 1994 (Robbins & Loudermilk, 1994). However, the compensation for physician executives—physicians who manage costs of care and physician performance—has increased among HMOs, group practices, and hospital/medical centers (Robbins & Loudermilk, 1994). Thus, one of the most profound metacontingencies operating to influence medical care, including preventive services, is cost containment. However, there is growing evidence that cost reductions may be limited to short-term, apparent cost reductions that are achieved by compromising quality and quantity of medical care. Further, cost reductions may be achieved in the short term, without preventing more expensive treatment costs in the long term, and may not lower overall medical care costs in the United States (Elliott, 1996; Reeder et al., 1993).

What Attracts Physicians to Managed Care Institutions?

HMOs and other managed care institutions seemingly reduce the physician's income and much of his/her leadership normally associated with FFS private practice. Given these apparent reductions in typical reinforcers for private practice, what are the probable offsetting reinforcers for practicing medicine in the context of managed care?

Relative Response Cost and Differential Rates of Reinforcement

There are two very important contextual variables that increase the likelihood of joining an HMO. One is the extreme cost of buying or starting a practice from scratch. This can be well over $200,000, with overhead exceeding income for the first two to three years. In the new competitive market, the ability to start a new practice and assure a profit at all is substantially reduced. Thus, costs to enter private practice can be overwhelming. Physicians who are interested in joining an ongoing practice may find few or none interested in hiring, especially if the existing practice is suffering loss of income due to managed care inroads. Overall, the probability of profit and the ratio of profit to workload for private practice has been severely reduced, essentially decreasing the reinforcement available for private practice.

Fee-for-service private practice increasingly requires business skills and substantial time and work directed to managing a practice. For many practitioners these tasks are aversive and are avoided if possible. With increasing paperwork and barriers to independent practice, as occurs with insurance overseers, the reinforcement value of the FFS system is decreasing for physicians. In contrast, many managed care systems, especially HMOs, provide clerical and administrative staff who manage all of the billing and personnel management for the delivery of medical services. The physician need only attend to patients.

Traditional private practice also entails long hours, hospital duties in the middle of the night, and the sacrifice of weekends, holidays, and time for a private life with family and friends. Managed care systems often offer an established pool of patients, job security, stable compensation, malpractice insurance, set daytime working hours and time off, interaction with colleagues, equipment, and work benefits. These conditions provide the practicing physician a somewhat lower income, but a higher quality of life. These privileges tend to be available immediately upon taking a position with an HMO; they are never certain and always delayed in an FFS private practice.

Medicine, Motherhood, and Family Life

The practice of medicine is changing, in part, due to cultural shifts among the adults who become physicians, and due to shifts in traditional male/female roles in the family. Increasingly, fathers are interested in flexible time off from work to attend to children and family needs. Some of these fathers may be physicians. These types of reinforcers may be more powerful for women planning to have children. The proportion of physicians who are women is rising (Montague, 1994). The most recent medical school classes are more than 50% female, suggesting that medicine will become a predominantly female profession if trends continue. For female professionals, time off for pregnancy and child care as well as family activities may be as reinforcing as practicing medicine, or total income. Managed care systems often provide the opportunity to practice medicine full- or part-time, thereby meeting the cultural contingencies of motherhood and accommodating the increasingly female physician population. These changes increase the pool of physicians available at modest cost to managed care institutions. As more patients and physicians move into managed care, the ability for other physicians to continue in FFS systems is reduced.

PREVENTIVE MEDICINE UNDER MANAGED CARE

Although these changes in systems are directed predominantly toward primary care, they affect the practice of preventive medicine as well. In some respects preventive services may be increased and in others decreased.

Facilitating Preventive and Primary Care Services

Managed care coverage of preventive services allows patients greater opportunity to access and use such services than if they have no medical insurance. Low-income workers who acquire their medical care from their employers' group purchase of an HMO service may obtain more primary care and preventive services than would normally be true of the FFS system. Managed care avoids annual deductibles and involves a minimal copayment per visit. These reduced costs, theoretically, should suppress preventive services less than the charges that are part of FFS plans by reducing response costs to the patient for seeking acute care, in the context of which preventive services may be delivered. However, this hypothesis remains to be supported empirically.

Decreasing the Likelihood of Preventive Services

Empirical evidence of access to and use of primary care (the most likely context of preventive services) suggests that, in reality, physicians reimbursed in FFS plans are more likely to provide preventive services than those in managed care systems (Hickson, Altemeier, & Perrin, 1987). This may be due to the relatively direct relationship between physician service and fees in FFS systems, while HMO doctors are paid salaries regardless of services provided: approximating the distinction between ratio and interval schedules, respectively. As noted earlier, copayment requirements may reduce the use of preventive services (Lurie et al., 1987; Woolhandler & Himmelstein, 1988). Both insurance-supported FFS and managed care systems have used copayments to decrease "overuse" of medical services. This is especially likely to decrease the use of medical care for preventive purposes—contacts in absence of definitive pain, disability, or functional limitations. Despite the greater social acceptance of health promotion and disease prevention, patient history of seeking curative over preventive treatment suggests that preventive services might not be requested even if provided for free.

Reinforcing Limited Care

Gatekeepers within FFS and HMO systems decrease the number of visits to specialists, as well as overall use of primary care (Hurlye, Freund, & Gage,

1991; U.S. DHHS, 1984). In managed care systems, it may be impossible to deny a patient the privilege of seeing a physician and this makes it difficult to reduce the number of patient visits needed to ensure profits. Managers compensate for numbers of visits by reducing the length of visits and the breadth of services provided.

The RAND Health Insurance Experiment (HIE) showed that HMOs reduced costs by decreasing consumption of services (primarily hospitalization), and increased use of preventive services compared to FFS systems (Brandon, 1995; RAND, 1995). HIE and other studies showed that clinical services vary with income; low-income people receive more preventive services in FFS systems (Brandon, 1995; RAND, 1995; Ware et al., 1986; Woolhandler & Himmelstein, 1988). This is important since poor and near-poor populations are at higher risk yet are less likely to be screened for preventable illness (Bobrow, 1987; Rudov & Santangelo, 1979; Subcommittee on Cancer in the Economically Disadvantaged, 1986). When physicians are randomly assigned to groups to separate the effect of reimbursement from patient characteristics, FFS and salaried physicians do not differ in total patient visits, but FFS physicians see more patients for well-child care than salaried physicians (Hickson et al., 1987). These data suggest that specific groups or specific preventive services may be more reliably provided by FFS practices than managed care systems. Again, this may be due to the relatively direct link between physician service and payment for services that is true of FFS practices, but less true for managed care practices. Managed care systems to date are promoted, in part, to prevent disease, but may actually decrease the rate of preventive services available.

Because most patients do not visit physicians while they are well, most preventive medicine must be provided in the context of curative care visits. The availability of physicians creates the demand for care and thus patients' use of services (Hickson et al., 1987; Holahan et al., 1979). In managed care systems, the contingencies controlling physicians' behavior are designed to reduce the amount of time and services delivered in each visit, with little attention to long-term consequences. De facto rationing of medical services for cost containment is almost certainly at the cost of preventive services; and may cost the health care institution more in the long run. Salary systems produce a lower rate of physician activity, usually observed as decreased patient visits (and lower costs for HMOs) (Hickson et al., 1987; Roemer, 1962; Wolinsky, 1970). However, even with supervision, salaried physicians will provide more care than the managed care system can tolerate. This has given rise to the use of bonus pay incentives for physicians who see fewer patients, conduct fewer diagnostic tests, and provide fewer medical treatments. From 1991 to 1994, the use of incentive pay systems in HMOs grew by 500% (Robbins & Loudermilk, 1994). Compared to hospitals and group practices, variable compensation and rewards to reduce physician use of certain procedures or services are most often used by HMOs (Robbins & Loudermilk, 1994).

Continuity, Rapport, and Quality of Care

Next to reducing medical care costs, the intended outcome of managed care systems is continuity of care. Continuity of the patient-physician relationship relates to numerous cost-containment and patient and physician satisfaction outcomes: faster problem identification, fewer physician visits and diagnostic tests, shorter hospitalizations, increased patient adherence to treatment procedures and scheduled appointments, better patient communication of problems (Becker, Drachman, & Kirscht, 1972, 1974a, 1974b, 1974c; Charney et al., 1967; Poland, 1976; Starfield et al., 1976; Wasson et al., 1984). These results suggest how continuity of care might improve clinicians' provision and patients' practice of prevention activities. Continuity of care might improve clinician provision and patient adherence to annual physical exams, immunizations, Pap smears, and other recommended services. Repeated patient-physician contact over time builds rapport as a basis for discussing sensitive lifestyle issues (e.g., risks of sexually transmitted diseases) and opportunities to prompt and reinforce preventive behaviors. Theoretically, the salary and gatekeeping contingencies found in managed care were designed to reduce care costs while providing better quality of care. The salary system should allow more time and energy for patient-physician interaction by reducing physicians' administrative responsibilities. The gatekeeper system should provide patients with one physician responsible for all their needs and continuity of care.

However, empirical results show otherwise. Compared to FFS systems, patient-physician continuity is reduced in prepaid systems (Davies et al., 1986; Mechanic, Weiss, & Cleary, 1983; Murray, 1988; Safran, Tarlov, & Rogers, 1994). Salaried physicians see their patients less often and personally attend patient visits less often than FFS physicians (Hickson et al., 1987). Patients not seen by a physician may be seen by a nurse or other medical practitioner, or may not be seen at all (i.e., patients of salaried physicians may tend to avoid seeking care for less serious concerns). These reductions decrease the probability of provision of, and reinforcement for, preventive services.

Compared to the FFS groups, the RAND HIE group randomly assigned to HMO care reported significantly greater dissatisfaction with access (e.g., travel time, convenience), availability of hospitals and specialists, continuity of care, and interpersonal aspects of care (Brandon, 1995; RAND, 1995). Over 40% of patients who end managed care membership report dissatisfaction with their ability to see the physician of their choice (Mechanic et al., 1983). Whereas the fees in FFS systems constitute "financial barriers" to access treatment, prepaid systems, lacking this disincentive (excepting the minimal copayment in some systems), may compensate by instituting "organizational barriers" (the "HMO hassle factor": Safran et al., 1994) to decrease utilization rates (Held & Reinhard, 1979; Mechanic et al., 1983; Wolinsky & Marder, 1983). Compared to FFS, patients in managed care systems are less satisfied with the amount of physician time and the interpersonal aspects (e.g., physicians' personal concern and accountability for their needs) of visits (Davies et al., 1986; Mechanic et al., 1983; Murray, 1988; Rubin et al., 1993; Safran et al., 1994). Patient dissatisfaction with interpersonal aspects of care is a primary reason for discontinuity of care in managed care systems (Kasteller, Kane, & Olsen, 1975; Marquis, Davies, & Ware, 1983; Mechanic et al., 1983; Rubin et al., 1993; Ware & Davies, 1983).

Iatrogenic Disease

Overall these patterns suggest less preventive care is delivered in managed care systems than in FFS practices. However, this is not the whole picture, nor are the past data necessarily representative of a quickly developing future. The physician's Hippocratic oath calls for "first, do no harm." Traditional FFS medicine runs the very real risk of overprescribing and inadvertently doing harm (cf. Illich, 1976). HMOs and other managed care systems reduce this risk and in this sense effect a kind of preventive service. Namely, they reduce the incidence of disease or injury caused by medical care—iatrogenic diseases. Thus, the process of curtailing costs and limiting services is not all bad for the patients. Unfortunately, going from one extreme to the other may not be the best medicine or the best management of costs, either. As discussed elsewhere (Hovell et al., 1991), research focused on reinforcement systems that are contingent on balanced costs and effective services is needed.

Rationing, by Any Other Name, May Be Managed Care

Health maintenance organizations (HMOs), preferred provider plans (PPOs), and other systems that provide discounted care do so without making rationing obvious. Two general approaches are employed to contain costs, and both employ rationing. The first is use of copayments, as noted earlier. The second entails "medically approved" diagnostic and treatment services. This takes place when the clinician's recommended testing or treatment is reviewed prior to authorization for payment. This is most commonly employed in PPO or insurance-based systems of care. Often, the diagnostic test or treatment recommended by the physician is not allowed. Disallowance is presumably due to inadequate justification for the individual patient's treatment. This type of restriction is an attempt to curtail physicians from casually ordering too many or inappropriate tests and from ordering inappropriate treatment. For example, a magnetic resonance imaging (MRI) test, which can cost many thousands of dollars, can provide detailed information regarding a possible spinal defect or injury. It might be ordered on the basis of minor or one-time back pain; it might be ordered on the basis of extensive and less expensive evaluation for a long-term back problem. The former would not be approved, while the latter would. This is a form of cost containment and rationing. Arguably, this type of rationing is reasonable. However, if the rationing is extended to patients for whom the test is clearly indicated, it becomes more than inappropriate cost containment. Even when "appropriate," it may suppress preventive medicine services. An MRI or other relatively expensive examination might rule out certain types of diseases and thereby redirect the physician to pursue exercise training to prevent future back pain. Alternatively, it could show early signs of bone degeneration for which vitamins and exercise could be prescribed as preventive measures. Either way, the practitioner could use the information to initiate preventive services. These are least likely to be forthcoming for the patients most suitable for preventive interventions because they are the least likely to be approved for testing. Physicians who order tests for possible preventive care, and are rebuked for doing so, learn not to order such tests in the future. Their discontinuation tends to reinforce such policymaking and validates the judgment that such rationing is reasonable and good medicine—further perpetuating a rationing system and delimiting preventive medical care services. These service feedback loops may represent metacontingencies designed by organizations that will attain profits by cost reductions, even if attained by rationing, rather than organizations that will attain profits (or other reinforcers) based on effecting improved health of patients.

Physician as Employee

Rationing also takes place as a function of direct physician supervision. As presented earlier, HMO physicians are salaried employees who report to a medical director or sometimes a health service administrator. These supervisors set standards for the number of patients to be seen per day, the number of expensive tests to be prescribed, treatments to be ordered, and the number of patients to be hospitalized. Clinicians who fail to meet these standards are provided criticism, may be assigned new duties, and can be fired from the medical care service. These contingencies direct clinicians toward one problem or complaint per patient, with limited review of other possible medical problems concurrently taking place. Emphasis is placed on moving the patient through the examination and treatment contact as quickly as possible. Physicians who take too long with one patient will be criticized by their supervisors and/or colleagues who may inherit their backlog of patients.

Systems of overbooking patients inherently cause the practitioner to focus on the most acute problem and delimit diagnostic work, including rapport building and assessing the need for or providing preventive medicine services. Analyses that compare the cost of providing preventive services relative to the costs of letting preventable disease develop have yet to determine the overall cost-benefit ratios of one procedure versus the other. Regardless of the cost balance, the patients receive less and possibly worse care; physicians operating under such contingencies are taught to avoid costs rather than provide the most effective care.

POLITICAL AND PROFESSIONAL POLICIES AND ACCOUNTABILITY

Politics and Law

Federal, state, and local governments influence the practice of medicine and preventive medicine substantially. Ultimately, government defines who can practice medicine and the limits of their service, privileges, and responsibilities. Government also sets standards to be met for government-funded medical service programs, such as Medicare. These systems can be viewed as meta-contingencies defining the range of services to be provided and the compensation rates to be attained in exchange.

Typically, government-based programs also include routine reporting or accountability checks that assess the degree to which the services provided meet the standards set by government. These may be informal billing audits, formal chart audits, or formal site reviews of practice patterns. These systems of checks serve to qualify the medical practice for inclusion or exclusion from the government-funded program. Usually, the standards or practice guidelines employed for quality assurance are set by the American Medical Association or other professional associations. These typically emphasize traditional medical services, but have increasingly included preventive services.

Practice Guidelines

Practice guidelines can interact with government-based medical care programs, as noted above. They also interact with insurance compensation systems, by setting the standards for compensation for specific services. Professional guidelines also can set the stage for certification of a hospital or medical practice group as qualified to be reimbursed for specific services or services to specific groups of patients. Application and site visit reviews determine whether a particular medical service qualifies for inclusion. HMOs, PPOs, and even individual private practices come under these contingencies.

Political Action Groups and Foundations

Government and professional policies are determined within a political influence system, with many competing groups vying for control. Among these are special interest groups: businesses are interested in lowering worker health care costs; the American Association of Retired Persons (AARP) is interested in services for the elderly; the American Lung Association is interested in care for lung diseases, and so on. The collection of special interest groups includes endowed philanthropic foundations such as the Ford, Robert Wood Johnson (RWJ), and other foundations. Many of these organizations direct funds to the design of legislation or to influence professional policies/guidelines for medical care, including preventive medicine.

A Case Example

Recently, the RWJ Foundation has been working with the Center for the Advancement of Health to promote new tobacco control guidelines, particularly among governmental agencies such as the CDC, and professional organizations such as the American Medical Association, American Public Health Association, and Society for Behavioral Medicine ("Integrating Tobacco Control into Managed Care," 1996). Ongoing facilitation of such policy promotion activities has resulted in increased action among governmental health agencies. Among recent developments which may be partially attributable to such activities are the development by the U.S. Agency for Health Care Policy Research of new clinical practice guidelines that emphasize the control of tobacco use. The new guidelines call for all practicing physicians to assess the smoking status of all patients and to promote cessation for those who are smokers (Smoking Cessation Clinical Practice Guideline Panel and Staff, 1996). The guidelines extend to the use of medical supports, such as nicotine replacement therapies (gum or patches), and the referral to formal cessation programs. These new guidelines are considered preventive medicine services, as they are designed primarily to prevent tobacco-related diseases. It is too soon to know the effect of these guidelines, but they verge on the revolutionary, and are likely to have a profound effect on medical care.

For private practices, PPOs, and HMOs, these guidelines and physicians' compliance with them determine whether the medical service will qualify for reimbursements. This contingency is blunt in that most medical services qualify and retain certification without invasive review or threats. However, as guidelines for an ever-increasing number of primary care services and a gradually increasing number of preventive services are added to existing standards of care, the ability of the medical service to comply with standards becomes questionable; the ability of the medical service to comply and make a profit becomes even more questionable. In short, quality assurance standards are blunt, aversive contingencies operating to ensure high quality curative and preventive medicine. These contingencies are in opposition to most contingencies designed to reduce the cost of care.

How will the combination of practice guidelines and managed care work? Ultimately, the combination may yield an efficient system of both primary and preventive care, but the developmental period is likely to be long and harsh. In the short run, the two systems will clash. Managed care systems call for less time to be spent with patients; quality assurance guidelines call for extensive review of possible risk conditions, such as tobacco use, and follow-on care as appropriate. Presently, these are incompatible contingencies. How they will be resolved is uncertain. Hence, the great experiment is underway.

A Second Case Example

California Governor Pete Wilson represents a fiscally conservative and pro-business party. This has placed him as more an ally of the tobacco industry than an opponent. He also has been working toward reducing the state's obligations for funding medical care to the indigent. These political agendas merged in 1993. The Proposition 99 tobacco tax initiative discussed earlier was designed to prevent tobacco use, support antitobacco research, and fund indigent medical care. Governor Wilson attempted to move funds from the Tobacco Related Disease Research Program and from that of the Tobacco Control Education account to increase funds for medical services for the indigent. To justify this move, he required that all patients who receive state funding for medical care be screened for tobacco use. Those found to be smokers or who exposed their children to passive smoke were to be advised to quit. This administrative decision was contested in the state courts, and the governor's use of the funds was declared illegal (Begay, Traynor, & Glantz, 1993; Skolnick, 1994). However, while the case is on appeal, the governor's use of the funding prevails, and tobacco-related disease research has been all but discontinued in the state.

This situation, too, is an experiment within the larger experiment with regard to the source of funding and type of services to be provided. However, inspection of the governor's disagreement with the original law suggests interesting consequences. First, his requirement for tobacco screening for all indigent care patients is a major change in primary and preventive care medicine, especially for the poor. Even if the courts reverse his use of funds, there is a very good chance that these screening procedures will remain in place, as most clinics have incorporated screening tools and have added clinical data to patients' medical charts and treatment plans. If the tobacco-use screening continues, the resulting data may provide the basis for demanding additional resources from the state's general fund to sustain tobacco-related control services in the context of indigent care. Although Wilson's intention was both to limit the damage to the tobacco industry and to fund indigent care by means other than the state's general fund, his actions may result in greater tobacco control than expected. The effects of such tinkering with large-scale metacontingencies is difficult to predict, especially for political leaders operating without advice from behavioral specialists.

Social Darwinism as Applied to Medical Care

These examples show that the operations of government and professional policies serve as important metacontingencies. Normally, laws, funding policies, and professional standard guidelines represent relatively stable contingencies. However, in the process of revolutionary changes in welfare, managed care, and overall deficit reduction by the federal government, and the increasing freedom to experiment with new systems of care by the states, these contingencies are no longer stable and much greater variance can be expected. From this variance will come significant discoveries regarding efficient means of delivering medical care, including preventive medicine services; these gains will come at the likely expense of equally great tragedies in the failure to deliver effective primary or preventive care. In this social Darwinism, even the tragedies will serve as consequences selecting for alternative medical systems and from which it may be expected that a reasonable system of care will evolve—but at what cost?

FORMAL EXPERIMENTATION

Operant Specialists

The processes described above are but a few of the most obvious and probably the most powerful metacontingencies operating to determine the nature of medical and preventive medicine care. As described, there is an ongoing natural experiment. This experiment is driven by physicians to a limited extent, by health service administrators to a greater extent, and by business leaders to a still greater extent, with complications coming from lobbying by professional associations and special interest–driven politicians. In all of these agencies there are few professionals who understand the principles of behavior and procedures of behavior change, who serve as advisors to the architects for managed care or preventive medicine. The experiment is underway with one of the most important specialists left out. This will probably delimit the nature of systems planned and tried, and will make the learning process longer and harsher than it might otherwise be. The costs in terms of disease, dysfunction, and human misery may be far greater with the present uncontrolled experiment than they need be.

Professionals in operant conditioning and contingency control of behavior are not likely to be invited to participate in groups who are designing health care systems. The only means of inclusion is for professionals in applied behavior analysis to join related professional groups, conduct small-scale studies of health care services, and prepare presentations and professional writings to be published in the medical and health services literature. The addition of behavior analysts to the process might make the ongoing experiment somewhat more effective, efficient, and humane. It might also contribute to the formal testing of possible contingency systems likely to effect preventive medicine practice patterns.

Applied Experimentation

It is most difficult to conduct formal experiments of preventive medicine services. The research costs can be extreme and professional physicians tend not to volunteer as subjects of study. Nevertheless, formal controlled experiments are as critical to our understanding and verification of reliable determinants of physician practice patterns as they are for any other application of science. Presently, there are limited metacontingencies available to promote formal study of preventive medicine. The Agency for Health Care Policy Research (AHCPR, formerly National Center for Health Services Research) within the federal Public Health Service (PHS) provides funding for health policy research, including practice patterns and quality assurance systems. Unfortunately, it is one of the smallest agencies within the PHS and it has suffered severe budget cuts in the context of threats from Congress of abolition.

These actions, too, represent some of the interlocking political contingencies that are operating. Research promoted by the AHCPR provides empirical findings regarding medical services that are at odds with special interest groups and political parties/representatives in Congress. Congressional action may ultimately support the special interest groups and result in the curtailment of funding such research. Nevertheless, the AHCPR and some foundations (e.g., RWJ) support medical policy and quality assurance studies and could serve as a foundation for operant-related investigations of preventive medicine.

The need for formal investigations of medical care and preventive medicine contingencies is critical. Failure to prevent latent tuberculosis today will ensure at least a localized epidemic of active disease in about 30 years. Failure to prevent tobacco use today will guarantee over 400,000 deaths annually as the current adolescents enter middle age. These trends represent very serious loss of human life and quality of life prior to death. Even if preventive services do not provide cost savings relative to curative care medicine, the improvement in human function and longevity may warrant the investment. The application of science to this end may be expected to increase our understanding and assist in the design of preventive medical systems more reliably than any other approach.

CONCLUSIONS

The practice of medicine in the United States is undergoing a major natural experiment. The ultimate form to be taken by medical care services in this country, including the provision of preventive medical services, is yet to be determined. We have summarized some of the major contingencies and meta-contingencies operating to influence the practice of medicine as well as preventive medicine. Several of these contingencies are due to the nature of disease and the effectiveness of drug treatment and vaccine prevention. Other contingencies and systems of contingencies include the availability of financial reinforcement for delivery of quality curative care or preventive services, the role of audience and other feedback systems of reinforcement, the role of government and professional agencies for setting laws, and policy-based contingencies in effect. These contingencies are viewed as operating in an ongoing stream of change, an evolution which may ultimately arrive at a relatively efficient and effective medical care system that includes preventive medicine services. However, the evolution is likely to be long and expensive in terms of human suffering. The present managed care contingencies appear to be driven predominantly by cost reduction for businesses at the expense of quality of care and at the expense of preventive services. The appearance of managed care appears to have redirected profits toward new recipients, such as nonmedical executives, management, and stockholders of HMOs or insurance providers, and also to inexpensive, nonprofessional service providers such as medical assistants. Whether this results only in a shift of wealth from physicians to business leaders with no overall reduction in cost to the nation is yet to be seen.

This experiment is taking place with essentially no guidance from applied behavior analysts and, hence, no guidance regarding the design of contingencies for behavior change purposes. We believe the addition of behavioral science to the process of designing managed care systems could enhance the effectiveness of delivering preventive as well as primary care, and still reduce costs. If specialists in applied behavior analysis direct research (and distribution of its results to the scientific and lay audience) concerning the effects of contingencies that promote both improvements in health and lower costs for medical services, possible damage from our ongoing national managed care experiment might be mitigated. If such study were advertised to the public, public reactions could provide audience contingencies to counter actions now driven by organized special interests. The public should be informed as to the processes taking place (e.g., managed care), the likely beneficiaries (e.g., business executives), the cost (e.g., compromises in medical services and health status), and to possible alternatives. Failing to study medical care and preventive medicine contingencies, and failing to activate public involvement may lead to tragic outcomes—from which the public reaction is a virtual certainty.

REFERENCES

Becker, M. H., Drachman, R. H., & Kirscht, J. P. (1972). Predicting mothers' compliance with pediatric medical regimens. *Journal of Pediatrics, 81*, 843–854.
———. (1974a). Continuity of pediatrician: New support for an old shibboleth. *Journal of Pediatrics, 84*, 599–605.
———. (1974b). A field experiment to evaluate various outcomes of continuity of physician care. *American Journal of Public Health, 64*, 1062–1070.
———. (1974c). A new approach to explaining sick-role behavior in low-income populations. *American Journal of Public Health, 84*, 599–605.
Begay, M. E., Traynor, M. P., & Glantz, S. A. (1993). The tobacco industry, state politics, and tobacco education in California. *American Journal of Public Health, 83*, 1214–1221.
Bobrow, R. S. (1987). Colorectal cancer at a public health center. *Journal of the American Medical Association, 257*, 782–783.
Bore, V. M. (1992). Health care costs tied to many issues. *Physician Executive, 18*, 23–29.
Brandon, W. P. (1995). A large-scale social science experiment in health finance: Findings, significance, and value. *Journal of Health Politics, Policy and Law, 20*, 1051–1061.
Charney, E., Bynum, R., Eldredge, D., Frank, D., MacWhinney, J. B., McNabb, N.,

Scheiner, A., Sumpter, E. A., & Iker, A. (1967). How well do patients take oral penicillin? A collaborative study in private practice. *Pediatrics, 40*, 188–195.

Corley, D. L., Gevirtz, R., Nideffer, R., Cummins, L. (1987). Prevention of postinfectious asthma in children by reducing self-inoculatory behavior. *Journal of Pediatric Psychology, 12*, 519–531.

County of San Diego, Department of Health Services. (1992, February 7). *Infant Immunization Initiative (1–3)*. San Diego, CA.

Davies, A. R., Ware, J. E., Brook, R. H., Peterson, J. R., & Newhouse, J. P. (1986). Consumer acceptance of prepaid and fee-for-service medical care: Results from a randomized controlled trial. *Health Services Research, 21*, 429–452.

Donelan, K., Blendon, R. J., Benson, J., Leitman, R., & Taylor, H. (1996). All payer, single payer, managed care, no payer: Patients' perspectives in three nations. *Health Affairs, 15*, 254–265.

Elliott, W. J. (1996). The costs of treating hypertension: What are the long-term realities of cost containment and pharmacoeconomics? *Postgraduate Medicine, 99*, 241–248, 251–252.

Feder, B. J. (1996, August 29). Major chain drops cigarettes. *San Diego Union-Tribune*, pp. C1, C3.

Garrett, L. (1994). *The coming plague*. New York: Penguin Books.

Glenn, S. S. (1988). Contingencies and metacontingencies: Toward a synthesis of behavior analysis and cultural materialism. *The Behavior Analyst, 11*, 161–179.

Hanks, G. E. (1992). The crisis in health care cost in the United States: Some implications for radiation oncology. *International Journal of Radiation Oncology, Biology, Physics, 23*, 203–206.

Held, P., & Reinhard, U. (1979). *Analysis of economic performance in medical group practices*. Princeton, NJ: Mathematica Policy Research.

Hickson, G. B., Altemeier, W. A., & Perrin, J. M. (1987). Physician reimbursement by salary or fee-for-service: Effect on physician practice behavior in a randomized prospective study. *Pediatrics, 80*, 344–350.

Holahan, J., Hadley, J., Scanlon, W., Lee, R., & Bluck, J. (1979). Paying for physician services under Medicare and Medicaid. *Milbank Memorial Fund Quarterly, 57*, 183–211.

Hovell, M. F., Elder, J. P., Blanchard, J., & Sallis, J. F. (1986). Behavior analysis and public health perspectives: Combining paradigms to effect prevention. *Education and Treatment of Children, 9*, 287–306.

Hovell, M. F., Kaplan, R., & Hovell, F. (1991). Analysis of preventive medical services in the United States. In P. A. Lamal (Ed.), *Behavioral analysis of societies and cultural practices* (pp. 181–200). New York: Hemisphere.

Hovell, M. F., Russos, S., Beckhelm, M. K., Jones, J. A., Burknam-Kreitner, S. M., Slymen, D. J., Hofstetter, C. R., & Rubin, B. (in press). Compliance with primary prevention in private practice: Creating a tobacco-free environment. *American Journal of Preventive Medicine*.

Hurlye, R. E., Freund, D. A., & Gage, B. J. (1991). Gatekeeper effects on patterns of physician use. *The Journal of Family Practice, 32*, 167–174.

Illich, I. (1976). *Medical nemesis*. New York: Pantheon.

Integrating tobacco control into managed care. (1996, Spring). *SBM Outlook*.

Kasteller, J., Kane, R. L., & Olsen, D. (1975). Issues underlying prevalence of "doctor-shopping" behavior. *Journal of Health and Social Behavior, 17*, 328–339.

Lamal, P. A. (1991). *Behavioral analysis of societies and cultural practices*. New York: Hemisphere.

Lurie, N., Manning, W. G., Peterson, C., Goldberg, G. A., Phelps, C. A., & Lillard, L. (1987). Preventive care: Do we practice what we preach? *American Journal of Public Health, 77*, 801–804.

Marquis, M. S., Davies, A. R., & Ware, J. E. Jr. (1983). Patient satisfaction and change in medical care provider: A longitudinal study. *Medical Care, 21*, 821–829.

Mechanic, D., Weiss, N., & Cleary, P. D. (1983). The growth of HMOs: Issues of enrollment and disenrollment. *Medical Care, 21*, 338–347.

Montague, J. (1994). Safe and sound: Security, improved lifestyles and driving physician recruiting. *Hospitals & Health Networks, 68*, 48–50.

Mori, M. (1995). Problems of national health insurance reimbursement revision, especially for laboratory tests. *Japanese Journal of Clinical Pathology, 43*, 660–664.

Morrow, R. W., Gooding, A. D., & Clark, C. (1995). Improving physicians' preventive health care behavior through peer review and financial incentives. *Archives of Family Medicine, 4*, 165–169.

Murray, J. P. (1988). A follow-up comparison of patient satisfaction among prepaid and fee-for-service patients. *Journal of Family Practice, 26*, 576–581.

O'Connor, S. J., & Lanning, J. A. (1992). The end of autonomy? Reflections on the postprofessional physician. *Health Care Management Review, 17*, 63–72.

Pierce, J. P., Evans, N., Farkas, A. J., Cavin, S. W., Berry, C., Kramer, M., Kealey, S., Rosbrook, B., Choi, W., & Kaplan, R. M. (1994). *Tobacco use in California: An evaluation of the tobacco control program, 1989–1993. A report to the California Department of Health Services*. San Diego: University of California, San Diego, Cancer Prevention and Control Program.

Poland, M. L. (1976). The effects of continuity of care on the missed appointment rate in a prenatal clinic. *Journal of Obstetric, Gynecologic, and Neonatal Nursing, 5*, 45–47.

RAND. (1995). *The health sciences program*. Santa Monica, CA: RAND Corporation.

Reeder, C. E., Lingle, E. W., Schulz, R. M., Mauch, R. P. Jr., Nightengale, B. S., Pedersen, C. A., Watrous, M. L., & Zetzl, S. E. (1993). Economic impact of cost-containment strategies in third party programmes in the U.S. (part 1). *Pharmacoeconomics, 4*, 92–103.

Robbins, M. M., & Loudermilk, R. C. (1994). Lining up their shots: Exclusive new Hay survey shows the impact of integration on M.D. compensation. *Hospitals & Health Networks, 68*, 30–36.

Roemer, M. I. (1962). On paying the doctor and the implications of different methods. *Journal of Health and Human Behavior, 3*, 4–14.

Rubin, H. R., Gandek, B., Rogers, W. H., Kosinski, M., McHorney, C. A., & Ware, J. E. Jr. (1993). Patients' ratings of outpatient visits in different practice settings: Results from the Medical Outcomes Study. *Journal of the American Medical Association, 270*, 835–840.

Rudov, M. H., & Santangelo, N. (1979). *Health status of minorities and low income groups*. (Publication HPA 79–627). Washington, DC: Department of Health, Education, and Welfare.

Russos, S., Hovell, M. F., Keating, K., Jones, J. A., Burkham-Kreitner, S. M., Slymen, D. J., Hofstetter, C. R., & Rubin, B. (in press). Clinician compliance with primary prevention of tobacco use: The impact of social contingencies. *Preventive Medicine.*

Russos, S., Keating, K., Hovell, M. F., Jones, J. A., Slymen, D. J., & Hofstetter, C. R. (1995, November). *Clinician anti-tobacco counseling: Cessation versus prevention.* Poster presented at the meeting of the American Public Health Association, San Diego, CA.

Safran, D. G., Tarlov, A. R., & Rogers, W. H. (1994). Primary care performance in fee-for-service and prepaid health care systems: Results from the Medical Outcomes Study. *Journal of the American Medical Association, 271*, 1579–1586.

Saver, B. G., & Pirzada, S. R. (1995). Effects of physician payment method on procedural activity in a large health maintenance organization. *AHSR/FHSR Annual Meeting Abstract Book, 12*, 90.

Skinner, B. F. (1953). *Science and human behavior.* New York: Macmillan.

Skolnick, A. (1994). Antitobacco advocates fight ''illegal'' diversion of tobacco control money. *Journal of the American Medical Association, 271*, 1387–1390.

Smoking Cessation Clinical Practice Guideline Panel and Staff. (1996). The Agency for Health Care Policy and Research Smoking Cessation Clinical Practice Guideline. *Journal of the American Medical Association, 275*, 1270–1280.

Starfield, B. H., Simborg, D. W., Horn, D. S., & Yourtree, S. A. (1976). Continuity and coordination in primary care: Their achievement and utility. *Medical Care, 14*, 625–636.

Subcommittee on Cancer in the Economically Disadvantaged. (1986). *Cancer in the economically disadvantaged: A special report.* New York: American Cancer Society.

Tenover, F. C. (1995). Emerging problems in antimicrobial resistance. *Journal of Intravenous Nursing, 18*, 297–300.

Triomphe, A. (1993). Economic analysis and public health. Why does one need economic evaluation applied to diabetes? What methods does one choose: Cost effectiveness, cost utility, cost benefit? Are such studies useful in terms of public health? *Diabete et Metabolisme, 19*, 376–473.

U.S. Department of Health and Human Services. (1984). *Consumer choice and cost containment: SAFECO's United Healthcare Plan* (HCFA Pub. No. 03183). Washington, DC: U.S. Government Printing Office.

U.S. Department of Health and Human Services. (1995). *Healthy People 2000: Midcourse review and 1995 revisions.* Washington, DC: U.S. Public Health Service.

Vess, R. W., Anderson, R. L., Carr, J. H., Bond, W. W., & Favero, M. S. (1993). The colonization of solid PVC surfaces and the acquisition of resistance to germicides by water micro-organisms. *Journal of Applied Bacteriology, 74*, 215–221.

Ware, J. E., Brook, R. H., Rogers, W. H., Keeler, E. B., Davies, A. R., Sherbourne, C. D., Goldberg, G. A., Camp, P., & Newhouse, J. P. (1986). Comparison of health outcomes at a health maintenance organization with those of fee-for-service care. *Lancet, 1*, 1017–1022.

Ware, J. E. Jr., & Davies, A. R. (1983). Behavior consequences of consumer dissatisfaction with medical care. *Evaluation and Program Planning, 6*, 291–297.

Wasson, J. H., Sauvigne, A. E., Mogielnicki, R. P., Frey, W. G., Sox, C. H., Gaudette, C., & Rockwell, A. (1984). Continuity of outpatient medical care in elderly men: A randomized trial. *Journal of the American Medical Association, 252*, 2413–2417.

Willems, E. B. (1974). Behavioral technology and behavioral ecology. *Journal of Applied Behavior Analysis, 7*, 151–165.

Wolinsky, F. D. (1970). The performance of health maintenance organizations: An analytic review. *Milbank Memorial Fund Quarterly, 58*, 537–587.

Wolinsky, F. S., & Marder, W. D. (1983). Waiting to see the doctor: The impact of organizational structure of medical practice. *Medical Care, 21*, 531–542.

Woolhandler, S., & Himmelstein, D. U. (1988). Reverse targeting of preventive care due to lack of health insurance. *Journal of the American Medical Association, 259*, 2872–2874.

Wu, Z. C., & Jiang, X. J. (1992). The effects of chlorine disinfection on the resistance of E. coli in water. *Chinese Journal of Preventive Medicine, 26*, 23–24.

2

Compliance, Health Service, and Behavior Analysis

JOEL GREENSPOON

A major problem in health services involves compliance by the patient with the treatment program. There are well over 4,000 references to compliance in PsycLit. Compliance with a treatment program may involve some of the same principles and procedures as compliance with a law, court decision, or parental mand. We shall discuss the issue of compliance only with a treatment program and appointments with the practitioner. These issues are critical in the outpatient setting where the practitioner can exercise limited control over the patient's behavior. The issue is very important to the behavior analyst who is functioning in the outpatient environment. The behavior analyst functioning in this environment may exercise less control over the patient's behavior than his or her institutional counterpart.

The behavior analyst functioning in the outpatient environment designs behavior-change programs that are to be implemented by the client or client-surrogate. If a behavior analyst designs a weight control program, it is the client who has to emit the behaviors of the program. The behavior analyst is placed in the position that s/he may be held responsible for the failure of the program, even though the client did not emit the specified behaviors. More than one behavior analyst, on describing a behavior-change program, has been told, "I have tried behavior modification stuff and it does not work." It is quite possible that the "behavior modification stuff" did not work because the client did not comply with the program.

The compliance issue of keeping appointments is also very important to the practitioner. Subsequent appointments with the practitioner are critical in a behavior-change program. Behavior change rarely occurs overnight except in fiction and movies; it may take weeks or months. The problem of the client's keeping an appointment is akin to the problem of the researcher who may have subjects returning for many sessions over time. The subject's not appearing may ruin an important research project. The client who fails to keep an appointment may not benefit from the behavior-change program. The client who does not keep an appointment makes the monitoring of the program, essential to success of the program, more difficult.

Not keeping an appointment also means that someone else who may be in need of the practitioner's services may be denied the opportunity. This situation has led some practitioners to charge the client for the time unless the client cancels in sufficient time to schedule another client. Charging the client and collecting are not the same behaviors, however.

ARE TWO PROGRAMS NECESSARY?

It appears that a practitioner needs to develop two programs. The behavior change program is obvious. The other program is a different behavior control program. This program is designed to increase the probability that the client will comply with the behavior change program and keep appointments. Fawcett (1995) proposed changing the term from compliance to adherence and assigned the burden of complying with the program to the practitioner. It is readily apparent that no clinician is able to control directly the pre- and postenvironments in which the client is behaving. In the absence of this control the behavior analyst may provide verbal reinforcement for any behavior that conforms to the demands of the program. There is a very real danger in this situation since the clinician may be reinforcing appropriate verbal behavior with no assurance the target behavior was actually emitted. This danger is greater in some behavior change programs than others. For example, the behavior analyst may compute the calories and fat calories of food reported eaten by the client in a weight control program. If the total calorie counts indicate the client should be losing weight but is not, then the behavior analyst may suspect the client's report is inaccurate.

It is essential that the behavior analyst design a behavior change program that enables the analyst to make observations that reduce the dependency on the client's verbal reports. If the client is a child who is doing poorly in school, the behavior analyst may request reports of the child's academic performance provided by the teacher(s). Teachers' reports may be requested for a disciplinary problem in school.

There are many other behavior change problems that may enable the behavior analyst to make direct or indirect observations. Indirect observations are made by third parties of the products of the behavior change program. These observations may not clearly indicate that the client is following the program, but may indicate the outcomes expected of the program. It is difficult to attribute behavior change to a program unless a design has been used to enhance such attributions. Behavior change in the appropriate direction suggests the program is being followed.

There may be many other behavior change programs that do not lend themselves to observations other than the verbal behavior of the client. This situation requires devising ways of increasing the likelihood that the client will comply with the demands of the program. We shall examine some research that has been designed to increase the likelihood that the client emits the behavior demanded by the program. Much of this research involves techniques designed to increase the likelihood that the patient will comply with the medication regimen prescribed by a physician. In some instances the research has been designed and conducted by behavior analysts. We plan to review a few pertinent studies. We shall examine some research concerned with increasing compliance with demands, primarily with children, since this research may include behavior analytic procedures that can be adapted to increasing compliance with programs developed by behavior analysts. We shall not examine research concerned with compliance to legislative and judicial actions as they involve consequences such as heavy monetary fines, contempt of court citations, and jail or prison sentences for noncompliers. One final disclaimer is concerned with research involving demographic, personality, or cognitive variables. We are concerned with research involving manipulable variables as they apply to compliance with a treatment regimen and/or keeping appointments.

RESEARCH ON COMPLIANCE WITH MEDICATION REGIMENS

A major problem in medicine is getting patients to adhere to a medication regimen. Hammond and Lambert (1994) reported approximately 1.5 billion prescriptions are filled each year. Approximately one-third of all patients fail to take their medication. About 7% of all prescriptions are never filled and of those filled about 4% are never picked up. Of those picked up about 20% are never taken. If the medication is necessary for a patient to be successfully treated, it becomes apparent that if the patient's condition does not improve, it may be related to noncompliance with the medication regimen.

A very popular approach to increasing compliance with a medication regimen is an educational program. Many of these programs include a description of the medical condition plus information about the medication and its relationship to the medical condition. There is usually some admonition about complying with the medication regimen. Sackett et al. (1975) developed an educational program that involved a description of the medical condition and the importance of adherence to the medication regimen. Over a six-month period the compliance rate ranged from 50 to 56%, indicating that the program was not particularly effective. It may be contended that the compliance may have been much lower if the education program had not been used. Nevertheless, because only about half the patients adhered to the regimen, the education program cannot be considered very effective. Lin et al. (1995) reported similar results for an education message for patients on an antidepressant regimen. The compliance rate was not very impressive, as 44% of the patients stopped taking the medication by the third month.

Somewhat related to the use of educational material to gain compliance is the use of instructions to enhance compliance with safety regulations. Zeitlin (1994) investigated the effect of safety warnings included in operating instructions. A posttest of knowledge of the safety warnings was also conducted. Although the subjects were knowledgeable about the safety warnings, the safety warnings did not increase compliance. Although education programs have not been very effective, Jackson (1994) found that an educational booklet containing a physician-related, credibility-enhancing cue produced greater compliance with a back pain exercise program than the same booklet without the enhancement or a control group that did not receive the booklet. On the other hand, Moseley et al. (1993) used an education program and social reinforcement for compliance with fluid restriction in a chronically noncompliant patient. The social reinforcement program was effective in increasing compliant behavior, but the educational program was not. The gain in compliance was maintained at a three- and six-month follow-up.

Developing an educational message or safety warning that is effective with all patients on the same regimen or training is a very difficult task. The educational message is designed to effect the verbal control of behavior. Since verbal control of behavior is acquired, it is difficult to find a single set of verbal behaviors that is effective in controlling the same behavior in patients who have very different histories with respect to the verbal behavior used in the educational message. There may be sufficient similarity of histories in enough patients to justify using educational messages, but the effectiveness of the message may be enhanced if it is adapted to the history of verbal control of the patient. It is conceivable that behavior analysts may be helpful in developing materials that would be more effective in controlling the desired behavior of a larger percentage of patients. Zefferblatt (1975) stated that noncompliance with a medication regimen was a behavior problem and could be best attacked through the application of behavior analysis.

Epstein and Masek (1978) investigated compliance with a Vitamin C regimen among college students. Two identical Vitamin C tablets were used, except that one contained phenazopyridine, which produced urine discoloration. Compliance was indicated by the time of the report of urine discoloration and the time it should occur if the vitamin was taken as prescribed. The 40 most noncompliant subjects were selected and randomly assigned to four treatment conditions: (1) self-monitoring, (2) taste–no recording, (3) taste plus self-monitoring and recording, and (4) control. Differently flavored Vitamin C tablets were used to evaluate increasing saliency of medicine-taking on compliance. Subjects recorded the flavor of the tablet. If the subject took the tablet and recorded the taste correctly it would indicate compliance. Self-monitoring and self-monitoring plus taste and recording had the highest rates of compliance. In the second part of the experiment each subject deposited $9 at the outset and lost $1/week if his/her compliance score was less than 2. The addition of the response cost to all treatments and the control increased the level of compliance. The results are impressive in demonstrating the effectiveness of a behavioral approach to compliance.

Much research from the area of noncompliant behavior shows that behavior consequences are effective in reducing noncompliant behavior and increasing compliant behavior. Bourne (1993) found that noncompliant behavior involving aversive and coercive behavior was negatively reinforced for both mother and child. A positive reinforcement program resulted in a sharp reduction in noncompliant behavior by the child and negative comments by the mother. Huguenin (1993) reported that positive reinforcement for compliant behavior both at school and home coupled with a five-minute nonexclusionary time-out was effective in increasing compliant behavior. Montgomery (1993) found that praise and physical contact for complying with requests reduced aggressive behavior during the treatment period but aggressive behavior rebounded, albeit below baseline level during nontreatment follow-up. Little and Kelley (1989) instructed mothers in the use of a response cost technique for noncompliance with demands. The child was given free points at the beginning of the training sessions several times during the day. Points were lost for noncompliance with a demand. Minimal point loss could be exchanged for daily and weekly privileges. Noncompliance to parental demands declined.

Although we have reviewed only a few studies concerned with the use of consequences to affect rate of compliance, the evidence is impressive. The literature of behavior analysis is replete with controlled experiments showing the effects of consequences on the modification and maintenance of a variety of human behaviors.

There is impressive literature describing the use of consequences to effect compliance with many different behavior change programs. Higgins, Budney, Bickel, and Foerg (1994) gave an experimental group of cocaine users vouchers to purchase retail items for every cocaine-free urine sample. Control subjects received the same behavioral treatment program but no vouchers. Seventy-five percent of the experimental subjects and only 40% of the control subjects completed the 24-week treatment program. Experimental subjects consistently exceeded control subjects in continuous cocaine abstinence. Elk et al. (1995) gave monetary reinforcers to cocaine-dependent, pregnant women for reduced cocaine metabolites and cocaine-free samples. Cocaine metabolites decreased and prenatal medical visits increased. Kadden and Mauriello (1991) provided positive and aversive consequences for several different categories of behavior of substance-abusing patients. Appropriate behaviors resulted in privileges. Inappropriate behaviors received demerits that required emission of additional appropriate behaviors before privileges could be earned. Patient involvement in the treatment program increased.

The ketogenic diet is a treatment for intractable epilepsy, but it requires such strict adherence that it is seldom used. Amari, Grace, and Fisher (1995) had intractable epileptic subjects assess relative food preferences of 33 items in the diet. Highly preferred foods were made contingent on the consumption of lower-preferred foods. The subjects increased their appropriate food from 60% during baseline to 99 to 100%. The treatment generalized across caregivers and settings. There was also a 40% reduction in seizures. Stock and Milan (1993) increased the selection of healthier meals by three members of a retirement home through the use of prompts, feedback, and social consequences.

Consequences for one behavior frequently have a beneficial effect on other behaviors. Soutor, Houlihan, and Young (1994) provided reinforcement for compliant behavior in twin boys with multiple behavior problems. Compliant behavior increased as did attending behavior and directed verbalizations. This covariation may be related to the fact that if one behavior declines in frequency other behaviors are going to increase in frequency. The use of positive reinforcement may be a critical factor in increasing other appropriate behaviors.

Behavior analysts have been interested in compliance with weight control programs. Many diet and weight loss programs have promised virtually miraculous reductions in weight. Although many of these diet plans are seemingly effective in enabling individuals to lose weight, many people have regained all of the lost weight plus additional pounds. Most behavior analytic weight control programs emphasize the acquisition of a different set of eating behaviors. The behavior analyst usually cannot observe the eating behaviors. Consequently, many weight control studies tend to rely on weight loss as the critical dependent variable. Mavis and Stoffelmayr (1994) used monetary reward, monetary response cost, monetary reward with lottery system, and response cost with lottery system. A fifth condition was attendance-contingent positive reinforcement, to serve as a control. Dependent variables included weight loss, attendance, contract adherence, dropout rate, and several nonbehavioral measures. Each subject signed a contract at the outset and deposited $40, matched by the experimenter. They also signed a contract each week acknowledging adherence to the contract as well as stating their weight loss. Subjects in the attendance-contingent condition were paid $8 for each meeting attended. Monetary reward involved payment of $8 each meeting if the subject met the stated weight loss goal. Monetary response cost involved docking the subject $8 if the weight loss goal was not met. The lottery-monetary reward involved a lottery chance each week the subject achieved the weight loss goal. Lottery-response cost involved losing one of ten lottery chances each time the weight loss goal was not attained. The monetary response group had a 55% dropout rate but the attendance-contingent group had a 25% dropout rate. Attendance-contingent had the highest attendance rate, but the consequence was for attendance. The attendance-contingent group had the poorest performance of meeting weekly weight loss. These results suggest that consequences, to be effective, must be contingent on the behavior of interest. Contingent-specific consequences may have positive or negative effects on behaviors that are not specifically consequated. Chang (1994) reported that clients who were provided positive feedback to interviewer questions consistently complied more with interviewer requests and recommendations, lost more weight, and returned more often than clients who received neutral feedback.

COMMITMENT TO COMPLY

In a commitment to comply procedure, the patient makes an oral or written commitment to comply with the program. Putnam et al. (1994) reported that subjects who made written and oral commitments for adherence to a ten-day antibiotic regimen and completed tasks designed to increase adherence to the program showed greater adherence to the program than control subjects who made no commitment but performed tasks similar to the experimental subjects. Adherence to the program was measured through unannounced pill counts. Whether an oral or written commitment would be effective for other kinds of behavioral compliance or a longer regimen was not addressed in this study. Taylor and Booth-Butterfield (1993) randomly selected fifteen subjects in a bar who were asked to sign a petition against drunk driving and given an informational pamphlet. The fifteen control subjects were not approached. For six weeks all participants were asked to call a taxi when they became alcohol impaired (that is political correctness for being drunk). Subjects who signed the petition against drunk driving significantly more often called a taxi when alcohol impaired. Levy and Clark (1980) found that getting subjects to commit in writing to keep appointments did not significantly affect their compliance rate.

The issue of oral and/or written commitment to comply with some facet of a treatment program is related to the control of behavior by verbal behavior. In this case the control of compliance behavior is related to the control exercised over the individual's behavior by his/her own verbal behavior. Saying or writing that one will emit certain behaviors does not ensure the behavior will be emitted. Some clients' written or oral commitment to emit certain behaviors will be effective as a source of control over those behaviors.

The oral and/or written commitment is a form of contract but it rarely contains any consequences for noncompliance. Presumably, complying will ultimately result in some positive or negative reinforcement, but that reinforcement may be long delayed. If there are no immediate consequences for complying, then the effectiveness of the commitment will depend almost totally on the verbal behavior of the individual as an effective source of control over his/her own behavior. Trinkaus (1993) made a number of fifteen-minute observations of customers at a supermarket and their compliance with the limit of items in the express lane. About 15% of the customers complied with the item limit. There were no aversive consequences, but probably positive or negative reinforcement provided for noncompliant behavior. The customers with more than the limit were able to avoid standing in the more time-consuming lines of customers with many items.

A contingency contract is a formal set of verbal behaviors that specify the behavior(s) to be emitted, the environmental conditions in which the behavior(s) is to be emitted, and the consequences for the behavior(s). The contract describes the three-term contingency. All conditions are clearly described to avoid any disagreements that may arise about the terms of the contract. When the terms have been agreed upon, the contract is written down and the involved parties sign it. The contract may include some aversive consequences, but it is extremely important that the bases for these consequences are clearly described. This provision is necessary, since the aversive consequences usually generate the most arguments.

It is generally assumed that the demanded behavior is in the individual's repertoire but is not occurring in appropriate environment(s). The appropriate environment is not functioning as a discriminative stimulus (S^D) or the behavior would be occurring. By stating the consequences for emitting the behavior in that environment, the behavior analyst assumed the environmental event has acquired S^D properties. A contingency contract is a set of rules created to control behavior. Skinner (1969) stated, "As a discriminative stimulus (S^D), a rule is effective as a part of a set of contingencies of reinforcement" (p. 148). Glenn (1987) echoed Skinner's position when she said that rules are verbal stimuli that "specify at least two events (more usually, classes of events) and a relation between them (a contingency)" (p. 31). Schlinger and Blakely (1987) and Blakely and Schlinger (1987) prefer to discuss rules in the framework of contingency-specifying stimuli (CSS) that do not evoke behavior as the S^D purportedly does, but alter the effectiveness of stimuli, including S^Ds and reinforcing stimuli. If a contingency contract is a set of rules, then it functions as function-altering rather than as evocative of events. Whether the contingency contract functions as S^Ds or function-altering stimuli, this form of control has to be acquired and is certainly not inherent in the specific set of words used to describe the terms and conditions of the contract. This control has to be acquired if the contingency contract is to have any chance of success. The behavior analyst who is developing a contract on behalf of a client will have more success if he/she has a knowledge of the history of the individuals when selecting the verbal behavior to describe the terms and conditions of the contract. Other individuals must provide the consequences associated with those specified behaviors if emitted. One problem that may arise is that the target individual emits the specified behavior(s), but the consequences are not provided. This situation has a deleterious effect on the behavior of the target individual.

Contingency contracting has been used extensively and successfully with a wide variety of behaviors, a large number of environmental events, and an extensive array of consequences. Some uses of contingency contracting include alcohol treatment (Hodgson, 1994), illicit drug use (Allen et al., 1993), with significant others of cocaine users (Higgins et al., 1994), parent-child contracts for school-related behaviors (Smith, 1994), homework performance (Miller & Kelley, 1994), reduction of HIV/AIDS risk among drug users (Rhodes & Humfleet, 1993), serious behavior disorders (Dupree, 1993), sexual problems (Lund, 1992), nutritional habits (Nelson & Heknat, 1991), attention-deficit hyperactivity

(DuPaul, 1991), juvenile delinquency (Zimpfer, 1992), exercise regimen (Leslie & Schuster, 1991), personal hygiene (Allen & Kramer, 1990), and glucose monitoring (Wysocki, Green, & Huxtable, 1989) to name a few. This list illustrates the widespread use of contingency contracting. Heinssen, Levendusky, and Hunter (1995) proposed the therapeutic contract as an integral part of a treatment program for the seriously mentally ill. Although the therapeutic contract differs in many features from the contingency contract, there are some features common to both.

The foot-in-the-door technique is designed to increase compliance. The technique, developed by Freedman and Fraser (1966), involves making a request that has a high probability of compliance. Then the individual is requested to meet a low probability request. Katzev and Johnson (1983) asked homeowners to fill out an energy conservation questionnaire prior to asking them to reduce their energy consumption by 10%. The initial high probability of compliance request is usually related to the low probability of compliance request. The high probability request may be to reduce energy consumption by 1% followed by the low probability request of reducing energy consumption by 10%.

The results of research on the foot-in-the-door technique have been equivocal. Sharkin, Mahalik, and Claiborn (1989) reported the technique to be reasonably effective as did Katzev and Johnson (1983), Goldman et al. (1981), Dolin and Booth-Butterfield (1995), and Hornik, Zaig, and Shadmon (1991). DeJong and Funder (1977) reported the foot-in-the-door technique was increasingly effective if compliance with a small request was accompanied by a promise of a $2 payment. This result tends to be congruent with principles and procedures of behavior analysis.

Many studies (e.g., Beaman et al., 1988; Brownstein & Katzev, 1985; Grace, Bell, & Sugar, 1988; Wang, Brownstein, & Katzev, 1989) reported the foot-in-the-door technique was not very effective in increasing compliance. Foss and Dempsey (1979) concluded that the technique may be effective when a verbal response has to be made, such as agreeing to give blood, but may not be very effective when the behavior is much more demanding than a verbal response.

A behavior analytic variation of this technique involves making a number of requests that have a high probability of compliance followed by a low probability request. This set of procedures, called behavioral momentum (Nevin, 1974; Nevin, Mandell, & Atak, 1983), involves the manipulation of density of reinforcement. As the probability of reinforcement of a behavior increased so did the probability that the behavior would continue to occur in the absence of additional reinforcement (extinction). Mace et al. (1988) reported that preceding a low probability of compliance instruction with high probability of compliance instructions increased the probability of compliance with the low probability instruction.

Using a variation of the Mace et al. (1988) procedures, Houlihan, Jacobson, and Branden (1994) found that a shorter interprompt time resulted in greater compliance than a longer interprompt time between the high and low probability of compliance demands. Kennedy, Itkonen, and Lindquist (1995) obtained similar results with the time variable as related to interspersed social comments. However, Zarcone et al. (1993) and Zarcone et al. (1994) did not get this effect working with severely retarded individuals. Zarcone et al. (1993) reported that adding an extinction of escape behavior component enabled the high probability instructional sequence to be effective, although the extinction of the escape component alone was also effective in increasing compliance to the low probability request. Zarcone et al. (1994) reported similar results.

It seems as though some magical properties are being ascribed to verbal behavior. Is there any particular behavioral principle that accounts for a positive effect on low probability of compliance demands if preceded by high probability of compliance demands? The momentum phenomenon relates to the persistence of a behavior that has a history of high reinforcement density. One problem arises because a continuous reinforcement schedule provides the highest density of reinforcement but the least persistence of the behavior. It may be that providing a few high probability of compliance requests is not the basis for establishing behavioral momentum. If it is, what is the momentum related to? Does having the individual emit a behavior to a high probability of compliance request maintain compliance regardless of the request? Compliance is not a behavior; it is the relationship between some antecedent event and the emission of some behavior. The issue of what momentum refers to becomes rather critical. Nevin's (1974) momentum referred to the same behavior that was reinforced. The behavior involved in complying with a low probability of compliance request may be considerably different from the behavior of the high probability of compliance request.

We believe the issue of compliance relates to control. Any control exercised by a request has to be acquired. Whether this control has been acquired depends on the behavioral history of the individual. One set of words describing a behavioral request may be effective for many but not necessarily for all people. We reported a study (Trinkaus, 1993) that showed about 15% of the customers in a supermarket complied with the restrictions on the number of items at the checkout lane. Frantz (1993) reported more subjects read and complied with warning labels when they were included in the Directions for Use than the Precautions section on the label of the container. Compliance with the warnings increased from 48% to 83% when the statement was moved from the Precautions to the Directions for Use section.

The environment in which the request or instructions are presented may affect the probability of compliance. An individual under serious time constraints may go through the express checkout line with an excess of items but would go through a regular checkout line if time is not a critical factor. The same situation may be applicable to compliance with other demands relating to therapeutic regimens, behavior change programs, or other treatment programs. Tuberculosis patients are notorious for complying with the medication regimen when first admitted to the hospital but become increasingly noncompliant as their condition improves. It appears that it is necessary not only to select words that may have high probability of controlling the emission of the compliant behavior but also to consider other factors and conditions that may prevail in the individual's environment that could affect compliance.

THE BEHAVIOR CHANGE PROGRAM

One important factor confronting the behavior analyst with respect to compliance with a behavior change program is that behavior change is usually a slow process. Assuming that behavior change in the desired direction reinforced the behavior(s) involved in the compliance with the behavior change program, it means that this reinforcement may be long delayed. Much of the research in delayed versus immediate reinforcement indicates clearly that immediate reinforcement is more powerful than delayed reinforcement. It is thus necessary to build into behavior change programs some reinforcement for complying with the behavioral demands of the program. A weight control program illustrates these points. If a client states a desire to lose 25 pounds, this weight loss is not going to occur quickly. The loss of a few pounds necessitates emitting a number of different behaviors over a period of time. The development of effective eating behaviors takes considerable time, especially if the client has emitted counter-productive eating behaviors that have been strongly reinforced, a high probability event. For the client to acquire and/or emit effective eating behaviors over the time necessary to lose a few pounds, it is necessary to provide reinforcement for effective eating behaviors before the reinforcing effects of the weight loss will occur. The behavior analyst may provide some verbal reinforcement when the client reports emitting the specified behaviors. This reinforcement is also delayed so far as the specific behaviors are concerned. What is reinforced is the verbal behavior describing the specified eating behaviors. If the client is to provide reinforcement immediately following emission of the specified eating behaviors, then the behavior analyst is dependent on the client to provide the reinforcement only when it is appropriate. The behavior analyst is not in a position to monitor the program, although being able to monitor the program is considered essential to the success of a behavior change program. Monitoring the weight of the client by having the client weighed in the analyst's presence is not the most desirable arrangement. There may be no effective way of monitoring the program unless there is another person who is always present in the client's environment. This problem is present in any behavior change program for an outpatient and is often present even in the institutional setting.

The behavior analyst may reinforce the verbal behavior of the client in the absence of any data to show there is a congruency between the verbal behavior of the client and the emission of the behavior specified in the behavior change program. This is an easy trap for the behavior analyst because the analyst is dependent on information and data provided by the client. This situation can occur in the institutional environment if the behavior analyst has to rely on others for the observation and recording of the client's behavior. It is much easier for the behavior analyst in the institution to observe the behavior of the client than it is for the behavior analyst in the outpatient setting, unless the behavior analyst has the time, money, and/or trained staff who can observe the client in the natural environment.

Having the client emit the behaviors specified in the behavior change program is a problem of control. The source of this behavior control is the verbal behavior of the behavior analyst. The behavior analyst will have some clients whose behavior is well controlled by the verbal behavior of others. These clients will probably emit the behaviors specified in the behavior change program. There will be many clients whose behavior is not very well controlled by the verbal behavior of others. The behavior analyst may find it necessary to develop his/her verbal behavior as a source of control over the client's behavior. If the behavior analyst is effective in this endeavor, there may be an increased likelihood that the client will emit the behaviors specified in the behavior change program.

An alternative for some behavior problems is to have the desired behavior occur in the presence of a verbal description of an environment in which the client reports emitting the behavior described in the behavior change program. Assume a client has requested assistance from a behavior analyst to help him say "no" to requests from fellow employees, especially when he has a lot of work to do. His failure to say "no" had led to his being passed over for promotion, as he frequently failed to meet deadlines because he was busy helping others. His self-report indicates that he has shown considerable improvement. The behavior analyst may describe a situation that could arise at work resulting in a request of him by a colleague. The behavior analyst may add that the client has a major report due in the morning. The analyst may add that the colleague agrees to remain after work and help the client with his report. That the colleague has emitted similar verbal behavior in the past but never helped is also described. The client is asked to respond to this situation. If he emits the desired behavior, then the behavior analyst may reinforce the behavior.

Although these procedures are less preferred than direct observation of the behavior in the actual environment, it may provide some additional information. An alternative but related procedure involves role playing. The behavior analyst in the situation described above plays the part of the colleague asking the client to do a favor that interferes with the client's completing his/her own work. The behavior analyst may make the demands that conceivably could be made and notes how the client reacts. The behavior analyst instructs the client to refuse the colleague's request regardless of what the colleague may say or offer to do. The behavior analyst can observe how the client reacts, but more importantly whether the client's behavior is being brought under the control of the behavior analyst. If the client refuses the "colleague's" request, the behavior analyst may provide reinforcement for the behavior. If these procedures are effective, the behavior analyst may repeat the procedures until the client is emitting the behavior at a high rate. The client has attained fluency (Johnson & Layng, 1992). Fluency presumably has a beneficial effect on the emission of a fluent behavior and the behavior analyst may have established his/her verbal behavior as a source of control over the client's behavior. It may be possible for the behavior analyst to exercise sufficient control over the client's behavior that the client will emit the behavior(s) specified in the program.

Establishing control over the client's behavior is not the ultimate end. The ultimate objective is to fade out the behavior analyst's control as the program's effectiveness increases. The objective of the behavior change program is to establish the client's environment as the source of control over the client's behavior so that positive reinforcement is maximized and aversive consequences are minimized. The procedures necessary to attain this objective are built into the behavior change program, or at least they should be. The behavior analyst, in developing a behavior change program, must consider how he/she will terminate the program and what procedures will maximize the maintenance of the behavior changes. Shifting control of the behavior from the behavior analyst to the client's environment becomes an important component of the behavior change program.

Another significant factor confronting the behavior analyst in the client's compliance with a behavior change program is the slow rate of behavior change. As mentioned previously, delayed reinforcement is usually less effective than immediate reinforcement, especially in the uncontrolled environment. In the uncontrolled environment the individual may emit a large number of behaviors between the time desired behavior occurs and the reinforcement from the behavior change occurs. Some of these intervening behaviors may be considered undesirable in the environments in which they are occurring. It is necessary for the behavior analyst to devise ways and means for providing immediate reinforcement for the desired behavior. Any conditioned reinforcer that has been developed in the client's past available to the behavior analyst may be used to provide reinforcement for any behavior deemed to be related either to the terminal behavior(s) or compliance with the behavior change program. If there are no available conditioned reinforcers, then the behavior analyst may find it necessary to develop such reinforcers in the sessions with the client. The behavior analyst can ill afford to leave compliance with the behavior change program to chance.

COMPLIANCE WITH APPOINTMENTS

The issue of keeping appointments is very important to any practitioner, but it is especially critical for the behavior analyst. Although most practitioners find it necessary to have the client return a number of times, they may function so differently from behavior analysts that they may have a greater likelihood that the client will keep the next appointment. These practitioners tend to analyze and interpret what the client reports. They also tend to gather information about the "psychological" development of the client. The client is usually not asked to do anything specific before the next appointment. The nonbehavior analytic practitioner tends to do most of the work involved in dealing with the client's problems. The behavior analyst usually uses the time of the first appointment to collect information that may be used to develop a behavior change program. One of the consequences of the initial appointment is that the client is usually instructed to collect data. This procedure is foreign to most clients, whose conception of what happens when one sees a "shrink" is based on the movies or television. They may leave the behavior analyst's office puzzled and perplexed by what is happening. Most clients probably assume the clinician is going to do the work of "curing" them. But behavior analysts operate from the premise that the analyst cannot breathe for the client, eat for the client, sleep for the client, or behave for the client. The client must emit behavior if behavior change is to occur. When the client is apprised of this situation, he/she may decide to see a clinician who operates from a different perspective. The client rarely tells the behavior analyst about this decision, but makes another appointment and simply fails to keep it.

The appointment problem extends to the very first appointment. Many clients contact the clinician or clinic by phone and make an appointment for a subsequent date. Sometimes individuals are informed there are no openings at the time and they are put on a waiting list. These two situations are somewhat comparable in that the individual is not seen immediately by a clinician, although the waiting list condition is not as definite as the specific future appointment. There are variations of these situations such as people who undergo screening for some condition at a public event. Sometimes there are health fairs and people may have their cholesterol checked, have a mammogram taken, blood pressure checked, and so forth. These people, when notified of the results, are frequently urged to make an appointment with a professional if the results suggest a potential or actual problem. All of these situations have a common thread of inducing individuals to keep or make an appointment. Although initial appointment and subsequent appointment compliance may seem to require different solutions, and perhaps they do, similar procedures have been used in both situations. We shall not distinguish between these two situations, although we shall note, if appropriate, whether the procedures were used for initial or follow-up appointments.

One factor reported to affect the probability of keeping an initial appointment is whether the individual is seen immediately or placed on a waiting list. Stern and Brown (1994) found a significant relationship between the failure to keep an initial appointment and the length of time between referral and appointment dates. As the time between referral and appointment dates increased, so did the incidence of failure to keep the initial appointment. Chen (1991) obtained comparable results and recommended shortening the waiting period to increase compliance with the appointment.

Maiman et al. (1992) offered a coupon along with a referral reminder to increase physician visits by individuals who attended a public cholesterol screening. Some individuals were referred by a lay communicator and some by a health professional. Only the coupon was effective in increasing visits to a physician. Reiss, Piotrowski, and Bailey (1976) reported a single written prompt plus a $5 incentive was the most effective, and a single written prompt was least effective in getting parents to initial dental care for their children. A series of three prompts consisting of a written note, a telephone call, and a home visit was almost as effective as the written prompt plus incentive and was cheaper. Reiss and Bailey (1982) found that a multiple contact procedure with no incentive increased parents' seeking dental care for their children and was most cost-effective.

Ross, Friman, and Christopherson (1993) investigated several different procedures to determine their effect on keeping and canceling appointments. One procedure involved a mailed reminder, plus a parking pass, plus a telephone reminder. Another procedure included a mailed reminder plus a parking pass. A telephone only reminder and a control were the other procedures. All the procedures produced better compliance than the control but did not differ among themselves. The interventions increased cancellations but did not significantly increase appointments kept, although all three interventions had a lower number of not-kept appointments than the control. They also found that as the time when the appointment was made and the appointment date increased, so did the failure to keep appointments.

Although some researchers (Ross et al., 1993) reported that reminders may be somewhat better than no contact in reducing ''no shows,'' West, DuRant, and Pendergast (1993) reported that reminder cards failed to improve compliance of adolescents with dental appointments. Kendall and Hailey (1993) found that a reassuring letter was effective in getting over 50% of women to comply with a mammogram screening test, while only 42% of the women receiving an anxiety provoking letter and 38% of those receiving a standard hospital letter scheduled appointments for the screening test. Moser (1994) reported that a postcard reminder was ineffective in increasing compliance with appointments or notifying the clinic of a cancellation.

A number of investigators have reported that a written and/or telephone prompt increased compliance with appointments. Gates and Colborn (1976) found that both letters and telephone prompts increased appointment compliance. Similar results were reported by Shepard and Moseley (1976) who found the telephone prompt was a little more effective than the letter prompt. Carrion et al. (1993) suggested that letter and phone prompts may improve compliance with appointments by schizophrenic patients. Campbell et al. (1994) reported a letter or postcard that described the content of an upcoming appointment resulted in better compliance than a no-postcard or letter group. Lombard, Lombard, and Winett (1995) found that more frequent phone prompts were more effective in getting individuals to continue a health fitness walking program. Forty-six percent of the individuals who were called once a week continued while only 13%

of those called every three weeks continued. Even the weekly phone calls were not effective in getting half of the individuals to continue.

If an intervention is effective in increasing compliance with appointments, it is also necessary to determine if the cost of the intervention may be greater than the revenue, if any, that would be generated by the individuals' complying with the appointments. Although one may express concern that people who may need some form of health care may not receive it because they do not keep appointments, the cost issue is becoming increasingly important. Facilities offering health care services are cutting every conceivable corner to reduce costs. Sometimes the cost cutting may be pennywise and pound foolish.

Rice and Lutzker (1984) investigated several different procedures designed to increase appointment compliance as well as to assess the cost of the procedures. They found that free follow-up and reduced rate procedures were more effective in increasing compliance than a no-treatment control or modified appointment card. The reduced rate procedure was continued for an additional six weeks and produced a significantly better compliance rate than the no-treatment control. Although the reduced rate procedure cost more per patient than the no-treatment control or modified appointment card, it actually generated more revenue than either of these two conditions. The free follow-up was the most expensive.

It appears there are some procedures that may increase the compliance rate with appointments. The procedures cost time, effort, and money to develop or effect control over the individuals' keeping appointments. Unkept appointments also cost money in that the appointments go unfilled and generate no revenue. Private clinics and private practitioners as well as tax-supported facilities can ill afford to lose too much revenue as a function of unkept appointments.

Complying with appointments is a form of rule-governed behavior. No rule or verbal request is inherently effective. The high incidence of noncompliance is prima facie evidence of the absence of inherent control in a particular verbal behavior. Like so many other forms of environmental control, the verbal behavior has to acquire the control. Specifying something as a rule does not ensure that it will exercise the desired control. A ready solution to this situation is to state that if the verbal behavior does not control the appropriate behavior, it is not a rule. That may solve one problem, but it does not solve the more important problem of compliance with appointments. The same is true with respect to contingency-specifying stimuli. Simply specifying some verbal behavior as a contingency-specifying stimulus does not ensure that the appropriate or desired behavior will occur.

The research in this area suggests that there may be procedures that will increase the probability that control over compliant behavior can occur. The fact that no intervention increased the control over compliance in all individuals is another indication that the control is acquired and is a reflection of the behavior history of the individual. There are no readily available means of determining what verbal behavior will effectively control the appointment compliance behavior of a particular individual. Without going into any of the details of the research, there have been many studies of demographic variables, some of which indicate there is a higher compliance rate among certain groups than other groups. Perhaps research that combined demographic variables and manipulable variables may shed some light on this problem.

IN CONCLUSION

It is readily apparent that the compliance issue in the health care services has not been adequately solved. We do not know how to increase reliably the probability that a client will keep an appointment, much less carry out the regimen created to deal with the presenting problem. There may be some practitioners who do not consider the compliance of a patient with the prescribed regimen to be their concern. They may contend that diagnosis and prescription are their only concerns. And perhaps that is a tenable position. But if the practitioner is concerned that the prescribed regimen be effective, then he/she must address the issue of compliance.

Despite the large number of references to compliance from a variety of disciplines, there is still a need for procedures that are readily available to the health provider, to enhance the probability of compliance either with a treatment regimen and/or appointments. The procedures have to be adaptable to the individual. At the same time the procedures have to be cost-effective. There are probably procedures that would increase the probability of compliance with an appointment, but the cost of such procedures may be too excessive to be adopted. From the behavior analytic standpoint the issue of compliance is the issue of control. Control simply means that in the presence of a particular event, it may be an intraorganismic or an extraorganismic event, there is an increased probability that a particular behavior will occur. The clinician has to discover the kind of verbal behavior that has a high probability of controlling the behavior of the client necessary to comply with the clinician's requests. One of the objectives of the initial interview with the client may be to discover some of the verbal behavior that seemingly controls the behavior of the client. What kinds of clinicians' verbal behaviors are effective in getting the client to respond appropriately? The clinician may find it worthwhile to conduct some exercises designed to determine the extent, if any, of the clinician's control over the client's behavior. What kinds of situations described by the client seem to be effective in controlling the client's behavior? A child-client may state that when his/her father or mother tells him/her to do something, he/she does it. If the other parent makes the same demand, the child does not comply. If this situation should evolve in the course of talking to the child, then the clinician may involve the parent as the one who describes the regimen to be followed by the child. If the clinician can identify individuals in the client's environment who can exercise control over the client's behavior, then it may be advisable to involve these individuals, if possible, in the program.

The research in the area of client compliance is not especially impressive in identifying variables or factors that may increase the probability of compliance by the client. At the same time the general public will assess the quality of applied behavior analysis by the effectiveness of the behavior analytic programs to effect behavior change. Since compliance with the program is essential to the effectiveness of the program, it behooves the behavior analyst to be attentive to the client's compliance with the program.

REFERENCES

Allen, L. J., Howard, V. F., Sweeney, W. J., & McLaughlin, T. F. (1993). Use of contingency contracting to increase on-task behavior with primary students. *Psychological Reports, 72*, 905–906.

Allen, S. J., & Kramer, J. J. (1990). Modification of personal hygiene and grooming behaviors with contingency contracting: A brief review and case study. *Psychology in the Schools, 27*, 244–251.

Amari, A., Grace, N. C., & Fisher, W. W. (1995). Achieving and maintaining compliance with the ketogenic diet. *Journal of Applied Behavior Analysis, 26*, 379–387.

Beaman, A. L., Stebley, N. M., Preston, M., & Klentz, B. (1988). Compliance as a function of elapsed time between first and second requests. *Journal of Social Psychology, 128*, 233–243.

Blakely, E., & Schlinger, H. (1987). Rules: Function-altering contingency-shaping stimuli. *The Behavior Analyst, 10*, 183–187.

Bourne, D. F. (1993). Over-chastisement, child non-compliance and parenting skills: A behavioral intervention by a family centre social worker. *British Journal of Social Work, 23*, 481–499.

Brownstein, R. J., & Katzev, R. D. (1985). The relative effectiveness of three compliance techniques in eliciting donations to a cultural organization. *Journal of Applied Social Psychology, 15*, 564–574.

Campbell, J. R., Szilagyi, P. G., Rodenwald, L. E., & Doane, C. (1994). Patient-specific reminder letters and pediatric well-child-care show rates. *Clinical Pediatrics, 33*, 268–272.

Carrion, P. G., Swan, A., Kellert-Cecil, H., & Barber, M. (1993). Compliance with clinic attendance by outpatients with schizophrenia. *Hospital and Community Psychiatry, 44*, 764–767.

Chang, P. (1994). Effects of interviewer questions and response type: An analogue study. *Journal of Counseling Psychology, 41*, 74–82.

Chen, A. (1991). Noncompliance in community psychiatry: A review of clinical interventions. *Hospital and Community Psychiatry, 42*, 282–287.

DeJong, W., & Funder, D. (1977). Effect of payment for initial compliance: Unanswered questions about the foot-in-the-door phenomenon. *Personality and Social Psychology Bulletin, 3*, 662–665.

Dolin, D. J., & Booth-Butterfield, S. (1995). Foot-in-the-door and cancer prevention. *Health Communication, 7*, 55–66.

DuPaul, G. J. (1991). Attention deficit-hyperactivity disorder: Classroom intervention strategies. *School Psychology International, 12*, 85–94.

Dupree, L. W. (1993). Treatment of paranoid ideation and hostile verbalizations in an elderly woman using thought-stopping, assertiveness training and marital and discharge contracting. *Clinical Gerontologist, 13*, 29–43.

Elk, R., Schmitz, J., Spiga, R., Rhoades, H., Andres, R., & Grabowski, J. (1995). Behavioral treatment of cocaine-dependent pregnant women and TB-exposed patients. *Addictive Behaviors, 20*, 533–542.

Epstein, L. H., & Masek, B. J. (1978). Behavioral control of medicine compliance. *Journal of Applied Behavior Analysis, 11*, 1–9.

Fawcett, J. (1995). Compliance: Definitions and key issues. Compliance strategies to optimize antidepressant treatment outcomes. *Journal of Clinical Psychiatry, 56*, 4–10.

Foss, R. D., & Dempsey, C. B. (1979). Blood donation and the foot-in-the-door technique: A limiting case. *Journal of Personality and Social Psychology, 37*, 580–590.

Frantz, J. P. (1993). Effect of location and presentation format on attention to and compliance with product warnings and instructions. *Journal of Safety Research, 24*, 131–154.

Freedman, J. L., & Fraser, S. L. (1966). Compliance without pressure: The foot-in-the-door technique. *Journal of Personality and Social Psychology, 4*, 195–202.

Gates, S. J., & Colborn, D. K. (1976). Lowering appointment failures in a neighborhood health center. *Medical Care, 14*, 263–267.

Glenn, S. S. (1987). Rules as environmental events. *The Analysis of Verbal Behavior, 5*, 29–32.

Goldman, M., Creason, C. R., Christopher, R., & McCall, C. G. (1981). Compliance employing a two-feet-in-the-door procedure. *Journal of Social Psychology, 114*, 259–265.

Grace, C. R., Bell, P. A., & Sugar, J. (1988). Effects of compliance techniques on spontaneous and asked-for helping. *Journal of Social Psychology, 128*, 525–532.

Hammond, S. L., & Lambert, B. L. (1994). Communicating about medications: Directions for research. Special Issue: Communicating with patients about their medications. *Health Communications, 6*, 247–251.

Heinssen, R. K., Levendusky, P. G., & Hunter, R. H. (1995). Client as colleague: Therapeutic contracting with the seriously mentally ill. *American Psychologist, 50*, 522–532.

Higgins, S. T., Budney, A. J., Bickel, W. K., Foerg, F. E., Donham, R., & Badger, G. J. (1994). Incentives improve outcome in outpatient behavioral treatment of cocaine dependence. *Archives of General Psychiatry, 51*, 568–576.

Hodgson, R. L. (1994). Treatment of alcohol problems. Special Issue: Comparing drugs of dependence. *Addiction, 89*, 1529–1534.

Hornick, J., Zaig, T., & Shadmon, D. (1991). Reducing refusals in telephone surveys on sensitive topics. *Journal of Advertising Research, 31*, 49–56.

Houlihan, D., Jacobson, L., & Branden, P. K. (1994). Replication of a high-probability request sequence with varied interprompt times in a preschool setting. *Journal of Applied Behavior Analysis, 27*, 737–738.

Huguenin, N. H. (1993). Reducing chronic noncompliance in an individual with severe mental retardation to facilitate community integration. *Mental Retardation, 31*, 332–339.

Jackson, L. (1994). Maximizing treatment adherence among back-pain patients: An experimental study of the effects of physician-related cues in written medical messages. *Health Communication, 6,* 173–191.

Johnson, K. R., & Layng, T. V. J. (1992). Breaking the structuralist barrier: Literacy and numeracy with fluency. *American Psychologist, 47,* 1475–1490.

Kadden, R. M., & Mauriello, I. J. (1991). Enhancing participation in substance abuse treatment using an incentive system. *Journal of Substance Abuse Treatment, 8,* 113–124.

Katzev, R. D., & Johnson, T. R. (1983). A social psychological analysis of residential electricity consumption: The impact of minimal justification techniques. *Journal of Economic Psychology, 3,* 267–284.

———. (1984). Comparing the effects of monetary incentives and foot-in-the-door strategies in promoting residential electricity conservation. *Journal of Applied Social Psychology, 14,* 12–27.

Kendall, C., & Hailey, B. J. (1993). The relative effectiveness of three reminder letters on making and keeping mammogram appointments. *Behavioral Medicine, 19,* 29–34.

Kennedy, C. H., Itkonen, T., & Lindquist, K. (1995). Comparing interspersed requests and social comments as antecedents for increasing student compliance. *Journal of Applied Behavior Analysis, 28,* 97–98.

Leslie, M., & Schuster, P. A. (1991). The effect of contingency contracting on adherence and knowledge of exercise regimens. *Patient Education and Counseling, 18,* 231–241.

Levy, R. L., & Clark, H. (1980). The use of an overt commitment to enhance compliance: A cautionary note. *Journal of Behavior Therapy and Experimental Psychiatry, 11,* 105–107.

Lin, E. H., Von Korff, M., Katon, W., & Bush, T. (1995). The role of the primary care physician in patients' adherence to antidepressant therapy. *Medical Care, 33,* 67–74.

Little, L. M., & Kelley, M. L. (1989). The efficacy of response cost procedures for reducing children's noncompliance to parental instructions. *Behavior Therapy, 20,* 525–534.

Lombard, D. N., Lombard, T. N., & Winett, R. A. (1995). Walking to meet health guidelines: The effect of frequent prompting frequency and prompt structure. *Health Psychology, 14,* 164–170.

Lund, C. A. (1992). Long-term treatment of sexual behavior problems in adolescent and adult developmentally disabled persons. *Annals of Sex Research, 5,* 5–31.

Mace, F. C., Hock, M. L., Lalli, J. S., Belfiore, P., Penter, E., Brown, D. K., & West, B. (1988). Behavioral momentum in the treatment of noncompliance. *Journal of Applied Behavior Analysis, 21,* 123–141.

Maiman, L. A., Hildreth, N. G., Cox, C., & Greenland, P. (1992). Improving referral compliance after public cholesterol screening. *American Journal of Public Health, 82,* 804–809.

Mavis, B. E., & Stoffelmayr, B. E. (1994). Multidimensional evaluation of monetary incentive strategies for weight control. *The Psychological Record, 44,* 239–252.

Miller, D. L., & Kelley, M. L. (1994). The use of goal setting and contingency contracting for improving children's homework performance. *Journal of Applied Behavior Analysis, 27,* 73–84.

Montgomery, R. W. (1993). The collateral effect of compliance training on aggression. *Behavioral Residential Treatment, 8*, 9–20.

Moseley, T. H., Eisen, A. R., Bruce, B. K., & Brantley, P. J. (1993). Contingent social reinforcement for fluid compliance in a hemodialysis patient. *Journal of Behavior Therapy and Experimental Psychiatry, 24*, 77–81.

Moser, S. E. (1994). Effectiveness of post card appointment reminders. *Family Practice Research Journal, 14*, 281–288.

Nelson, L. J., & Heknat, H. (1991). Promoting healthy nutritional habits by paradigmatic behavior theory. *Journal of Behavior Therapy and Experimental Psychiatry, 22*, 291–298.

Nevin, J. A. (1974). Response strength in multiple schedules. *Journal of the Experimental Analysis of Behavior, 21*, 389–408.

Nevin, J. A., Mandell, C., & Atak, J. R. (1983). The analysis of behavioral momentum. *Journal of the Experimental Analysis of Behavior, 39*, 49–59.

Putnam, D. E., Finney, J. W., Barkley, P. L., & Bonner, M. J. (1994). Enhancing commitment improves adherence to a medical regimen. *Journal of Consulting and Clinical Psychology, 62*, 191–194.

Reiss, M. L., & Bailey, J. R. (1982). Visiting the dentist: A behavioral community analysis of participants in a dental screening and referral program. *Journal of Applied Behavior Analysis, 15*, 353–362.

Reiss, M. L., Piotrowski, W. D., & Bailey, J. S. (1976). Behavioral community psychology: Encouraging low-income parents to seek dental care for their children. *Journal of Applied Behavior Analysis, 9*, 387–397.

Rhodes, F., & Humfleet, G. L. (1993). Using goal-oriented counseling and peer support to reduce HIV/AIDS risk among drug users not in treatment. *Drugs and Society, 7*, 185–204.

Rice, J. M., & Lutzker, J. R. (1984). Reducing noncompliance to follow-up appointment keeping at a family practice center. *Journal of Applied Behavior Analysis, 17*, 303–311.

Ross, L. V., Friman, P. C., & Christopherson, E. R. (1993). An appointment-keeping improvement package for outpatient pediatrics: Systematic replication and component analysis. *Journal of Applied Behavior Analysis, 26*, 461–467.

Sackett, D. L., Haynes, R. B., Gibson, E. S., Hackett, B. C., Taylor, D. W., Roberts, R. S., & Johnson, A. L. (1975). Randomized clinical trial of strategies for improving medication compliance in primary hypertension. *Lancet, 1*, 1205–1207.

Schlinger, H., & Blakely, E. (1987). Function-altering effects of contingency-specifying stimuli. *The Behavior Analyst, 10*, 41–45.

Sharkin, B. S., Mahalik, J. R., & Claiborn, C. D. (1989). Application of the foot-in-the-door effect to counseling. *Journal of Counseling Psychology, 36*, 248–251.

Shepard, D. S., & Moseley, T. A. E. (1976). Mailed versus telephoned appointment reminders to reduce broken appointments in a hospital outpatient department. *Medical Care, 14*, 268–273.

Skinner, B. F. (1969). *Contingencies of reinforcement: A theoretical analysis*. New York: Appleton-Century-Crofts.

Smith, S. E. (1994). Parent-initiated contracts: An intervention for school-related behaviors. *Elementary School Guidance and Counseling, 28*, 182–187.

Soutor, T. A., Houlihan, D., & Young, A. (1994). An examination of response covariation on the behavioral treatment of identical twin boys with multiple behavioral disorders. *Behavioral Interventions, 9*, 141–155.

Stern. G., & Brown, R. (1994). The effect of waiting list on attendance at initial appointments in a child and family clinic. *Child Care, Health and Development, 20*, 219–230.

Stock, L. Z., & Milan, M. A. (1993). Improving dietary practices of elderly individuals: The power of prompting, feedback, and social reinforcement. *Journal of Applied Behavior Analysis, 26*, 379–387.

Taylor, T., & Booth-Butterfield, S. (1993). Getting a foot in the door with drinking and driving: A field study of healthy influence. *Communication Research Reports, 10*, 96–101.

Trinkaus, J. (1993). Compliance with the items limit of the food supermarket express checkout lane: An informal look. *Psychological Reports, 73*, 105–106.

Wang, T., Brownstein, R., & Katzev, A. (1989). Promoting charitable behaviour with compliance techniques. *Applied Psychology: An International Review, 38*, 165–183.

West, K. P., DuRant, R. H., & Pendergast, R. (1993). An experimental test of adolescents compliance with dental appointments. *Journal of Adolescent Health, 14*, 384–389.

Wysocki, T., Green, L., & Huxtable, K. (1989). Blood glucose monitoring by diabetic adolescents: Compliance and metabolic control. *Health Psychology, 8*, 267–284.

Zarcone, J. R., Iwata, B. A., Hughes, C. E., & Vollmer, T. R. (1993). Momentum versus extinction effects in the treatment of self-injurious behavior. *Journal of Applied Behavior Analysis, 26*, 131–136.

Zarcone, J. R., Iwata, B. A., Mazaleski, J. L., & Smith, R. G. (1994). Momentum and extinction effects on self-injurious escape behavior and noncompliance. *Journal of Applied Behavior Analysis, 27*, 649–658.

Zefferblatt, S. M. (1975). Increasing patient compliance through the applied analysis of behavior. *Preventive Medicine, 4*, 173–182.

Zeitlin, L. R. (1994). Failure to follow safety instructions: Faulty communication or risky decisions. *Human Factors, 36*, 172–181.

Zimpfer, D. G. (1992). Group work with juvenile delinquents. *Journal for Specialists in Group Work, 17*, 116–126.

3

Activity Anorexia: The Interplay of Culture, Behavior, and Biology

W. DAVID PIERCE AND W. FRANK EPLING

This chapter addresses the interrelationships among culture, behavior, and biology for an analysis of human self-starvation. Unusual behavior of animals may occasionally be analogous to disordered behavior of humans. An example comes from our work on activity anorexia (e.g., Epling & Pierce, 1996a). Animals self-starve and die of starvation when food deprivation is combined with excessive physical activity. This phenomenon is similar to seemingly willful starvation by humans. In the animal laboratory, food restriction and the opportunity to exercise are arranged by the experimenter. Humans, on the other hand, go on diets and exercise because of social contingencies of reinforcement for this behavior. Regardless of whether food restriction and physical activity are imposed, or chosen by the individual on the basis of prevailing social contingencies, severe dieting and excessive exercising can trigger a biobehavioral process that results in self-starvation and death of the organism.

BIOBEHAVIORAL AND TRADITIONAL VIEWS

The biobehavioral approach to anorexia contrasts with the traditional model of the disorder. Anorexia nervosa is a psychiatric disorder involving a voluntary refusal to eat, extreme loss of weight, and in some cases, death. The disorder poses a serious health problem to otherwise healthy adolescents and young adults, especially for those who uphold white middle-class values (Crago, Shisslak, & Estes, 1996). The incidence of anorexia is as high as 3% for the population at risk, and mortality for diagnosed patients is between 5% and 21% (Yates, 1990). The *Diagnostic and Statistical Manual of Mental Disorders* (1994), published by the American Psychiatric Association, indicates that primary criteria for a diagnosis of anorexia nervosa include behavior directed at

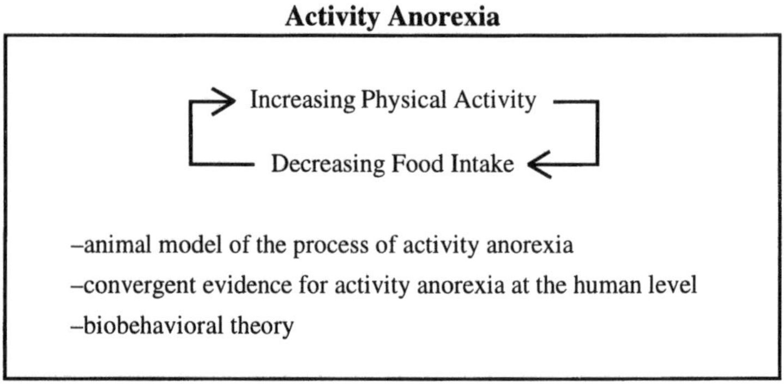

Activity Anorexia

Increasing Physical Activity

Decreasing Food Intake

–animal model of the process of activity anorexia

–convergent evidence for activity anorexia at the human level

–biobehavioral theory

Figure 3.1. A simplified model of the interrelations of physical activity and food intake. The negative feedback loop is related to the animal model of activity anorexia, is substantiated by convergent evidence at the human level, and is the basis for a biobehavioral theory of anorexia.

losing weight, weight loss, unusual ways of handling food, intense fear of gaining weight, body image disturbance, and, in females, irregular or absent menstrual cycles (amenorrhea). Secondary features are not required for diagnosis, but occur at some frequency. These include denial of illness and resistance to therapy, delayed psychosexual development in adolescents, and, in adults, loss of sexual interest. Clinical researchers have suggested additional or alternative diagnostic criteria, but all have viewed anorexia as a mental or cognitive disorder that results in self-starvation (Bruch, 1965; Crisp et al., 1980; Garner & Garfinkel, 1980).

Notably, stringent dieting and excessive exercise are associated with up to 75% of the cases of anorexia nervosa (Kron et al., 1978). One possibility is that many of these cases of self-starvation are, in fact, cases of activity anorexia. In this view, a significant number of people in our society could suffer from activity anorexia who are incorrectly labeled neurotic. These people are diagnosed as having anorexia nervosa. Moreover, there are individuals in athletics and physical fitness who appear to self-starve as a result of the combined effects of dieting and exercising. Instances of eating disorders in athletics and sports could be additional cases of activity anorexia (see Wheeler, 1996; Yates, 1996).

A basic premise of the biobehavioral view is that people go on diets that lead to excessive physical activity. The dieting athlete may increase training, the sedentary person may begin jogging, the person with anorexia nervosa may be hyperactive. Paradoxically, excessive exercise or hyperactivity begins to interfere with eating and the loss of weight results in further physical activity. Thus, as shown in Figure 3.1, declining food intake produces accelerating physical activity and excessive exercise suppresses appetite. The process is a vicious cycle that is not consciously controlled by the person. Social contingencies related to diet and exercise as well as evolution, natural selection, and physiological processes provide a scientific account of the activity-anorexia cycle.

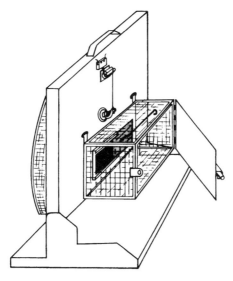

Figure 3.2. The basic Wahmann running wheel used to study activity anorexia. The figure depicts the attached side-cage, the sliding door to the running wheel, and the wheel itself. See text for a description of the basic procedures to induce self-starvation in rats. Reprinted from W. F. Epling and W. D. Pierce (1991), *Solving the anorexia puzzle: A scientific approach.* Toronto: Hogrefe & Huber. Reprinted with the permission of Hogrefe & Huber Publishers, Seattle, Toronto, Bem Gottingen.

ACTIVITY ANOREXIA: AN ANIMAL MODEL

In the laboratory, rats stop eating and die of starvation when food restriction is linked with high-rate physical activity (see Epling, Pierce, & Stefan, 1983; Routtenberg & Kuznesof, 1967). A typical experiment begins when adolescent male or female rats are placed in a cage that is attached to a running wheel. As shown in Figure 3.2, the wheel and side cage can be separated by closing a sliding door. During the first five days of an experiment, the door that separates the side cage from the wheel is closed. Food is freely available in the cage, and each animal can eat as much as it wants. The amount eaten is measured daily and the rats are also weighed each day (see Pierce & Epling, 1991, for a more complete description).

The food and weight measures provide baseline data for the experimental interventions. The experimental procedures combine food restriction and the opportunity to run on a wheel. In a typical experiment, the rats are restricted to a single 90-minute daily meal. Following the meal, the doors to the wheels are opened, and experimental animals are allowed to run. Control animals receive the same treatment, but the wheels are locked and will not turn.

Figure 3.3 shows that animals given a single 90-minute daily meal and the opportunity to exercise on a wheel escalate running over days, reduce food intake, and decline in body weight—a process described as activity anorexia

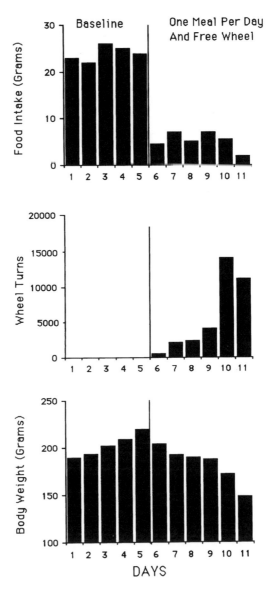

Figure 3.3. Effects of changing from free food (baseline) to one 90-minute meal a day and an opportunity to run on a wheel. Food intake (top) is suppressed, wheel running (middle) accelerates over days, and body weight declines. The ultimate result of the activity anorexia process is starvation and death. Reprinted from W. F. Epling and W. David Pierce, An overview of activity anorexia (1996b), in W. F. Epling & W. D. Pierce (Eds.), *Activity anorexia: theory, research and treatment* (p. 6). Mahwah, NJ: Lawrence Erlbaum. Reprinted with permission.

(Epling, Pierce, & Stefan, 1983; Epling & Pierce, 1988, 1991, 1996b). Notice that food intake (top) drops to less than 5 g/day, partially recovers, and then falls to 1 g or less a day. The downward turn in food intake is accompanied by an acceleration in wheel running (middle) that can exceed 20 km/day. Figure 3.3 (bottom) shows that excessive exercise and low food intake result in a substantial loss of body weight. If allowed to continue, animals become weaker and weaker, activity subsides, and they die of starvation. Control animals exposed only to the 90-minute food restriction, but not given the opportunity to run, increase their food intake over days and survive in a healthy condition. Additional experimental evidence indicates that the greater the acceleration in physical activity the higher the likelihood of self-starvation and death (Epling & Pierce, 1984).

One way to establish functional similarity between our animal model of activity anorexia and the human disorder is to gather convergent evidence. Pierce and Epling (1994, pp. 9–11) documented the evidence for five levels of functional similarity by convergent evidence as follows: (1) Excessive physical activity is associated with anorexia in humans; (2) physical activity decreases the food intake of humans; (3) lower food consumption increases the physical activity, exercise, and hyperactivity of humans; (4) the onset of anorexia in humans and animals develops in a similar manner; and (5) reproductive function is disrupted for physically active rats, athletes, and anorexic patients. Overall, Pierce and Epling (1994) concluded that the convergent evidence for activity anorexia is strong. Based on more than twelve years of research, we proposed a biobehavioral analysis of activity anorcxia (see Epling & Pierce, 1988, 1989, 1991, 1996a; Epling, Pierce, & Stefan, 1981, 1983).

In the following section of this chapter, the roles of culture and social contingencies of reinforcement are examined as initiating conditions for the activity-anorexia cycle. Although cultural pressures encourage people to combine dieting with exercise, a biobehavioral analysis shows that activity anorexia is a ''self-maintaining'' process based on evolution and natural selection. One implication is that once the process is initiated, the person is not free to stop; motivational and physiological factors work to maintain the cycle even though family, friends, and professionals no longer support the anorexic behavior.

THE CULTURAL CONTEXT OF ACTIVITY ANOREXIA

Figure 3.4 shows the interrelations among culture, behavior, and biology that account for activity anorexia. The theory explains how the physical and psychological symptoms attributed to anorexia nervosa are by-products of starvation and social learning. Activity anorexia is hypothesized to result from behavioral and biological processes that, in Western societies, are initiated by cultural practices based on the values of fitness and thinness.

A BIOBEHAVIORAL MODEL OF ACTIVITY ANOREXIA

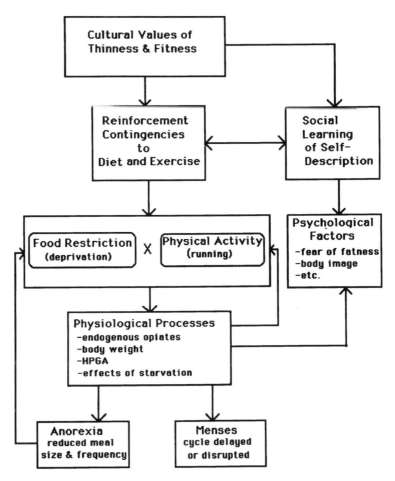

Figure 3.4. The biobehavioral theory of activity anorexia. The values of thinness and fitness of Western culture results in social contingencies of reinforcement for diet and exercise. These contingencies, as well as social learning of self-description, are sex-biased and increase the risk of activity anorexia in women more than men. Sociocultural factors predispose some people to combine food restriction with physical activity, resulting in physiological processes that maintain the activity anorexia cycle. In this model, psychological factors are viewed as the result of social learning or starvation itself, but are not the causes of anorexia. Reprinted from W. F. Epling and W. D. Pierce (1991), *Solving the anorexia puzzle: A scientific approach* (p. 201). Toronto: Hogrefe & Huber. Reprinted with the permission of Hogrefe & Huber Publishers, Seattle, Toronto, Bem Gottingen.

Culture, Contingencies, and Appearance

From a behavioral perspective, culture refers to the common, everyday practices of people. Such practices are often called customs in the sense that they are usual or customary actions of many individuals. An important aspect of culture involves teaching people to value particular ideals, symbols, and standards. For example, in the United States children are taught to value freedom, the flag, and a high standard of living. Children learn to talk about, and actively pursue, these values. The socialization of values occurs when an individual receives approval for acceptable behavior and censure for unacceptable conduct. This social conditioning ensures that most people behave in accord with, and uphold, the values of the community.

A thin and fit woman represents the current beauty standard of Western society (Orbach, 1986). Social rewards are given when women attempt to achieve this cultural standard by dieting or exercising. A slim woman is told that she looks attractive and she receives a number of social rewards that are not given to other women. Women who weigh more than the ideal standard are criticized and are often told they need to lose a few pounds. Job promotions, being asked out on a date, reactions from friends and family, and many other social rewards are given to women who take care of their appearance. These rewards and sanctions encourage many women to alter their appearance toward contemporary standards of beauty.

Sex Differences in Perceiving and Altering Appearance

Social contingencies of reinforcement regulate the customary practices of women with regard to beauty. This means that young girls and mature women learn self-descriptions based on the reactions of others. Self-descriptions as verbal stimuli can prompt behavior to alter appearance (see Figure 3.4, social learning of self-description). Young women of normal weight for height often describe themselves as too heavy (Davies & Furnham, 1986). Also, experts in the treatment of anorexia nervosa point to the distorted body perceptions of such women. These researchers recognize the social pressure to be thin, but prefer to talk about the person's perceptions as determinants of ''the relentless pursuit of thinness.'' From a biobehavioral view, however, both the perceptions (i.e., self-descriptions) and the active attempts to achieve the beauty standard are caused by social contingencies of reinforcement. This point is exemplified in a study of mothers and expectations for children's appearance (Hodes, Jones, & Davies, 1996). Mothers of British origin (Western culture) found slimmer girls attractive more than mothers of South Asia, the Mediterranian or Caribbean regions, and sub-Saharan Africa. Presumably, mothers who associate physical attractiveness with slimness prompt and reinforce the regulation of body weight by their daughters. Because of these (and other) social contingencies many young women in Western culture combine dieting and exercising, and are susceptible to the activity anorexia cycle.

The cultural practices of Western society also affect the behavior of men. Although there are no clear standards of beauty for men, there is evidence that obesity is not acceptable (Harris, Harris, & Bochner, 1982). In addition, men are expected to be physically fit. Women respond positively to an athletic appearance that involves thin legs, a slim waist, and broad shoulders (Beck, Ward-Hull, & McLear, 1976). Thus, social approval and sexual interest are some of the rewards obtained by men who attain a physically fit appearance. These social reinforcement contingencies induce many men to exercise, but the pressure to diet is not as extreme as for women. For this reason, exercise is less often combined with food restriction and the incidence of activity anorexia is less for men.

Social Construction of Beauty and Appearance

Standards of beauty and fitness have changed over the centuries. Ancient portraits of Venus and Aphrodite portray an ideal woman who is somewhat chubby by today's standards. At other times artists have depicted the perfect woman as almost fat. In contemporary American and European culture, women who are thin and fit are beautiful. At the turn of the century, however, women in this culture were expected to be somewhat overweight, and during the 1940s and 1950s a curvaceous figure was in vogue. Today a beautiful woman is tall and slim.

One index of beauty ideals in America is the body measurements of beauty-queen contestants. The average height of Miss America contestants has increased since 1940 and average weight has decreased. A similar trend was reported for Miss U.S.A. contest finalists for 1983 and 1984. The average Miss U.S.A. finalist weighed 120 pounds and was 68 inches tall. During the 1960s, Miss America contestants also weighed 120 pounds but they were only 66 inches tall—two inches shorter. Insurance statistics indicate that for maximum life span a woman who is 64 inches tall should weigh 124 to 138 pounds. According to these health standards, both Miss U.S.A. and Miss America contestants would be considered very thin and unhealthy (Mazur, 1986).

Lakoff and Sherr (1984) have commented about social standards of appearance and the conditions that produce and change such ideals. These authors point to the large-scale economic factors that affect the values of beauty. They remark:

Why are different (body) types in vogue at different times? Is the choice governed by larger social forces? It has been pointed out that in periods when starvation is a real threat, and only the wealthy can look plump and well-fed, large women tend to be idealized: in a period when the Madonna represents the feminine ideal, the large-bellied look of pregnancy—whether or not the woman is in fact pregnant—is most desirable:

and at a time when it is easier to be sedentary, and food, especially of a calorific kind, is readily available to almost everyone, only the wealthy can afford the time and money required to be slim and/or athletic, and therefore these looks will be "in." (pp. 63–64)

In this passage, Lakoff and Sherr (1984) propose that ideals of beauty result from the prevailing economic conditions. When food is scarce the wealthy still eat well, become fat, and fatness becomes a symbol of prosperity. When food is abundant, as in current Western culture, the wealthy separate themselves from the common mass by pursuing slimness and athleticism. In our society, the middle, upper-middle, and rich classes predominantly have the leisure time and money to attend health clubs, buy special low-calorie foods, and exercise during the time when most people are working. Under these conditions, thinness or slimness is associated with money, power, and status, becoming a valued conditioned reinforcer. One implication is that any behavior (e.g., sufficient exercising) that results in a thin appearance is strengthened and maintained.

It is difficult to be sure that food abundance and wealth are the only factors contributing to changes in beauty standards. There are probably other economic and social conditions that influence beauty trends. Mazur (1986) suggests that standards of beauty in Western society are influenced by the fashion industry. He states that "the Great War ended an epoch in fashion as waistlines were let out and hemlines rose. . . . Dresses of the 1920s and the ideal bodies underneath, became curveless, almost boylike" (p. 285). More recently, high fashion models have become extremely thin, to match clothing designs that require a slender body. Many women read fashion magazines and attempt to emulate the appearance of these models.

There is also a huge sports, fitness, and health industry that pushes, and may help create, the values of thinness and fitness. This industry generates billions of dollars each year and requires consumers who are concerned with fitness, health, and slimness. Although there are considerable benefits for those who follow such a fitness standard—for instance, reduced chances of heart disease—it is important to realize that the pursuit of fitness increases the likelihood of activity anorexia in Western society.

Western Culture and the Value of Fitness

The value of exercise and physical fitness is upheld by people in North America and Europe. This is a peculiar and modern practice. The effects of vigorous exercise have been disputed for a long time. For example, the Greek physician Hippocrates claimed that exercise and competition shortened the life span of athletes (Montoye, 1967, p. 815). This view of exercise as an unhealthy practice was maintained until the mid-nineteenth century. In fact, the Surgeon General of the United States Navy in 1911 attempted to discourage recruits from participation in sports by suggesting that "the prolonged rigorous course of physical exercises necessary to excellence in physical sports is believed to be dangerous in its after effects upon those who indulge in athletic sports sufficiently to excel therein'' (Montoye, 1967). During the last twenty years, this negative view of exercise has been replaced by a zealous concern with the benefits of physical activity and fitness.

Time magazine (July 25, 1988) documented the popular interest in physical fitness in the United States. According to the article, Americans in the 1970s spent a little over $5 million a year on exercise equipment. Subsequently, sales in this area skyrocketed and by 1987 Americans spent over $700 million on weights, exercise bikes, treadmills, and exercise benches. Additionally, in this same year, young-adult Americans spent $5 billion on health club fees.

A cultural fascination with fitness is reflected in the immense popularity of long distance running. In recent years, the Boston Marathon has attracted over 30,000 participants. Runners come from diverse lifestyles and travel considerable distances to compete in the marathon. The 26 miles covered in a marathon is an exceptional distance to run. In fact, the Greek soldier who ran to Marathon to warn his comrades of an imminent attack dropped dead of exhaustion after delivering his message.

Each year in North America there are hundreds of long distance races, as well as events that combine strenuous swimming, bicycling, and running (e.g., Iron Man Competitions). This fitness ``craze'' has been accompanied by an explosion in sales of athletic clothing and equipment. In 1987, Americans spent over $6 billion on quality running shoes. This means that roughly 60 million pairs of elite athletic shoes were purchased by American consumers. The evidence clearly shows the value and pursuit of fitness in North America.

The Fitness Subculture and Anorexia. The number of cases of anorexia has increased along with the rise of the fitness culture. From a biobehavioral viewpoint this makes sense; in fact, Epling et al. (1983) hypothesized that excessive physical activity would predispose people to anorexia. This hypothesis followed from the research on activity anorexia in animals. Clinical researchers have since documented this effect in humans (Beumont, Beumont, & Touyz, 1996; Davis, 1996; Katz, 1996). In fact, Katz (1986) described two male patients ``in whom participation in long distance running clearly preceded the appearance of anorexia nervosa and appeared to play a role in its onset'' (p. 75). The onset of activity anorexia in males who exercise excessively is noteworthy, indicating that the cycle can occur as readily in males as in females when the appropriate conditions occur. In addition, Katz (1986) reported that the men developed the classic symptoms of anorexia nervosa, but only after excessive activity had reduced their food intake. That is, the symptoms followed from self-starvation induced by long distance running and were not the causes of the men's anorexia.

According to Katz (1986), the patients' initial involvement with jogging appears to have resulted from their acceptance of the cultural value of physical fitness. In humans, the social environment prompts and reinforces people who engage in strenuous exercise. Many people who begin a program of long distance running (or some other sport) become part of a subculture that is even more concerned with body form, trimness, and exercise. This subculture selectively reinforces increasing weekly mileage, speed, and use of training techniques to enhance performance.

Garner and his associates have suggested that the growing emphasis on fitness has different implications for women than for men (Garner et al., 1985). As we have noted, women are subjected to the cultural standards of beauty involving a slim appearance. In our culture women exercise for different reasons than men. For women, fitness is associated with achieving a thin and curveless body shape. According to Garner et al. (1985), a survey by *Glamour* magazine found that 95% of the female respondents had used exercise for the sole purpose of weight control. In contrast, men usually exercise for sports, toning of the body, or cardiovascular fitness. An important implication of this difference is that women are more likely to combine exercise with dieting than men—increasing females' risk for activity anorexia.

Western Culture, Appearance, and Body Weight

As previously stated, "thin and trim" is the contemporary beauty standard for women. There has been much discussion of the unrealistic nature of such a standard and the pressures to achieve it. The media promote the message that personal success and happiness come to those women who are thin. Bruch (1978) mentioned that movies, magazines, and television advocate the view that "one can be loved and respected only when slender" (p. viii). One suggestion is that the media are fabricating a message that has little basis in reality (see also Wolf, 1991). That is, women believe that social acceptance is based on their beauty, when in fact it is not (reality distortion). An alternative view, and one that we favor, is that the media present an exaggerated, but accurate, reflection of social reactions to beauty in our culture. In other words, people do reward the performance of women depending on their body weight and other aspects of ideal beauty (see Averett & Korenman, 1996).

Contingencies Based on Attractiveness and Body Weight. Physical attractiveness has a strong impact on our social relationships (Collins & Zebrowitz, 1995). When men and women meet socially, the attractiveness of the other person affects the behavior of both sexes (Hatfield & Sprecher, 1986). Physical attractiveness affects judgments of desirability of a person as a date (Sprecher & Duck, 1994); additional research indicates that attractive women are more likely to be chosen as dates (Green, Buchanan, & Heuer, 1984). Men and women state that physically attractive people are also sociable, independent, interesting, poised, exciting, sexually warm, well-adjusted, and successful (Brigham, 1980; Dion & Dion, 1987; Moore, Graziano, & Miller, 1987). Unattractive people are judged to be socially deviant in a number of ways; they are seen as mentally ill, politically radical, and homosexual (Agnew & Thompson, 1994; Jones, Hannson, & Philips, 1978; Unger, Hilderbrand, & Madar, 1982).

These responses of others to physical appearance affect an individual's behavior. People who are seen as attractive learn positive self-evaluations and show confidence in a variety of social settings. Attractive people expect to do well in social situations and they generally do (Abbott & Sebastian, 1981; Reis, Nezlek, & Wheeler, 1980). On the other hand, those who are judged as unattractive learn negative self-evaluations. To illustrate, one study showed that unattractive college students believed that they were more likely to become mentally ill in the future (O'Grady, 1982).

Obesity is a physical feature that is currently viewed as unattractive by both men and women (Harris, Harris, & Bochner, 1982; Larkin & Pines, 1982). This prejudice begins at an early age; grade school children judge obese people as stupid, dirty, sloppy, lazy, mean, and ugly (Allon, 1975; Staffieri, 1967, 1972). In a comprehensive review, Wooley and co-workers found that professional mental health workers, including psychiatrists, psychologists, and social workers, judged obese persons as less desirable than normal weight individuals (Wooley, Wooley, & Dyrenforth, 1979). Experimental manipulation of physical appearance by computer simulation can make normal weight individuals appear overweight (Gardner & Tockerman, 1994). A stranger whose image appeared overweight was rated as less sincere, honest, intelligent, friendly, humorous, pleasant, ambitious, talented, neat, and so on—and as more aggressive, lonely, envious, obnoxious, and cruel—than the same stranger at normal or thin body weight (see also Lundberg & Sheehan, 1994). These findings provide support for the contention that the stigma of obesity is one of a few socially accepted prejudices based solely on appearance (Fitzgerald, 1981).

The social rewards for beauty and sanctions for unattractiveness teach women to modify their appearance. Social psychologists have found that attractive people do better in school; attractive individuals also have higher incomes and more occupational prestige than less attractive persons (Umberson & Hughes, 1984). There is no biological basis for the connection between physical appearance and achievement. This fact strongly suggests that in our culture academic and work performance is differentially reinforced on the basis of appearance. Differential reinforcement based on beauty is clearly seen when the more attractive cocktail waitress receives higher tips for her services than other waitresses.

As attractiveness leads to rewards, unattractiveness leads to punishment. In medieval times, if two people were accused of the same crime, the uglier person was regarded as more likely to be guilty (Alcock, Carment, & Sadava, 1987, p. 243). This overt discrimination does not exist today, but more subtle forms of sanctions continue. Effran (1974) reported that unattractive people who were accused of cheating on an exam or committing a burglary were less liked, seen as more guilty, and given more severe punishment than attractive defendants.

The negative treatment of people who are judged as unattractive due to being overweight extends to many social contexts. Overweight children are teased and ostracized by other children and may not receive as much positive attention from parents and other caretakers. As adults, obese people are frequently denied housing, jobs, promotions, and educational opportunities (Bray, 1976; Canning

& Mayer, 1966; Karris, 1977). Gortmaker et al. (1993) found that obese women suffered disadvantages in household income, years of education, probabilities of marriage, and graduating from college. Obesity in men did not result in the same level of disadvantages as for obese women.

Obesity has other socioeconomic consequences. Register & Williams (1990) observed that obese women are paid 12% less, and obese men 5% less than normal weight workers (see also Hamermesh & Biddle, 1993; Sargent & Blanchflower, 1994; however, Loh, 1993, reports no differences). A recent study by Averett and Korenman (1996) further investigated income, marital status, and hourly pay differentials of obese persons. In their sample of 23- to 31-year-olds, obese women had low family incomes that were, at least paritally, due to low probabilities of marriage and weak earnings of their spouses. Extremely overweight white (and Hispanic) women earned about 20% less in hourly wages than their normal weight counterparts. These socioeconomic consequences did not occur at the same level for obese men, suggesting that social reactions to body weight are sex-typed.

Sex Bias, Appearance, and Weight. There is other evidence that men, more than women, discriminate on the basis of weight and appearance. Women less often judge men on the basis of appearance (Feingold, 1990; Pierce, 1992) and are more likely to emphasize personality and social position (Berscheid & Walster, 1974; Huston & Levinger, 1978). In contrast, men are more interested in the appearance and body shape of women (Mazur, 1986). Also, men from Western cultures (Euro-American) prefer women with thinner figures to a greater extent than males from different cultural backgrounds (African-American). Additionally, Euro-American men more often indicate that they would like their girlfriends to lose weight than do African-American males (Epel et al., 1996). One implication is that males in Western culture reinforce weight regulation by women, and differentially reinforce the behavior of women based on body weight. Generally, then, the evidence indicates that women reward men based on performance and acquired status, and men reward women on the basis of appearance. Mazur (1986) states that this sex bias may arise from either biology or socialization. In either case, it has profound implications for women.

Whether because of genetic differences . . . or a persistent bias in socialization, men are reliably more visually interested than are women in the bodies of the other sex. As a result, women are under more pressure than men to conform to an ideal of beauty because they quickly learn that their social opportunities are affected by their beauty, and a sense of beauty (or lack of it) becomes an important facet of a young woman's self-concept. (p. 282)

The arrangement of rewards and sanctions based on a woman's beauty has resulted in many women conforming to current conceptions of physical appearance. In the past, women have modified their appearance by increasing or decreasing bust size, by wearing corsets to give an "hour glass" appearance, and by altering facial appearance with cosmetics. Today, the ideal beauty standard is a very thin and athletic body type. The acceptance of this standard is reflected by evidence on breast enlargement and reduction through cosmetic surgery. Research indicates that, in recent years, there has been a decline in the incidence of breast enlargement medical procedures and an increase in operations to reduce the size of breasts, hips, thighs, and buttocks (Biggs, Cukier, & Worhing, 1982).

Thinness and Weight Regulation. Acceptance of the thin standard of beauty by women has been accompanied by an excessive concern with weight regulation. Garner and his co-workers reviewed six women's magazines for the years 1959 to 1978 (Garner et al., 1985). They found a 70% increase in articles concerned with dieting over the last ten years of their review. Social conditioning toward thinness has resulted in many normal weight women describing themselves as overweight and many thin women failing to recognize that they are underweight (Gray, 1977; Halmi, Falk, & Schwartz, 1981).

The value of thinness is clearly seen in a study of British school girls. Davies and Furnham (1986) found that 47% of the girls in their study considered themselves overweight, although only 4% were heavier than normal. The concern with weight increased as the girls reached maturity. At all ages, at least 80% of the girls who described themselves as overweight had thought about dieting and 36% of these girls were actually doing so. Surprisingly, about 10% of the youngest girls (12–14 years) were dieting even though they thought their weight was ''just right.'' In the oldest category (18 years), 11% of the women who saw themselves as underweight were on diets. Most women in this age group (59%) described themselves as overweight and 35% of these women were dieting. These findings are not unusual and are replicated in numerous studies (Dwyer, Feldman, & Mayer, 1970; Jakobovits et al., 1977; Miller, Coffman, & Linke, 1980).

Davies and Furnham (1986) also reported on the girls' use of exercise to control weight. Within the youngest age group, 40% of the girls who thought their weight was ''just right'' had at one time considered exercise as a method of weight loss and 54% were currently exercising. In this same age group, 75% of the girls who saw themselves as overweight had previously considered exercise for weight loss and 83% were on an exercise program. More girls were using exercise to lose weight than would admit a desire to be thin. By age eighteen, 81% of the women who felt they were ''just right'' had considered exercise as a method of weight control and 27% were actually exercising. Ninety-six percent of the 18-year-olds who thought they were overweight had contemplated using exercise for weight control; 74% were currently exercising.

In terms of activity anorexia, it is notable that these young women were frequently combining dieting with exercise. The severity of the diet and the intensity of exercise were probably quite variable; however, the chances of anorexia are expected to be higher in this adolescent female population. In fact, Kalucy et al. (1977) reported that 1 in 100 adolescent British school girls from London were suffering from anorexia nervosa. This figure is the highest reported incidence of the disorder in the general population. The high incidence of an-orexia, in the context of dieting and exercise, suggests that girls in this popu-lation are experiencing activity anorexia, not anorexia nervosa.

Social Contingencies as Predisposing Events

Western culture has evolved standards of beauty and fitness that favor a thin and trim appearance. Based on these standards, women are reinforced for be-havior directed at achieving or maintaining a slim body type. Women who attain a slim and trim appearance are more likely to be successful in life and interact more frequently and positively with the opposite sex. In contrast, women who fail to meet the ideal standard experience social disapproval and are less likely to attain a high social position. These social contingencies of reinforcement regulate the behavior of women and produce the extreme concern with diet and exercise to lose weight. Thus, women choose to combine dieting and exercise because of the social reactions of others.

The person who is subjected to these social consequences does not voluntarily starve to death. Although food is abundant in Western society, a cultural famine is arranged for many women. For example, a young woman can easily go to the refrigerator and eat what she wants. However, repeated choices to eat may result in weight gain and social disapproval. On this basis, young women fre-quently choose to restrict their food intake.

Although it is tempting to attribute anorexia to cultural pressures to be thin (and current cognitions based on these pressures), this is not an adequate ex-planation. In our view, the culture establishes the preconditions to diet and exercise, but does not directly cause loss of appetite and severe starvation. In laboratory animals food is also restricted, but animals do not die from this imposed reduction. Only those animals that exercise excessively become ano-rexic. An adequate analysis of activity anorexia must, therefore, include refer-ence to the roles of evolution, natural selection, and physiological factors (i.e., contingencies of survival) in the regulation of eating and physical activity.

EVOLUTION, MOTIVATION, AND ACTIVITY ANOREXIA

Eating has obvious survival value; the survival value of not eating is less obvious. There are, however, anorexias that occur in many species as a result of natural selection (see Mrosovsky & Sherry, 1980 for a review and discussion). For these animals, anorexias often occur when the organism is engaged in other biologically relevant behavior (i.e., defending young, defending territory, molt-ing, etc.). Animals exposed to fluctuations in food supply (e.g., due to regular seasonal variation) may also become anorexic. Thus, ground squirrels hibernate during the winter and will not eat when aroused. Anorexia during hibernation contributes to energy efficiency. During a period of hibernation, body temper-ature decreases and the kidneys do not function well. The kidneys remove waste products from the bloodstream and the animal must remain awake for efficient kidney function. Staying awake is energy expensive because the animal must heat its body to normal temperature. Refusal to eat during hibernation therefore relates to the energy cost of waking. In fact, the more squirrels eat the sooner they come out of hibernation (Mrosovsky & Barnes, 1974).

Our biobehavioral analysis proposes that activity anorexia also had survival value. That is, the interrelationships between physical activity and food intake are based on evolved structural features of organisms (i.e., physiological characteristics). Generally, natural selection favored those individuals (of some species) who became active during severe and unexpected food shortages. Animals that traveled to a new location contacted food, survived, and reproduced.

Anorexia induced by travel or migration to a new food patch likely had survival value. During a famine, food would be difficult to obtain and stopping to eat small amounts could be more energy costly than efficient. In other words, there would be a net negative energy balance between foraging for scarce (and difficult to obtain) food items and traveling to a more abundant food source. These assumptions about evolution and anorexia suggest that physical activity and food intake are motivationally interrelated; we tested these relationships in a number of experiments.

Motivational Relationships and Activity Anorexia

As shown in Figure 3.4 (lower), activity anorexia results from the interrelations of (a) deprivation and food schedule on physical activity, and (b) physical activity on food consumption. Briefly stated, food deprivation increases the reinforcement effectiveness of exercise and greater physical activity decreases the reinforcement value of food. Thus, a feedback loop based on the principle of reinforcement generates anorexia.

Reinforcement Value of Wheel Running. Pierce, Epling, and Boer (1986) used nine adolescent rats to test the reinforcement effectiveness of wheel running as food deprivation changed. Rats were trained to press a lever to obtain 60 s of wheel running. When the animal pressed the lever, a brake was removed and the running wheel was free to turn. After 60 s, the brake was again activated and the rat had to press the lever to obtain more time to run.

Once lever pressing for wheel running was consistent, each animal was tested when it was food deprived and when it was at free-feeding weight. In order to measure the reinforcement effectiveness of wheel running, the animals were required to press the lever on a progressive fixed-ratio schedule for each opportunity to run. Specifically, the rats were required to press 5 times to obtain 60 seconds of wheel running, then 10, 15, 20, 25, and so on. The point at which they gave up lever pressing for an opportunity to wheel run was used as an index of the reinforcement effectiveness of physical activity. Figure 3.5 shows the main results of this experiment and indicates that the reinforcement effectiveness of wheel running increased with food deprivation for all animals.

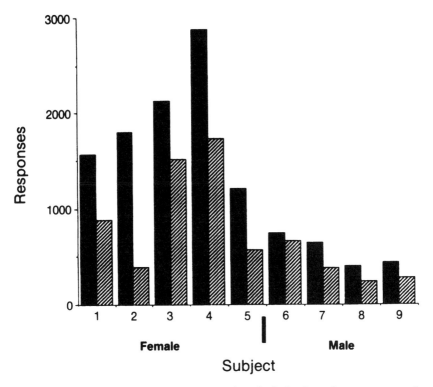

Figure 3.5. Number of responses for 60 seconds and of wheel running on a progressive ratio schedule. Female and male rats were tested at 100% (striped bars) and 75% (black bars) of ad libitum body weight. The reinforcement effectiveness of wheel running is consistently greater under conditions of food restriction. Reprinted from W. F. Epling & W. D. Pierce, Excessive activity and anorexia in rats (1989), in K. M. Pirke, W. Wuttke, & U. Schweiger (Eds.), *The menstrual cycle and its disorders: Influences of nutrition, exercise, and neurotransmitters* (p. 84). New York: Springer Verlag. Copyright 1989 by Springer Verlag. Reprinted with permission.

Female rats pressed more for the opportunity to run than male rats. Although it is tempting to suggest that this is in accord with a proportionally high number of women anorexics when compared to males, there are other explanations. Female rats are considerably lighter than males and the deprivation operation likely had a stronger impact on them. Also, female rats become highly active during the estrus cycle and this may have affected the reinforcement value of wheel running.

Overall, these results indicate that the reward value of wheel running is sensitive to food allocation and deprivation (i.e., the behavior is food related). When food is restricted the reinforcement effectiveness of wheel running increases, and when food supply is reinstated the reinforcement value of wheel running declines. The results support an evolutionary hypothesis that travel or migration is induced by reduction in food supply. Travel occurs because the reinforcement value of physical activity increases at times when food supply is diminished (also see Boer, 1989 and Russell et al., 1987, on sensitivity of wheel running to variation in daily food supply).

Reinforcement Value of Food. A second experiment, by Pierce, Epling, and Boer (1986, Experiment 2), investigated the effects of physical activity on the reinforcement value of food. Four male rats were trained to press a lever for food pellets. When lever pressing reliably occurred, the effects of exercise on each animal's willingness to work for food was tested. In this case, it was expected that a day of exercise would decrease the reinforcement effectiveness of food on the next day.

Reinforcement effectiveness of food was assessed by counting the number of lever presses for food as food became more and more difficult to obtain. To illustrate, an animal had to press 5 times for the first food pellet, 10 for the next, then 15, 20, 25, and so on. As in the first experiment, the "giving up" point was used to measure reinforcement effectiveness. Presumably, the more effective or valuable the reinforcer (i.e., food) the harder the animal would work for it.

As shown in Figure 3.6, when test days were preceded by a day of exercise, the reinforcement effectiveness of food decreased sharply. Three of the four rats pressed the lever more than 200 times when they were not allowed to run but no more than 38 times when running preceded test sessions. Food no longer supported lever presses following a day of moderate wheel running, even though a rest period in the home cage preceded the test. Although wheel running was moderate, it represented a large change in physical activity, since these animals were previously sedentary.

One rat refused to run (Subject 40), but was forced to do so on a motor-driven wheel. As shown in Figure 3.6, this animal sharply reduced lever pressing for food after forced exercise. Because the reinforcement effectiveness of food decreased with forced exercise, it may be concluded that both forced and voluntary wheel running produce a decline in the value of food reinforcement.

These findings support an evolutionary hypothesis that animals become anorexic during times of travel or migration. This conclusion is based on the assumption that wheel running in the laboratory shares functional similarity to an animal's travel or migration in natural habitats. In this view, loss of appetite (anorexia) occurs because increases in physical activity reduce the reinforcement effectiveness of food (also see Epling and Pierce, 1984 for data on the relationship between eating and the opportunity for physical activity). In terms of human behavior, people who increase their physical activity due to occupational requirements (e.g., ballet dancers) or for recreation may value food less and increase their chances of developing anorexia.

These motivational relationships between eating and physical activity explain, at a behavioral level, why organisms do not eat on a famine-induced migration and why they eventually abort travel when a new food patch is contacted. During a famine (or drought), food is difficult to obtain and caloric intake is reduced.

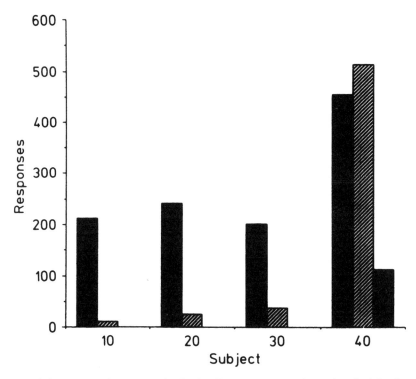

Figure 3.6. Number of responses for food pellets on a progressive ratio schedule. Compared with a locked running wheel (black bars), rats 10, 20, and 30 showed less responses for food after a day of exercise (striped bars). Rat 40 did not run when given the opportunity and subsequently was forced to run. Forced running resulted in a decrease in responses for food (third bar, black). Results indicate that the reinforcement effectiveness of food declines with either voluntary or forced physical activity. Reprinted from W. D. Pierce and W. F. Epling, Activity anorexia: An interplay between basic and applied behavior analysis (1994), *The Behavior Analyst,* 17, p. 14. Copyright 1994 by the Association for Behavior Analysis. Reprinted with permission from *The Behavior Analyst* and the Association for Behavior Analysis.

Because food is infrequently obtained physical activity is highly reinforcing and the organism begins to move. As the animal increases physical activity, food becomes less effective as reinforcement and the organism is unlikely to respond for food items that require extended effort. When food becomes abundant and more easily obtained, it is eaten. As food from easily acquired sources is taken, the reinforcement value of traveling declines and the organism stops moving. For these reasons, animals stop migrating once a new food patch is contacted. The behavioral relationships between eating and activity are a function of the organism's evolutionary history. Natural selection has resulted in physiological processes that are part of the contingencies regulating activity anorexia.

PHYSIOLOGY AND ACTIVITY ANOREXIA

Epling and Pierce (1988, 1991) noted that the excessive physical activity associated with anorexia could be maintained by the release of endogenous opiates. Recent evidence also implicates the dopaminergic system and neuropeptide Y (NPY) in the regulation of physical activity and food intake. Finally, there is evidence that neural opiates can modulate the impact of dopamine on both eating and running.

Activity Anorexia and Endogenous Opiates

Physical Activity, Opiates, and Reinforcement. As we have noted, the release of endogenous opiates may function as reinforcement for physical activity. There is evidence of a dose-response relation between intensity of exercise and plasma β-endorphin (Radosevich et al., 1989). This implies that β-endorphin release in the central nervous system (CNS) is increased. As aerobic fitness increases, more and more exercise is required to attain maximal release of endogenous opiates (McMurray et al., 1989). Thus, physical activity is partially maintained on a schedule of reinforcement for endorphin release that requires greater and greater amounts of exercise.

The endogenous reinforcement hypothesis suggests that injection of an opiate antagonist will decrease the intense wheel running of food-restricted animals. This is because the euphoric effects of opiates are diminished by antagonizing opioid receptors. We tested the effects of the opiate antagonist (or blocker), naloxone, on the food-restricted running of male rats (Boer et al., 1990; Pierce et al., 1996). In the Pierce et al. (1996) experiments, male and female rats were made hyperactive by feeding them a reduced amount of food and providing a running wheel. Once wheel running exceeded 5,000 revolutions per day (5 km), each animal was given injections of naloxone (50 mg/kg in saline) or saline (0.5 ml) on alternate days. The results of four female rats are presented in Figure 3.7. The graph shows wheel turns in meters for the one-hour period following the injection of the opiate antagonist. For each animal, wheel running is reduced on days of naloxone treatment compared with days of saline (control) injections. These findings support the hypothesis that food-restricted running is strengthened and maintained by the release of endogenous opiates (see also Arnsten & Segal, 1979; DeRossett & Holtzman, 1982; Potter, Borer, & Katz, 1983; Rodgers & Deacon, 1979).

Opiates, Anorexia, and Food-Seeking. Beta endorphin (β-endorphin) and the *mu* receptor appear to have some involvement in the relationship between increasing physical activity and decreasing food intake in both rats and humans (e.g., Aravich et al., 1993; Doerries et al., 1989; also see Epling & Pierce, 1991, pp. 158–164 for a review; see Aravich, 1996 for evidence against this hypothesis). Recently, Aravich et al. (1993) reported elevated levels of plasma β-endorphin and anterior pituitary β-endorphin in rats exposed to the activity

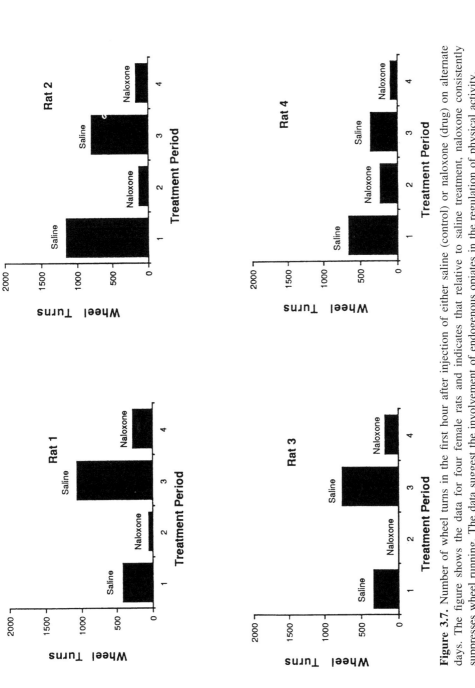

Figure 3.7. Number of wheel turns in the first hour after injection of either saline (control) or naloxone (drug) on alternate days. The figure shows the data for four female rats and indicates that relative to saline treatment, naloxone consistently suppresses wheel running. The data suggest the involvement of endogenous opiates in the regulation of physical activity.

anorexia procedure. After reviewing the relevant evidence, Marrazzi and Luby (1986) suggested that anorexia nervosa in humans results from addiction to opioids. In terms of activity anorexia, it is significant to note that anorexic patients show high plasma levels of β-endorphin (Kaye et al., 1982). Also, β-endorphin reduces the motivation of anorexic patients to eat (Kaye, 1987; Moore, Mills, & Forester, 1981; Nakai et al., 1987) as well as for rats that are forced to exercise (Davis et al., 1985).

Although β-endorphin is implicated in the regulation of activity anorexia, there is other evidence that points to dynorphin and the *kappa* receptor as playing a role. Aravich et al. (1993) reported a reduction of supraoptic hypothalamic dynorphin-A in rats exposed to the activity anorexia procedure. Nencini and Graziani (1990) reported a result that is apparently at odds with the Aravich et al. experiment. They found that the *kappa* agonist U50 did not increase food intake, but accelerated running down a runway for food. This effect was blocked by a dose of naloxone (5 mg/kg). Thus, in the context of food restriction and wheel running a reduction in *kappa* stimulation is associated with excessive running; in a maze learning experiment, elevation of *kappa* stimulation leads to accelerated running for food. These findings on the *kappa* receptor and food-related running are not yet clarified, but the research does suggest involvement of dynorphin and *kappa* in the regulation of this behavior.

Dynorphin and the *kappa* receptor are also implicated in the regulation of food intake. In a review of the neurobiological basis of eating disorders, Morely and Blundell (1988) noted several studies with rats that pointed to the involvement of the *kappa*-opioid receptor in the regulation of feeding behavior (e.g., Morely et al., 1983). Recent evidence indicates that the *kappa*-opioid system plays a role in NPY-induced feeding. Neuropeptide Y and dynorphin have additive effects on food intake, suggesting that a component of NPY-induced feeding may be mediated by the *kappa*-opioid system (Lambert et al., 1993).

Morely and Blundell (1988) speculated that opioids such as dynorphin and β-endorphin were involved in the control of food-related behavior (i.e., food seeking) as well as feeding. One possibility is that deprivation-induced wheel running (or exercise) functions as food-seeking behavior; this behavior could be partially maintained through its effects on the β-endorphin and the *mu* receptor. At the same time, changes in the level of physical activity may reduce the uptake of dynorphin by the *kappa* receptor. Together, the two opioid effects could (at least partially) account for increased travel (or exercise) during periods of food restriction and suppression of eating during the trek for a stable food supply (or during exercise brought on by stringent dieting).

Endogenous Opiates and Fertility. Disruption of menstrual cycle is a major physical symptom of anorexia nervosa. Evidence suggests that increased levels of endorphins produced by physical activity disrupts hormones that regulate the menstrual cycle (Cumming & Rebar, 1983, 1985; Petraglia et al., 1986; Ropert, Quigley, & Yen, 1981; Warren, 1989) and testosterone production in males

(Wheeler et al., 1991). Simply stated, it makes sense that sexual reproduction should decrease during a time of food shortage and travel to a new food patch

In terms of fertility and anorexia, the issue is whether hyperactivity contributes directly to late onset of menstruation and amenorrhea (e.g., by altering endorphin, luteinizing hormone, and/or GnRH levels), or whether excessive physical activity works indirectly on body composition (i.e., fat to lean ratio) and/or nutrition (Frish, 1988; also see Cumming, 1996, and Geer & Warren, 1996 for more on fertility and activity anorexia). The role of exercise or physical activity in the regulation of menstrual cycle continues to be an important area of research related to activity anorexia.

Activity Anorexia and the Dopaminergic System

Although there is evidence implicating the endogenous opiates with activity anorexia, there is other research that suggests an involvement of the dopaminergic system. More specifically, there is evidence that dopamine and its receptors in the hypothalamus play a role in the reward value of physical activity. In addition, research indicates that dopamine is an antagonist for NPY in the perifornical region of the hypothalamus. Neuropeptide Y elicits eating, and a hypothesis is that physical activity (induced by food restriction) causes a release of dopamine that blocks the effects of this neuropeptide. Thus, suppression of eating based on excessive physical activity may be mediated by dopamine's effects on NPY.

Physical Activity, Dopamine, and Reinforcement. Animal research also shows that dopamine, a neurotransmitter, is implicated in reinforcement processes and affects physical activity (Belke, 1996). Dopamine agonists (i.e., amphetamine, cocaine) increase running (Evans & Vaccarino, 1986; Glavin et al., 1981; Jakubczak & Gomer, 1973; Tainter, 1943) while dopamine antagonists (i.e., pimozide, chlorpromazine) decrease this behavior (Beninger & Freedman, 1982; Routtenberg, 1968; Routtenberg & Kuznesof, 1967). In terms of deprivation-induced wheel running, Routtenberg and Kuznesof (1967) and Routtenberg (1968) found that 1 mg/kg or 2 mg/kg doses of chlorpromazine (CPZ) decreased wheel running in rats. This effect presumably accounted for the increased survival of animals exposed to their self-starvation paradigm. Recently, Belke (1993) injected rats with amphetamine (0.5, 1.0, and 2.0 mg/kg) and chlorpromazine (0.5, 1.0, and 2.0 mg/kg) and measured the effects on lever pressing for wheel-running reinforcement. His procedures separated the motoric effects of the drug from its effects on the reinforcement effectiveness of wheel running (i.e., motivation). Results showed that both amphetamine and chlorpromazine decreased running. Further analysis showed that chlorpromazine decreased motivation to run while amphetamine affected both motivation to run and motor performance. Considering both opioid and dopamine systems, the neurochemical basis for the reinforcing properties of running may be a function of either an opiate mechanism, a dopamine mechanism, or a mechanism involving both systems (Belke, 1996).

Eating, Neuropeptide Y, and Dopamine. The dopamine system may be implicated in the regulation of eating through its effects on hypothalamic NPY (Stanley & Gillard, 1994). Neuropeptide Y is the most abundant neurotransmitter in the human brain and the peptide is highly concentrated within the hypothalamic nuclei (Adrian et al., 1983). When NPY is injected into hypothalamic sites, rats and other animals show excessive and prolonged eating (Stanley, 1993). There is a dose-response relationship between the level of the neurotransmitter and eating. Low doses of NPY elicit normal eating while higher doses induce gorging (in one hour rats may eat more than a half of their daily intake). Also, repeated injections of the peptide result in sustained overeating and weight gain, without signs of tolerance. Generally, the evidence suggests that hypothalamic NPY is one of the most important neurochemicals in regulation of eating.

Recent experiments have shown that NPY elicits eating through its effects on the perifornical hypothalamus region of the brain, the most sensitive site. In terms of anorexia, it is interesting to note that the perifornical hypothalamus is the primary site for the suppression of eating by endogenous dopamine and epinephrine (two catecholamine neurotransmitters) when activated by injections of amphetamine.

An important experiment by Gillard, Dang, and Stanley (1993) investigated whether these catecholamine neurotransmitters interact antagonistically with NPY-elicited eating. That is, would amphetamine activation of dopamine or epinephrine within the perifornical hypothalamic region suppress eating induced by NPY injections? Results indicated that amphetamine reduced or eliminated the eating response elicited by NPY, suggesting an antagonistic effect between these catecholamines and the NPY neurotransmitter. The suppression effects on NPY-elicited eating could be dopaminergic or adrenergic (i.e., via epinephrine). Further experiments with selective blockers of catecholamine receptors attempted to reverse the suppression of eating by amphetamine. Neither alpha- nor beta-adrenergic antagonists blocked the suppression of eating by amphetamine, as would be expected if epinephrine were involved. In contrast, the dopamine antagonist, haloperidol, blocked amphetamine's suppressive effects. That is, the feeding response to NPY was restored by blocking the dopamine receptors. Thus, the evidence indicates that dopamine and NPY interact antagonistically to control eating, especially in the perifornical hypothalamus.

In terms of activity anorexia, it is possible that physical activity induced by food restriction is strengthened or reinforced by an increase in dopamine (Belke, 1996). Gillard, Dang, and Stanley's (1993) experiments show that activation of the dopamine receptors will suppress eating by blocking the response to NPY in the perifornical hypothalamus. Thus, the role of dopamine as a mediator of activity anorexia would be twofold: a neurotransmitter implicated in the reward value of physical activity and an antagonist for the eating response elicited by NPY.

Opioid Modulation of the Dopaminergic System. Although the direct effects of dopamine could account for activity anorexia, there is reason to believe that neural opiates modulate the dopaminergic system. In the naloxone and wheel-running experiments (see above, Boer et al., 1990; Pierce et al., 1996), a relatively large dose of naloxone (50 g/kg) systematically reduced physical activity of food-deprived rats. These results are contrary to the findings of Carey, Ross, and Enns (1981), who reported that 1 mg/kg and 10 mg/kg doses of naloxone had no effect on wheel running by rats. Schnur and Barela (1984) also found no effect on wheel running of the opiate blocker, naltrexone, between doses of 0.3 to 10 mg/kg in golden hamsters. Finally, our laboratory has not found suppression of wheel running in food-deprived rats with either 1 or 20 mg/kg doses of naltrexone (unpublished).

Taken together, the current research indicates that naltrexone has no effect on physical activity for doses up to 20 mg/kg. In contrast, naloxone seems to have a dose-response relationship to the wheel running of rats. Lower doses of naloxone have no effect on wheel running, but higher doses reduce physical activity. Naloxone has a high affinity for the *mu* receptor and even low doses of the drug would effectively block the binding of β-endorphin at these sites. If *mu* is effectively blocked, but wheel running is unchanged, it is difficult to conclude that high-rate running is mediated by the effects of β-endorphin and the *mu* receptor (i.e., "runners' high" hypothesis).

One possibility is that the suppression of wheel running by high doses of naloxone indicates opioid modudation of the dopaminergic system (see Wood, 1983). Opioid receptors have been identified on dopaminergic neurons of the nigrostriatal and mesolimbic tracts (Goodman, Aider, & Pasternak, 1988; Mansour et al., 1988; Sharif & Hughes, 1989; Wood & Iyengar, 1988). Hooks et al. (1992) demonstrated that naloxone blocked amphetamine-induced increases in extracellular dopamine levels in the striatum and nucleus accumbens of rats. At the same time, naloxone attenuated the increased gross-motor movements caused by the administration of amphetamine. Additional research by Jones and Holtzman (1992) showed that a selective delta antagonist (naltrindole, NTI) blocked the gross-motor movements induced by amphetamine, but other *mu* and *kappa* antagonists did not have this effect. These results indicated that the delta receptor (and endogenous enkephalins) is involved in opioid regulation of the behavioral stimulant effects of amphetamine. A reasonable hypothesis is that deprivation-induced wheel running is increased and maintained by the release of dopamine. Naloxone could bind to the delta receptors of dopamine neurons and thereby attenuate prolonged high-rate running.

In terms of activity anorexia, it is possible that physical activity (induced by food restriction) stimulates endogenous enkephalins that bind to the delta receptors of dopamine neurons. Activation of the dopamine neurons could function to maintain or increase the level of physical activity. At the same time, higher levels of dopamine would inhibit the release of NPY (see above) and lead to a suppression of appetite. Opioid modulation of the dopaminergic system would provide a more complete physiological account of activity anorexia.

REFERENCES

Abbott, A. R., & Sebastian, R. J. (1981). Physical attractiveness and expectations of success. *Personality and Social Psychology Bulletin, 7*, 481–486.

Adrian, T. E., Allen, J. M., Bloom, S. R., Ghatei, M. A., Rosser, M. N., Crow, T. J., Tatemoto, K., & Polak, J. M. (1983). Neuropeptide Y distribution in human brain. *Nature, 306*, 584–586.

Agnew, C. R., & Thompson, V. D. (1994). Causal inferences and responsibility attributions concerning an HIV-positive target: The double-edged sword of physical attractiveness. *Journal of Social Behavior and Personality, 9*, 181–190.

Alcock, J. E., Carment, D. W., & Sadava, S. W. (1987). *Social psychology.* Scarborough, Ont.: Prentice-Hall.

Allon, N. (1975). Latent social services in group dieting. *Social Problems, 32*, 59–69.

American Psychiatric Association. (1994). *Diagnostic and statistical manual of mental disorders* (4th ed.). Washington, DC: Author.

Aravich, P. F. (1996). Adverse effects of exercise stress and restricted feeding in the rat: Theoretical and neurobiological considerations. In W. F. Epling & W. D. Pierce (Eds.), *Activity anorexia: Theory, research and treatment* (pp. 81–98). New York: Lawrence Erlbaum.

Aravich, P. F., Rieg, T. S., Lauterio, T. J., & Doerries, L. E. (1993). Beta-endorphin and dynorphin abnormalities in rats subjected to exercise and restricted feeding: Relationship to anorexia nervosa? *Brain Research, 622*, 1–8.

Arnsten, A. T., & Segal, D. S. (1979). Naloxone alters locomotion and interaction with environmental stimuli. *Life Sciences, 25*, 1035–1042.

Averett, S., & Korenman, S. (1996). The economic reality of The Beauty Myth. *The Journal of Human Resources, XXXI*, 304–330.

Beck, S. B., Ward-Hull, C. I., & McLear, P. M. (1976). Variables related to women's somatic preferences of the male and female body. *Journal of Personality and Social Psychology, 43*, 1200–1210.

Belke, T. W. (1996). Investigating the reinforcing properties of running: Or running as its own reward. In W. F. Epling & W. D. Pierce (Eds.), *Activity anorexia: Theory, research and treatment* (pp. 45–56). New York: Lawrence Erlbaum.

———. (1993). *A matching law analysis of the effects of environmental and pharmacological agents on the reinforcing properties of wheel running in rats.* Unpublished doctoral dissertation, Department of Psychology, Harvard University.

Beninger, R. J., & Freedman, N. L. (1982). The use of two operants to examine the nature of pimozide-induced decreases in responding for brain stimulation. *Physiological Psychology, 10*, 409–412.

Berscheid, E., & Walster, E. (1974). Physical attractiveness. In L. Berkowitz (Ed.), *Advances in experimental social psychology*, Vol. 7 (pp. 158–216). New York: Academic Press.

Beumont, C. C., Beumont, P. J. V., & Touyz, S. W. (1996). The problem of excessive physical activity in patients with anorexia nervosa. In W. F. Epling & W. D. Pierce (Eds.), *Activity anorexia: Theory, research and treatment* (pp. 189–198). New York: Lawrence Erlbaum.

Biggs, T., Cukier, J., & Worthing, L. (1982). Augmentation mammaplasty: A review of 18 years. *Plastic and Reconstructive Surgery, 69*, 445–450.

Boer, D. P. (1989). *Determinants of excessive running in activity anorexia.* Unpublished doctoral dissertation, Department of Psychology, University of Alberta.

Boer, D. P., Epling, W. F., Pierce, W. D., & Russell, J. C. (1990) Suppression of food deprivation–induced high-rate wheel running in rats. *Physiology and Behavior, 48*, 339–342.

Bray, G. A. (1976). The risks and disadvantages of obesity. *Major Problems in Internal Medicine, 9*, 215–251.

Brigham, J. C. (1980). Limiting conditions of the "physical attractiveness stereotype": Attributions about divorce. *Journal of Research in Personality, 14*, 365–375.

Bruch, H. (1978). *The golden cage.* Cambridge, MA: Harvard University Press.

———. (1965). Anorexia nervosa: Its differential diagnosis. *Journal of Mental and Nervous Disorders, 141*, 555–556.

Canning, H., & Mayer, J. (1966). Obesity: Its possible effect on college acceptance. *New England Journal of Medicine, 275*, 1172–1174.

Carey, M. P., Ross, J. A., & Enns, M. P. (1981). Naloxone suppresses feeding and drinking, but not wheel running in rats. *Pharmacology, Biochemistry, and Behavior, 14*, 569–571.

Collins, M. A., & Zebrowitz, L. A. (1995). The contributions of appearance to occupational outcomes in civilian and military settings. *Journal of Applied Social Psychology, 25*, 129–163.

Crago, M., Shisslak, C. M., & Estes, L. S. (1996). Eating disturbances among American minority groups: A review. *International Journal of Eating Disorders, 19*, 239–248.

Crisp, A. H., Hsu, L. K. G., Harding, B., & Hartshorn, J. (1980). Clinical features of anorexia nervosa: A study of a consecutive series of 102 female patients. *Journal of Psychosomatic Research, 24*, 179–191.

Cumming, D. C. (1996). The female athlete triand and the critical body fat hypothesis. In W. F. Epling & W. D. Pierce (Eds.), *Activity anorexia: Theory, research and treatment* (pp. 137–146). New York: Lawrence Erlbaum.

Cumming, D. C., & Rebar, R. W. (1985). Hormonal changes with acute exercise and with training in women. *Seminars in Reproductive Endocrinology, 3*, 55–64.

———. (1983). Exercise and reproductive function in women. *American Journal of Industrial Medicine, 4*, 113–125.

Davies, E., & Furnham, A. (1986). The dieting and body shape concerns of adolescent females. *Journal of Child Psychology and Psychiatry, 27*, 417–428.

Davis, C. (1996). The interdependence of obsessive-compulsiveness, physical activity, and starvation: A model for anorexia nervosa. In W. F. Epling & W. D. Pierce (Eds.), *Activity anorexia: Theory, research and treatment* (pp. 209–217). New York: Lawrence Erlbaum.

Davis, J. M., Lamb, D. R., Yim, G. K., & Malvern, P. V. (1985). Opioid modulation of feeding behavior following repeated exposure to forced swimming exercise in male rats. *Pharmacology and Biochemistry of Behavior, 23*, 709–714.

DeRossett, S. E., & Holtzman, S. G. (1982). Effects of naloxone and diprenorphine on spontaneous activity in rats and mice. *Pharmacology, Biochemistry, and Behavior, 17*, 347–351.

Dion, K. L., & Dion, K. K. (1987). Belief in a just world and physical attractiveness stereotyping. *Journal of Personality and Social Psychology, 52*, 775–780.

Doerries, L. E., Aravich, P. F., Metcalf, V. A., Wall, J. D., & Lauterio, T. J. (1989). Beta endorphin and activity-based anorexia in the rat: Influence of simultaneously initiated dieting and exercise on weight loss and beta endorphin. *Annals New York Academy of Sciences, 575*, 609–610.

Dwyer, J. T., Feldman, J. J., & Mayer, J. (1970). The social psychology of dieting. *Journal of Health and Social Behavior, 11*, 269–287.

Effran, M. G. (1974). The effect of physical appearance on the judgment of guilt, interpersonal attraction, and severity of recommended punishment in a simulated jury task. *Journal of Research in Personality, 8*, 45–54.

Epel, E. S., Spanakos, A., Kasi-Godley, J., & Brownell, K. D. (1996). Body shape ideals across gender, sexual orientation, socioeconomic status, race, and age in personal advertisements. *International Journal of Eating Disorders, 19*, 265–273.

Epling, W. F., & Pierce, W. D. (1996a). *Activity anorexia: Theory, research and treatment.* Mahwah, NJ: Lawrence Erlbaum.

———. (1996b). An overview of activity anorexia. In W. F. Epling & W. D. Pierce (Eds.), *Activity anorexia: Theory, research and treatment* (pp. 3–12). New York: Lawrence Erlbaum.

———. (1991). *Solving the anorexia puzzle: A scientific approach.* Toronto: Hogrefe & Huber.

———. (1989). Excessive activity and anorexia in rats. In K. M. Pirke, W. Wuttke, & U. Schweiger (Eds.), *The menstrual cycle and its disorders: Influences of nutrition, exercise and neurotransmitters* (pp. 79–87). New York: Springer-Verlag.

———. (1988). Activity-based anorexia: A biobehavioral perspective. *International Journal of Eating Disorders, 7*, 475–485.

———. (1984). Activity-based anorexia in rats as a function of opportunity to run on an activity wheel. *Nutrition and Behavior, 2*, 37–49.

Epling, W. F., Pierce, W. D., & Stefan, L. (1983). A theory of activity-based anorexia. *International Journal of Eating Disorders, 3*, 27–46.

———. (1981). Schedule-induced self-starvation. In C. M. Bradshaw, E. Szabadi, & C. F. Lowe (Eds.), *Quantificaton of steady-state operant behavior* (pp. 393–396). Amsterdam: Elsevier/North Holland Biomedical Press.

Evans, K. R., & Vaccarino, F. J. (1986). Intra-nucleus accumbens amphetamine: Dose-dependent effects on food intake. *Pharmacology, Biochemistry, and Behavior, 25*, 1149–1151.

Feingold, A. (1990). Gender differences in effects of physical attractiveness on romantic attraction: A comparison across five research paradigms. *Journal of Personality and Social Psychology, 59*, 981–993.

Fitzgerald, F. T. (1981). The problem of obesity. *Annual Review of Medicine, 32*, 221–231.

Frisch, R. E. (1988). Fatness and fertility. *Scientific American, 258*, 88–95.

Gardner, R. M., & Tockerman, Y. R. (1994). A computer-TV methodology for investigating the influence of somatotype on perceived personality traits. *Journal of Social Behavior and Personality, 9*, 555–563.

Garner, D., & Garfinkel, P. (1980). Sociocultural factors in the development of anorexia nervosa. *Psychological Medicine, 10*, 646–656.

Garner, D. M., Rockert, W., Olmsted, M. P., Johnson, C., & Coscina, D. V. (1985).

Psychoeducational principles in the treatment of bulimia and anorexia nervosa. In D. M. Garner & P. Garfinkel (Eds.), *Handbook of psychotherapy for anorexia nervosa and bulimia* (pp. 513–572). New York: Guilford Press.

Geer, E. B., & Warren, M. P. (1996). Nutrition, physical activity, menstrual cycle, and anorexia. In W. F. Epling & W. D. Pierce (Eds.), *Activity anorexia: Theory, research and treatment* (pp. 125–136). New York: Lawrence Erlbaum.

Gillard, E. R., Dang, D. Q., & Stanley, B. G. (1993). Evidence that neuropeptide Y and dopamine in the perifornical hypothalamus interact antagonistically in the control of food intake. *Brain Research, 628*, 128–136.

Glavin, G. B., Pare, W. P., Vincent, G. P., & Tsuda, A. (1981). Effects of d-amphetamine on activity-stress ulcers in rats. *Kurume Medical Journal, 28*, 223 226.

Goodman, R. R., Aider, B. A., & Pasternak, G. W. (1988). Regional distribution of opioid receptors. In G. W. Pasternak, (Ed.), *The opiate receptors* (pp. 197–228). Clifton, NJ: The Humana Press.

Gortmaker, S. L., Must, A., Perrin, J. M., Sobol, A. W., & Dietz, W. H. (1993). Social and economic consequences of overweight in adolescence and young adulthood. *New England Journal of Medicine, 329*, 1008–1012.

Gray, S. H. (1977). Social aspects of body image: Perception of normalcy of weight and affect of college undergraduates. *Perceptual and Motor Skills, 45*, 1035–1040.

Green, S. K., Buchanan, D. R., & Heuer, S. K. (1984). Winners, losers, and choosers: A field investigation of dating initiation. *Personality and Social Psychology Bulletin, 10*, 502–511.

Halmi, K. A., Falk, J. R., & Schwartz, E. (1981). Binge-eating and vomiting: A survey of a college population. *Psychological Medicine, 11*, 697–706.

Hamermesh, D. S., & Biddle, J. E. (1993). Beauty and the labor market. *American Economic Review, 84*, 1174–1194.

Harris, M. B., Harris, R. J., & Bochner, S. (1982). Fat, four-eyed, and female: Stereotypes of obesity, glasses, and gender. *Journal of Applied Social Psychology, 12*, 503–516.

Hatfield, E., & Sprecher, S. (1986). *Mirror, mirror . . . the importance of looks in everyday life*. Albany, NY: State University of New York Press.

Hodes, M., Jones, C., & Davies, H. (1996). Cross-cultural differences in maternal evaluation of children's body shapes. *International Journal of Eating Disorders, 19*, 257–263.

Hooks, M. S., Jones, D. N. C., Justice, J. B. Jr., & Holtzman, S. G. (1992). Naloxone reduces amphetamine-induced stimulation of locomotor activity and in vivo dopamine release in the striatum and nucleus accumbens. *Pharmacology, Biochemistry, and Behavior, 42*, 765–770.

Huston, T. L., & Levinger, G. (1978). Interpersonal attraction and relationships. *Annual Review of Psychology, 29*, 115–156.

Jakobovits, C., Halstead, P., Kelley, L., Roe, D. A., & Young, C. M. (1977). Eating habits and nutrient intakes of college women over a thirty-year period. *Journal of the American Dietetic Association, 71*, 405–411.

Jakubczak, L. F., & Gomer, F. E. (1973). Effects of food deprivation and initial levels on a wheel response to methamphetamine. *Bulletin of the Psychonomic Society, 1*, 343–345.

Jones, D. N. C., & Holtzman, S. G. (1992). Interaction between opioid antagonists and amphetamine: Evidence for mediation by central delta opioid receptors. *The Journal of Pharmacology and Experimental Therapeutics, 262,* 638–645.

Jones, W. H., Hannson, R., & Philips, A. L. (1978). Physical attractiveness and judgments of psychotherapy. *Journal of Social Psychology, 105,* 79–84.

Kalucy, R. C., Crisp, A. H., Lacy, I. H., & Harding, B. (1977). Prevalence and prognosis in anorexia nervosa. *Australian and New Zealand Journal of Psychiatry, 11,* 1401–1407.

Karris, L. (1977). Prejudice against obese renters. *Journal of Social Psychology, 101,* 159–169.

Katz, J. L. (1996). Clinical observations on the physical activity of anorexia nervosa. In W. F. Epling & W. D. Pierce (Eds.), *Activity anorexia: Theory, research and treatment* (pp. 199–207). New York: Lawrence Erlbaum.

————. (1986). Long distance running, anorexia nervosa, and bulimia: A report of two cases. *Comprehensive Psychiatry, 27,* 74–78.

Kaye, W. H. (1987). Opioid antagonist drugs in the treatment of anorexia nervosa. In P. E. Garfinkle & D. M. Garner (Eds.), *The role of drug treatments for eating disorders* (pp. 150–160). New York: Bruner/Mazel.

Kaye, W. H., Picker, D. M., Naber, D. & Ebert, M. H. (1982). Cerebrospinal fluid opioid activity in anorexia nervosa. *American Journal of Psychiatry, 139,* 643–645.

Kron, L., Katz, J. L., Gorzynski, G., & Weiner, H. (1978). Hyperactivity in anorexia nervosa: A fundamental clinical feature. *Comprehensive Psychiatry, 19,* 433–440.

Lakoff, R. T., & Scherr, R. L. (1984). *Face value: The politics of beauty.* Boston: Routledge & Kegan Paul.

Lambert, P. D., Wilding, J. P., al-Dokhayel, A. A., Gilbey, S. G., & Bloom, S. R. (1993). The effect of central blockade of kappa-opioid receptors on neuropeptide Y-induced feeding in the rat. *Brain Research, 629,* 146–148.

Larkin, J. C., & Pines, H. A. (1982). No fat person need apply. *Sociology of Work and Occupations, 6,* 312–327.

Loh, E. S. (1993). The economic effects of physical appearance. *Social Science Quarterly, 74,* 420–438.

Lundberg, J. K., & Sheehan, E. P. (1994). The effects of glasses and weight on perceptions of attractiveness and intelligence. *Journal of Social Behavior and Personality, 9,* 753–760.

Mansour, A., Khachaturian, H., Lewis, M. E., Akil, H., & Watson, S. J. (1988). Anatomy of CNS opioid receptors. *Trends in Neuroscience, 7,* 308–314.

Marrazzi, M. A., & Luby, E. D. (1986). An auto-addiction opioid model of chronic anorexia nervosa. *International Journal of Eating Disorders, 5,* 191–208.

Mazur, A. (1986). U.S. trends in feminine beauty and overadaptation. *The Journal of Sex Research, 22,* 281–303.

McMurray, R. G., Hardy, C. J., Roberts, S., & Forsythe, W. A. (1989) Neuroendocrine response of type A individuals to exercise. *Behavioural Medicine, 15,* 84–92.

Miller, T. M., Coffman, J. G., & Linke, R. A. (1980). Survey on body image, weight and diet of college students. *Journal of the American Dietetic Association, 77,* 561–566.

Montoye, H. J. (1967). Participation in athletics. *Canadian Medical Association Journal, 96,* 813–820.

Moore, J. S., Graziano, W. G., & Miller, M. G. (1987). Physical attractiveness, sex role orientation, and the evaluation of adults and children. *Personality and Social Psychology Bulletin, 13*, 95–102.

Moore, R., Mills, I. H., & Forester, A. (1981). Naloxone in the treatment of anorexia nervosa: Effect on weight gain and lipolysis. *Journal of the Royal Society of Medicine, 74*, 129–131.

Morely, J. E., & Blundell, J. E. (1988). The neurobiological basis of eating disorders: Some formulations. *Biological Psychiatry, 23*, 53–78.

Morely, J. E., Levine, A. S., Plotka, E. D., & Seal, U. S. (1983). The effects of naloxone on feeding and spontaneous locomotion in the wolf. *Physiology and Behavior, 38*, 331–334.

Mrosovsky, N., & Barnes, D. S. (1974). Anorexia, food deprivation and hibernation. *Physiology and Behavior, 12*, 265–270.

Mrosovsky, N., & Sherry, D. F. (1980). Animal anorexias. *Science, 207*, 837–842.

Nakai, Y., Kinoshita, F., Koh, T., Tsujii, S., & Tsukada, T. (1987). Perception of hunger and satiety induced by 2-deoxy-D-glucose in anorexia nervosa and bulimia nervosa. *International Journal of Eating Disorders, 6*, 49–57.

Nencini, P., & Graziani, M. (1990). Opiatergic modulation of preparatory and consummatory components of feeding and drinking. *Pharmacology, Biochemistry, & Behavior, 37*, 531–537.

O'Grady, K. E. (1982). Sex, physical attractiveness, and perceived risk for mental illness. *Journal of Personality and Social Psychology, 43*, 1064–1071.

Orbach, S. (1986). *Hunger strike*. London: Faber and Faber.

Petraglia, F., Porro, C., Facchinetti, F., Cicoli, C., Bertellini, E., Volpe, A., Barbieri, G. C., & Genazzani, A. R. (1986). Opioid control of LH secretion in humans: Menstrual cycle, menopause and aging reduce the effect of naloxone but not of morphine. *Life Sciences, 38*, 2103–2110.

Pierce, C. A. (1992). *The effects of physical attractiveness and height on dating choice: A metaanalysis*. Unpublished master's thesis, State University of New York at Albany, Albany.

Pierce, W. D., & Epling, W. F. (1994). Activity anorexia: An interplay between basic and applied behavior analysis. *The Behavior Analyst, 17*, 7–23.

————. (1991). Activity anorexia: An animal model and theory of human self-starvation. In A. Boulton, G. Baker, & M. Martin-Iverson (Eds.), *Neuromethods, Vol. 18: Animal models in psychiatry 1* (pp. 267–311). Clifton, NJ: Humana Press.

Pierce, W. D., Epling, W. F., & Boer, D. P. (1986). Deprivation and satiation: The interrelations between food and wheel running. *Journal of the Experimental Analysis of Behavior, 46*, 199–210.

Pierce, W. D., Morse, A., Russell, J. C., & Epling, W. F. (1996). *Opioid involvement in food deprivation-induced high-rate wheel running of rats*. Paper presented at the annual meeting of the Association for Behavior Analysis, San Francisco, May.

Potter, C. D., Borer, K. T., & Katz, R. J. (1983). Opiate-receptor blockade reduces voluntary running but not self-stimulation in hamsters. *Pharmacology, Biochemistry, and Behavior, 18*, 217–223.

Radosevich, P. M., Nash, J. A., Lacy, D. B., O'Donovan, C., Williams, P. E., & Abumrad, N. N. (1989). Effects of low- and high-intensity exercise on plasma and cerebrospinal fluid levels of β-endorphin, ACTH, cortisole, norepinephrine, and glucose in the conscious dog. *Brain Research, 498*, 89–98.

Register, C. A., & Willians, D. R. (1990). Wage effects of obesity amoung young workers. *Social Science Quarterly, 7*, 130–134.

Reis, H. T., Nezlek, J., & Wheeler, L. (1980). Physical attractiveness in social interaction.
Journal of Personality and Social Psychology, 38, 604–617.

Rodgers, R. J., & Deacon, R. M. J. (1979). Effect of naloxone on the behavior of rats
exposed to a novel environment. *Psychopharmacology, 65*, 103–105.

Ropert, J. F., Quigley, M. E., & Yen, S. S. C. (1981). Endogenous opiates modulate
pulsatile luteinizing hormone release in humans. *Journal of Clinical Endocrinology and Metabolism, 52*, 583–585.

Routtenberg, A. (1968). ''Self-starvation'' of rats living in activity wheels: Adaptation
effects. *Journal of Comparative and Physiological Psychology, 66*, 234–238.

Routtenberg, A., & Kuznesof, A. W. (1967). Self-starvation of rats living in activity
wheels on a restricted feeding schedule. *Journal of Comparative and Physiological Psychology, 64*, 414–421.

Russell, J. C., Epling, W. F., Pierce, W. D., Boer, D. P., & Amy, R. (1987). Induction
of voluntary prolonged running by rats. *Journal of Applied Physiology, 63*, 2549–
2553.

Sargent, J. D., & Blanchflower, D. G. (1994). Obesity and stature in adolescence and
earnings in young adulthood: Analysis of a British birth cohort. *Archives of Pediatrics and Adolescent Medicine, 148*, 681–687.

Schnur, P., & Barela, P. (1984). Locomotor activity and opiate effects in male and female
hamsters. *Pharmacology, Biochemistry & Behavior, 21*, 369–374.

Sharif, N. A., & Hughes, J. (1989). Discrete mapping of brain *mu* and *delta* opioid
receptors using selective peptides: Quantitative autoradiography, species differences, and comparison with *kappa* receptors. *Peptides, 10*, 499–522.

Sprecher, S., & Duck, S. (1994). Sweet talk: The importance of perceived communication
for romantic and friendship attraction experienced during a get-acquainted date.
Personality and Social Psychology Bulletin, 20, 391–400.

Staffieri, J. R. (1972). Body build and behavior expectancies in young females. *Developmental Psychology, 6*, 125–127.

———. (1967). A study of social stereotype of body image in children. *Journal of
Personality and Social Psychology, 7*, 101–104.

Stanley, B. G. (1993). Neuropeptide Y in multiple hypothalamic sites controls eating
behavior, endocrine, and autonomic systems for body energy balance. In W. F.
Colmers & C. Wahlestedt (Eds.), *The biology of neuropeptide Y and related
peptides*. Totowa, NJ: Humana Press.

Stanley, G., & Gillard, E. R. (1994). Hypothalamic neuropeptide Y and the regulation
of eating behavior and body weight. *Current Directions in Psychological Science,
3*, 9–15.

Tainter, M. L. (1943). Effects of certain analeptic drugs on spontaneous running activity
of the white rat. *Journal of Comparative Psychology, 36*, 143–155.

Umberson, D., & Hughes, M. (1984). *The impact of physical attractiveness on achievement and psychological well-being*. Paper presented at the Meetings of the American Sociological Association, San Antonio, Texas, August.

Unger, R. K., Hilderbrand, M., & Madar, T. (1982). Physical attractiveness and assumptions about social deviance: Some sex-by-sex comparisons. *Personality and Social Psychology Bulletin, 8*, 293–301.

Warren, M. P. (1989). Reproductive function in the ballet dance. In K. M. Pirke, W.

Wuttke, & U. Schweiger (Eds.), *The menstrual cycle and its disorders: Influences of nutrition, exercise, and neurotransmitters* (pp. 161–170). New York: Springer-Verlag.

Wheeler, G. (1996). Exercise, sports, and anorexia. In W. F. Epling & W. D. Pierce (Eds.), *Activity anorexia: Theory, research and treatment* (pp. 159–175). New York: Lawrence Erlbaum.

Wheeler, G. D., Singh, M., Pierce, W. D., Epling, W. F., & Cumming, D. C. (1991). Endurance training decreases serum testosterone levels in men without change in luteinizing hormone pulsatile release. *Journal of Clinical Endocrinology and Metabolism, 72,* 422–425.

Wolf, N. (1991). *The beauty myth.* New York: Doubleday.

Wood, P. L. (1983). Opioid regulation of CNS dopaminergic pathways: A review of methodology, receptor types, regional variations and specific differences. *Peptides, 4,* 595–601.

Wood, P. L., & Iyengar, S. (1988). Central actions of opiates and opioid peptides. In G. W. Pasternak (Ed.), *The opiate receptors* (pp. 307–356). Clifton, NJ: The Humana Press.

Wooley, O. W., Wooley, S. C., & Dyrenforth, S. R. (1979). Obesity and women. II. A neglected feminist topic. *Women's Studies International Quarterly, 2,* 67–79.

Yates, A. (1996). Athletes, eating disorders, and the overtraining syndrome. In W. F. Epling & W. D. Pierce (Eds.), *Activity anorexia: Theory, research and treatment* (pp. 179–188). New York: Lawrence Erlbaum.

———. (1990). Current perspectives on eating disorders: 1. History, psychological and biological aspects. *Journal of Childhood and Adolescent Psychiatry, 6,* 813–828.

4

A Behavioral Analysis of Collaborative Partnerships for Community Health

STERGIOS RUSSOS, STEPHEN B. FAWCETT,
VINCENT T. FRANCISCO, JANNETTE Y. BERKLEY,
AND CHRISTINE M. LOPEZ

INTRODUCTION

Culture refers to the shared practices of members of a community and the social contingencies which shape and maintain those practices (Skinner, 1953). Cultural and community practices, such as collaboration or competition, occur in the context of personal, group, and environmental factors and contingencies that allow and select for such behavior. Communities, as groups of people who share common turf or experience, evolve as they identify and solve problems that threaten their survival and development. Problem-solving practices in a community may be strengthened as members collaborate in activities that result in community-wide benefits.

Community partnerships are innovative mechanisms for problem solving at the community level (Fawcett, Paine-Andrews et al., 1995; Fawcett, Paine, Francisco, & Vliet, 1993). They involve alliances between representatives of different community sectors, organizations, or constituencies collaborating for a common purpose or mission (Gray, 1991; Wolff, 1992). A community partnership to reduce adolescent pregnancy, for example, might engage adolescents, their families, and others affected by the problem, as well as community members and groups who might contribute or hinder solutions to the problem, such as educators, religious leaders, and business people. Community partnerships target a variety of societal concerns including substance abuse (Fawcett et al., in press; Hawkins & Catalano, 1992; Lewis et al., in press; Paine-Andrews et al., in press), cardiovascular disease (Harris, Paine-Andrews et al., 1996; Harris, Richter et al., 1996; Johnston et al., 1996; Samuels, 1990), adolescent pregnancy

(Paine-Andrews et al., 1995; Vincent, Clearie, & Schulchter, 1987), and youth violence (Wilson-Brewer et al., 1991).

Many societal problems, such as death and disability due to cardiovascular disease, represent consequences too distal to affect the behaviors contributing to them, such as prolonged use of tobacco products or eating foods high in fat. A community partnership aims to change the environmental context of behavior so that distal consequences bear on the environmental factors and behaviors leading to them. This role might be analogous to maintaining functional connections between interlocking operants of a metacontingency through socially arranged contingencies of reinforcement (Glenn, 1988). For example, a community partnership with the long-term goal of reduced incidence of cardiovascular disease might attempt to alter the contingencies on tobacco use, physical activity, and intake of dietary fat (Harris, Richter et al., 1996). The partnership may effect the social contingencies for appropriate behaviors by modifying an array of programs (e.g., establish intramural sports clubs), policies (e.g., enact policies in conjunction with local government promoting access to healthy foods at restaurants, schools, and worksite cafeterias), and practices (e.g., provide incentives for employees to exercise) throughout the community. By selecting multiple and diverse changes within multiple community settings (e.g., agencies, institutions, citizen organizations, and informal community networks) and across the entire community, the partnership may increase the density of antecedents and consequences for appropriate behaviors (Hovell et al., 1994). This strategy may increase the probability of an individual's exposure to social contingencies connected to the long-term outcome of reduced cardiovascular disease.

This chapter examines contingencies of reinforcement affecting collaborative partnerships for community health. First, we describe a support system for community partnerships including grantmakers (e.g., federal and state agencies, private foundations) and a university-based research team involved in a case study in Kansas. The aim of such support systems—to build a community's capacity to solve local problems—and their topography and function are described. Examples are presented using case studies of community partnerships served by the authors. Second, we describe some broad classes of operants, such as collaborative planning or community action, associated with community partnerships. Third, we describe practices associated with supporting community partnerships, such as enhancing experience and competence or enhancing environmental support and resources. Fourth, we outline broader societal contingencies that affect the grantmakers, state and federal agencies, professional associations and networks, and university-based centers that comprise an ideal support system for community partnerships. Finally, the discussion concludes with challenges in and recommendations for enhancing the practice of collaborative partnerships based on theory and field practice.

A BROAD COLLABORATIVE PARTNERSHIP FOR
COMMUNITY HEALTH: A CASE STUDY IN KANSAS

A broad collaborative partnership for community health was established in Kansas beginning in 1989, under the auspices of the Kansas Health Foundation. Although other parties were involved in this initiative, this section features a case study involving three primary partners: local community partnerships, the Kansas Health Foundation, and a university-based research and technical assistance organization (the Work Group on Health Promotion and Community Development) with which the authors are affiliated. The methods and practices of this broad partnership are shaped by the interactions among the partners and with communities toward progress for a common end—to build communities' capacities to address local health concerns and goals.

The Kansas Health Foundation is a statewide health foundation committed to improving the health of the people of Kansas. Toward this aim, the Foundation began the Kansas Initiative—a comprehensive effort to address the state's major health concerns, such as cardiovascular disease, adolescent substance abuse, and adolescent pregnancy. Community assessments across the state identified communities prepared to create partnerships for addressing community health concerns. The Foundation helped facilitate the establishment of community partnerships by convening diverse partners, leveraging funding, and brokering access to material and other resources. To encourage production and outcomes, the Foundation set contingencies on grant renewal based on evidence of community partnership progress in becoming a catalyst for community change.

Community partnerships were formed, each one targeting specific issues relevant in its community. Target health issues included cardiovascular disease, adolescent substance abuse, and adolescent pregnancy. Community partnerships were selected from among those responding to requests for proposals by the Foundation. Criteria for selection included commitment to creating and changing programs, policies, and practices related to behaviors associated with the health concern. Each community partnership agreed to incorporate evaluation methods in its activities, and to seek ways to sustain its efforts. To increase the likelihood that these community partnerships would become effective catalysts for community change, the researchers at the Work Group on Health Promotion and Community Development (hereater Work Group) were also funded to provide support and monitoring of the community partnerships.

The Work Group at the University of Kansas provided technical assistance and evaluation for community partnerships of the Kansas Initiative. The mission of the Work Group is to enhance community health and development through collaborative research, teaching, and service. A primary strategy is to develop the capacities of communities to address their health concerns over time and across concerns. The Work Group developed materials to facilitate community planning (e.g., action planning guides for the prevention of substance abuse, chronic disease, teen pregnancy, and violence among youth) (Fawcett, Francisco,

Paine-Andrews, Fisher et al., 1994; Fawcett, Harris et al., 1995; Fawcett, Paine-Andrews, Francisco, Richter, Lewis, Harris et al., 1994; Fawcett, Paine-Andrews, Francisco, Richter, Lewis, Williams et al., 1994). It also developed and implemented evaluation procedures to assess the process of implementation (e.g., satisfaction with program implementation), intermediate outcomes (e.g., community change), and impacts on the community (e.g., community-level indicators such as rates of teen pregnancy) (Fawcett, Francisco, Paine-Andrews, Lewis et al., 1994; Fawcett, Sterling et al., 1996; Francisco, Paine, & Fawcett, 1993). The Work Group faculty, students, and staff also researched the effectiveness of particular community partnership interventions. Successful programs, practices, and policies were disseminated among community partnerships throughout the state (Lewis et al., in press; Paine-Andrews, Francisco, & Fawcett, 1994). The Work Group's evaluation results and other research findings were shared with the community leadership and the Kansas Health Foundation to help shape the problem-solving capacities of each partner in this collaborative system.

The next section of this chapter describes the classes of operants of community partnerships, support system contingencies for community partnership practices, and the broader societal contingencies on practices in a support system. More detailed descriptions of intervention and evaluation within this system can be found elsewhere (Fawcett, Paine-Andrews et al., 1996; Fawcett, Paine-Andrews et al., 1995; Francisco et al., 1993; Fawcett et al., 1993).

PRIMARY CLASSES OF BEHAVIOR ASSOCIATED WITH COMMUNITY PARTNERSHIPS

A community partnership attempts to effect distal outcomes, such as the incidence and prevalence of death, disability, or other outcomes related to health and development. It does so by arranging more proximal social contingencies, such as new or modified programs, policies, and practices related to those outcomes. Community partnerships function as catalysts for community change by convening, leveraging, and brokering resources needed to engage the community in a change process. The primary classes of behavior associated with community partnerships include: (a) collaborative planning, (b) community action, (c) community change, (d) community capacity and outcomes, and (e) adaptation and maintenance. The following brief description of these classes of community partnership practices is detailed extensively in Fawcett, Paine-Andrews et al. (1995).

Collaborative planning describes an array of community practices for identifying local goals, adapting local goals to attract resources held by grantmakers, and tailoring efforts to the assets and needs of the local context. Collaborative planning can help identify and clarify local problems, the contingencies supporting those problems, and the local contingencies of reinforcement to address those problems. Practices in this class include assessing public health data, implementing listening sessions or town meetings, conducting behavioral surveys (both self-report and direct observation), conducting surveys to identify issues and options of local importance (Schriner & Fawcett, 1988), and formal and informal interviewing of community members. The behaviors of collaborative planning may be proximally reinforced by identifying shared aspirations that reflect reinforcing and punishing stimuli. For example, planning information might indicate what community members find valuable (e.g., neighbors looking out for each other), what does not work well (e.g., local criminal activity is unreported by neighbors), and what might work better (e.g., a neighborhood "watch" program). The degree to which those participating in collaborative planning are representative of the whole community may affect the function of the other classes of behavior in community partnerships and, consequently, the associated outcomes.

Community action describes a class of practices for effecting relevant changes in a variety of sectors of the community (e.g., businesses, schools, faith institutions). The desired product of community action is community change: new or modified programs, policies, and practices to address the mission, objectives, and strategies outlined in the process of collaborative planning. Functionally, community leaders or groups of persons with shared interests work to resolve problems resulting from ineffective or misplaced contingencies of reinforcement. For example, a community partnership targeting contingencies related to reduced cardiovascular disease may organize a meeting with fast-food restaurant owners, schools lunch officials, and health care providers to develop a social marketing campaign to promote healthy food choices by youth. The intended proximal consequence of community action is community change related to the longer-term outcome, reduced incidence or prevalence of the problem. The contingencies of reinforcement for community actions (i.e., consequent community changes) presume that conditions that affect community health are multiple and interconnected with those affecting other concerns. By organizing efforts and building collaborations across community sectors, a community partnership increases the probability of new or modified community changes, thereby affecting the probability of individuals' exposure to social contingencies (e.g., a work exercise room or nutrition curriculum in schools) controlling behaviors related to the health outcome.

Community change describes the class of events that, taken together, may effect proximal and distal outcomes of interest. These events include new or modified programs (e.g., after-school peer tutoring programs), policies (e.g., raising the age for legal tobacco purchases to 18 or 21 years), and practices (e.g., moving tobacco products behind the checkout counter to eliminate shoplifting or easy access by minors). A community change results from actions taken to bring about changes in the community that were planned by the community partnership. For example, a planning objective to increase children's consumption of fruits and vegetables to improve nutrition might result in a new practice of stocking such items in salad bars of schools. Community change is the outcome of community actions, or rather the embodiment of new contingencies of reinforcement which may result in new and more functional patterns of behavior for sufficient numbers of people to affect community-level outcomes.

Community change practices may be categorized by type of strategy for behavior change. These strategies may include antecedent events, such as providing information or enhancing skills, and consequent events, such as providing incentives and disincentives or facilitating support from influential others. Change strategies may also include modifying the physical design of the environment to increase the response requirement (e.g., moving tobacco products out of sight or access to youth) or decrease it (e.g., enhancing availability of condoms for people at higher risk for HIV/AIDS). Other strategies, such as providing services, may enhance the opportunity to respond. Finally, strategies to change contingencies of reinforcement may include modifying policies related to one or more sectors of the community or providing public feedback on a community's goal attainment.

The experimental analysis of behavior helps select for demonstrably functional community changes (i.e., independent variables) worthy of maintenance and widespread adoption (Fawcett, 1990; Fawcett, Mathews, & Fletcher, 1980). The rate of community changes and the distribution of community changes across community sectors (e.g., businesses, schools, faith institutions) may be promising indicators of the functioning of community partnerships (Fawcett et al., 1993; Francisco et al., 1993). A community's capacity to facilitate change may be evidenced in consistent rates of community change over time and across concerns. Future research must clarify the relationship between unique patterns of community change and change in community-level indicators of problems experienced by community members (e.g., the incidence and prevalence of youth violence, adolescent pregnancy, or cardiovascular disease). Preliminary evidence indicates that this connection is at least correlational (Fawcett et al., in press).

Community partnerships learn to address new problems (e.g., moving from substance abuse to violence) and function under different conditions (e.g., shift in available resources) over time. As new ways of planning collaboratively, developing new programs and policies, and providing feedback on goal attainment unfold in the community, members of the partnerships and communities may be reinforced for their efforts by public recognition or enhanced access to resources. Accordingly, the occurrence of activities for sustaining partnerships (e.g., increased funding for new programs, increased citizen participation in community change) may be more probable. Consider, for example, the diet and exercise programs implemented by Kansas LEAN (Low-fat Eating for America Now), community partnerships with a mission to change practices associated with cardiovascular disease. The programs became so successful that they expanded to new populations and attracted additional funding (Harris, Richter et al., 1996). However, community partnerships may dissolve and the old ways of interacting may continue when the grant ends. The identification of processes for adapting and sustaining successful community efforts must be a key component of future community research.

These community practices represent complex chains of behaviors that may reinforce each other and may lead to new and continuing ways of interacting that would prevent and address community health problems. Although discrete operants in each class of community practice have a unique consequence, all operants in a class share a common consequence. For example, holding community-wide listening sessions and engaging representatives from multiple sectors of the community each result in collaborative community planning. Outcomes of an operant in one class (e.g., community change) might reinforce operants in other classes (e.g., community action, collaborative planning). This might be observed when the goals established during collaborative planning come to fruition in new community actions and changes. All the classes of behaviors associated with community partnerships have the common consequence of enhanced community capacity to influence local community health outcomes. These theoretical relationships call for empirical demonstration beyond the case studies presented in this chapter.

PRIMARY CLASSES OF BEHAVIOR ASSOCIATED WITH SUPPORTING COMMUNITY PARTNERSHIPS

Practices of community partnership are established and strengthened by activities of grantmakers, university-based research and technical assistance teams, and other parts of the support system (Chavis, Florin, & Felix, 1993). An analysis of how support system activities may shape and maintain community problem-solving practices is presented using examples of collaborations among community partnerships, the Kansas Health Foundation, and the Work Group. These support system practices may be grouped into three categories based on the similarity in their intended outcomes for community partnerships: (a) enhancing experience and competence, (b) enhancing group structure and capacity, and (c) enhancing environmental support and resources. Table 4.1 shows a list of practices within these groups. A more extensive description of support system practices can be found in Fawcett, Paine-Andrews et al. (1995).

The extent to which practices within each category are reinforced by a common group outcome is undemonstrated. More likely, each support practice (e.g., conducting focus groups to assess interests of community members) represents a class of support system operants. The classes may share the common outcome of effective and sustained community capacity to address community health concerns. Two questions help set the occasion for support system practices and their reinforcement: Does the support system practice enhance the community's capacity to address local problems? Is this capacity evidenced with new problems? For purposes of this analysis, these support system practices are exemplified through people representing the grantmaker or university-based research and technical support team. These practices might be increasingly observed of

Table 4.1
Some Contingencies of a Support System for Community Partnerships

A. Enhancing Experience and Competence

Encouraging listening sessions to identify local issues, resources, barriers, and alternatives

Conducting surveys to identify community concerns and needs

Creating an inventory of community assets and resources

Using records and surveys to determine the incidence and prevalence of identified problems

Identifying potential targets (e.g., youth) and agents of change (e.g., teachers)

Providing information about community partnerships as catalysts for change and impact

Promulgating guidelines for selecting leadership and membership (e.g., inclusion, diversity, experiential knowledge, capacity to influence change)

Providing training in leadership skills (e.g., analyzing problems, strategic planning, conflict resolution)

Providing technical assistance in creating action plans (i.e., identifying important changes)

Conducting focus groups to assess interests of community members

Locating meetings and activities in diverse communities (e.g., low-income neighborhoods, ethnic churches)

Providing consultation in selection, design, and implementation of early project

Encouraging involvement of potential opponents as well as allies

B. Enhancing Group Structure and Capacity

Providing technical assistance in strategic planning (i.e., identifying vision, mission, objectives, strategies, and action plans)

Helping develop an organizational structure (i.e., committees, task forces, bylaws) that facilitates community change in a variety of relevant sectors (e.g., schools, businesses)

Encouraging involvement of key influentials (e.g., school superintendent, police chief) from important community sectors

Encouraging inclusion of people affected by the problem (e.g., low-income people, people of color, youth)

Providing technical assistance in recruiting, developing, and supporting members and volunteers

Providing technical assistance in developing plans for financial sustainability (i.e., leveraging positions in established agencies)

Brokering access to other financial resources (e.g., arranging contacts with funders)

Providing technical assistance in securing financial resources (e.g., writing grant applications)

Promoting coordination, cooperative agreements, and collaborative arrangements

Developing media campaigns to counter arguments of opponents

Table 4.1 continued

C. Enhancing Environmental Support and Resources

Providing ongoing information and feedback about community change, behavior change, community satisfaction, and community-level impact (e.g., teen pregnancy rates)

Helping develop ties to existing community sectors, organizations, and groups

Reinventing and adapting to fit local needs, resources, and cultural traditions

Arranging opportunities for networking among those with relevant experiential knowledge

Providing access to outside experts in areas of local concern

Establishing a microgrants program (i.e., $50–$1,000) to support grassroots efforts

Promoting celebration and recognition of community change and accomplishment

Helping advocate for policies and resource allocations consistent with the partnership goals

Source: S. B. Fawcett, A. Paine-Andrews, V. T. Francisco, J. A. Schultz, K. P. Richter, R. K. Lewis, and E. L. Williams et al., Using empowerment theory in collaborative partnerships for community health and development, *American Journal of Community Psychology, 23* (1995), pp. 686–687. Copyright 1995 by Plenum Press. Adapted with permission of the author.

a community partnership as it improves its function as a catalyst for community change.

Enhancing experience and competence (see Table 4.1, A). Support systems may enhance experience and competence of community partnerships by encouraging and assisting with the collection and analysis of information. During the initial period of planning, community partnerships seek to understand local issues related to the problem, locate resources and assets, and identify potential barriers to solutions. The Work Group provided training and help for staff of local partnerships with methods of collaborative planning. Listening sessions, town meetings, and surveys were used to identify local issues, concerns, resources, and barriers—contingencies of reinforcement for problem solving. The Work Group staff prompted for and taught partnership staff how to involve a representative group of the community in collaborative planning so as to improve the identification of local reinforcers (e.g., construction of a recreation center) for community action and change. For example, a community partnership located in a college town, and with a mission to reduce youth substance abuse, held listening sessions in libraries, community centers, public housing, and the university campus. A partnership's adaptation of recommended procedures is shaped by their immediate consequences (e.g., large citizen participation in a town meeting) and by evaluation results of adapted procedures by the Work Group (e.g., low response rate of mail survey procedures). Engaging community members in identifying problems and solutions may increase the likelihood of their participation in implementing and sustaining contingencies for solutions. The grantmaker established grant contracts to encourage participation of people of different ages, races, and economic groups. Collaborative planning contingencies may be designed to evoke a partnership's inclusion of potential opponents, allies, and those most affected by the issue. Support system encouragement of diverse participation may facilitate community-wide cooperation and support for community partnerships.

Support system evaluations and research activities were designed to enhance experience and competence in the community partnerships. For example, the Work Group's summary of empirical findings related to substance abuse prevention helped a community partnership identify community changes for the prevention of substance abuse among adolescents. The Work Group monitored self-reported and observed community changes (e.g., new or modified programs, policies, and practices) facilitated by each community partnership. Monitoring data were used to establish contingencies for the classes of behaviors of community partnerships (Francisco et al., 1993). Routine feedback on progress, such as bar graphs of number of community changes across categories of objectives defined during the planning process, differentially reinforced collaborative planning practices. Similar feedback on community changes across types of strategies (e.g., providing information, modifying policies, changing the physical environment) shaped practices to include strategies more likely to result in community change. Line graphs of cumulative community changes over time were used to shape partnerships' community change activity: a small or zero slope in the community change curve provided an opportunity to prompt higher rates of activity; a large slope set the occasion for celebration of group and individual efforts. Results from random-digit dialed behavioral surveys and summaries of health department epidemiological data suggested health issues requiring greater attention and impact of community efforts. Partnerships used data on community change and community-level impact to prompt additional community actions and changes and to gain reinforcement, such as recognition articles in local news, recruitment of volunteers, and collaborations with influential groups. These examples suggest that consistent contingencies established by the support system contingencies may help create community-controlled conditions for a partnership's use of data and evaluation methods.

Enhancing structure and capacity (see Table 4.1, B). A community partnership's function as a catalyst for change in addressing local concerns is greatly influenced by its structure. Local partnerships must decide how to best organize their human and material resources to bring about desired community outcomes. Practices that identify problems and probable solutions, discussed earlier in collaborative planning, contribute to decisions of structure. The Work Group helped partnerships develop guidelines for organizational structure appropriate to their mission, community resources, and available paid and volunteer staff. Given that health-related behaviors are influenced by multiple contingencies in multiple settings, community partnerships were encouraged to organize so as to maximize community change in a variety of community sectors which may influence targeted outcomes. Consider, for example, the case of a community partnership for prevention of cardiovascular diseases with an objective to promote healthy eating behaviors in children. It organized committees to implement new or modified policies and practices in schools, homes, fast-food stores, and supermarkets. This partnership organized similar structures to induce changes related to its physical activity and tobacco use objectives. Regular feedback from the Work Group on rate and distribution of community changes across committees, strategies, and objectives further helped shape the structure of community partnerships. Involvement of influential community members (e.g., school superintendent, clergy, newspaper editors) from important community sectors facilitated community changes. Such involvement was enhanced through personal contact and technical assistance materials (e.g., training and reference materials) for volunteer recruitment and development and through grantmaker incentives contingent on support from community leaders for a community partnership.

The capacity of a community partnership to maintain and adapt its structure and function may be enhanced through contingencies for financial sustainability provided by the support system. For example, grants from the Kansas Health Foundation were designed to prompt and shape community partnership planning for financial sustainability. A sustainability plan outlines a partnership's practices for financial and community support following the end of the grant period. A written sustainability plan was required of all funded projects. Community partnerships were required to submit periodic status reports on progress to the Foundation. The frequency of status report requirements might be varied in order to shape a community partnership's performance. The status reports are also an opportunity to identify areas for training and technical assistance. Based on the needs reflected in status reports and financial sustainability plans, the Work Group communicated grant opportunities to community partnerships, provided training for staff in how to seek and apply for grants, and arranged contacts with potential funders.

Enhancing environmental support and resources (see Table 4.1, C). The support system seeks to establish social and environmental contingencies that contribute to the function of community partnerships. Examples included arranging opportunities for networking among partnerships and allies, providing access to outside experts in matters of local concern, establishing and improving sources of local data on issues of community health and development, and providing sources of financial, material, and human resources. The Work Group collaborated with the Foundation to provide regional conferences on topics of interest to community partnerships, organize workshops with experts, and plan group discussions and retreats involving groups of community partnerships. These networking activities exposed community partnerships to new practices and innovations (e.g., volunteer recruiting techniques) as well as contingencies of reinforcement for continuing partnership efforts (e.g., links to new funding sources, models of long-running partnerships). With support from the Foundation and the Work Group, several partnerships created a minigrants program, offering $50 to $1,000 grants to grassroots efforts consistent with community partnership objectives, establishing conditions for immediate and long-term community support (Paine-Andrews, Francisco, & Fawcett, 1994). The Work Group collaborated with the Foundation to provide training grants and fellowships that enhanced community leadership and reinforced community problem solving. A support system enhances environmental support and resources to improve the effectiveness of community partnerships.

Providing ongoing information and feedback on proximal outcomes (e.g., community changes, citizen satisfaction) and distal consequences (e.g., incidence and prevalence of disease, disability, injury, and other societal problems in the community) supported the development of partnership capacity to better serve the needs of the community. For example, monitoring data suggested that a community partnership was spending greater efforts toward providing direct services than contributing to community change. This information helped partnership staff redirect its efforts as a catalyst for community change and decrease service provision efforts.

BROADER SOCIETAL CONTINGENCIES ON A SUPPORT SYSTEM FOR COMMUNITY HEALTH

The creation and maintenance of a comprehensive support system for community partnerships is affected by broader contingencies of reinforcement. For example, grantmakers' investments in collaborative partnerships for community health may be a function of antecedent events, such as new ideas about collaboration as a means to address societal concerns, and consequent events, including social reinforcement from colleagues in other foundations for adopting the strategy of collaboration. This section outlines some of the broader contingencies that may affect key parties in a comprehensive support system for community health: grantmakers, state and federal agencies, professional associations and networks, and academic and research institutions.

Contingencies affecting grantmakers. Many grantmakers or private foundations with the mission of improving community health and development, such as the John D. and Catherine T. MacArthur Foundation or the Kansas Health Foundation, serve as catalysts for change (Gerzon, 1995). They convene key stakeholders, such as leadership in the business or religious community, by identifying health or development issues that may be worthy of community attention. They also broker connections among and between those who have the concern, such as grassroots community organizations committed to preventing violence or injury, and those who have the resources to help address local concerns. Finally, using grants as incentives, they leverage human and financial resources for the commonly shared purpose.

Social contingencies affect these broad classes of behavior—convening, brokering, and leveraging—displayed by senior leadership and program officers of foundations. For example, the decision to convene or bring people together around the community issue of child abuse and neglect may be affected by a variety of contingencies of reinforcement mediated by an array of relevant audiences. Antecedent events, such as new data showing increased incidence of cases of abuse and neglect or prompts from foundation board members to do something about this issue, may increase the likelihood that a request for proposals will be announced for communities to address the issue. Similarly, consequent events, such as social reinforcement from senior program officers within the philanthropy or criticism from board members, may increase or decrease the chances that investments in this priority area will be maintained for sufficient time to have an effect on the problem, as evidenced by community-level indicators, such as the reported incidence of child abuse and neglect.

Contingencies affecting state and federal agencies. State and federal agencies, such as state departments of health or the U.S. Centers for Disease Control and Prevention, set priorities for attention and provide resources and other support for local, state, and national efforts to promote community health and development. For example, a state commissioner for health may select childhood immunizations as a high priority for maternal and child health, promulgating information about the level of the problem and effective strategies for addressing it. State public health officials may also provide access to new grants, technical assistance for planning and implementation, and other resources for meeting a new state goal such as that every child is fully immunized by age two.

These broad classes of behavior—setting priorities and more specific health objectives, promulgating information about the problem and its consequences, developing grant programs to address the issue, and providing technical assistance and other supports—may also be affected by contingencies of reinforcement. For example, the decision to choose childhood immunization as a priority area over domestic violence may be affected by a variety of contingencies of reinforcement mediated by actors who control contingencies for those making these decisions. Some antecedent events, such as data on dollars saved in health costs per dollar invested (e.g., for immunization a ratio of 11:1 is sometimes given), may be functional in controlling priority setting (Schauffler, 1993). When relevant data for other candidate issues, such as domestic violence, are unavailable or viewed as inaccurate or insensitive, these may be even less likely to attain media attention, agenda status, and resources. Similarly, consequent events, such as social reinforcement from constituents or other officials within the state or federal agency, may help maintain allocation of resources for this priority area (Schauffler, 1993). By contrast, criticism from elected officials or others for including reductions in access to weapons as a core component of a prevention initiative in youth violence, for instance, may lead to adjustments in priorities.

Contingencies affecting professional associations and networks. Professional associations, such as the American Psychological Association, the American Public Health Association, or the American Medical Association, help set standards for what is considered good science and practice. For example, by announcing themes for conferences or special issues of main scholarly journals, professional associations and networks may help set the agenda for research or practice. Smaller networks or communities of scholars, such as those interested in prevention of violence or substance abuse, may be particularly influential. They may also provide leads about new grants, technical support for planning and implementation of research and intervention projects, and other resources for enhancing research and practice.

These broad classes of behavior of professional associations and networks—setting guidelines and priorities for research and practice, sharing information about opportunities, and providing technical support—may similarly be affected by contingencies of reinforcement. For example, the decision to choose a conference theme of "creating community partnerships for health" may be affected by a variety of contingencies of reinforcement controlled by those in leadership positions in professional associations. Some antecedent events, such as anticipated changes in the health care system that favor investment in prevention over treatment, may be influential in choosing "creating community partnerships" as a professional development activity for membership. Similarly, consequent events, such as increased access to grant opportunities for conducting collaborative research with community partnerships, may increase the likelihood of this type of applied research. By contrast, consistent rejection of journal manuscripts describing such work or other criticism from colleagues in professional networks may result in the choice of other, more traditional forms of scholarship and professional activity.

Contingencies affecting academic and research institutions. Leadership in universities, such as the chancellor or senior administrators or scientists, may encourage or discourage research and practice relevant to collaborative partnerships for community health and development. University-based centers, such as applied research institutes or training units, help model legitimate forms of integrating research, teaching, and public service. For example, announcing a university initiative supporting collaborative research, teaching, and service relevant to community health may increase the probability of such activity by academic or research administrators. They may also provide leads about available grant funds in related areas, technical support for planning and implementation of related research and intervention projects, and other resources for enhancing research, teaching, and service of social relevance.

These broad classes of behavior of academic and research administrators—setting priorities for research, teaching, and service, communicating information about opportunities, and providing technical support—are likely affected by past histories and prevailing contingencies of reinforcement. For example, the decision to use new communication technologies to provide distance learning courses for citizens working in community partnerships throughout the state may be affected by contingencies of reinforcement mediated by prominent donors, alumni, senior faculty and administrators, and others who control contingencies for academic and research administrators. Some antecedent events, such as anticipated loss of federal funding for basic research, may encourage allocation of university resources for community health, an area in which opportunities for extramural grant support appear to be on the rise. Similarly, consequent events, such as foundation endowments for conducting collaborative research with community partnerships, may increase the likelihood of this type of work. By contrast, discrediting of this type of research during promotion and tenure review or other criticism from colleagues in local academic departments or research centers may decrease collaboration with community partnerships in favor of other, more traditional forms of university research, teaching, and service.

In summary, this analysis suggests an array of broader contingencies that may affect the support available for partnerships for community health and development. By working together, state and community partnerships, grantmakers, state and national agencies, professional associations and networks, and academic and research institutions can create a comprehensive and integrated support system for community health and development. Under such conditions, state and community partnerships may be more successful in facilitating locally valued improvements in community health and development.

CONCLUSION

A behavior analysis of cultural innovations, such as collaborative partnerships for community health, should be measured by the degree to which it contributes to the understanding, prediction, and enhancement of such cultural practices. Collaborative partnerships for community health illustrate the contingencies for establishing effective and sustainable community practices for addressing locally valued health concerns. This chapter examined how community partnerships may effect community health outcomes by establishing contingencies of reinforcement that mediate long-term consequences and individual behaviors contributing to them. A support system for community partnerships may help establish sustainable partnerships by convening, leveraging, and brokering social and environmental resources. The innovation known as collaborative partnerships offers an important context for future experimental research and analysis of cultural practices.

There are a number of methodological challenges in the study of collaborative community partnerships. Most importantly, there is considerable difficulty in defining the dependent variables. As an example, for the outcome ''sustained community capacity for problem solving,'' definitions of ''community'' and ''capacity'' may vary with the internal validity of procedures to identify the behaviors and contingencies that describe them. Funding conditions usually define a community in terms of geographic boundaries (e.g., town, city, county) with the assumption of similar social contingencies on inhabitants' behaviors. Future studies might clarify this definition by examining the variability in social contingencies' strength with a geographic community's square area, population diversity and density, type and density of available social activities, and prox-imity to neighboring communities.

A definition of capacity might include many combinations of measures of practices within the classes of behavior associated with community partnerships (e.g., number of planning objectives accomplished, number of sustained com-munity changes over time, number of partnership-initiated intervention studies). As an independent variable, the capacity of a community to address local health concerns may be defined by changes in community-level outcomes. This defi-nition is limited by the lack of reliable and valid community-level health out-comes (e.g., epidemiological and behavioral survey data at the county and city level). For example, despite its modest sensitivity and accuracy, the monthly rate of single, nighttime vehicular crashes is among the more commonly used community-level indicators of impact of a community partnership for prevention of substance abuse among adolescents. Such deficiencies weaken the contingen-cies of reinforcement represented by feedback on process and impact. Future research should help establish more accurate and sensitive measures for inter-mediate and more distal health outcomes.

Internal validity issues in community-based research and action include chal-lenges of experimental design and methodology (Biglan, 1995, ch. 11; Robinson & Hill, 1995). Several questions suggest areas of future research. What com-munity practices and conditions affect changes in the community-level out-comes? What amount (dose) or combination of the independent variables (e.g., community capacity variables or community changes facilitated by a partner-ship) results in what level of effect? How do we measure variables not related to, but occurring concurrently, during the life of the community partnership? What are the side effects of community partnerships? One of the most common challenges reflected in these questions is how to identify a valid control com-munity or comparison condition. For example, what are the most important variables representative of a community (e.g., population density, existing ma-terial resources, baseline level of problem-solving capacity) to match or control for? How is citizen reactivity to measurement of community resources and prob-lems controlled for in comparison communities? Issues of social significance also inform questions of internal validity. What are the costs and benefits related to addressing local concerns and building local capacities? Do the benefits out-weigh the costs? What is the appropriate balance of input from community members, grantmakers, and researchers in deciding appropriate procedures, methods, and goals of community intervention?

Enhancement of the capacity of community partnerships and the support sys-tem may necessitate a change in traditional practices of community partnerships, grantmakers, and researchers. In this developmental perspective, the goal of grantmakers and researchers cannot be to make a single, post hoc decision on the effectiveness of community partnerships. Instead, they must provide ongoing support to shape effective and sustained community problem-solving practices. Maintaining this balance may result in a struggle between researcher and community values. For example, researchers might desire to disseminate proven interventions cautiously in order to ensure their continued effectiveness while community members may seek to adapt interventions to fit local conditions. This situation requires that researchers develop the skills to disseminate effective interventions and provide support for community members to adapt innovations to fit local conditions while preserving effectiveness (Fawcett, 1991b). Social validity assessments of procedures and effects may help select for more functional and durable support practices (Fawcett, 1991a; Wolf, 1978).

The conceptual analysis and case study presented in this chapter highlight the value of an agenda for studying the processes of community health and development. Future conceptual analyses can inform us about the broad contingencies that affect attempts of community groups, and their support systems, to effect mutually desired outcomes. A science agenda can draw on the analytic methods of the experimental analysis of behavior to refine our understanding of environmental conditions that affect the practice and support of community research and action. Such collaborative efforts between behavioral scientists and community practitioners may enhance the cultural practice of problem solving in local communities.

NOTE

Preparation of this chapter was supported by a grant from the Kansas Health Foundation (Grant 9501005) to the Work Group on Health Promotion and Community Development at the University of Kansas. We thank our colleagues at the Work Group, the Kansas Health Foundation, and the collaborating communities for providing the understanding and encouragement for this work. Correspondence should be addressed to Stergios Russos and Stephen B. Fawcett, 4084 Dole Center, University of Kansas, Lawrence, KS 66045.

REFERENCES

Biglan, A. (1995). *Changing cultural practices: A contextual framework for intervention research*. Reno, NV: Context Press.

Chavis, D. M., Florin, P., & Felix, M. R. J. (1993). Nurturing grassroots initiatives for community development: The role of enabling systems. In T. Mizrahi & J. Morrison (Eds.), *Community organization and social administration* (pp. 41–67). New York: Haworth Press.

Fawcett, S. B. (1990). Some emerging standards for community research and action. In P. Tolan, C. Keys, F. Chertok, & L. Jason (Eds.), *Researching community psychology: Issues of theory and methods* (pp. 64–75). Washington, DC: American Psychological Association.

———. (1991a). Social validity: A note on methodology. *Journal of Applied Behavior Analysis, 24*, 235–239.

———. (1991b). Some values guiding community research and action. *Journal of Applied Behavior Analysis, 24*, 621–636.

Fawcett, S. B., Francisco, V. T., Paine-Andrews, A., Fisher, J., Lewis, R. K., Williams, E. L., Richter, K. P., Harris, K. J., & Berkley, J. Y. (1994). *Preventing youth violence: An action planning guide for community-based initiatives.* Lawrence, KS: Work Group on Health Promotion & Community Development, University of Kansas.

Fawcett, S. B., Francisco, V. T., Paine-Andrews, A., Lewis, R. K., Richter, K. P., Harris, K. J., Williams, E. L., Berkley, J. Y., Schultz, J. A., Fisher, J. L., & Lopez, C. M. (1994). *Work Group evaluation handbook: Evaluating and supporting community initiatives for health and development.* Lawrence, KS: Work Group on Health Promotion & Community Development, University of Kansas.

Fawcett, S. B., Harris, K. J., Paine-Andrews, A., Richter, K. P., Lewis, R. K., Francisco, V. T., Arbaje, A., Davis, A., Chang, H., & Johnston, J. (1995). *Reducing risk for chronic disease: An action planning guide for community-based initiatives.* Lawrence, KS: Work Group on Health Promotion & Community Development, University of Kansas.

Fawcett, S. B., Lewis, R. K., Paine-Andrews, A., Francisco, V. T., Richter, K. P., Williams, E. L., & Copple, B. (in press). Evaluating community coalitions for the prevention of substance abuse: The case of Project Freedom. *Health Education Quarterly.*

Fawcett, S. B., Mathews, R. M., & Fletcher, R. K. (1980). Some promising dimensions of behavioral community psychology. *Journal of Applied Behavioral Analysis, 13,* 505–518.

Fawcett, S. B., Paine, A. L., Francisco, V. T., & Vliet, M. (1993). Promoting health through community development. In D. S. Glenwick & L. A. Jason (Eds.), *Promoting health and mental health in children, youth, and families* (pp. 233–255). New York: Springer Publishing.

Fawcett, S. B., Paine-Andrews, A., Francisco, V. T., Richter, K. P., Lewis, R. K., Harris, K. J., & Williams, E. L. (1994). *Preventing adolescent pregnancy: An action planning guide for community-based initiatives.* Lawrence, KS: Work Group on Health Promotion & Community Development, University of Kansas.

Fawcett, S. B., Paine-Andrews, A., Francisco, V. T., Richter, K. P., Lewis, R. K., Williams, E. L., Harris, K. J., & Winter-Green, K. (1994). *Preventing adolescent substance abuse: An action planning guide for community-based initiatives.* Lawrence, KS: Work Group on Health Promotion & Community Development, University of Kansas.

Fawcett, S. B., Paine-Andrews, A., Francisco, V. T., Schultz, J. A., Richter, K. P., Lewis, R. K., Harris, K. J., Williams, E. L., Berkley, J. Y., Lopez, C. M., & Fisher, J. L. (1996). Empowering community health initiatives through evaluation. In D. M. Fetterman, S. J. Kaftarian, & A. Wandersman (Eds.), *Empowerment evaluation: Knowledge and tools for self-assessment and accountability* (pp. 161–187). Thousand Oaks, CA: Sage.

Fawcett, S. B., Paine-Andrews, A., Francisco, V. T., Schultz, J. A., Richter, K. P., Lewis, R. K., Williams, E. L., Harris, K. J., Berkley, J. Y., Fisher, J. L., & Lopez, C. M. (1995). Using empowerment theory in collaborative partnerships for community health and development. *American Journal of Community Psychology, 23,* 677–697.

Fawcett, S. B., Sterling, T. D., Paine-Andrews, A., Harris, K. J., Francisco, V. T., Richter, K. P., Lewis, R. K., & Schmid, T. L. (1996). *Evaluating community efforts to prevent cardiovascular diseases*. Atlanta, GA: Centers for Disease Control and Prevention, National Center for Chronic Disease Prevention and Health Promotion.

Francisco, V. T., Paine, A. L., & Fawcett, S. B. (1993). A methodology for monitoring and evaluating community health coalitions. *Health Education Research: Theory and Practice, 8*, 403–416.

Gerzon, M. (1995). Reinventing philanthropy: Foundations and the renewal of civil society. *National Civic Review, 8*, 188–195.

Glenn, S. S. (1988). Contingencies and metacontingencies: Toward a synthesis of behavior analysis and cultural materialism. *The Behavior Analyst, 11*, 161–179.

Gray, B. (1991). *Collaborating: Finding common ground for multiparty problems*. San Francisco: Jossey-Bass.

Harris, K. J., Paine-Andrews, A., Richter, K. P., Lewis, R. K., Johnston, J. A., James, V., Henke, L., Fawcett, S. B. (1996). *The effects of school lunch modification, nutrition education, and physical activity interventions on the behavior and environment of school children in two communities*. Manuscript submitted for publication.

Harris, K. J., Richter, K. P., Paine-Andrews, A., Lewis, R. K., Johnston, J., James, V., & Henke, L. (1996). *Evaluating school and community partnerships for reducing risks for chronic diseases among children*. Manuscript submitted for publication.

Hawkins, J. D., & Catalano, R. F. (1992). *Communities that care*. San Francisco: Jossey-Bass.

Hovell, M. F., Hillman, E., Blumberg, E. J., Sipan, C. L., Atkins, C. J., Hofstetter, C. R., & Myers, A. (1994). A behavioral-ecological model of adolescent sexual development: A template for AIDS prevention. *Journal of Sex Research, 31*, 267–281.

Johnston, J. A., Marmet, P. F., Coen, S., Fawcett, S. B., & Harris, K. J. (1996). Kansas LEAN: An effective coalition for nutrition education and dietary change. *Journal of Nutrition Education, 28*, 115–118.

Lewis, R. K., Paine-Andrews, A., Fawcett, S. B., Francisco, V. T., Richter, K. P., Copple, B., & Copple, J. E. (in press). Evaluating the effects of a community coalition's efforts to reduce illegal sales of alcohol and tobacco products to minors. *Journal of Community Health*.

Paine-Andrews, A., Fawcett, S. B., Richter, K. P., Berkley, J. Y., Williams, E. L., & Lopez, C. M. (in press). Community coalitions to prevent adolescent substance abuse: The case of the ''Project Freedom'' replication initiative. *Prevention in Human Services*.

Paine-Andrews, A., Francisco, V. T., & Fawcett, S. B. (1994). Assessing community health concerns and implementing a mircrogrant program for self-help initiatives. *American Journal of Public Health, 84*, 316–318.

Paine-Andrews, A., Vincent, M. L., Fawcett, S. B., Campuzano, M. K., Harris, K. J., Lewis, R. K., Williams, E. L., & Fisher, J. L. (1995). Replicating a community initiative for preventing adolescent pregnancy: From South Carolina to Kansas. *Family and Community Health, 19*, 14–30.

Robinson, G. H., & Hill, J. (1995). *Problems in the evaluation of community-wide initiatives*. New York: Russell Sage Foundation.

Samuels, S. E. (1990). Project LEAN: A national campaign to reduce dietary fat consumption. *American Journal of Health Promotion, 4*, 435–440.

Schauffler, H. H. (1993). Disease prevention policy under Medicare: A historical and political analysis. *American Journal of Preventive Medicine, 9*, 71–77.

Schriner, K. F., & Fawcett, S. B. (1988). Development and validation of a community concerns report method. *Journal of Community Psychology, 16*, 306–316.

Skinner, B. F. (1953). *Science and human behavior.* New York: Macmillan.

Vincent, M. L., Clearie, A. F., & Schlichter, M. D. (1987). Reducing adolescent pregnancy through school and community-based education. *Journal of the American Medical Association, 257*, 3382–3386.

Wilson-Brewer, R., Cohen, S., O'Donnell, L., & Goodman, I. F. (1991). *Violence prevention for young adolescents: A survey of the state of the art.* Washington, DC: Carnegie Council on Adolescent Development.

Wolf, M. M. (1978). Social validity: The case for subjective measurement or how applied behavior analysis is finding its heart. *Journal of Applied Behavior Analysis, 11*, 203–214.

Wolff, T. (1992). *Coalition building: One path to empowered communities.* Amherst, MA: Community Partners.

5

Behavior Analysis and Demographics: Government Control of Reproductive Behavior and Fertility in the Province of Quebec, Canada

---

CATHERINE KRULL AND W. DAVID PIERCE

The analysis of contingencies regulating cultural practices is a fundamental problem for behavior analysis (Skinnner, 1953). There is evidence that the infrastructural requirements of a society, in terms of production and reproduction, set contingencies of survival for a culture (Harris, 1979). In terms of reproduction, problems of cultural survival arise when human populations show dramatic increases or decreases in fertility. Overpopulation uses up, or contaminates, limited resources; underpopulation threatens cultural transmission because there are insufficient new members to learn and propagate the customs and traditions. Moreover, underpopulation of a specific cultural group increases the likelihood of assimilation within the majority group. Faced with such problems, governments have often attempted to control the reproductive behavior of group members, implementing policies and programs to reduce or augment the number of births (e.g., Krull, 1996a, 1996b; Pierce, 1991). One way to study the cultural control of reproductive behavior is to analyze social interventions that influence the fertility rate of a population. Demographers are noted for studying the relationship between social factors and fertility rates of diverse populations, but have been less concerned with analyzing the contingencies of reproduction. The study of fertility rates and the cultural contingencies for reproduction integrates demographic issues with those of behavior analysis.

The present chapter addresses the recent attempt by the government of Quebec, Canada, to increase the extremely low fertility levels in the province. Quebec's low fertility rates have been interpreted by government officials and academics as a threat to the survival of French Canadian culture and language in the province. Research on the reproductive contingencies arranged by the Quebec government's pronatal policies and programs, and the resulting changes in fertility, is therefore an important step toward an understanding of government's role in the design and evolution of a culture.

In order to appreciate the importance of fertility to the survival of French Canadian culture in Quebec, we begin this chapter with a brief historical overview. Subsequently, the current situation and perspectives on Quebec's pronatal policies are outlined. In addition, the monetary incentives arranged by the Quebec government to increase fertility are analyzed as contingencies for reproduction. Next, results are presented on the effectiveness of these contingencies in the regulation of reproductive behavior and fertility. The findings suggest that the baby bonus policies are having a positive effect for third and subsequent births and, as such, are in accord with the specified contingencies. However, the effect has not been large enough to substantially affect the total fertility rate, suggesting that changes to the graded method of payment may be in order. The chapter is concluded with a consideration of demographic issues related to the social control of fertility in Quebec. As part of this conclusion, we address the roles of local and remote contingencies and relative rates of reinforcement in the management of human reproduction. Overall, we demonstrate the utility of combining behavioral and demographic analyses to enhance our understanding of cultural practices such as reproduction.

A BRIEF HISTORY OF FERTILITY AND FRENCH CANADIAN CULTURE

Historically, fertility has been central to the survival of French Canadian culture in Quebec. Recently, the province has gone from having one of the highest fertility rates in the world to having one of the lowest. These changes in fertility have coincided with the socioeconomic transformation of Quebec society that took place gradually over time, and more intensively after the rapid modernization during the early 1960s (Krull, 1996a).

Before the 1960s, Quebec maintained high fertility for over two centuries due to the substantial influence of the Catholic Church and the pronatal policies of the provincial government. Indeed, very few societies "have ever exhibited such prolific childbearing for so long a period of time" (Beaujot & McQuillan, 1982, p. 4). Women were educated toward domestic activities, encouraged to marry young and to have large families. Henripin (1994) estimates that in the period from 1711 to 1865, women who married at fifteen years of age and who lived until the end of their reproductive years had between twelve and thirteen children. However, this is probably an overestimation, as not everyone married at age fifteen. Moreover, the maternal mortality rates were higher in New France (what is now the province of Quebec) than in most European countries, which means that many women died before the end of their reproductive years. Taking these factors into account, the average number of children per married woman was approximately 7.1 (Henripin & Péron, 1972). However, this rate was still much higher than for married women in any of the European countries.

Several factors account for the high birth rates in Quebec until 1865. Economically, Quebec was a rural society and survival on the agricultural *seigneuries* depended on the work of large family units. Moreover, the number of land concessions made to parents often depended on the number of male children that they had. Consequently, high fertility was intricately tied to economic survival. Pronatal attitudes were further reinforced by the French government, which offered an annual monetary reward to couples who had at least ten legitimate children. Marriages at an early age were also encouraged by government policies. Financial rewards were given to females who married under the age of sixteen and to males who married under the age of twenty. It was not uncommon for girls to marry as early as age twelve or thirteen. Compared to most European societies during this period, the average age at marriage for females in New France was exceptionally young (Beaujot & McQuillan, 1982, p. 7). Marriage was viewed as a natural state, one that everyone would eventually enter and remain in until their death. Divorce was forbidden by the Roman Catholic Church and in 1659, celibacy was forbidden by law (Peters, 1990).

Quebec society continued to be characterized as primarily rural and traditional until the late 1950s. Urbanization in Quebec did increase during this period, but the province did not experience the modernization effects of the industrial revolution as did the rest of Canada. Pestieau suggests that in contrast to the rest of the industrializing world, "Quebec was almost completely cut off from important nineteenth-century currents, particularly those of industrialization and female emancipation" (in Wilson, 1986, p. 147). An important mechanism in Quebec's delayed modernization was the omnipresent authority of the Roman Catholic Church, instrumental in keeping the province tied to a rigidly traditional ecclesiastical system. French Canadians attached great importance to the Catholic Church and to the family but saw little significance in education and individual prosperity (Lachapelle & Henripin, 1982).

Both the political elite and the clergy in Quebec were aware of the political importance of high fertility to traditional French Canadian society. They promoted an ideology of "strength in numbers," often referred to as *la revanche des berceaux* (the revenge of the cradles) as a means of overcoming the Quebecois's subordination to the English (Gratton, 1992). This strategy was effective for approximately two centuries. Quebec's pattern of fertility remained distinct from that of English Canada and other industrialized countries until 1960 (Beaujot & McQuillan, 1982). Between 1760 and 1960, the world population tripled and the European population quadrupled; in the same period, the French Canadian population increased 80 times despite losing approximately 800,000 people to emigration (Beaujot & McQuillan, 1982, pp. 183–184).

It is important to note that although fertility was significantly higher in Quebec than in the rest of Canada until 1960, it nonetheless had been declining since the 1850s. However, it did so at a much slower rate than it did for the rest of Canada. From 1851 to 1921, the number of births per woman in Quebec decreased by 23% compared to a 51% decrease in the rest of Canada. In 1921, for example, women in Quebec had an average of 5.3 children and more than half of the women living in rural areas of Quebec continued to have at least 7 or more children (Beaujot & McQuillan, 1982). These fertility rates are very high in comparison to Ontario (Quebec's neighboring province) and Canada where the total fertility rates (TFRs) were 3.2 and 3.5, respectively. Quebec's birth rates remained higher than those of Canada or Ontario until the early 1960s.

MODERNIZATION AND THE DECLINE OF FERTILITY IN QUEBEC

The Quiet Revolution[1] began with the election of a new Liberal provincial government in Quebec on June 22, 1960. This revolution has been described as both a political and an intellectual attempt on the part of Quebec society to catch up to the rest of Canada in social and economic development (Krull & Trovato, 1994). The intellectual elite of Quebec advocated a new vision for the society, no longer based on the authority of the church but on the philosophy of liberalism and secularization. This vision was reflected in government-instituted policies that promoted industrial development and urban growth (Behiels, 1986). According to Cormier and Klerman (1985):

during this time period, social troubles and strong popular pressures forced the newly elected liberal government to adopt new policies based on such social-democratic ideas as income security, public ownership of natural resources, democratization of education, universal health care, etc. Following an era of ultraconservative social climate, two important phenomena occurred during this time period, namely, the rapid adoption of new liberal policies and the drastic change in social behavior. (p. 112)

Throughout the next three decades, the province transformed from a traditional, rural society to a modern industrial state. As part of this transformation, the control of education was removed from the church as schools were placed under the secular regulation of government. Where once individuals were discouraged from pursuing education or personal gain, they were now encouraged to advance their education and actively engage in productive labor for a capitalist economic system. The overall result of this process of modernization has been a gradual rise in individualism and a corresponding decline in traditional institutions such as marriage and religion. Since the early 1960s, there have been substantial increases in the rates of cohabitation, divorce, and married female labor force participation, accompanied by a staggering decline in fertility:

although traditional Quebec could and knew how to resist change in order to assure its *survival* after the conquest . . . , today's Quebec has, so to speak, taken its revenge in the form of an impulse toward economic and political independence in which the family, once so dear to traditional Quebec, has borne all the cost. (Houle, 1987, p. 5)

Coinciding with the onset of the Quiet Revolution, the 1960s marked the peak in family planning and the beginning of the fertility collapse in Quebec. From 1961 onward, the use of contraceptive methods became the norm for the majority of sexually active couples in Quebec. Moreover, voluntary sterilization and abortion increased considerably (Fréchet, 1992). By 1982, more than 42% of people in the reproductive ages had undergone some form of sterilization, while the total abortion rate increased from 178.5 per 1,000 women in 1978 to 411.3 in 1990.

The family planning movement had a dramatic effect on Quebec's fertility rates. In the course of a few decades, Quebec's total fertility rate (TFR) has gone from being the highest in the industrialized world to the lowest. The TFR indicates the expected number of children that women will have throughout their reproductive years (15 to 49 years). A total fertility rate of 2.1 is required in order for a society to ensure replacement of the generations (Trovato, 1994). In 1961, Quebec had a total fertility rate of 3.7 (well above replacement level) but by 1970, the TFR in this province had decreased to below replacement level (1.97). Interestingly, Quebec, which historically had the highest TFRs in Canada, was the first province in the country to report a TFR below replacement level. By 1986, the TFR in Quebec reached an unprecedented low of 1.4. Quebec's fertility rate has therefore been insufficient to replace its population since 1970, and the survival of French Canadian culture has consequently become a central political issue.

Fertility is the most critical component of population change and the sharp decline in Quebec's fertility rates have concerned many government officials. If Quebec's influence in Canada is directly related to the size of its population, then a continuing decline in fertility could threaten the province's cultural, social, and political well-being. In fact, as early as 1967, federal and provincial government officials were pressured by the leaders of the Council of French Life to offer financial inducements for higher fertility.

The most crucial problem that confronts Quebec is not political, economic or educational, but one concerning family size. If births continue to decline in Quebec, neither independence, nor wealth, nor immigration can assure the survival of the French Canadian people. The Quebec government must be asked without delay for a birth-rate policy, and more broadly a family policy. (Council on French Life in America, 1971:6)

The Council closed its report with the telling comment: ''The conclusion is cruelly obvious: French Canada is on its way to losing the demographic battle which it had so successfully fought for three centuries, and even in Quebec'' (Council on French Life in America, 1971, p. 11). Despite these concerns, it was not until 1988 that the Quebec government implemented policies to increase births.

PERSPECTIVES ON QUEBEC'S PRONATAL POLICIES

The dramatic decline in Quebec's fertility rates has generated two diverse reactions from academics and government officials. The interventionists, primarily composed of demographers, journalists, and government officials, argue that low birth rates in Quebec have reached crisis levels that can only be alleviated through government pronatal policies. According to the interventionists, "too few babies were being born to *francophones 'de vieille souche'* ['of the old stock'] for political and economic stability, and that new immigration would lead to failures of assimilation" (Disparaitre, 1988, in Maroney, 1992, p. 7). Two prominent demographers, Henripin and Lapierre-Adamcyk, were instrumental in bringing about Quebec's current birth incentive policies. Lapierre-Adamcyk, for example, identified the lack of a third child as the cause of Quebec's low fertility levels and determined that the major impediment to childbearing was financial. Henripin urged government officials to offer benefits, in the form of both fiscal rewards and services, based on the number of children in a family. These assessments have shaped Quebec's birth incentive policies since 1988.

The critical school, which has recently emerged in the social science literature, makes up the second perspective on Quebec's low fertility rates. Adherents of this position argue that Quebec's low fertility levels do not constitute a crisis but rather reflect the historical trends of all industrializing societies. Advocates of the critical perspective charge that any crisis that has emerged over Quebec's fertility levels has been manufactured by the pronatal interventionists who favor government regulation of women and reproduction. For example, Maroney (1992) argues that against "the background of an unresolved national question, and with the intervention of journalists, demographers, and politicians, data and predictions that were at least five years old were invoked to create a renewed sense of demographic crisis" (p. 7). She charges that in pairing nationalism with pronatalism, demographers (notably Jacques Henripin) have used science to manufacture the potential threat of cultural genocide if women in Quebec continue to have few children. "Henripin's normative bias was made especially clear when he more recently asserted that human birth rates below reproduction should be read through ethological theory as an index of social sickness" (Maroney, 1992, p. 20). Maroney also charges that the policy recommendations put forward by Quebec demographer Lapierre-Adamcyk reinforced women's subordinate status within the family. She concludes her analysis by stating that the monetary incentive policies initiated by the interventionists and adopted by the Quebec government marginalized women, eliding them as objects of demographic policy. According to her views, women have not benefited from the incentive policies primarily because "child care remains inadequate, expensive and inconvenient, women continue to bear the brunt of the double day, and one estimate suggests that 100,000 Montreal children live in poverty" (Maroney,

1992, p. 28). She claims that in creating a crisis over Quebec's declining fertility rates, demographers have been the only ones to benefit.

All of this meant not only a chance to lobby for more funding for more studies, and greater access to government files, but also an opportunity to publicize the importance of their field. No longer plagued by the image problems of the early 1970s—''The demographer? A strange little man.''—the demographer became a celebrity. (Maroney, 1992, p. 25)

The remainder of this chapter outlines a behavioral analysis perspective on Quebec's current baby bonus policies, and is an alternative view to those cited above. While emphasizing the design and engineering of social systems, this perspective differs from the interventionists' in that it is experimental and emphasizes the importance of behavioral contingencies. Unlike the critical perspective, a behavioral approach asserts that government policies and incentive programs set up contingencies of reinforcement for individual behavior and that the modification of these contingencies either increases or decreases the targeted behavior.

GOVERNMENT CONTROL OF REPRODUCTION AND FERTILITY

In 1988 the government of Quebec implemented a monetary incentive program to increase levels of fertility in the province. In terms of behavior analysis, the policies that stipulate the allocation of the monetary payments to Quebec families set out the behavioral contingencies arranged by the government to solve the problem of low birth rate.

Monetary Contingencies for Reproduction

The policies that govern the Birth Allowance program are outlined in the Quebec Pension Board's document *Les Allocations D'Aide Aux Familles* (1994). According to this document, a family is defined as at least one adult with a child who is receiving benefits in a given month. Table 5.1 shows that the monetary payments for births began in 1988 and with minimal payments of $500 for first and second births, and more substantial payments of $3,000 for third births and each subsequent birth. Notice that the amount paid for second births increased to $1,000 in 1989 and the payments for third or more births continued to increase until 1992, leveling off at $8,000 for each higher-order birth. From 1992 through 1995 the Quebec government paid for births on a progressive schedule—$500 for first births, $1,000 for second births, and $8,000 for each birth of three or more children.

Birth allocations are tax-free payments at the provincial and federal levels of taxation. A payment of $500 for the birth of a first child is currently given at

Table 5.1
Birth Allowance by Birth Order, Quebec: 1988–1995

Year	First Child	Second Child[a]	Third and Subsequent Children[b]
1988	$500	$500	$3,000
1989	$500	$1,000	$4,500
1990	$500	$1,000	$6,000
1991	$500	$1,000	$7,500
1992	$500	$1,000	$8,000
1993	$500	$1,000	$8,000
1994	$500	$1,000	$8,000
1995	$500	$1,000	$8,000

[a]$500 is paid at the time of birth and $500 also is paid on the child's first birthday. In 1988, $500 was paid only at the time of birth.

[b]In 1988, the birth allowance was paid in quarterly payments of $375 until the child reached the age of two. In May of 1989, the quarterly payments were extended until the child was three and in May of 1991, until the child was five years of age. In May 1992, the quarterly payments were increased to $400 and were paid until the child was five years of age.

Source: Quebec Pension Board (1994), *Les allocations d'aide aux familles: Statistiques 1994.* Province of Quebec, Canada, p. 16.

the time of birth (cf. Table 5.1). The $1,000 allowance for the birth of a second child is allocated in two equal payments of $500; one payment at the time of birth and the second on the child's first birthday. The $8,000 allowance for the birth of a third and subsequent children is paid in twenty quarterly installments of $400, ending on the child's fifth birthday. Thus, families who have a third birth gain an extra $1,600 a year of tax-free income for five years. A family who had a third and fourth child in close proximity could receive an extra $3,200 a year, during the period when the twenty installments overlap. Clearly, the birth allocation policies and program set up contingencies that favor larger family sizes (three or more children) and motivate families to have their higher-order births closer together. Table 5.2 indicates that this program began in May of 1988 with a cost of about $48 million but by 1994, the government of Quebec spent approximately $186 million on this program.

Supplementary Contingencies for Having Children

The Birth Allowance program is part of a more general system of aid to families in Quebec. Table 5.2 shows the amount spent on family assistance

Table 5.2
Amounts Paid by Type of Allowance, Quebec: 1971–1994 (in thousands of dollars)

Year	Family Allowance $	Young Child Allowance $	Birth Allowance $	Total $
1974	92,292.4	-	-	92,292.4
1975	100,990.9	-	-	100,990.9
1976	110,427.4	-	-	110,427.4
1977	135,568.3	-	-	135,568.3
1978	151,423.8	-	-	151,423.8
1979	159,400.2	-	-	159,400.2
1980	168,749.4	-	-	168,749.4
1981	180,510.1	-	-	180,510.1
1982	176,069.6	-	-	176,069.6
1983	181,717.9	-	-	181,717.9
1984	187,328.6	-	-	187,328.6
1985	185,107.1	-	-	185,107.1
1986	191,203.7	-	-	191,203.7
1987	197,653.7	-	-	197,653.7
1988	205,179.6	-	[a]47,688.7	252,868.3
1989	213,726.6	106,067.5	100,454.8	420,248.9
1990	225,888.5	111,301.7	136,082.8	473,273.0
1991	239,768.0	118,165.5	162,946.8	520,880.3
1992	254,482.8	126,167.2	177,168.8	557,818.8
1993	258,537.5	132,437.7	182,326.1	573,301.3
1994	258,792.7	135,321.5	186,361.5	580,475.7

[a]These amounts were paid for children who were born between May and December 1988, and for third and subsequent birth-order children who were less than two years of age on May 1, 1988.
Source: Quebec Pension Board (1994), *Les allocations d'aide aux familles,* p. 22.

Table 5.3
Payable Allowances by Number of Children, Quebec: 1994

		Number of Children		
Allowance	1	2	3	4+
Family	$10.91	$14.54	$18.18	$21.78
Child	$9.77	$19.53	$48.83	$48.83
Birth	$500.00	$1,000.00[a]	$8,000.00 [b]	$8,000.00 [b]

[a]Payable in two $500.00 payments.
[b]Payable in twenty $400.00 payments.
Source: Quebec Pension Board, *Les allocations d'aide aux familles,* p. 12.

programs (excluding handicap allowance) by the Quebec government for the years 1974 to 1994. It is important to note that payments from each of these three sources of assistance (Family Allowance, Young Child Allowance, and Birth Allowance) are tax-free income that may be allocated concurrently, as long as the child is eligible for the respective programs.

The Family Allowance program is a sum paid monthly to each child who is less than eighteen years of age. This program has been in effect since 1974 and does not represent a new intervention by the Quebec government to increase family size. Currently, the monthly payment ranges from $11 for a single child to around $22 for four and more children (see Table 5.3). Inspection of Table 5.2 indicates that the Quebec government spent about $260 million on the Family Allowance program in 1994.

Another source of assistance to Quebec families is the Young Child Allowance. This program began in 1989 and is supplementary to the money received for Birth Allowances or Family Allowances. As indicated in Table 5.3, the monthly payment for this program increases with the number of children under the age of six. Families with one child under six years of age receive approximately $10 a month, but families with four or more children under six receive approximately $50 per month. Table 5.2 indicates that the Young Child Allowance program began in 1989 with yearly payoffs of close to $106 million and by 1994 this program cost the Quebec government approximately $135 million.

Overall, the government of Quebec spent more than half a billion dollars on the three family assistance programs in 1994. Table 5.3 shows the actual monetary allocations to a family in Quebec by the number of children they had in 1994 (assuming they qualified for the three programs of assistance). The short-run financial benefits for third and fourth births is apparent and suggests that an assessment of the effectiveness of the government's contingencies should focus on the reproductive behavior and fertility of women at higher levels of parity.

EFFECTIVENESS OF REPRODUCTION CONTINGENCIES

In this section, we provide a preliminary descriptive analysis of the effectiveness of the Quebec government's monetary-incentive policies and programs that are directed at increasing the number of births in the province. We begin with a brief overview of the data and design. Next, we present the results of our analysis, emphasizing the effects of the government interventions on the birth rates and reproductive behavior of women of third and fourth parities. This section is concluded with a consideration of the limitations of our analysis and possible sources of invalidity for inferences about the effectiveness of the Quebec government's contingencies.

Data and Design

The data were compiled from official statistics on the populations of the province of Quebec and Canada excluding Quebec (the rest of Canada). The total fertility rates (1971–1994) and fertility rates by birth order (1982–1993) were calculated from Statistics Canada publications by Dumas and Belanger (1995) on the demographic situation in Canada, 1995, and Statistics Canada's Vital Statistics on *Births* (Annual). The proportion of births by parity (birth order) for Quebec (1982–1994) was taken from the Quebec Pension Board (1994) publication *Les Allocations D'Aide Aux Familles* and the rest of Canada proportions (1982–1993) were calculated from Statistics Canada's Vital Statistics on *Births* (Annual). Data on the use of the birth control pill (1987 and 1992–93) were taken from *Rapport de l'Enquete Social et d'Sante* (1992–93, Vol. 1). At the present time, we have been unable to find data on contraceptive use for Quebec and the rest of Canada broken down by the number of existing children that a woman has for comparable years before and after the government's birth interventions.

The study is conceptualized as a quasi-experimental interrupted time series design, appropriate for a behavioral analysis of cultural contingencies (Pierce, 1991). In the present study, the fertility rates and the percentages of births by birth order before the government interventions serve as baselines for comparison of Quebec's fertility levels relative to the rest of Canada. In 1988, the Quebec government implemented the monetary incentives for births and so this year is taken as the point of intervention (interruption) of the time series. If the fertility levels of Quebec show an increase compared with the rest of Canada, subsequent to the intervention (1988), we infer that the incentive program was effective. It is not possible, at this point, to provide a statistical analysis of the time series data because of few data points prior to, and after, the intervention (see Glass, Wilson, & Gottman, 1975). We are currently establishing a more substantial data set on fertility and contraceptive use for both Quebec and the rest of Canada which will permit stronger inferences to be drawn about the effectiveness of the Quebec government's birth programs.

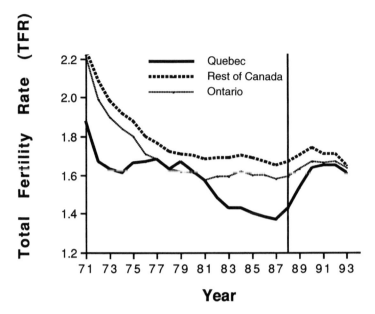

Figure 5.1. Total fertility rates (TFRs) from 1971 to 1993 for Quebec, rest of Canada, and Ontario. TFR is interpreted as the average number of children women will have over their reproductive years (15–49 years). *Sources:* J. Dumas and A. Belanger (1995), *Report on the demographic situation in Canada, 1995* (Table 10). Statistics Canada Catalogue #91-209E Annual; Statistics Canada, Health Statistics Division, Health Status and Vital Statistics Section, *Births,* Catalogue #84-210, Annual; and calculations by authors.

Results of the Quebec Government's Interventions

Total Fertility Rates. Figure 5.1 shows the total fertility rates (TFRs) for Quebec, the rest of Canada, and the neighboring province of Ontario for the period 1971 to 1993. The vertical black line indicates the year when the Quebec government's birth program was implemented. Notice that the TFR for Quebec is declining relative to the rest of Canada and Ontario prior to the intervention, reaching a low in 1987. Following the onset of the birth incentive program, the TFR for Quebec increased compared with the rest of Canada and Ontario, and then leveled off as Quebec's TFR approximated the Canadian trend. This suggests that the Quebec incentive program had a temporary impact on total fertility that dampened out over time. It is for this reason that many demographers have concluded that the incentive programs have been unsuccessful. However, a behavioral analysis of the contingencies set up by the incentive program suggest that this conclusion may be premature.

Fertility Rates by Parity. Figure 5.2 shows the fertility rates for first parity women in Quebec and the rest of Canada. Fertility rates by first parity can be interpreted as the probability of a first birth for women aged 15 to 49 years.

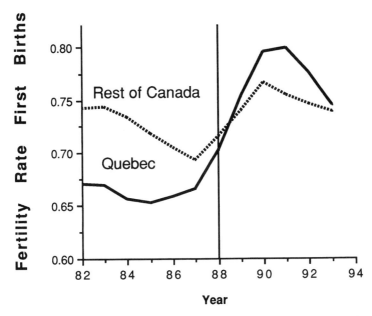

Figure 5.2. Fertility rate for first births in the province of Quebec and the rest of Canada. This rate is interpreted as the probability of having a first birth for women in their reproductive years (15–49 years). *Source:* J. Dumas and A. Belanger (1995), *Report on the demographic situation in Canada, 1995* (Table 10). Statistics Canada Catalogue #91-209E Annual.

Prior to the government's intervention, the probability of first births in Quebec remained below the rest of Canada. The probability of first births increased from 1987 to 1990, but the rest of Canada also showed a less substantial increase in fertility for first parity women. For the years 1991 to 1994, fertility rates for first births declined in Quebec and less so in the rest of Canada. The covariation of Quebec's first parity rate with the rate for the rest of Canada indicates that the changes in first births were probably not due to the Quebec government's intervention. This is in accord with the contingencies of the program, as it is unlikely that a payment of $500 would persuade a woman to have a child that she had not planned on having.

Results for second parity fertility rates are shown in Figure 5.3. Before the 1988 birth incentive program, the probability of having a second child in Quebec declined from about 0.53 in 1982 to around 0.48 in 1987. During this same period, the probability of having a second child in Canada remained fairly stable between 0.57 and 0.59 values. Following the onset of the Quebec government's birth program, second parity births increased from 1988 to 1994 to approximate the rate for the rest of Canada. Second parity births remained fairly stable for the rest of Canada during this same period. The evidence indicates that the government's birth incentives, combined with the supplementary payoffs for

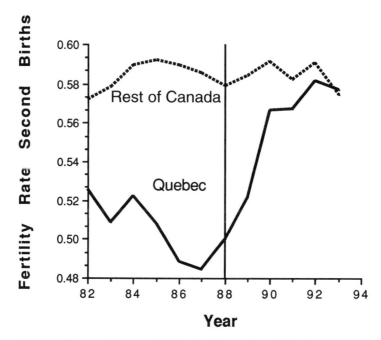

Figure 5.3. Fertility rate for second births in the province of Quebec and the rest of Canada. This rate is interpreted as the probability of having a second birth for women in their reproductive years (15–49 years). *Source:* J. Dumas and A. Belanger (1995), *Report on the demographic situation in Canada, 1995* (Table 10). Statistics Canada Catalogue #91-209E Annual.

Family and Young Children, were effective, increasing the probability of second births for Quebec women.

Analysis of the contingencies indicated that the payoffs for reproduction and births were targeted at third and higher births. Figures 5.4 and 5.5 show the fertility rates for women of third and fourth parities, in the province of Quebec. In the baseline periods (1982–1987), the probability of third and fourth and subsequent births declined in Quebec whereas in the rest of Canada, baseline birth rates remained stable and higher than in Quebec. Coinciding with the Quebec government's birth program, the probability of women having a third birth increased from 1988 to 1992 (Figure 5.4). A similar, but less substantial, effect is observed for fourth and subsequent births (Figure 5.5). Overall, the increases in fertility rates of third and fourth and subsequent parities is in accord with the monetary contingencies arranged by the Quebec government.

Percentage of Total Births by Parity. In order to further clarify the impact of the Quebec government's interventions, we conducted an analysis on the percentages of total births by parity in Quebec and the rest of Canada. Compared with the baseline periods (1982 to 1987), Figures 5.6 and 5.7 show that the percentages of third and fourth and subsequent births continued to increase in

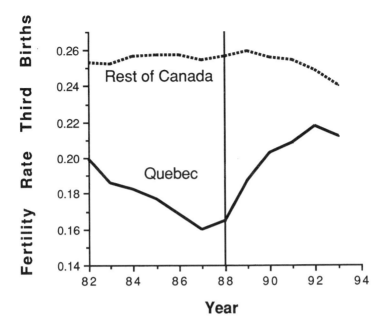

Figure 5.4. Fertility rate for third births in the province of Quebec and the rest of Canada. This rate is interpreted as the probability of having a third birth for women in their reproductive years (15–49 years). *Source:* J. Dumas and A. Belanger (1995), *Report on the demographic situation in Canada, 1995* (Table 10). Statistics Canada Catalogue #91-209E Annual.

Quebec (1988–1994) compared with the rest of Canada (1988 to 1993). The increase in the percentage of third and fourth and subsequent births is in accord with the Quebec government's birth incentives that targeted higher order births. Similar analyses (not shown) indicated a decline in the percentage of first births and no change in the percentage of second births, compared with the rest of Canada.

Percentage of Births Aborted. From a behavioral perspective, increases in fertility of the population due to the Quebec government's incentives involve changes in reproductive behavior at the individual level. Since the 1960s, the province of Quebec has shown a dramatic increase in the number of abortions. It is assumed that if fewer women chose to abort their pregnancies, fertility levels would rise. An examination of the percentages of third and fourth or more pregnancies aborted indicates a decline in abortions that coincides with the birth incentives. Figure 5.8 shows that the percentage of third pregnancies aborted in Quebec underwent a substantial decline from 1988 to 1989 and then leveled off at approximately 13%. In the rest of Canada, we can see that during this time period, the percentage of third pregnancies aborted actually rose and decreased slightly in 1992. Likewise, the percentage of four or more pregnancies aborted

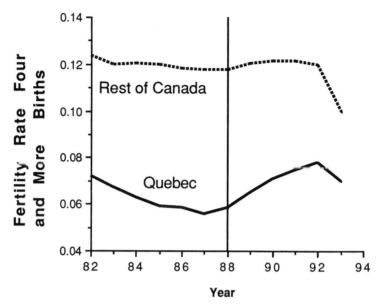

Figure 5.5. Fertility rate for fourth or subsequent births in the province of Quebec and the rest of Canada. This rate is interpreted as the probability of having a fourth or subsequent birth for women in their reproductive years (15–49 years). *Source:* J. Dumas and A. Belanger (1995), *Report on the demographic situation in Canada 1995* (Table 10). Statistics Canada Catalogue #91-209E Annual.

in Quebec declined from 21% in 1987 to 16% in 1988 and to 15% in 1992 (see Figure 5.9). Whereas the percentages of four or more pregnancies aborted in Quebec were considerably higher in the baseline period compared to the rest of Canada, they were lower following the incentives. These results suggest that the Quebec government's interventions may have affected women's decisions to terminate unwanted or unexpected pregnancies at higher-order births.

Use of the Birth Control Pill. Another indicator of changes in reproductive behavior involves decisions to use contraceptive techniques. Table 5.4 shows the use of the birth control pill by age for women in Quebec for the years 1987 (before intervention) and 1992–93 (after intervention). With the exception of the youngest age group, 15–19, there was a decrease in the percentage of women between the ages of 20 and 44 using the birth control pill. Overall, there was approximately a 6% decrease between 1987 and 1992–93 with the largest decrease occurring for women between the ages of 20 and 24 (approximately a 9% decrease) and for women between the ages of 25 and 34 (approximately a 7% decrease).

It is important to note that decreases in the use of the birth control pill do not necessarily imply the abandonment of all contraceptive use. Women in Quebec could have shifted to other means of birth control. However, studies have

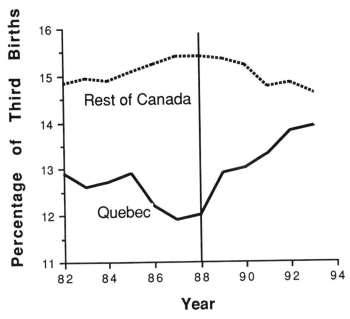

Figure 5.6. Percentage of third births to all births in Quebec and the rest of Canada. *Sources:* Statistics Canada, Health Statistics Division, Health Status and Vital Statistics Section, *Births,* Catalogue #84-210, Annual; calculations by authors; and Quebec Pension Board (1994), *Les allocations d'aide aux familles,* Table 38.

shown that the birth control pill is the preferred form of contraceptive technique. The observed decrease in its use, which coincides with the birth incentive policies, suggests a change in reproductive behavior. It would have been desirable to be able to compare the changes in birth control use in Quebec with that in the rest of Canada, but the data are not available at this time. Presently, we are obtaining data on contraceptive sales for both Quebec and the rest of Canada, which should provide a more robust measure of changes in reproductive behavior.

DISCUSSION OF DEMOGRAPHIC AND BEHAVIORAL ISSUES

The evidence presented here indicates that the Quebec government's birth incentive program was effective in altering women's reproductive behaviors. Although the contingencies did not specify the requisite behavior, fewer women chose to have abortions or to use the birth control pill. These behaviors, and possibly others not measured in this study, increased fertility rates for second and higher births. The effectiveness of the birth incentives is particularly noticeable for third and fourth births where fertility rates and percentages of births

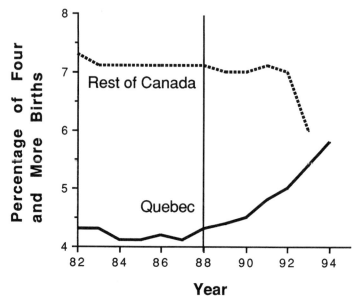

Figure 5.7. Percentage of fourth or subsequent births to all births in Quebec and the rest of Canada. *Sources:* Statistics Canada, Health Statistics Division, Health Status and Vital Statistics Section, *Births,* Catalogue #84-210, Annual; calculations by authors; and Quebec Pension Board (1994), *Les allocations d'aide aux familles,* Table 38.

increased with the implementation of the birth incentive program. Such increases are in accord with the contingencies set up by the birth incentive program (the progressively increasing payments for higher-order births).

Demographic Issues about Birth Incentives

From a behavioral point of view, the birth incentive program was effective in changing the reproductive behavior of women in Quebec. That is, the Quebec government's birth program was successful as a behavioral intervention. However, the contingencies have been less effective when viewed from a demographic perspective. Demographers emphasize the ultimate outcome of the government's intervention in terms of the overall fertility level. Recall that a total fertility rate (TFR) of 2.1 is necessary for replacement of a population. To the extent that population replacement is tied to the survival of French Canadian culture, the incentives program fell short of its target.

Quebec women currently are expected to have 1.6 children over their reproductive years—a level well below replacement. A major impact on TFR would occur if more women in Quebec chose to have a first birth (as opposed to not having children), and had their first child at an earlier age. Given this reality,

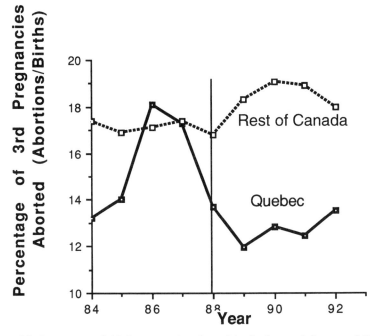

Figure 5.8. Percentage of third pregnancies aborted in Quebec and the rest of Canada. The percentage is based on the number of abortions for women with two previous births divided by the number of third births. *Sources:* Statistics Canada, Catalogue #82-211 Annual, *Therapeutic abortions* (Province of Residence); Statistics Canada, Health Statistics Division, Health Status and Vital Statistics Section, *Births,* Catalogue #84-210, Annual; calculations by authors; and Quebec Pension Board (1994), *Les allocations d'aide aux familles*, Table 38.

incentives for early marriage and first births would have to be superimposed on the current birth program in order to push the TFR to replacement levels. Incentives for first births would result in women having a first birth shortly after they entered into marriage. The additional economic costs of early marriage and first birth programs would have to be weighed against the possible benefits in terms of survival of French Canadian language and culture. Also, birth incentive programs raise ethical issues in terms of the government's right to control the reproductive behavior of women. These important issues concerning individual freedom could prevent the implementation of birth programs, even though the programs were effective as behavioral and demographic interventions.

A Behavior Analysis of Reproduction and Fertility

Many governments throughout the world are faced with increasing populations and declining resources. Social scientists, economists, and demographers

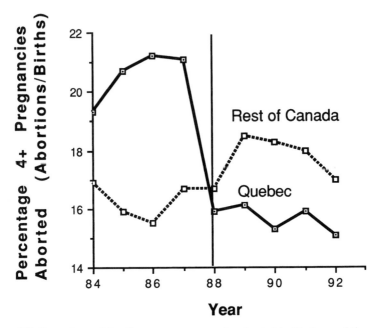

Figure 5.9. Percentage of fourth or more pregnancies aborted in Quebec and the rest of Canada. This percentage is based on the number of abortions for women with three or more previous births divided by the number of fourth or more births. *Sources:* Statistics Canada, Catalogue #82-211 Annual, *Therapeutic abortions* (Province of Residence); Statistics Canada, Health Statistics Division, Health Status and Vital Statistics Section, *Births,* Catalogue #84-210, Annual; calculations by authors; and Quebec Pension Board (1994), *Les allocations d'aide aux familles,* Table 38.

provide advice to government agencies to curb the growth of human populations. A variety of birth control programs have been devised, but current evidence indicates that these measures are usually ineffective (Hernandez, 1981). A behavioral approach to enhance contraceptive use has been proposed (Wiest & Squier, 1974), but the recommendations of this analysis have never been carried out by government agencies. Rather, government agencies have typically relied on the recommendations of demographers, who tend to focus on the consequences of policy rather than on the contingencies of the policies. This can often lead to the abandonment of policies prematurely. Taking a behavioral approach and assessing whether the contingencies are working, even if only minimally, can lead to the development of more effective policies. The situation in Quebec is interesting because the birth incentive program was devised to increase the French Canadian population, and reduce the use of birth control techniques. In this context, progressive monetary payments by birth order seems to have been effective in controlling reproductive behavior and fertility.

Local and Long-Term Contingencies. In terms of behavior principles, it is useful to distinguish between local and long-term contingencies arranged by the

Table 5.4
Use of Birth Control Pill by Age, for the Population of Women 15 to 44 Years, in Quebec: 1987 and 1992–1993

Age Group	1987 (%)	1992-1993 (%)	Change (%)	Population 1992-1993
15-19	42.2	45.6	+3.4	94,566
20-24	58.0	49.2	-8.8	113,205
25-34	30.0	23.4	-6.6	142,205
35-44	4.6	2.9	-1.7	17,864
Total	27.5	21.9[a]	-5.6	367,840

[a]Coefficient of variation is between 15 and 25%; interpret with caution.
Source: Sante Quebec, et la sante, ca va en 1992–2993? *Rapport de l'Enquete sociale et d'sante 1992–1993,* Vol. 1. Public sou la direction de Carmen Dellcrose, Claudette Lavallee, Lucie Chanard, et Madeleine Levasseur.

birth incentive program. Clearly, the payoffs of the program cannot function as immediate reinforcement for unprotected sexual intercourse. That is, the reproductive behavior is far removed from the birth of a child and the eventual monetary returns.

The long-term contingencies for births could, however, be mediated by more local reinforcement contingencies. The announcement of the birth incentive program and the progressive nature of the payoffs could have motivational effects (Michael, 1982), especially for women who were already planning to have children in the near future (i.e., they function as establishing events). One such effect would involve a temporary increase in the probability of talking about having more children and practicing unprotected sexual intercourse. A temporary increase in talking about having children could provide the opportunity for family, friends, and spouses to reinforce this verbal behavior. If "talking about having babies" is correlated with "unprotected sexual intercourse" (e.g., in the same response class), then social reinforcement of talking about having children could further increase unprotected sexual intercourse (and reduce the use of birth control devices). At the same time, family, friends, and spouses would be more inclined to approve of (reinforce) conversations about having more children when they learned of the government incentives, especially for higher-order births. Thus, immediate social contingencies of reinforcement would mediate the long-term contingencies for births arranged by the government.

Choice, Preference, and Childbirth. Another way of looking at the birth incentive program involves an analysis of reproductive choice and preference. Behavior analysts model choice and preference in terms of concurrent schedules of reinforcement (de Villiers, 1977; Pierce & Epling, 1983). When two or more schedules provide reinforcement for behavior, humans and other organisms distribute their responses to match the relative rates of reinforcement from the alternatives (Baum, 1974a; Herrnstein, 1961). In simple language, if 60% of the reinforcement for behavior is obtained from one of two alternatives, then 60% of the organism's responses will be allocated to that alternative (all other things being equal).

In the present case, the choice is between protected or unprotected sexual intercourse. For this analysis, each opportunity for sexual intercourse arranges two concurrent schedules that reinforce protected or unprotected sexual intercourse, respectively. Each alternative arranges immediate and long-term consequences for the sexual behavior. For example, the immediate consequences of unprotected sex could involve less interruption of sexual stimulation, greater tactile stimulation during intercourse, or less monitoring of birth control (''did I take the pill?''). The long-range consequences of unprotected sexual intercourse could involve becoming pregnant, the social responses to pregnancy, the economic costs of raising a child, as well as the reduction in social and economic opportunities (loss of freedom). In terms of protected sexual intercourse, the short-term consequences are usually less positive (i.e., monitoring of birth control and protection), but the long-term consequences can be substantial, such as obtaining an education, having a career, or having more social and economic opportunities (greater freedom).

Notice that in terms of immediate consequences unprotected sex has higher positive payoffs, but in the long run protected sex produces greater positive outcomes. In terms of matching theory (McDowell, 1988), both immediate and long-range (obtained) consequences regulate the distribution of behavior on two or more alternatives. Immediate consequences, however, would be expected to exert more control over behavioral choice than the longer-term payoffs (see Logue et al., 1986). On this basis, unprotected sexual intercourse would have a relatively higher rate of occurrence than protected sexual intercourse.

Consideration of the short-term relative payoffs for unprotected sex provides a behavioral account of why interventions to increase the use of birth control could fail. Use of birth control reduces the immediate relative reinforcement for protected sex and matching theory requires that the person distribute more behavior to the unprotected-sex alternative. This means that birth control programs could backfire, and birth rates could continue to rise. At the same time, this analysis indicates that government incentives to increase births and unprotected sexual intercourse could be effective. This is because the long-range payoffs for unprotected sex support the more immediate positive consequences, increasing the relative rate of reinforcement for this behavior. Generally, matching theory provides a behavioral account of why government attempts to limit family size are less successful than attempts to increase the number of births.

Although matching theory is usually applied to individual choice, Baum (1974b) has shown that molar matching equations also describe the aggregate behavior of groups. This finding suggests that it may be possible to describe the reproductive choices of human populations by a form of matching or distribution equations. Subsequent research on matching and fertility could be directed at quantification of human reproductive choice. This analysis would detail the relationship between sexual behavior at the individual level and fertility at the level of human populations. A quantitative formulation of matching and fertility eventually could provide specific predictions about the effects of birth incentives and new technologies to alter the fertility levels of human populations.

CONCLUSION

Historically, the Quebec government has used a variety of incentives for early marriage and large family size in an attempt to maintain Quebec's population size and thus avoid subordination to English Canada. In other words, high fertility rates were synonymous with the survival of French Canadian culture. For over two centuries, Quebec had one of the highest fertility rates in the industrial world. However, since 1960, fertility rates have plummeted in Quebec and since 1970, Quebec's total fertility rates have been below the level needed to ensure replacement of the generations. As Caldwell and Fournier (1987) have observed, Quebec, "in achieving the much-sought-after modernism, has effectively liquidated the essential spring of its survival as a society, its demographic dynamism" (p. 118). Quebec's low fertility has been a central issue with government officials for the past few years now, resulting in several incentive programs in an attempt to reverse this downward trend in fertility rates.

In this chapter, we have described a recent attempt by this government to increase births, using graduated monetary payments based on birth order. An interrupted time-series design, with the rest of Canada as the control group, indicated that the Quebec incentives did increase reproductive behavior (i.e., less use of birth control devices). A behavioral analysis based on local reinforcement of verbal behavior and changes in the relative rate of reinforcement for unprotected sex provided a plausible account of how the Quebec government's incentives for births altered reproductive behavior. Generally, probirth (or birth control) programs indirectly arrange behavioral contingencies at the individual level. A birth program can succeed, be ineffective, or boomerang, depending on the behavioral contingencies set up for unprotected or protected sex. Once this is realized, there is reason for demographers and behavior analysts to work together toward a more complete analysis of reproduction and fertility. A behavioral demography could have a substantial impact at both the theoretical and practical levels.

NOTE

1. According to Thompson (1984), the term *Quiet Revolution* is standard among Canadian academics but scholars are uncertain who created the term. Thompson maintains

that the early 1960s have been referred to as a revolution because it marked a dramatic turning point in Quebec's history. Moreover, the social and economic transformations which took place in Quebec during this time occurred unexpectedly, almost "quietly" (Thompson, 1984).

REFERENCES

Baum, W. M. (1974a). On two types of deviation from the matching law: Bias and undermatching. *Journal of the Experimental Analysis of Behavior, 22,* 231–242.
————. (1974b). Choice in free ranging wild pigeons. *Science, 185,* 78–79.
Beaujot, R., & McQuillan, K. (1982). *Growth and dualism: The demographic development of Canadian society.* Toronto: Gage Publishing Ltd.
Behiels, M. D. (1986). *Prelude to Quebec's Quiet Revolution.* Kingston, Ontario: McGill-Queen's University Press.
Caldwell, G., & Fournier, D. (1987). The Quebec question: A matter of population. *The Canadian Journal of Sociology, 12,* 16–41.
Cormier, H. J., & Klerman, G. L. (1985). Unemployment and male-female labour force participation as determinants of changing suicide rates of males and females in Quebec. *Social Psychiatry, 20,* 109–114.
Council on French Life in America. (1971). The fertility crisis in Quebec. Translated by K. von Knorring. In C. F. Grindstaff, C. L. Boydell, & P. C. Whetehead (Eds.), *Population issues in Canada* (pp. 6–11). Toronto: Holt, Rinehart and Winston of Canada.
de Villiers, P. (1977). Choice in concurrent schedules and the quantitative formulation of the law of effect. In W. K. Honig & J. E. R. Staddon (Eds.), *Handbook of operant behavior* (pp. 233–287). Englewood Cliffs, NJ: Prentice-Hall.
Dumas, J., & Belanger, A. (1995). *Report on the demographic situation in Canada, 1995.* Statistics Canada. Catalogue #91–209E Annual.
Fréchet, G. (1992). Reproductive technologies. In S. Langlois, J. Baillargeon, G. Caldwell, G. Fréchet, M. Gautheir, & J. Simard (Eds.), *Recent social trends in Québec, 1960–1990* (pp. 129–134). Kingston, Ontario: McGill-Queen's University Press.
Glass, G. V., Wilson, V. L., & Gottman, J. M. (1975). *Design and analysis of time-series experiments.* Boulder: University of Colorado Press.
Gratton, Michel. (1992). *French Canadians: An outsider's inside look at Quebec.* Toronto: Key Porter Books.
Harris, M. (1979). *Cultural materialism.* New York: Random House.
Henripin, J. (1994). From acceptance of nature to control: The demography of the French Canadians since the seventeenth century. In F. Trovato & C. F. Grindstaff (Eds.), *Perspectives on Canada's population: An introduction to concepts and issues* (pp. 24–34). Toronto: Oxford University Press.
Henripin, J., & Péron, Y. (1972). The demographic transition of the province of Quebec. In D. V. Glass & R. Revelle (Eds.), *Population and social change* (pp. 213–232). London: Edward Arnold Publishers.
Hernandez, D. (1981). The impact of family planning programs on fertility in developing countries: A critical evaluation. *Social Science Research, 10,* 32–66.
Herrnstein, R. J. (1961). Relative and absolute response strength as a function of fre-

quency of reinforcement. *Journal of the Experimental Analysis of Behavior, 4*, 267–272.

Houle, G. (1987). Présentation/Introduction. *The Canadian Journal of Sociology, 12*, 1–7.

Krull, C. (1996a). From the King's Daughters to the Quiet Revolution: A historical overview of family structures and the role of women in Quebec. In M. Lynn (Ed.), *Voices: Essays on Canadian families* (pp. 369–396). Toronto: Nelson Canada.

———. (1996b). *Modernization and fertility change in Quebec*. Unpublished. Doctoral dissertation, Department of Sociology, University of Alberta, Edmonton, Alberta, Canada.

Krull, C., & Trovato, F. (1994). The Quiet Revolution and the sex differential in Quebec's suicide rates: 1931–1986. *Social Forces, 72 (4)*, 1121–1147.

Lachapelle, R., & Henripin, J. (1982). *The demolinguistic situation in Canada: Past trends and future prospects*. The Institute for Research on Public Policy, Montreal.

Logue, A. W., Pena-Correal, T. E., Rodriguez, M. L., & Kabela, E. (1986). Self-control in humans: Variation in positive reinforcer amount and delay. *Journal of the Experimental Analysis of Behavior, 46*, 159–173.

Maroney, H. J. (1992). Who has the baby? Nationalism, pronatalism and the construction of a "demographic crisis" in Quebec, 1960–1988. *Studies in Political Economy, 39*, 7–36.

McDowell, J. J. (1988). Matching theory in natural human environments. *The Behavior Analyst, 11*, 95–109.

Michael, J. (1982). Distinguishing between discriminative stimuli and motivational functions of stimuli. *Journal of the Experimental Analysis of Behavior, 37*, 149–155.

Peters, J. (1990). Cultural variations: Past and present. In M. Baker (Ed.), *Families: Changing trends in Canada* (pp. 166–191). Toronto: McGraw-Hill Ryerson.

Pierce, W. D. (1991). Culture and society: The role of behavioral analysis. In P. A. Lamal (Ed.), *Behavioral analysis of societies and cultural practices* (pp. 13–38). New York: Hemisphere.

Pierce, W. D., & Epling, W. F. (1983). Choice, matching and human behavior. *The Behavior Analyst, 6*, 57–76.

Quebec Pension Board, Régie des rentes du Québec. (1994). *Les allocations d'aide aux familles: Statistiques 1994* [Allocations of assistance to families: 1994 statistics]. Province of Quebe, Canada.

Rapport de l'Enquete Sociale et d'Sante. Sante Quebec, et la sante, ca va en 1992–1993? En C. Bellcrose, C. Lavellee, L. Chenard, & M. Levasseur (Eds.), *Rapport de l'Enquete sociale et d'sante 1992–1993, Volume 1*, Gouvernement du Quebec.

Skinner, B. F. (1953). *Science and human behavior*. New York: Free Press.

Statistics Canada, Health Statistics Division, Health Status and Vital Statistics Section, 1971–1993, *Births*, Catalogue #84–210, Annual.

Thompson, D. C. (1984). *Jean Lesage and the Quiet Revolution*. Toronto: Macmillan of Canada.

Trovato, F. (1994). Sociology and demography. In W. Meloff and W. D. Pierce (Eds.), *An introduction to sociology* (pp. 377–406). Scarborough: Nelson Canada.

Wiest, W. M., & Squier, L. H. (1974). Incentives and reinforcement: A behavioral approach to fertility. *Journal of Social Issues, 30*, 235–263.

Wilson, S. J. (1986). *Women, the family and the economy*. Toronto: McGraw-Hill Ryerson.

6

Women's Roles in Japan's Economic Success and in the Problems that Resulted

MIYAKO TAZAKI AND DONALD M. BAER

INTRODUCTION

A survey by Japan's Ministry of Foreign Affairs in 1989 showed that 90% of Japanese were glad to have been born Japanese (Gaimusyo Daijin Kanbo Kaigai Kohoka, 1989). How long that has been true is unknown, but current reasons for such pride are easy to find. In the 50 years since the Second World War, Japan quickly achieved and maintained a successful economy, and became the world's second largest market, with a gross domestic product (GDP) in 1993 of 421 trillion yen (U.S. $3.8 trillion). The Japanese standard of living has progressed greatly since the Allied occupation; the distribution of personal wealth is much more even, especially since the ''bubble'' economy of the 1980s ended (Nihon Keizai Shimbun, Inc., 1985, 1992). According to the Human Development Index of the United Nations Development Programme, Japan in 1993 was leading the world in providing education, increasing GDP, and extending life expectancy (The United Nations Development Programme, 1993).

The Japanese economic success is often attributed to the national industrial policy pursued by the Ministry of Finance and the Ministry of Planning, and to Japan's employment system. The cooperation between government ministries and private industries is distinctively strong in Japan, allowing the organization of intense and massive private efforts into a carefully planned national pattern (Japan Center for Economic Research, 1992; Nihon Keizai Shimbun, 1994). Perhaps the exemplary performance of Japanese workers results in part from the widespread belief that they will be employed until their retirement; for industry and government, that is a desirable form of worker self-instruction, and industry and government do not temper it with reality.

Yet the Japanese do not have a luxurious lifestyle. Other nations say that

Japan is rich but the Japanese are not. Indeed, since 1920, the average Japanese family lives in a smaller house than before—about 900 square feet, consisting of two rooms and a dining-room/kitchen (Somucho, 1988). Furthermore, a survey of fifteen developed nations by the World Health Organization (WHO) in 1995, centering on six domains of everyday life (health, psychological, independence, social relations, environment, and spirituality), showed that Tokyo offers the lowest quality of life in the social relationships and psychological aspects of its healthy citizens. Interestingly, while Japan has been at peace since the post–World War II occupation, Israel, which has always been prepared to fight for its life, is rated the best in these domains (Tazaki et al., in press).

This chapter will describe some of these problematic aspects of current Japanese society, relate them to the behaviors of various Japanese, and speculate about the subtle metacontingencies that support those behaviors. As will be seen, the analysis will rely in part on facts gathered by reasonably dependable survey techniques, and in part on unverifiable but at least plausible speculation about dependencies among behaviors, contingencies, and metacontingencies. The analysis will never rise to the level of proof; as will be seen, it hardly could.

It will be seen that women's roles in Japan are crucial to all the success the nation has achieved, and also are involved in six phenomena reported by surveyors to be current societal problems: (a) an unusual rate of business men's deaths from overwork ("Karoushi"); (b) the reported "examination hell" faced by students, with its high rates of bullying, apathy, dropping out, and suicide; (c) the reported sexual promiscuity of some Japanese women in foreign countries; (d) the vacuous criteria more and more Japanese women are reported to use in choosing husbands; (e) the reported increase of "sexless couples"; and (f) the apparent dysfunctional attraction of apocalyptic religious cults such as Omu Shinrikyo to at least a few of Japan's youth searching for meaning in life.

These six social problems are present in virtually every developed society. They can result from diverse causes; but in Japan, their origins may be distinctive. It may be that their primary causes are the metacontingencies that determine the roles of women. Those metacontingencies began with Japan's unprecedented economic success.

JAPAN'S ECONOMIC GROWTH

Japan's economic success seems incredible if we consider the obstacles it faced. Between 1953 and 1973, Japan shifted with unprecedented rapidity from agriculture and light manufacturing to heavy industry. The average yearly growth rate was 8% overall, and 10.6% during the 1960s. War procurements during the Korean conflict and a general expansion of world trade let Japan earn the foreign exchange to pay for the imports essential to its growth (Shimokawa, 1990). But that caused an average annual inflation rate of 5.8%, along with increasing pollution and pollution-related diseases. In 1973, the first oil crisis created double-digit inflation in Japan; the economy had its first decline since 1950, as severe restrictions on oil use made it quadruple in price (Gendai Nihon Keizai Kennkyu-kai, 1992; Nihon Keizai Shimbun, 1993).

Yet the Japanese economy recovered from that decline by systematic, nation-wide energy-saving, and by reforming industrial structures (the so-called Japanese-style rationalization); in the process, it recovered a comparatively low inflation rate (Nihon Keizai Shimbun, 1993; Shimokawa, 1990). The second oil shock of 1979 shifted the economy from heavy industry to high-technology industry. That increased trade friction with other industrialized countries; Japan had a huge trade surplus (Keizai Kikakucho, 1994; Komine, 1986).

In 1985 the Plaza Accord drove up the value of the yen to twice its 1984 value (Gendai Nihon Keizai Kennkyu-kai, 1992; Nihon Keizai Shimbun, 1993). As a result, the trade surplus gradually decreased; and as the Bank of Japan lowered the discount rate from 5.0% to 2.5%, consumption increased and corporate investment rose to 21.7% in 1989 (Keizai Kikakucho, 1994; Kojima, 1992). Some Japanese companies moved their operations to other cheap-labor Asian countries to remain competitive (Kojima, 1992; Nihon Keizai Shimbun, 1993). Thus, by the end of 1990, the Tokyo stock market had fallen 38% from its peak, and the Japanese economy was in recession. It shifted yet again, this time from the production of goods to service industries (Japan Center for Economic Research, 1992).

Thus, a small country with only human resources has shown amazing flexibility in overcoming two oil crises and exchange crises, which have been severe threats everywhere in the developed world. The cost of that successful flexibility must have been human, in the form of unusually intense behaviors. Japanese workers have let Japan weather the big world changes by several new starts, often from the bottom; to do that, the workers had to work very hard. The hard work that brought about economic success has created six serious social problems. The first of them, the apparent rate of death from overwork, derives immediately from that success; the remainder derive from the interaction between that success and the rules and contingencies it imposed on Japanese women and children.

Death from Overwork ("Karoushi")

The economy survived and expanded because people overworked, sometimes to death at an unusually early age. The Japanese term such deaths "Karoushi." Since the late 1980s, more and more cases of Karoushi have been reported (Nihon Karoushi Zenkoku Renraku-kai, 1991); in 1992, the number reported to the Karoushi Dial 110 reached 2,600 (Kashima, 1995). That 2,600 business men die in a year in a developed country of 130 million people is not remarkable; that they are in their forties or fifties and die from overwork is remarkable.

Karoushi is not a medical term; it is a social term used by insurers. The proximal diagnoses are cerebral hemorrhage, cardiac insufficiency, and coronary disease (Keizai Kikakucho, 1991). These diseases apparently can result from working long hours for very extended periods of time; medical authorities assume that an accumulation of "stress" and "fatigue" mediate between too much work and these fatal diseases. Still, the real cause of Karoushi is too much work: too often after 5 P.M., too often until midnight, and before 9:00 A.M., and on weekends, and sometimes all night.

According to Somucho (the Ministry of General Affairs) (1991), the employees of all the industries in Japan probably work an average of 49.3 hours every week ("probably," because companies forbid employees from formally reporting more than 40 hours per week, since they will not pay for more than 40 hours). That is 2,570 hours yearly. The yearly hours recommended by the International Labor Office are only 1,800 (Rodosho, 1991). The Japanese work 43% longer than that. And even that level of 2,570 was the outcome of governmental intervention to reduce work hours from their previous levels: the government was defending against Japan-bashing by its trading partners (Kashima, 1995).

A typical business man works late, gets home late, and goes straight to bed. His commuting time is spent crowded into a train that always seems fully packed, yet at each big station even more commuters will be jammed into it by pushers hired for the job (Kashima, 1995). A survey of these men (Nihon Keizai Shimbun, 1992) found a third of them feel overworked—usually the same men who profess themselves satisfied with their jobs!

Two-thirds of business people drink with their colleagues after work to make a better work relationship, and to do business; they do this usually more than once a week. Those who say they like their jobs do it more often than that. So, on a typical day, a typical business man gets up at 6:30 A.M., leaves home at 7:45 A.M., rushes to a crowded train station and is jammed in with an increasing number of people for nearly an hour; he is more likely to stand than sit for that time. He begins work at 9:00 A.M. and stops at 8:00 P.M. when a colleague invites him out for a drink. He probably accepts this invitation at least twice a week. He will spend at least two hours drinking and talking. That means he will rarely have enough sleep, because he often will not be home before 1:00 A.M. And on many weekends he must work, or play golf with clients, and so during those weeks he has no rest at all.

He probably feels tired all the time. The WHO research on quality of life (Tazaki et al., in press) shows that the average healthy Japanese, average age 48, says the important goals of life are to stop feeling tired, be healthy, rest, and relax, in that order. Indeed, according to a 1988 survey by Somucho, more than half the Japanese say that they would be glad to earn no more money if that would gain them more free time. Two surveys by the NHK TV channel, one in 1973 and the other in 1988, showed that the percentage of Japanese claiming work as most important in their lives decreased from 44% to 31%. Yet the more satisfied a business man says he is with his job, the more intense is this scenario of overwork without relaxation. This is the behavior pattern most likely to result in promotion.

This contingency is often backed up by corporate exercises in stimulus control: the company offers itself as employees' family, a portrayal based strongly on its failure to correct the workers' prevailing self-instruction that their employment is lifelong. Most Japanese companies recruit workers immediately upon their graduation, and do not correct these workers' self-instruction about continuing with the company until they retire. Furthermore, the company often trains them extensively to do their jobs, which may well enable the conclusion that their university education did not equip them for anything of practical value: if they had to be made valuable to this company, then presumably they are valuable only to this company.

Their pre-university education taught employees to work very hard; that usually was taught as both a performance and a rule. Now their company repeats the rule, modifying it only to mean working very hard at the job the company just taught them. If the company's equivalence training is effective, then maximizing the company's profit is maximizing their "family's" profit. Thus, quite likely, the company becomes their highest priority. The first morality rule of company membership is loyalty to the company: harmony, cooperation, and hard work make the company-family prosperous.

Corporate culture goes even further. It uses what appear to be induction routines, such as everyone singing a company song to start each day, and special greetings among co-workers. All stimulus controls support the rule that the co-workers are comrades in a long-term relationship—but the prevailing contingency is that they also are competitors, because they, too, are seeking promotion to the very few higher positions. Thus, companies create family rules that define excellence, status, and uniqueness, not as creativity or brilliance, but as working harder and longer, taking fewer holidays, and being more loyal to the company than anyone else—and never disturbing the harmony of the company. But, companies typically deny that they press their workers into too much overtime work (Kashima, 1995). And when men retire, they are badly surprised to discover that they have no skills for being at home, for contributing to the community network the women have created and maintained, or for using their time in a fulfilling way. In the same way, when men are laid off, for at least a month they are quite likely to pretend to go to work, rather than face the truth—or the fact that they have no function at home (Inoue & Ehara, 1995).

ROLES OF JAPANESE WOMEN

Because men are always at work, one way or another, wives must take charge of everything else. The man is considered to owe the wife his salary; she controls its use. Without wives who ask nothing more, men could not work as the company teaches. In this sense, it is wives who have made the success of Japan's economy. The costs of that success are the time of both the men and their women.

Most Japanese men still endorse the tradition that they *should* work outside the home, and that after marriage, women *should* devote themselves entirely to the home (Nihon Fujin Dantai Rengokai, 1992; Sorifu, 1988). A survey by the Yomiuri News in 1986 showed that 65% of its readers did not see the father as responsible for the children's education, because he is busy at work. Japanese men increasingly do not, and, they believe, *should* not, have much time for family. That is tradition—and also a good reason to avoid the formidable demands of family responsibility.

The father was also reported to avoid intimate relationship with the wife. Forty percent of couples in their forties had sex less than once a month (Tanaka, 1989). A survey by Rodosho (the Ministry of Labor) in 1986 showed that Japanese housework costs wives seven to eight hours a day—three hours longer than the average in other developed countries.

Many young Japanese are greatly influenced by Western culture; they want more romantic marriages than their parents had (Yoshikawa, 1996). Nevertheless, after a year or two of marriage, most couples settle into a pattern of separate social worlds and a clear-cut division of contingencies, skills, and repertoires. The husband's life is governed mainly by the company's contingencies, the wife's is governed mainly by the contingencies created by her children and their home and schooling. Most of the husband's social reinforcement will be given by his work group; most of the wife's by the people around her children and their schooling.

These facts are central to the problem of men's overwork; and they also give rise to a number of other social problems.

Examination Hell

Japanese women are given the responsibility to rear and educate their children (Nihon Fujin Dantai Rengokai, 1992; Tanaka, 1989). It is a task that does not allow for substitutes. Motherhood, defined as the careful nurturing of children, is a supreme value in Japan (Tanaka, 1989). Mother and child are usually inseparable when the child is young, and even in later years, mother-child relationships continue to be the strongest and closest within the family (Somucho, 1995).

In the Japan of today, the success of a child, whether boy or girl, requires the mother to spend a great deal of time and thought on the child's education. Her tool is, of course, the schools—all of them. The Japanese often complain about their schools' examination systems; and they often make fun of the so-called education mother (kyoikumama) who single-mindedly drives her children toward educational achievement. Even so, most middle-class mothers have no other way to answer the powerful social contingencies that mandate that a good job requires a degree from a good university.

Gossip and media teach constantly that Japanese schools have some degree of reputation. Large Japanese companies recruit new employees almost exclusively from those universities with the finest reputations (Nohara, 1996). Therefore, mothers want their children to graduate from at least a good university. To enter a good university, one must have graduated from a good high school; to enter a good high school, one must have graduated from a good junior high school; to enter a good junior high school, one must have graduated from a good primary school; to enter a good primary school, one must have attended a good nursery school. So, modern Japanese mothers begin their children's education at the age of one and a half (Ishii, 1987; Shishido & Hijikata, 1986).

In the Japanese educational system, entrance examinations are given heavy weight in the selection of students, especially for high schools and universities (Nohara, 1996). If an applicant fails a particular school's examination, which is given only once a year, there is no recourse or appeal. Therefore, students apply to more than one school. Nowadays, 97% of junior high school graduates go on to high schools, and 40% of high school graduates go on to universities (Nishio, 1992; Nohara, 1996). Since the early 1960s, each student has received a percentile ranking ("hensachi") from "practice" entrance examinations. As the Japanese are nearly homogeneous in their distribution of wealth, there is little besides a person's educational background to determine social status. Graduates from a school whose students tend to have higher percentiles ("hensachi") have higher status.

To prepare for that competition, 16.7% of nursery school children, 49.5% of primary school students, 64.2% of junior high school students, and 35.8% of high school students attend a private tutoring school ("juku") after regular school hours, which, by Western standards, are very long (Somucho, 1995). And private "cram schools" ("yobiko") offer to help those students who fail their first entrance examination for the universities.

University entrance examinations determine much of one's fate in Japan; the battle to qualify for the best schools is waged with such fierce intensity, the competition has come to be known as "examination hell."

As the examination hell became a regular path for all students these last ten years, juvenile delinquency, apathy, school allergy, dropping out, and bullying have exploded dramatically.

School violence emerged in the late 1980s (Shimada, 1987; Yoshida, 1993), and was suppressed by the authorities. It turned into bullying, reports of which reached 155,000 cases for seven months in 1987 (Maruki, 1985; Somucho, 1995). At the same time, suicides of junior high school students attributable to bullying also erupted all over Japan, in addition to the student suicides attributable to failing an entrance examination. When countermeasures against bullying were introduced, cases of school apathy increased (Sakano, 1990; Serizawa, 1994).

These phenomena are reminiscent of the behavioral contrast studied in behavior analysis: when several behaviors all serve the same function, and one is suppressed, another of them will increase (Honig & Staddon, 1977). The heavier the suppression, the more extreme the contrast.

As just described, some students resorted to violence. Others, good at school, became violent at home, bullying their mothers (Sano, 1984; Tagami, 1990). School authorities began to punish students with suspensions and expulsions. The victims of bullying who resorted to suicide began leaving "wills" naming their oppressors, to guarantee their severe punishment (Kuze, 1992). As bullying was suppressed, some students stopped attending school. The number of school apathy and dropout cases surpassed 10,000 in Japan in 1994 (Somucho, 1995).

Perhaps these problems share the same root. The schools taught students only the skills for higher scores in entrance examinations, which required little more than acquiring a great deal of knowledge too fast, and a highly regulated setting that restricted too many other activities. The nature of the entrance examinations made fact memorization paramount, problem solving unimportant, and discussions of the possible meanings of life irrelevant. Children found themselves valued for only one attribute—the status of the school their entrance examination scores could achieve: that was the essential stimulus control for admiration and acceptance by family and peers, and for avoiding disgrace. Mothers, wishing only for their children's future happiness, sent them only to a battle for academic achievement. In such conditions, healthy development must be at risk.

These problems probably will not cease until the examination hell is changed, which probably will not happen until the companies stop recruiting new employees based only on their university's status. Then mothers can have a different view of their children, and the children probably will not suffer so much.

"Yellow Cab" Sexual Promiscuity

In the last twenty years, many Japanese women have adopted a drastically different view of sexual behavior. In 1973, a survey found that 53% of 16-to-29-year-old Japanese women would engage in sexual offers before marriage; in 1988, another survey found that 78% would (Inoue & Ehara, 1995; Wada, 1991). Apparently most young women no longer see any taboo to premarital sexual behavior (More Report Group, 1985, 1986). In recent years, many junior high girls have been placed in protective custody because of prostitution. Clearly, many women have become free from the earlier Japanese tradition. There are fewer arranged marriages: in the early 1980s, 60% of marriages were arranged; today only 30% are (Yoshikawa, 1996). In an arranged marriage, the woman's virginity is a crucial if unspoken premise.

That context explains much of a phenomenon termed "Yellow Cab" promiscuity (Ieda, 1992, 1995). Ieda says the term emerged in the 1980s among American West Coast teenagers. They were said to look for young Japanese women tourists, because they found some of these women easily became lovers during their brief visits. Such women were said to be like a yellow cab, in that anyone can easily get in and get out. These women would leave after a few days; there would be no future problems, and new tourists always kept coming. This form of some young Japanese women's promiscuity was known at first only in the United States, until Shoko Ieda published the first documentary report, "Yellow Cab," in 1992.

Traditionally, Japanese girls were taught to become good wives; that was their rule for life. There were always familial approval and disapproval contingencies for them to marry by the age of 25, just as there were always strong governmental contingencies and stimulus controls, and much early education, to remain in the traditional women's roles (NHK Seronchosabu, 1995). Unmarried women older than 25 were ridiculed as "Christmas cakes." Just as no one wants a Christmas cake after December 25th, so it was said that no one wanted to marry a woman older than 25. Parents and relatives also strongly urged still unmarried daughters to consent to arranged marriages, which would become difficult after the woman reached 30.

Besides, the women had few alternatives. Until the 1995 Equal Employment Opportunity Law for Men and Women, women had never been seen as lifetime employees of a company. They had been given only secretarial work, and were often recruited as much to provide the lifetime male employees of the company some convenient candidates for wives as to be secretaries (Nihon Fujin Dantai Rengokai, 1992). So, when such a woman reached 25, her boss often urged her to quit. The woman who wanted something to do with her life, but was untrained for a profession, could turn to little else but marriage at that point.

In Japan, marriages, especially arranged marriages, assume the woman's virginity. Girls and young women faced with so much social pressure to marry and so few alternatives cannot seek sexual romances in their own neighborhoods and jeopardize the reputations they will need for their eventual marriage. Going abroad is their only chance for romantic sexual experience, hence the occasional "Yellow Cab" phenomenon. Abroad, they would find a great deal of sexual experience, much of it exploitative of their naivete, but very little romance.

The "Yellow Cab" behaviors of those Japanese women who were interested took a somewhat different turn when they began touring in other Asian countries. There, some of them might take the initiative in seeking out young men as sexual companions. They were no longer seeking romance (Ieda, 1995).

Characterizing these phenomena as a social problem is itself problematic. The magnitudes of these phenomena are difficult to estimate. On the one hand, many people today think the young Japanese woman should be as free to seek sexual experience as any man; for them, if this emancipation can be attributed to the Japanese economic success and its educational system, at least that is to its credit. On the other hand, this particular form of emancipation outrages many people. And it exposes the relatively naive young woman to the threat of sexually transmitted diseases, some of them fatal (e.g., AIDS) (Munakata, 1996).

Some Women's Criteria for Husbands ("Sanko")

In the last ten years, women's awareness has increased. After the passage of the Equal Employment Law, women pursued management and specialist positions in companies. They sometimes succeed, but usually are still excluded from the companies' mainstreams, and they are the first to be laid off in a recession (Owaki, 1993). Still, a new way of life for women has at least surfaced and been acknowledged in Japan.

Of course some women, even among those with high education, still follow the paths of their mothers. After a few years of work, they turn gladly to the housewife role. Some of them are said to choose their husbands then by the "sanko" criteria. "San" means three; "ko" means high: the "three highs" these women seek are husbands who are tall, rich, and well educated (Wada, 1991; Yashiro, 1994). These three criteria are interdependent. A man who is relatively wealthy even though young must have graduated from a privileged university. The fact that a company hired him for one of its best jobs makes it likely he is relatively good-looking (in that the companies to some extent also value this criterion).

People born in the 1960s have been brought up to judge people by the likelihood of their future success. The "three highs" are an easy, useful scale for that judgment about husbands. Those women using it need not find out a candidate's personality, values, loyalty, likelihood of personal support, or life history.

Sexless Couples

Married couples virtually without sexual relations have recently surfaced in Japan as a psychiatric phenomenon (Oshima et al., 1996); it is still difficult to estimate their prevalance. The typical sexless couple is the result of an arranged marriage between a daughter who hoped only for a "three highs" husband and a son who endorsed those criteria as the relevant tests he should pass. Both have good educations. Although they are healthy, some of them will not have any sexual relationship, presumably because the man, perhaps still a virgin, has none of the sexual skills usually acquired during adolescence: those skills are not part of the "three highs" criteria, and meeting the "three highs" criteria usually meant there was no time for development of sexual skills. But some of these couples will have an occasional sexual relationship, probably only until the first child is born (Ishiguro, 1995; Yamamoto, 1994; Yoshihiro, 1994).

The husband in such a couple is said to never have been independent from his parents; he probably lived in his parents' house some 30 years before he married. Equally probably, his only strong relationship is with his mother. Perhaps he married mainly for the social status of marriage, to have a son to carry on the family name, and to have another woman to take care of him.

In the same speculative spirit, perhaps, the woman of that couple wanted mainly to maintain the living standard in which she grew up. If so, then after the marriage, she may well remain as behaviorally and financially dependent on her parents as before.

Perhaps the husband spends most of his time at work in the company and socializing with his colleagues. Perhaps she devotes herself to the child and the child's education. If there is no child, she probably will have her own career. Both are busy at work. They rarely talk. When they come home, she is still expected to do all the housework (Kimoto, 1995), after which they go to their separate beds, as very likely they used to do at their parents' houses.

But Japanese men hate to fail at anything, and Japanese women do seek sexual satisfaction. So, modern Japan offers its men and women many telephone "shops" that mediate a random analog to computer dating: one telephones the shop, and is connected to the next person of the opposite sex who calls the shop. It is understood that the topic of conversation will be sex, and that if the parties like each other, they may simply discuss their mutual problems at length—or they may arrange to meet. (The Japanese refer to this service as "Dial Q2," which long ago was the term for a party line) (Inoue, 1993; Masada, 1991; Miyadai, Ishihara, & Otsuka, 1993). Each member of the sexless couple may know that the other has found sexual partners, but they do not acknowledge the fact, because they do not want to be divorced.

Such couples no doubt exist in all developed societies; their numbers increase at least because declining economies require both spouses to work if they are to maintain their expected standard of living. But perhaps the Japanese case reflects a different origin: the examination-oriented education they received. The modern Japanese school curriculum does not consider the social, human, family development of its students. It makes them too busy memorizing endless facts to have enough time for play with friends when they are young. They can only imitate their parents' behaviors, which usually were far from intimate, as far as the children could see.

Religious Cults

The year 1996 was a cruel one for Japan: over 5,000 people died in the Kobe earthquake, and more than 300 people were killed in a series of crimes by the religious cult Omu Shinrikyo.

The Japanese are often seen as only mildly religious. True, their religion does not show in their daily lives. For the most part, their religious practice is confined to celebrating New Year's Day in a shrine, visiting their ancestors' graves in a temple, having a Christmas party (although 95% are not Christian), getting married in a church, and being buried in a religion-determined manner.

However, since the late 1980s, a religious boom has swept Japan. The number of people who profess to believe in God or Buddha is increasing dramatically (Takao, 1988; Yoneyama, 1988). Some groups that not long ago were small cults now have become rich political forces (e.g., the Sokagakkai) (Itagaki, 1995).

For the Japanese, the ability to state a rule defining a meaning in life is very important. According to the NHK survey in 1988, the younger generation said they were fully satisfied with their material life, but also said they still searched for a meaning to it. They began to explore religion for that meaning (Kato, 1996; Okonogi, 1986).

What is meant by "meaning to life" is never clear in these surveys. Perhaps the point at issue is whether a person always has a worthy purpose to serve— something good that can be attained more and more as life progresses, but never is fully attained. If so, then another striking failure of the modern educational system is that it offers a series of worthy goals that require almost all of a student's behavior, but these goals can be fully attained fairly early in life: good grades, high scores on entrance examinations, degrees from fine universities, and placement with an important company. Such goals, once achieved, leave the student with only a "Now what?" response, somewhat reminiscent of the postreinforcement pause characteristic of ratio schedules (Honig & Staddon, 1977). By contrast, the goals posited by religious sects are something like securing a personal grace or the salvation of mankind, and they are lifetime tasks because they are never completely attained.

At first, the Omu Shinrikyo seemed to be just one more of the 1,000 Japanese cults that encourage asceticism (Itagaki, 1995). That made their subsequent crimes, especially their murders, all the more shocking. But most astonishing to many Japanese was that some members of the Omu who committed major crimes had graduated from the elite universities. They had been science majors (Egawa, 1995; Mainichi Shimbun Shakaibu, 1995; Tokyo Shimbun Shakaibu, 1995). How could *they* have lost their common sense and their fundamental human values, the newspapers asked. Had they been taught no rule to the contrary, the behavioral scientists might well have asked. Despite their small numbers, a statement to emphasize healthy mental development of science major students was strongly stated by the Minister of Education in front of more than 100 deans of Japanese National universities in an official meeting ("Monnbudaijinn," 1995). After all, a small number of highly educated people—chemists who understand poison gas, for example—can, given strange new convictions about what is necessary to "save" society, wreak great damage on it.

Apparently, the science curricula of the best universities did not contribute much to these students' ability to state rules summing up the meaning and the consequent course of life—but Omu did. (What is known of Omu's techniques suggests that, knowingly or intuitively, it used a wide variety of the most effective behavior-control techniques, many of them similar to the techniques the educational system had used to secure dedicated achievement from these students.)

These particular Omu members were a natural product of the Japanese economic success and the educational system that supports it. They were few in number, perhaps because random accidents of life have put them at the most vulnerable fringe of the student population, but the point is that such an educational system will always produce a large vulnerable fringe. Thus they are a natural phenomenon, and their numbers will probably grow if present trends in Japan continue. People whose societies and educations have left them without rules to define a meaning to life, that is, a set of goals worthy of a set of skills for a lifetime of behavior maximizing but never finishing those goals, may often have their behavior taken over by any agency wielding the appropriate symbols, even widely hateful symbols. A society devoted exclusively to its materialistic glory may not think to provide for meaning-of-life curiosities—but apparently it will pay an increasing price for that neglect.

CONCLUSION

None of these six problems is independent of the others. In particular, the role of Japanese women seems central in each of them, interactive with the power and roles of the companies, especially if the problems are summarized as the following topographies, interdependencies, and contingencies:

- Japan achieved economic success without many natural resources by recruiting a great deal of human labor and devotion.
- The men paid for that success with overwork, no family life, a social life based on work and drinking, and early deaths.
- To free the men for that overwork, the women paid for that success by taking all responsibility for family, children, and home, and entered a social life based only on their children's education.
- Finding that their children's education meant satisfying the companies' demands for graduates of the finest universities, the women, like the schools, had no choice but to urge their children into "examination hell."
- Both men and women pay for that success by sacrificing sex, romance, and mutual understanding and support during crises; and by perpetuating their childhood relationships with their parents.
- Their children pay for that success by having their education based on memorized facts, to the exclusion of being taught creative problem-solving skills and a worthy purpose to their lives, and some of them rebel into apathy, dropout, suicide, and aggression, and later some of them are vulnerable to any religious sect that claims to know the meaning of life.
- Women compensate by promiscuity abroad, men by acquiring mistresses.
- A culture emerges in which women value men only for their education, wealth, and good appearance, and men believe that if they gain education, wealth, and good appearance, they must be good men.

Clearly, the women are central to all this: they enable the men to overwork, they coerce their children to compete in the examination hell, and they seek husbands by such poor criteria that they teach men to consent to all that rather than resist it.

If a change is to occur, it follows that it must begin with the roles of women. Mothers are Japan's most important educators. They need to know that values more important than entrance to the best universities operate in life, and are ignored at great peril to their children and their society.

But that may be a difficult lesson to offer a loving mother, if companies continue their single-minded (and probably dysfunctional) recruitment of their most important employees from only the best universities. That will be dysfunctional to the extent that the best universities define *their* excellence as attracting the best companies, and the companies define their labor requirements only in terms of getting the graduates of the best universities. In traditional psychiatric terms, that has been termed a *folie a deux*, and it is, potentially, a path to inanity, and to irrelevance to the rest of the world.

Computerization means many things in the modern work world; one of them is that some workers are increasingly free to work at home. At present, some Japanese companies are establishing small offices away from their large offices, for work that depends only on a computer and a telephone line. If in the future some companies find an economic advantage to their men working at least sometimes at home, then, inadvertently, that may make men more vulnerable to housework, child care, and family life, and that may, inadvertently, contribute to some change in current Japanese patterns.

But a much more powerful force probably lurks in current economic trends. If those trends continue to make a decent standard of living more and more expensive in Japan, it will become inevitable that Japanese women work full-time and at the highest pay levels they can attain. Besides, the current Japanese family has only 1.43 children (Yoshikawa, 1996)—not enough to support the current working generation when they retire, unless many women work as remuneratively as men. And even that is verging on the problematic, in that the best-trained Japanese women are increasingly likely to leave Japan to work where they are more valued (Nakao, 1985; Tanabe, 1993; Yanagida, 1995).

Logic and an understanding of the metacontingencies that make or break societies might not cause a change in the status of women, but the contingencies of a down-turning economy in a society increasingly overwhelmed by an aging population will. Those contingencies are likely to break more and more of the traditional barriers against women. As women become as busy outside the home as men, they will lose much of their ability to support their husbands' potentially deadly overwork and much of their ability to commit their children to the "examination hell" of modern Japanese education. That might free the schools to teach problem solving as well as fact memorization, since they could then no longer guarantee to produce high scorers on university entrance examinations. That might provide the companies with employees who can create the new, unmemorized developments in science and engineering that competitive survival in the modern world increasingly requires. The companies might then redefine what an excellent university really is.

REFERENCES

Egawa, S. (1995). *Omu Shinri-kyo tsuiseki 2200 nichi* [2200 days of follow up of the Omu shinri-kyo]. Tokyo: Bungei Syunjyu.

Gaimusyo Daijin Kanbo Kaigai Kohoka. (1989). *EC 7 kakoku ni okeru tainichi seron chosa* [Public poll among seven EC countries on Japan]. Tokyo: Okurasyo In-satsu-kyoku.

Gendai Nihon Keizai Kennkyu-kai (Ed.). (1992). *Nihon keizai no genjyo* [Current situation of Japan's economy]. Tokyo: Gakubunsya.

Honig, W. K., & Staddon, J. E. R. (Eds.). (1977). *Handbook of operant behavior*. Englewood Cliffs, NJ: Prentice-Hall.

Ieda, S. (1992). *Yellow cab*. Tokyo: Koyusya.

———. (1995). *Kiken ga ippai* [Much of danger]. Tokyo: Kosaido.

Inoue, T. (1993). *Gendai bunka wo manabu hito no tameni* [For the people who learn modern culture]. Tokyo: Sekai Shisosya.

Inoue, T., & Ehara, Y. (1995). *Jyosei no Data Book* [Women's data book]. Tokyo: Yuhikaku.

Ishiguro, S. (1995). *Kekkon no okite* [Rule of marriage]. Bessatsu Takarajima, Tokyo: Takarajima.

Ishii, I. (1987). *Yoji ha minna tensai* [Every young child can be a genius]. Tokyo: Nihon Kyobunsya.

Itagaki, H. (1995). *Omu jiken to syuukyo senso* [Omu's crimes and religious war]. Tokyo: Sanichi-syobo.

Japan Center for Economic Research. (1992). *Nikkei Data guide. Nihon keizai no kiso chishiki* [Data of Japan's economy]. Tokyo: Nihon Keizai Shimbunsya.

Kashima, T. (1995). *Otoko no zahyo jiku* [Men's principles]. Tokyo: Iwanami Syoten, Inc.

Kato, N. (1996). *Gendai wo yomitoku rinri-gaku* [Ethics to figure out modern society]. Tokyo: Maruzen Inc.

Keizai Kikakucho. (1991). *Kojin seikatsu yusen wo mezashite* [In order to set private life as the highest priority]. Tokyo: Okurasyo Insatsu-kyoku.

———. (1994). *Heisei 6 nen-do keizai hakusyo* [Report of year 1988]. Tokyo: Okurasyo Insatsu-kyoku.

Kimoto, K. (1995). *Kazoku, gyenda, kigyo syakai* [Family, sex, cooperative society]. Kyoto: Mineruva-syobo.

Kojima, S. (Ed.). (1992). *'92 nen ban Nihon keizai key words* [Key words of Japan's economy 1992]. Tokyo: Keizaicyousa-kai.

Komine, T. (1986). *Keizaimasatu: Kokusaika to Nihon no sentaku* [End of century: International society and Japan's selection]. Tokyo: Nihon Keizai Shimbunsya.

Kuze, T. (1992). *Seinen no shinri to kyoiku* [Adolescent psychology and education]. Tokyo: Okurasyo Insatsu-kyoku.

Mainichi Shimbun Shakaibu. (1995). *Omu jiken* [Omu's crimes]. Tokyo: Mainichi Shimbunsya.

Maruki, M. (1985). *Mo ijimerarenainda* [No more bullying]. Tokyo: Jitsunichi Shinsyo.

Masada, N. (1991). *Business man, OL hakusyo* [Report of business men and office ladies]. Tokyo: Jiyu Kokuminsya.

Miyadai, S, Ishihara, H., & Otsuka, A. (1993). *Sub culture: Shinwa kaitai* [Sub culture: Desolving of myth]. Tokyo: PARCO Syuppan.

Monnbudaijinn ga syuuryou rinen nokyouiku wo youcyo. [The Minister of Education emphasizes the need of a new guidance of religion]. (1995, June 16). *Asahi Shimbun*, p. 13.

More Report Group (Ed.). (1985). *More Report A.* Tokyo: Shueisha.

———. (1986). *More Report B.* Tokyo: Shueisha.

Munakata, K. (Ed.). (1996). *Seisyonen no AIDS to sex* [Aids and sexual behaviors in adolescents]. Tokyo: Nihon Hyoronnsya.

Nakao, M. (1985). *Onna hitori de kurasu New York* [Single woman living alone in New York]. Tokyo: Shinchosya.

NHK Seronchosabu. (1995). *Gedai Nihonjin no ishiki kozo* [Awareness structure of modern Japanese]. Tokyo: Nihon Hoso Syuppan Kyokai.

Nihon Fujin Dantai Rengokai. (1992). *Fujin hakusyo* [Report of women]. Tokyo: Horupu Syuppan.

Nihon Karoushi Zenkoku Renraku-kai. (1991). *Karoushi* [Death from overwork]. Tokyo: Kodansya.

Nihon Keizai Shimbun, Inc. (1985). *Nikkei shasetsu ni miru sengo keizaino ayumi* [Development of Japanese economy appeared in Nikkei News after World War II]. Tokyo: Nihon Keizai Shimbun Inc.

———. (1992). *Salary-man no katei to shigoto ni kansuru ishiki cyosa* [Meaning of life on work and home among business men]. Tokyo: Nihon Keizai Shimbun, Inc.

Nihon Keizai Shimbun, Inc. (Ed.). (1993). *Zeminaru Nihon keizai nyumon* [Introduction of Japan's economy]. Tokyo: Nihon Keizai Shimbun, Inc.

———. (1994). *Basic Nihon keizai nyumon* [Basic introduction of Japanese economy]. Tokyo: Nihon Keizai Shimbun, Inc.

Nishio, K. (1992). *Kyoiku to jiyu* [Education and freedom]. Tokyo: Shinchosensyo.

Nohara, A. (1996). *Nihon no kyoiku* [Education in Japan]. Tokyo: Maruzen Inc.

Okonogi, K. (1986). *Gendai shakai no shinri kozo* [Psychological structure of modern society]. Tokyo: NHK Shuppan Kyokai.

Oshima, K., Nagata, H., Abe, H., & Matsuzawa, G. (1996). Sei no kodogaku [Behavioral pattern of sex]. *Gendai, 9*, 192–218.

Owaki, M. (1993). *Byodo no second stage he* [The second stage towards freedom]. Tokyo: Gakuyo-shobo.

Rodosho. (1986). *Keizai syakai kankyo no hennka to Nihon teki koyo kankei ni kansuru cyosa* [Research report on changes of economic social environments and Japanese style employment system]. Tokyo: Okura Insatsu-kyoku.

———. (1991). *Rodo hakusyo* [Report of work and business]. Tokyo: Okura Insatsu-kyoku.

Sakano, Y. (1990). *Tokokyohi, futoko* [Refusal of going to school and absences]. Tokyo: Dohosya.

Sano, K. (1984). *Sabakareru kodomo-tachi* [Children in court]. Tokyo: Eideru Kenkyujyo.

Serizawa, S. (1994). *Kaitai sareru kodomo-tachi* [Children who are a part]. Tokyo: Seiyusya.

Shimada, S. (1987). *Nimgen kankei no shinrigaku. Kazoku no nimgen kankei (II) kakuron*

[Psychology of human relationship. Family relationship (II)]. Tokyo: Buren Syuppan.

Shimokawa, K. (1990). *Nihon no kigyou hattenshi. Sengo fukkou kara 50nen* [Development history of Japanese economy. Reconstructed after the war 50 years ago]. Tokyo: Koudansya.

Shishido, K., & Hijikata, H. (Eds.). (1986). *Nyujino hoiku keikaku to jissen* [Plans and practice of taking care of infants]. Tokyo: Ayumi Syuppansya.

Somucho. (1988). *Nihon no jyutaku* [Japanese housing]. Tokyo: Okurasyo Insatsu-kyoku.

———. (1992). *Seishonen no yujin kankei ni kansuru kokusai hikaku* [International comparison of friendship among adolescents]. Tokyo: Okurasyo Insatsu-kyoku.

———. (1995). *Seishonenn hakusho* [Report on adolescents]. Tokyo: Okurasho Insatsu-kyoku.

Somucho Seisyonen Taisaku Hombu. (1991). *Nihon no chichioya to kodomo. Kodomo to chichioya ni kansuru kokusai hikaku* [Japanese children and fathers. International comparison of father-child relationship]. Tokyo: Okurasyo Insatsu-kyoku.

Sorifu. (1988). *Fujin ni kansuru seron-cyosa* [Public poll report on women]. Tokyo: Okurasho Insatsu-kyoku.

Tagami, F. (1990). *Tokokyohi, katei-nai boryoku* [Refusal of going to school and domestic violence]. Tokyo: Reimei-syobo.

Tanabe, A. (1993). *Onna ga hitoride hataraku-toki* [When a woman works alone]. Tokyo: Bungei Shunjyu.

Tanaka, K. (1989). *Hataraku josei no kosodate ron* [How to raise children by working women]. Tokyo: Shincyosya.

Takao, T. (1988). *Syukyo genron* [Religious]. Tokyo: Hyoronsya.

Tazaki, M., Nakane, Y., Miyaoaka, E., & Noji, A. (in press). *WHO/QOL yobi cyousahyo kaihatu kennkyu kekka houkoku* [Result of WHO/QOL instrument development research]. Tokyo: Nihon Kosyu Eisei Zasshi, *Japanese Journal of Public Health*.

Tokyo Shimbun Shakaibu. (1995). *Soshiki hanzai no nazo* [Mystery of organizational crimes]. Tokyo: Tokyo Shimbun Syuppan-kyoku.

The United Nations Development Programme. (1993). *The Human Development Index*. New York: Oxford University Press.

Wada, H. (1991). *Kosai annai* [Introduction of relationship]. Tokyo: Banseisya.

Yamamoto, N. (1994). *Jyukunen no sei* [Sex of middle-aged people]. Tokyo: Otsuki Syoten.

Yanagida, K. (Ed.). (1995). *Do jidai non-fiction sensyu. Kokusaika no senrei* [Nonfiction selection of modern society. Exposure to internationalization]. Tokyo: Bungei Syunjyu.

Yashiro, M. (1994). *Kekkon no keizai gaku* [Eonomy of marriage]. Tokyo: Futami-shobo.

Yoneyama, Y. (1988). *Syukyo jidai* [Religious era]. Tokyo: Syobunsya.

Yoshida, S. (Ed.). (1993). *Sono shinri to gakko no byori* [The mind and school's illness]. Tokyo: Kobunsya.

Yoshihiro, K. (1994). *Sexless couples*. Tokyo: NHK Shuppan.

Yoshikawa, S. (Ed.). (1996). *Kekkon* [Marriage]. Tokyo: Tokyo Daigaku Syuppan-kai.

7

Reworking Welfare: Untangling the Web

MARK A. MATTAINI AND
JENNIFER L. MAGNABOSCO

Despite the existing welfare system, one in five American children is growing up in poverty (and nearly half of African-American children are doing so) (U.S. House of Representatives, 1994). We are now at a cultural turning point, a truly dangerous opportunity. A central issue for the health and perhaps the survival of American society is whether we will allow poverty to deepen, or develop a set of cultural practices that will meet the minimum survival and developmental needs of children and families in ways that allow everyone to contribute; whether we advance toward becoming the proverbial village raising our children (Clinton, 1996), or regress to nineteenth-century Social Darwinism. There is no going back, and perhaps that is for the best; we shall see.

While the welfare debates have so far been driven largely by economists and policy analysts, the most difficult questions involved are primarily behavioral and cultural. Behavior analysts and cultural designers, therefore, are in a position to be central players in emerging systems, and perhaps bear some ethical responsibility to embrace that role. Both what we know of behavior, and our growing knowledge regarding acting as scientist-advocates within the political system (Fawcett et al., 1988; Mattaini, 1996a) are certainly critical to poor children and their families, and perhaps to the future of the nation as well.

The welfare system had its roots in the New Deal (and to some extent in the Progressive Era) (Trattner, 1989). Early in the twentieth century, many in society believed that mothers raising their children alone should be assisted to stay at home and care for them, as most middle-class women did at the time. Society has changed, of course, and the notion that anyone—even children—should be entitled to unconditional support has become controversial. The cultural ground is shifting, and this is therefore a challenging historical moment to write about welfare and welfare reform.

With the recent passage of the Personal Responsibility and Work Opportunity Reconciliation Act of 1996, we are entering a period in which every state's system is likely to be somewhat—or very—different from that of any other. The risks are enormous and should not be understated; the opportunities are perhaps substantial. There are only limited hard data currently available to guide many of the policy decisions that are being and will be made for the next several years, and essentially none dealing with shifts of statewide systems (Pear, 1996b). Nonetheless, the science of behavior has much to tell us about what approaches are most promising. We addressed some of these questions in a paper prepared several years ago (Opulente & Mattaini, 1993), when President Clinton began calling for "an end to welfare as we know it." Some useful data are available (e.g., Bloom & Butler, 1995; Ellwood, 1988; Ellwood & Summers, 1986; Gueron, 1995; Katz, 1989), and the interlocking contingencies involved have become increasingly clear.

Most of the recent welfare debates have not really been about data, however, but rather about "values"—basically rules believed by those who hold them to tact the connections among behavior and personal and cultural outcomes. These rules, largely untested by exposure to actual contingencies and meta-contingencies (see terminological note below and Glenn, 1991), are nonetheless strongly supported by particular verbal communities—political cultures—making rational decision making difficult. *Newsweek* columnist Joe Klein, himself no stranger to political rhetoric, states that "political demagoguery—not reality—is what has driven the debate about welfare reform" (Klein, 1996, p. 45).

Herbert J. Gans, the noted sociologist, recently argued that viewing some poor persons as "undeserving" fulfills multiple societal functions (Gans, 1995). Gans suggests that current practices may be selected by such outcomes as supplying moral legitimation for existing structures and institutions, providing jobs for those who work with the poor, forcing the poor out of the labor market, and even shortening their life spans, thus reducing the population of "less desirable" groups. Cultural outcomes like these, rather than those specified by political rules, may sometimes be those that participate in metacontingencies related to welfare reform.

Since rules once established can be remarkably resistant to change, achieving a data-based welfare system is exceptionally difficult. Nevertheless, the outcomes involved may be critical to the survival of our culture, so the issues involved deserve thoughtful analysis. It may be reasonable to begin by suggesting a rule of our own: a society to which everyone contributes is likely to have better overall outcomes than one in which only a portion do so (cf. Mead, 1986; note, however, that we argue that the issues are opportunity and contingencies, not obligation). This was certainly true when society was simpler, and biological selection probably has prepared humans for arrangements in which opportunities to act to obtain valued reinforcers are available (Skinner, 1975/1996). The real issues perhaps revolve around what forms of contribution are valued, and facilitating access to opportunities to make such contributions (by arranging the cultural antecedents and consequences required).

In the material that follows, we begin by outlining central provisions of the recent welfare bill, and a few key facts about welfare, welfare recipients, poverty, and jobs. We then turn to questions regarding the aggregate outcomes toward which welfare reform aims, and the extent to which there are feedback loops between those outcomes and interlocking cultural practices. Existing experiments and proposals focus particularly on two possible routes out of dependency: education and work. We will briefly discuss what is known about the interlocking contingencies involved in each of those routes. Finally, we briefly sketch a new vision, deeply rooted in cultural design, that appears consistent with existing data and that might enhance cultural outcomes.

First, a few brief terminological notes. The terms *incentives* and *coercion* are used extensively in this chapter, despite the imprecision they involve. Those terms can communicate with a wide audience, but it may be useful to clarify their usage here. By an incentive, we mean a reinforcer (of any kind) that participates in a rule like, "If you work every day, you will receive $8 per hour, and child care and medical coverage will be provided as benefits." (While the data suggest that such incentives are effective for many people, some persons lack the extensive rule-governed repertoires on which many welfare reform arrangements rely. We return to this issue below.) Regarding coercion, this chapter relies on Sidman's (1989) definition: "Our use of punishment and the threat of punishment to get others to act as we would like, and to our practice of rewarding people just by letting them escape from our punishments and threats" (p. 1). We will argue below that both data and theory suggest that relying on incentives, not only for welfare recipients but for all actors participating in the interlocking contingencies involved, is likely to produce better aggregate outcomes than relying on coercive strategies. This is not rhetoric, it is science.

The term *contingency* refers to the relationships among behaviors and their antecedents and consequences (Mattaini, 1996b). Such contingencies interlock in complex ways to support cultural practices (behaviors supported by, and transmitted among members and generations of, cultural entities). The term *metacontingency* refers to the connections between cultural practices and their aggregate outcomes (Glenn, 1991). The existence of a metacontingency requires not only that interlocking cultural practices produce such outcomes, but that a feedback loop exists so that those outcomes reciprocally affect the incidence of cultural practices.

THE PERSONAL RESPONSIBILITY AND WORK OPPORTUNITY RECONCILIATION ACT OF 1996 (P.L. 104–193)

The Personal Responsibility and Work Opportunity Reconciliation Act became law in 1996, with some provisions effective almost immediately, and others phasing in over a period of months. It is a complex bill, and many analyses of its provisions and implications (e.g., Center on Budget and Policy Priorities, 1996; National Association of Social Workers, 1996) are partial or still being completed. Readers interested in more specifics than can be provided here may wish to contact the Center on Law and Social Policy in Washington, DC, for the most recent analyses. A few key provisions, however, are important to the discussion in this chapter.

The Aid to Families with Dependent Children (AFDC) program as structured in recent years (DiNitto, 1991), in which families below state-established income levels were entitled to financial assistance, in essence has been discontinued. The program that replaces it provides Temporary Assistance for Needy Families (TANF) block grants to states. States are entitled to money from the federal government under the program (so long as they meet requirements), but the principle of individual entitlements has been eliminated. If a state program runs short of money, there is no longer a guarantee that an eligible person (regardless of age) will receive assistance. Adults in most families will need to work (though the definition of work will be variable) after two years on assistance, and in any case will be ineligible for more than five years of cumulative (lifetime) assistance. These deadlines can be shortened by individual states.

A number of specific provisions apply to particular groups of recipients. Unmarried minor parents must live with an adult and participate in education or training to be eligible for assistance. Recipients must cooperate with efforts to establish paternity of children and assign rights to child support to the state. Persons convicted of drug felonies are ineligible for assistance for life. Most single persons who receive food stamps will be required to work in order to remain eligible for more than 90 days.

There are exceptions and qualifications to some of these provisions, but the above summary captures the general intent of the legislation. A deeply disturbing feature of the legislation, which is not, however, central to this chapter, is the elimination of many benefits for legal residents who are not citizens. (There is some indication—but no assurance—as this is written that these may be eased somewhat in the future.)

Individual states have substantial flexibility within these broad guidelines, and in fact it is in the design of specific state programs that behavior analysts may have the most to contribute. States have substantial leeway in terms of the time limits that are implemented, the persons considered eligible, the level of benefits provided, the amount of support provided for child care and social services. Each state also has very broad flexibility in the way particular programs are designed, whether individualized ''Personal Responsibility Plans'' are developed with each family, whether to allow the drug conviction provision to go into effect, whether to provide additional support if additional children are born, and in numerous other areas.

These and other associated changes, currently being implemented, constitute an enormous social experiment; the aggregate outcomes are unknown and to a considerable extent unpredictable. In designing the emerging systems, policy and cultural analysts have some limited experimental data (see below) to rely on, but many decisions will be based on hypotheses; the science of behavior at least offers some well-established principles that can provide some guidance.

A FEW CRUCIAL FACTS

In 1960, 15% of American children were poor. Now over 20% are. Thirty-six percent of Hispanic children are poor. Forty-four percent of African-American children are poor. Children in families receiving AFDC and food stamps remain roughly 30% below the poverty line (U.S. House of Representatives, 1994). The Congressional Budget Office indicates that the recent changes will reduce assistance to the poor by approximately $55 billion over a six-year period, and the Urban Institute suggests that the severity of child poverty will increase by 20% under this legislation (National Association of Social Workers, 1996). The long-term implications of this deprivation for the nation are enormous; they include deep emotional, personal, and family costs, the vast loss of potential contributions to society, and the resentment and countercontrol that are inevitable under such conditions.

The average welfare mother has less than two children. Monthly AFDC checks under the previous system varied by state; a family of four might receive $660 a month in New York, and only a third as much in Mississippi (Welch, 1996). Most states have made cuts of varying magnitude in recent years, and the number of persons receiving AFDC has declined by about 9% in the past three years, to about 12.8 million persons at present (Pear, 1996a). AFDC in recent years constituted about 1% of the federal budget. (Much of the savings in the current bill comes from eliminating aid to legal residents who are not citizens.) Medicaid, the medical assistance program for the poor, now costs about ten times as much as did the now discontinued AFDC program; long-term care for the indigent elderly accounts for most of the recent dramatic growth in this program (Center on Budget and Policy Priorities, Center for Law and Social Policy, & Children's Defense Fund, 1992).

Given the emphasis placed on work in the recent reforms, it is important to recognize how the overall employment situation may affect persons who are hoping to transition off the welfare rolls. Clearly, there is enormous variability in this factor; in some areas of Wisconsin where early experiments were tried, the economy was expanding rapidly, and employment was often possible (Bloom & Butler, 1995). By contrast, in New York City, where there are nearly half a million adults on welfare, just over 20,000 new jobs are created each year, for many of which few welfare recipients are qualified (Finder, 1996). Gans (1995) suggests that there are six to ten times as many poor, jobless persons as there are vacancies they might fill nationwide.

These facts are important, not because they suggest that the situation is hopeless, but to demonstrate the enormous importance of addressing poverty, the multiple levels at which this needs to happen, and to hint at the tremendous challenges that will be involved in doing so. Simply placing arbitrary time limits on benefits is no more likely to be effective under such circumstances than is setting arbitrary academic "standards" within the educational system. What is required in either case is the confluence of the necessary resources and the necessary technologies for achieving desired outcomes.

CAN BEHAVIOR ANALYSIS AND CULTURAL DESIGN HELP?

Behavior analysts may be able to contribute to the design of adequate welfare reforms arrangements on at least two levels: assisting in the analysis and design of welfare programs, and assisting in the analysis and design of interlocking webs of contingencies required to establish and maintain such programs. As is described below, participation in educational and work-related activities can be encouraged by arranging appropriate antecedents and consequences. While this argument has been made in more detail elsewhere (Opulente & Mattaini, 1993), both theory and the existing experimental data (see below) suggest that programs that provide genuine incentives for working or going to school are likely to succeed, while those that are rooted in coercion are likely to lead to, at best, short-lived success, countercontrol, and emotional side effects (Biglan, 1995; Sidman, 1989). The data we have available suggest that these basic behavioral principles are as applicable in this area as in any other; people respond to meaningful incentives, while sanctions may save money in the short term, but do not produce long-term employment or adequate support for children and families.

Several specific programs developed by behavior analysts can contribute in significant ways. For example, job-finding clubs, developed as one component of the Community-Reinforcement Approach to substance abuse (Hunt & Azrin, 1973; Meyers & Smith, 1995), have been widely used in pilot projects to move welfare recipients toward employment. Similarly, a quite successful experiment in which community members received a fee for sharing information about available positions for which program participants could be hired may be an example that could be widely emulated (Jones & Azrin, 1973). However, such efforts by themselves do not increase the available pool of jobs. The rate of employment for program participants, therefore, could increase at the expense of other low-income persons, unless steps are also taken to increase total employment opportunities. Cultural designers, in some cases in collaboration with economists, may be in a position to begin an analysis of the required contingency interlocks to do so.

Not everyone can work in the competitive economy or complete school; we return to this issue below. But for those who can, education and work are the two most promising routes out of poverty (and off welfare) (Gueron, 1995; Opulente and Mattaini, 1993). The analysis that follows for each of these two

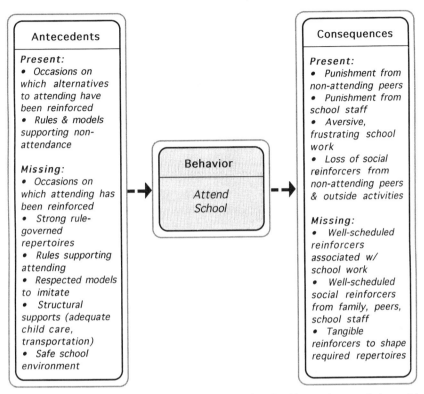

Figure 7.1. Common antecedents and consequences involved in contingent relations with school attendance for many young persons living in poverty. Multiple classes of antecedents (occasions, establishing operations, structural antecedents, rules, and models) and consequences (reinforcers and punishers) are listed together for simplicity of presentation.

behavior classes demonstrates that both are promising for some persons, but neither is easy to arrange for everyone.

EDUCATION AS A WAY OUT OF POVERTY

Education for the parent is commonly viewed as a hopeful way out of poverty for children in welfare families and particularly for the teenage welfare mothers. The contingencies supporting school attendance for many of these individuals, however, are quite weak, as shown in Figure 7.1. This simplified contingency diagram portrays the antecedents and consequences associated with school attendance for many young people, including young welfare mothers (Anderson, 1990; Mattaini, 1995). Attending school produces multiple concurrent consequences, including social aversives and, often, school work for which the young person is ill-prepared, and therefore produces frustration rather than reinforcement and the loss of social reinforcement from nonattending peers. Attending also produces, at best, limited social reinforcement from family, peers, or teachers for many young people. Rule-governed repertoires are sometimes weak, making working toward distant and uncertain reinforcers difficult. Existing rules and available models may in fact suggest that going to school produces few significant payoffs. The competing contingencies for young mothers, in particular, are often daunting. Many other cultural practices, in the school, the family, the peer culture, and even the media clearly interlock with school attendance, but few support it.

Current programs have not focused in any coherent way on changing the supporting practices. One approach, well-tested in Wisconsin and elsewhere, is "learnfare"—if kids do not go to school, the family's welfare check is cut. The evidence is now incontrovertible that learnfare is ineffective in increasing attendance (Johnson, 1996). This is not surprising. This approach does not address the existing contingencies as portrayed in Figure 7.1, but rather attempts to overlay a modest rule-governed analogue to a response-cost contingency on the existing situation. The procedure is coercive, the outcomes are cumulative and delayed, the person whose behavior is targeted for change (the child) is often not involved in the contingency, and reinforcers for alternatives remain unchanged. If learnfare doesn't work, why is it still being used and expanded? Perhaps because one outcome valued by many, saving the money that would otherwise go to the family, does participate in a metacontingency. Certainly the arrangement is consistent with the values—rules—of some political actors.

President Clinton recently spoke in support of an expansion of the Learning, Earning and Parenting (LEAP) program in Ohio, in which the checks for young welfare mothers who attend school are increased by $62 per month, while the checks of those who do not are cut by the same amount (Mitchell, 1996). The LEAP program has been widely lauded, since about 20% of young welfare mothers in the program, who would otherwise be expected to drop out, stay in school. Note, however, that the other 80% of teen mothers, and their children, simply have less to support themselves on, deepening poverty for most (DeParle, 1993).

This experiment to keep young welfare mothers in school is often described as encouraging, and the fact that even a poorly designed incentive arrangement may be of some value is important data. The magnitude of the effect, however, is not large. In the experimental group, 46% completed high school or a GED, as compared with 39% in the control group. Fifty-four percent of the experimental group, therefore, and 61% of the control group, did not complete even the very minimal requirements for a GED (Mitchell, 1996). This is far from universal success. Why is the LEAP program not more effective? The size and scheduling of the incentive are probably not optimal, and none of the other contingencies in place are affected by the program (Figure 7.1). What is perhaps frustrating is that in the current environment, it is difficult to implement an approach that relies on incentives, without a coercive component, even though this would probably be far more effective (Sidman, 1989).

Looking back at Figure 7.1, addressing the missing and competing contingencies is likely to produce better outcomes. For example, behavior analysts know a great deal about how to target educational programs at the right level, and how to arrange contingencies for learning (Greer, 1996). Work to change the rules within, and models and consequences provided by, cultural entities (families, peer groups) within which the child is embedded will be challenging, but it is likely to produce the most stable outcomes if changes can be achieved. Additional incentives, including money but also discount coupons for favorite fast-food restaurants, movies, or other desirable reinforcers, could be designed so that they are paid frequently and are of adequate magnitude.

Arrangements in which the equivalent of "lottery tickets"—chances to win larger awards—are offered may be of particular value. For example, through the efforts of the Renaissance Education Foundation, Toledo High School formed a partnership with a local McDonald's restaurant, in which attendance and achievement were reinforced with popular food items, as well as chances for larger prizes. The program improved attendance and achievement significantly, and no coercive component was required (Damico, 1992).

WORK AS A WAY OUT OF WELFARE

While education is critical to long-term life success, the primary focus of current welfare programs is on work. (In some cases this is short-sighted, of course; the new welfare legislation encourages recipients to take unskilled and unstable jobs, but does not support efforts to complete higher education.) Despite extensive political rhetoric suggesting that welfare recipients must be coerced to act more responsibly, the existing data indicate that if adequate jobs are available for which people have the skills, and if the necessary supports so people can take advantage of those jobs are in place, most people prefer to work (DeParle, 1992; Sack, 1992). Every welfare experiment suggests this is true; most people do not want to be on welfare (no doubt in part because there are many aversives associated with the system). The practice diagram in Figure 7.2 shows some of the necessary antecedents and consequences for "working" (which is actually a complex set of interlocking behaviors).

Nearly all of the required antecedents and consequences depicted are themselves cultural practices embedded in their own interlocking matrices of antecedents and consequences. For example, a business must make available a paying position, but businesspersons will hire only if doing so produces improved outcomes for themselves (and generally the organization). A child care provider must care for the children, but will do so only if the aggregate incentives from the parent and subsidizing agencies are large enough. Subsidies in turn will be provided only if doing so produces improved outcomes for the actors within the subsidizing organization, and so forth. There is no magic whatever here, just the basic principles of the science of behavior. If we provide the incentives required at each interlocking link of the web to arrange the contingencies effectively, people will work. Unfortunately, at the present time many

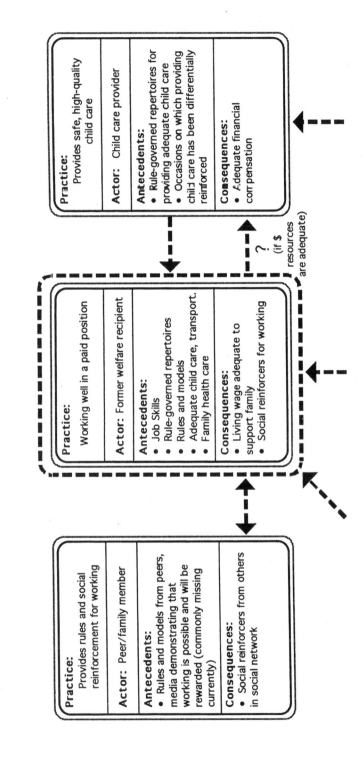

Practice:
Provides safe, high-quality child care

Actor: Child care provider

Antecedents:
• Rule-governed repertoires for providing adequate child care
• Occasions on which providing child care has been differentially reinforced

Consequences:
• Adequate financial compensation

Practice:
Working well in a paid position

Actor: Former welfare recipient

Antecedents:
• Job Skills
• Rule-governed repertoires
• Rules and models
• Adequate child care, transport.
• Family health care

Consequences:
• Living wage adequate to support family
• Social reinforcers for working

Practice:
Provides rules and social reinforcement for working

Actor: Peer/family member

Antecedents:
• Rules and models from peers, media demonstrating that working is possible and will be rewarded (commonly missing currently)

Consequences:
• Social reinforcers from others in social network

?
(if $ resources are adequate)

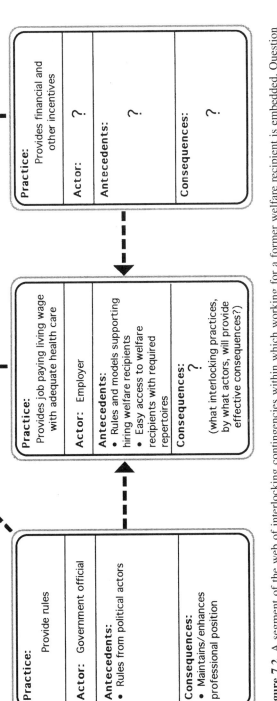

Figure 7.2. A segment of the web of interlocking contingencies within which working for a former welfare recipient is embedded. Question marks indicate essential antecedents and consequences for which a source does not currently appear to be available.

of the contingencies depicted in the figure are not present for many welfare recipients. While some (like government officials simply providing rules) are relatively easy to establish, others are very challenging.

As mentioned above, the availability of jobs for which the poor have the skills is a major issue. The actual jobless rate in this country (counting those who have given up looking) is about 15% (Gans, 1995), and it is higher in impoverished areas. Other necessary antecedents for working are also commonly missing. According to estimates from the Congressional Budget Office, there will be nearly a $14 billion shortfall in funds required to provide the child care and employment supports needed to meet employment goals over the next six years (National Association of Social Workers, 1996). Some have suggested that "workfare" programs, in which people perform some form of public service, are one way to begin to shape repertoires consistent with work. These programs have proven disappointing, however, in moving recipients into regular, paid employment; less than one-tenth of those who have participated in the New York City workfare program, for example, have reported that they have found (much less kept) regular jobs (Firestone, 1996).

The new legislation includes time limits for most recipients, both to begin work and to lose benefits completely. Recent experiments in several states may provide some lessons regarding how these may work. Work-based experiments recently conducted in several states were typically linked with time limits. Some experiments, like one in Vermont, ensured a public service job at the expiration of the time limit (30 months) (Bloom & Butler, 1995). In Wisconsin, by contrast, financial support basically ends after 24 months (there are exceptions and complexities, but this is the basic plan). There are attractive features in the Wisconsin plan, including an emphasis on helping people find jobs and other alternatives at the front end, so they need not go on welfare, but the underlying premise of the W2—Wisconsin Works—plan appears flawed. Preliminary experiments in the state were conducted in rural counties with booming economies; expansion of essentially the same program to areas with significant joblessness, including Milwaukee, involves a different level of challenge (Bloom & Butler, 1995).

Politically, time-limited programs are attractive, since supporting these plans leads to votes now, while the social disruption that may occur if the number of available jobs does not match the number of applicants is delayed. Will massive public service jobs programs be implemented when recipients begin to reach the time limits and lose benefits? Perhaps, but most policy analysts believe these would be more expensive to administer than the existing welfare system (Eckholm, 1992). In the experiments conducted so far, financial incentives and extensive work-related supports (including, among other things, training, job search, case management, child care, transportation, transitional medical coverage) seem to have been important, but will be limited in the present legislation. According to a study done by the Manpower Demonstration Research Corporation (MDRC), in states where experiments with time limits have begun, many recipients do not understand the details of the time limits and requirements, or see them as being too far off to be concerned about immediately, and staff are often confused and ambivalent themselves (Bloom & Butler, 1995).

The research that has been done in moving people from welfare to work in experimental programs is instructive. A rigorous, three-site evaluation of an intensive Job Opportunities and Basic Skills Training (JOBS) program in Atlanta; Grand Rapids, Michigan; and Riverside, California was recently completed by the MDRC (Freedman & Friedlander, 1995). In one stream of the program, extensive job search support and other resources (child care, transportation, and more) were provided, and the results were seen as very encouraging. But this is what the data showed: 43% of the experimental group were off welfare at the end of two years, versus 32% of the control group—an aggregate impact of 11%. Forty-two percent of the experimental group (versus 34% of the control group) were employed, and 14% (contrasted with 10%) were earning at least $10,000 per year. The average income of the experimental group was slightly although not significantly lower than that of the control group, however, and reached only 71% of the poverty line for a family of three. The children of most of these families were still poor, and most of the participants in both the experimental and the control groups were still on welfare.

These are high-visibility, well-supported experimental programs. The message seems to be that current projects can make a meaningful and socially significant difference, but that effective ways to provide the necessary antecedents and consequences to move *everyone* into employment, even at a poverty level, have yet to be devised. Small incentives appear to make some difference, primarily with those with the strongest existing repertoires. Additional supports and substantial efforts to construct the required repertoires will probably be necessary if other recipients are to work, even if positions are available. The challenges, in other words, are formidable.

A NEW CULTURAL VISION: CONSTRUCTING METACONTINGENCIES

Perhaps the major unrecognized challenges involved in welfare reform are achieving a coherent vision of the desired outcomes and finding ways to link those outcomes to the interlocking practices that produce them. The issues are commonly framed as requiring a choice among three competing goals: (a) protecting poor children, (b) encouraging self-sufficiency among their parents, and (c) saving money. So long as these outcomes are viewed as incompatible, there is only limited hope for designing a set of interlocking contingencies that lead to a stable social order, since shifting political pressures will favor one or another of these outcomes at any one time. A healthy society, of course, requires healthy children, productive adults, and control of social expenses, but the challenge is to develop a set of interlocking contingencies that produce all three. We believe that behavior analysis and cultural design can contribute to a different vision. We begin from the position that a healthy society requires healthy children, and that chronic and severe poverty is generally inconsistent with health. Whatever interlocking practices are constructed, therefore, should ensure that children are not left in abject poverty.

The next step in this alternative vision is to examine the contingencies within which the behaviors in which we are interested occur, and to develop experimental programs that rely on incentives and providing necessary support, rather than on coercion. Incentive-based programs have produced consistently positive, if modest, results, and with better design (to which behavior and cultural analysts could contribute) would probably produce stronger outcomes. There is so far no evidence that coercive strategies can produce either increased school attendance or consistent work, and theory suggests that any positive results they do produce are likely to be unstable. Existing experiments indicate that many welfare recipients will volunteer for programs that rely primarily on even fairly modest incentives. While there may be some initial increased expense, if the programs are successful people will be on welfare for shorter periods, so there should be savings over time.

Small changes in contingencies will probably keep those with the strongest repertoires in school, or move such persons into employment quickly. It may, in fact, be most practical to offer voluntary programs for those individuals, which would quickly reduce the welfare rolls substantially. Assisting those recipients with more significant skills deficits to learn the necessary repertoires and ensuring the availability of jobs for that group will be more expensive propositions, but can be done incrementally. A series of successively more intensive approaches would gradually move higher percentages of recipients into positions where they are self-sufficient and can contribute to society, and may be the most effective design for state programs. It is clear that in an adequate program, very few persons would ever reach the established time limits. In fact, for well-designed programs, time limits would be largely irrelevant.

There will always be some persons with very limited capacities whom society will need to subsidize, although nearly everyone can make some contribution (not necessarily through paid employment). If the economy genuinely requires a certain level of structural unemployment, supports for those who do us the favor of being unemployed will always be needed. But perhaps setting the economists, analysts, and policy makers the challenge of devising full-employment arrangements, in which everyone is allowed to make the contributions for which we are biologically and culturally programmed, should be part of an expanded vision.

Behavior analysts could have a role in constructing a better system in at least four ways. First, and very obviously, they could seek to have a voice in the design of incentive arrangements (and minimally coercive alternatives, if necessary), both using what they already know and assisting in the design of experiments to further refine what will work at acceptable cost. No one else is in a better position to contribute to the arrangements of antecedents and consequences, including issues like schedules and magnitudes of reinforcement provided. A task force of behavior analysts in every state could be enormously helpful in refining what will no doubt at first be only very rough approximations to working systems.

Second, behavior and cultural analysts could take actions that make the links between cultural practices and their outcomes clear to policy makers and the general public, and thus aid in constructing the feedback loops necessary to a metacontingency. Constructing widely used indices that balance adequate support for children, adequate levels of employment, and reasonable state expenditures is important in order to clarify the aggregate outcomes being produced. Behavior analysts might collaborate with economists and policy makers on construction of the indices, but even more important, in designing approaches for ensuring that changes in the indices function as effective establishing operations for political actors (legislators, administrators, and voters). How to do so is an experimental question, but media efforts aimed at making excellent performance reinforcing to those actors, and poor performance aversive, perhaps involving construction of new equivalence relations or relational frames, would be valuable.

''Consequence analysis'' (Sanford & Fawcett, 1980), a procedure in which members of classes of decision makers are given the opportunity to evaluate multiple consequences of decisions in detail, might also strengthen the links between aggregate outcomes like child poverty and employment and the matrices of interlocking practices constituting the welfare system. A major advantage of consequence analysis is that it does not involve distortion or coercion, but rather tends to lead to more thoughtful analyses.

We cannot afford to give up our commitment to the future of American families and children. ''Untangling the web'' of interlocking contingencies associated with this endeavor can contribute to building a better system for supporting both the working and the nonworking poor. This country can afford to feed, shelter, clothe, and educate our children. And we cannot afford not to.

REFERENCES

Anderson, E. (1990). *Streetwise: Race, class and change in an urban community*. Chicago: University of Chicago Press.

Biglan, A. (1995). *Changing cultural practices: A contextualist framework for intervention research*. Reno, NV: Context Press.

Bloom, D., & Butler, D. (1995). *Implementing time-limited welfare: Early experiences in three states. Report of the Cross-State Study of Time-Limited Welfare*. New York: Manpower Demonstration Research Corporation.

Center on Budget and Policy Priorities. (1996). *The new welfare law*. Washington, DC: Author.

Center on Budget and Policy Priorities, Center for Law and Social Policy, & Children's Defense Fund. (1992, February 21). *Selected background material on welfare programs*. Washington, DC: Authors.

Clinton, H. R. (1996). *It takes a village and other lessons children teach us.* New York: Simon & Schuster.

Damico, M. (1992). Incentives in our schools. *B&IS: Business and Incentive Strategies, 51,* 4–18. (As reported in S. Hersh, 1993, Business incentive program works for students and teachers, *Behavior Analysis Digest, 5 [1]* , pp. 1, 3.)

DeParle, J. (1992, April 22). Welfare plan linked to jobs is paying off, a study shows. *The New York Times,* pp. A1, D25.

————. (1993, April 12). Ohio welfare bonuses keep teen-age mothers in school. *New York Times,* p. A14.

DiNitto, D. M. (1991). *Social welfare politics and public policy.* Englewood Cliffs, NJ: Prentice-Hall.

Eckholm, E. (1992, July 26). Solutions on welfare: They all cost money. *New York Times,* pp. A1, A18.

Ellwood, D. T. (1988). *Poor support: Poverty in the American family.* New York: Basic Books.

Ellwood, D. T., & Summers, L. H. (1986). Poverty in America: Is welfare the answer or the problem? In S. H. Danziger & D. II. Weinberg (Eds.), *Fighting poverty: What works and what doesn't* (pp. 78–105). Cambridge, MA: Harvard University Press.

Fawcett, S. B., Bernstein, G. S., Czyewski, M. J., Greene, B. F., Hannah, G. T., Iwata, B. A., Jason, L. A., Mathews, R. M., Morris, E. K., Otis-Wilborn, A., Seekins, T., & Winett, R. A. (1988). Behavior analysis and public policy. *The Behavior Analyst, 11,* 11–25.

Finder, A. (1996, August 25). Welfare clients outnumber jobs they might fill. *New York Times,* pp. 1, 46.

Firestone, D. (1996, September 9). Workfare cuts costs but tracking new jobs poses problems. *New York Times,* p. B1.

Freedman, S., & Friedlander, D. (1995, September). *The JOBS evaluation: Early findings on program impacts in three sites.* U.S. Department of Health and Human Services, U.S. Department of Education. (Advance Pre-publication Copy, prepared by Manpower Demonstration Research Corporation).

Gans, H. J. (1995). *The war against the poor: The underclass and antipoverty policy.* New York: Basic Books.

Glenn, S. S. (1991). Contingencies and metacontingencies: Relations among behavioral, cultural, and biological evolution. In P. A. Lamal (Ed.), *Behavioral analysis of societies and cultural practices* (pp. 39–73). New York: Hemisphere.

Greer, R. D. (1996). The education crisis. In M. A. Mattaini & B. A. Thyer (Eds.), *Finding solutions to social problems: Behavioral strategies for change* (pp. 113–146). Washington, DC: APA Books.

Gueron, J. M. (1995, Summer). Work programs and welfare reform. *Public Welfare, 53,* 7–16, 40.

Hunt, G. M., & Azrin, N. H. (1973). A community-reinforcement approach to alcoholism. *Behaviour Research & Therapy, 11,* 91–104.

Johnson, D. (1996, May 19). Wisconsin welfare effort on schools is a failure, study says. *New York Times,* p. 20.

Jones, R. T., & Azrin, N. H. (1973). An experimental application of a social reinforcement approach to the problem of job-finding. *Journal of Applied Behavior Analysis, 6,* 345–353.

Katz, M. B. (1989). *The undeserving poor*. New York: Pantheon Books.

Klein, J. (1996, August 12). Monumental callousness. *Newsweek, 128*, p. 45.

Mattaini, M. A. (1995). Contingency diagrams as teaching tools. *The Behavior Analyst, 18*, 93–98.

———. (1996a). "Acting to save the world": The elements of action. In M. A. Mattaini & B. A. Thyer (Eds.), *Finding solutions to social problems: Behavioral strategies for change* (pp. 397–414). Washington, DC: APA Books.

———. (1996b). Public issues, human behavior, and cultural design. In M. A. Mattaini & B. A. Thyer (Eds.), *Finding solutions to social problems: Behavioral strategies for change* (pp. 13–40). Washington, DC: APA Books.

Mead, L. (1986). *Beyond entitlement: The social obligations of citizenship*. New York: Free Press.

Meyers, R. J., & Smith, J. E. (1995). *Clinical guide to alcohol treatment: The community reinforcement approach*. New York: Guilford.

Mitchell, A. (1996, May 5). Clinton tells of plans to keep mothers on welfare in school. *New York Times*, p. 22.

National Association of Social Workers (1996). *Personal Responsibility and Work Opportunity Reconciliation Act of 1996 (H. R. 3734), Public Law 104–193, Summary of provisions*. Washington, DC: Author.

Opulente, M., & Mattaini, M. A. (1993). Toward welfare that works. *Behavior and Social Issues, 3*, 17–34.

Pear, R. (1996a, August 1). Clinton to sign welfare bill that ends U.S. aid guarantee and gives states broad power. *New York Times*, pp. A1, A22.

———. (1996b, September 15). What welfare research? *New York Times*, p. 4:4.

Personal Responsibility and Work Opportunity Reconciliation Act, 110 U.S.C. § 2106. (1996).

Sack, K. (1992, June 11). Welfare experiment showing signs of success. *New York Times*, pp. B1, B4.

Sanford, F. L., & Fawcett, S. B. (1980). Consequence analysis: Its effects on verbal statements about an environmental project. *Journal of Applied Behavior Analysis, 13*, 57–64.

Sidman, M. (1989). *Coercion and its fallout*. Boston: Authors Cooperative.

Skinner, B. F. (1996). The ethics of helping people. In M. A. Mattaini & B. A. Thyer (Eds.), *Finding solutions to social problems: Behavioral strategies for change* (pp. 61–72). Washington, DC: APA Books.

Trattner, W. I. (1989). *From poor law to welfare state: A history of social welfare in America* (4th ed.). New York: Free Press.

U.S. House of Representatives, Committee on Ways and Means. (1994). *1994 Green Book, Overview of Entitlement Programs*. Washington, DC: GPO.

Welch, W. M. (1996, May 29). Shifting welfare to the states. *USA Today*, pp. 1–2.

8

Behavior Analysis and Social Welfare Policy: The Example of Aid to Families with Dependent Children (AFDC)

LARRY NACKERUD, R. JEFFERSON WALLER, KATHERINE WALLER, AND BRUCE A. THYER

> . . . that which should have been for their welfare, let it become a trap.
> Psalms, 69:22

A new era of welfare reform is upon us. On August 22, 1996, President Clinton signed into law the Personal Responsibility and Work Opportunity Reconciliation Act (H.R. 3743). Presidential candidate Bill Clinton had stated in 1992 that he would "end welfare as we know it" (Church, 1996, p. 19), and at first glance it appears as if he may have done so. It was, however, not merely a coincidence that President Clinton signed the new welfare reform legislation on the eve of the Democratic National Convention and the formal beginning of his bid for reelection. While it is clear that this new welfare reform effort is a lot about politics, it is also clear that the primary focus of the new law is on altering the behavior of persons in receipt of public assistance. What may prove to be problematic, however, is that the new welfare law, like many of its predecessors, appears to lack a comprehensive theory of behavior change (Thyer, 1996).

As is typical of past welfare reform efforts, this new effort includes changes in elements of other programs (e.g., Emergency Assistance and JOBS), but focuses primarily on one cash assistance program. That one program, which is the program most people in the country think of when they hear the term "welfare," is Aid to Families with Dependent Children (AFDC) (Ginsberg, 1996). Social welfare programs, like AFDC, and modifications in those programs are designed to change human behavior. As noted by Heffernan (1992, p. 17):

government and private social agencies respond . . . to social welfare problems and that those responses result in . . . *regulation* of behavior of persons and groups. (emphasis in original)

The primary mechanism by which this is accomplished is through the contrived governmental establishment of contingencies of reinforcement and punishment which are intended to reward or deter selected behavior on the part of welfare recipients. Unfortunately, punitive contingencies are more often employed than reinforcing ones.

Behavior analysis, the science of attempting to account for human behavior primarily in terms of contingencies of reinforcement and punishment, among other mechanisms of learning, has been rarely evoked as a viable conceptual framework for designing and implementing social welfare programs. As a result, perverse incentives sometimes reinforce dependent, nonproductive behavior among those receiving welfare benefits and punish efforts at achieving self-sufficiency. In this chapter one major welfare program, AFDC, is examined in detail for illustrations of how contingencies of reinforcement and punishment affect the behavior of recipients. Statements obtained from AFDC legislation, including the most recent Personal Responsibility and Work Opportunity Reconciliation Act, and program policy manuals and anecdotal evidence from actual AFDC recipients and eligibility caseworkers, are used to exemplify how this program can exert deleterious effects on impoverished persons. A behavior analytic perspective is used to develop suggestions to improve the contingencies associated with AFDC, and how such modifications should be pilot tested in real life, small-scale experiments prior to being implemented at the national or state level.

A BRIEF HISTORY OF AFDC

The federalization of mother's or widow's pension laws, established in most of the individual states between 1910 and 1926 (Miller, 1983), laid the foundation for what proved to be one of the more significant parts of the federal Social Security Act of 1935. Title IV of the Social Security Act established Aid to Dependent Children (known now as Aid to Families with Dependent Children, AFDC), as a federal program of cash payments to mothers deprived of their husbands' support. An important holdover from the widow's pension laws was the inclusion of the principle of *adequate aid* for these mothers. It was the provision of adequate aid which was intended to allow/encourage mothers to stay at home and devote themselves to housekeeping and caring for their children (Trattner, 1994). This is one of the earliest examples of a contingency of reinforcement established by the federal government, intended to reward or deter selected behavior on the part of recipients of the cash benefits of AFDC. The AFDC program was started with the intent of reinforcing the behavior of mothers remaining at home with their dependent children.

AFDC was conceived of as a short-term device to assist financially needy children. The program was intended to diminish and eventually become outmoded as more and more families came to qualify for assistance under the social insurance programs of the Social Security Act (DiNitto, 1995). In reality, nothing could be further from the truth. During its 60 years, the number of people receiving AFDC, considered both as total number of recipients and total number of families, has grown dramatically. For example, in the ten-year period between 1968 and 1978, the number of families receiving AFDC doubled (DiNitto, 1995). Between 1965 and 1985, the number of recipients of AFDC increased by 270% (Moffitt, 1992). Although the number of recipients stabilized from the mid-1970s through the 1980s, increases occurred in the early 1990s. In 1992, 13.6 million individuals (4.8 million families) received AFDC, representing just under 5% of the total population. Enrollment figures peaked at over 14 million individuals and 5 million families in the early 1990s. In 1940, AFDC benefit expenditures totaled $134 million; by 1960 they were $1 billion; in 1970 they were $4.9 billion, and by 1980 they had risen to $12.5 billion. In 1990, the total bill for AFDC benefits was $18.5 billion and in 1992 the benefits reached $22 billion (DiNitto, 1995).

Even though AFDC originated in response to a major structural failure, the national economy and the Great Depression, recipients have still often been viewed as characterologically deficient or immoral. If recipients were not immoral they were probably lacking in initiative and receipt of public monies was viewed as only rewarding dependency. Although not in any sort of comprehensive manner, behavioral contingencies intended to reinforce work behavior have always had a part in the AFDC program. In some places, receipt of benefits was not available during harvest times, when such families were expected to work in the fields (an early example of ''workfare''). In some states, surprise visits by eligibility workers into the homes of the recipients were the norm. The visits, sometimes occurring in the night, were conducted to determine whether there was a man living in the house of an AFDC recipient. Not only a husband, but any man, who had a relationship with the recipient was expected to support her and her children (DiNitto, 1995; Miller, 1983).

With the realization that the nature of the AFDC caseload had changed came a new concern over the breakdown of the family and community structures. A study commissioned in 1960 by President Eisenhower stated that AFDC made financial assistance available for the protection and care of 2.34 million homeless, dependent, or neglected children, but also that assistance provision was occurring where a parent was not only dead or physically incapacitated, but also in families where there was desertion, divorce, or indeed, where there was no marriage. More and more poverty theorists came to believe that the AFDC program did little to deal with family or community breakdown and quite possibly, the regulations of AFDC may actually be encouraging families to separate. A large group of current and potential AFDC recipients have found that a mother and father living separately could do better financially than could a family living together. If the parents were separated, AFDC allowed the parent with the child to collect benefits; the family that lived together had less access to public assistance. In 1961, in an effort to address this counterproductive reinforcement of separation of parents, the Kennedy administration led a reform effort which resulted in an amendment to add a provision for unemployed parents to the AFDC program (Berkowitz & McQuaid, 1992).

In 1962, and in another effort to influence the behavior of AFDC recipients, Congress passed public welfare amendments to the Social Security Act that provided federal matching funds to help the states give social services to AFDC recipients. The social welfare lobby, comprised primarily of social workers, convinced Congress that social services would somehow get the welfare recipients off the rolls. The social service movement was built on the notion that people were poor because of some psychological flaw. With social work treatment and social service programs, the dependent could become independent. The provision of social services not only did not serve to decrease the numbers of persons receiving AFDC but shortly thereafter the AFDC rolls started rising (Miller, 1983). To address the problem of possible family breakup caused by AFDC, two changes were made in the AFDC program. In 1961 a new component called the ADC-Unemployed Parent (UP) program was enacted. This component allowed for an unemployed parent, most often the father or another man, to be present in the home and AFDC receipt to continue. In 1962 the program name, Aid to Dependent Children, was officially changed to Aid to Families with Dependent Children (DiNitto, 1995).

The original AFDC program was designed in an era when the preference for mothers to stay at home to care for their children was strong. Requiring mothers to work or forcing fathers to pay child support had not yet been strongly considered. "Rehabilitating" AFDC recipients had been tried, but as AFDC rolls continued to grow, Americans became less inclined to provide cash assistance to those who seemed capable of working. The focus shifted to decreasing welfare dependency through more incentives and tougher requirements to work (DiNitto, 1995; Moffitt, 1992). In 1967, Congress passed a new set of amendments which tied continued receipt of AFDC benefits to employment-related activities. Under the Work Incentive Program, or WIN, all able-bodied adults were given the opportunity to acquire vocational skills and work experience. But not much happened (Berkowitz & McQuaid, 1992).

In the early 1970s income maintenance and social services became distinctly separated from one another in the social welfare system. The notion that dependency was caused by receipt of AFDC benefits and could be altered by the provision of social services was weakened. The ideology that welfare was an entitlement right was strengthened. In 1969, additional work incentives were built into the AFDC program. Previous to this time, a recipient's grant was reduced, dollar for dollar, by any amount earned. New legislation also provided for deductibles for child care and work expenses (Miller, 1983). This benefit-reduction rate (BRR) has been altered a number of times in the history of the

AFDC program. For example, the nominal BRR was 100% until 1967, when Congress lowered it to 67% to theoretically provide incentives to AFDC recipients. Congress increased the BRR again to 100% in 1981 (Moffitt, 1992). The BRR has also been the focus of much debate in regard to whether it created an incentive to work or failed to overcome the presumed disincentives to work for AFDC participants. Congress passed the Talmadge Amendments in 1971 and then all able-bodied AFDC recipients without responsibilities for children under age six were required to register for WIN services, and program administrators were required to spend one-third of their budgets on subsidized training and employment. The trouble was that employment was in short supply, particularly for single mothers without a high school diploma. Again, nothing much happened (Berkowitz & McQuaid, 1992).

In 1975, President Ford's administration could find little to say that was positive about the WIN program. The data for fiscal year 1974 showed that while 1,811,466 people registered for WIN, only 534,885 people reached the stage of program participant, only 177,271 obtained employment, and only 51,627 left welfare! The WIN program was a flop, as was President Nixon's previous attempt at consolidating the nation's many assistance programs into a guaranteed annual income program, the Family Assistance Plan. Nixon's, as well as Ford's and Carter's, "negative income tax" proposals to reform welfare were based on the concept of economic efficiencies. The major form of efficiency centered on building work incentive into welfare programs. The basic insight came from what economists called the theory of labor supply. According to this theory, a person faced a choice between work and leisure. If she were given money not to work, she might well prefer leisure over working, providing the financial sacrifice was not too great. Welfare represented money that was paid to people who agreed not to work. If a person decided to go to work anyway, she often found her welfare grant reduced by the amount of her wages. Under such a system work was not reinforced. In the economists' jargon, the marginal tax on welfare recipients' earnings was too high. The solution, then, was to lower the marginal tax rate and in that manner encourage a welfare recipient to work. As a form of guaranteed annual income and in place of AFDC, there would be a minimum cash payment to all families with dependent children (Berkowitz & McQuaid, 1992).

The explicit requirements that AFDC mothers should work started in earnest with the Omnibus Budget Reconciliation Act (OBRA) of 1981. Under OBRA states were allowed to develop a variety of programs to mobilize AFDC mothers to work. Work supplementation and community work-experience programs were the two most common responses by states. The Job Opportunities and Skills Training (JOBS) program, as the centerpiece of the Family Support Act, followed in 1988. JOBS required nonexempt AFDC mothers to participate in education and job training programs and to look for jobs as long as day care is available. As a transitional feature, JOBS provided day care and medical care for one year after AFDC benefits ended (Ozawa, 1994).

Similar to welfare reform efforts in other periods of history, the Clinton administration's efforts at welfare reform during 1992–1996 tended to focus on two elements; (a) work requirements, and (b) sanctions of women's reproductive behavior while on AFDC. A two-year limit on benefits, family caps (like the one instituted in New Jersey), and workfare programs (like the one instituted in Wisconsin) were the most popular forms of waivers and experiments tried by states. The two-year limit and the workfare programs included the assumption that the majority of single mothers with children and on AFDC could work. However, critics of workfare plans argue that such an assumption is unrealistic. For instance, among the general population of married women with preschool children, 40% are out of the labor force, and of all women who work, only two out of three work full-time. Thus one can infer that fewer than four out of every ten married mothers with children work full-time. It is difficult to expect that low-income single mothers will behave much differently. Furthermore, if single mothers have health problems or if their children are disabled, these mothers' earnings capabilities decline drastically. Because AFDC mothers are a diverse group, the universal application of the two-year limit for the receipt of benefits may be an inappropriate public policy. Without the imposition of the two-year limit rule, 48% of AFDC families are off AFDC within two years, and only 17% stay on AFDC eight years or longer. The rest, 35%, leave AFDC within three to seven years (Ozawa, 1994). Jencks and Edin (1995) state the issue more directly when they discuss whether poor women have the right to bear children and how AFDC reform efforts often mistakenly assume they do not. They contend that if a mother wants to stay off welfare, the most important issue is that she has to find a husband who can pull his weight economically. Marrying a man with an unstable work history or low wages is not a good formula for avoiding welfare (Jencks & Edin, 1995). Put another way, female headship of families is increasing because men are losing their relative economic advantage as breadwinners. Divorce may push some women into poverty and thus force them to depend on AFDC as a transitional measure, but these women's quest for economic self-sufficiency need not be questioned (Ozawa, 1994).

One of the problems is that we cannot predict in advance which children might eventually need welfare. Nearly half the children on AFDC in any given month were born to parents who were married at the time of birth. Also, while it may be possible to get the poor to delay childbearing for a few years by making the economic or social contingencies of contraception more reinforcing, and having children more punishing, it is hard to imagine that many poor women would voluntarily go to their graves childless. The alternative of a lifetime of minimum wage work is not likely to be effective. Adults are usually poor because their services are of little value to employers (Jencks & Edin, 1995).

Earning a general equivalency diploma and short-term job training seem to have little impact on the ability of a poor woman or man to earn enough to stay off AFDC. More important to an inability to get off or stay off AFDC are the difficulties of securing affordable day care and the unavailability of health insurance while employed in a minimum wage job. Single mothers who earn $5.00 an hour cannot afford to pay market rates for child care. At present, therefore, those who cannot persuade a relative to watch their children or find subsidized child care seldom work. That is a main difference between AFDC recipients and single mothers in low-wage jobs, many of whom get either free or very cheap child care from their relatives (Jencks & Edin, 1995).

AFDC OFTEN REINFORCES DEPENDENCY AND PUNISHES EMPLOYMENT

A major concern is the high number of individuals and families in receipt of AFDC. An additional concern, however, is the implication that long-term welfare "dependency," work disincentives (Moffitt, 1992), female-headed households, and children being born to unmarried teenagers are so closely associated with AFDC (Ozawa, 1988). Moffitt (1992) conducted an extensive analysis of the reinforcing contingencies of the U.S. welfare system. He concluded that because the benefits are primarily paid to female heads of households with children, but with no spouse present, AFDC encourages the delay of marriage, increases divorce/marital dissolution, delays *re*marriage, and reinforces having children outside of a marital union. The cumulative effect is to lower the percentage of the population that is married.

In his book *Losing Ground*, Charles Murray (1984) coalesced the sentiments of AFDC critics by arguing that receipt of AFDC exacerbates poverty by encouraging the poor to leave the work force, to become dependent on federal aid, and to have numerous out-of-wedlock children. His recommended solution was, and continues to be, to abolish welfare (Murray, 1994). Other sociologists, economists, and poverty theorists agree with Murray that overly generous means-tested programs, like AFDC, increase poverty by encouraging female headship of families and welfare dependency. The questions they raise are: Do poor women have children to receive AFDC? Does welfare provision to the nonelderly discourage work and encourage dependency (Sanders, 1991)?

THE IMPACT OF AFDC ON BEHAVIOR

The goal of social welfare policy, in this instance AFDC policy, is to shape, reinforce, or punish the behavior of individuals or groups within the jurisdiction under which those policies were enacted. With that understanding, it is possible to evaluate the impact of specific policy components using empirical data that are available about the behavior of organisms, make some predictions about the outcomes of those policies, and identify reasons that AFDC policy does not impact human behavior in the ways that policy makers originally intended. The following question may occur at this point, "If it is possible to identify policy components that result in behaviors that are diametrically opposed to those that were originally intended, why were the policies enacted as they are written?"

Before proceeding with this analysis, it is incumbent upon us to distinguish between the behaviors of those to whom policy is addressed, and the behaviors of those who are writing the policies. While the principles of reinforcement apply to both groups, the contingencies that shape the behaviors of the policy makers are entirely different from the contingencies that shape the behaviors of AFDC recipients. The behaviors of policy makers are shaped by such contingencies as favorable publicity, campaign contributions, and reelection to office (e.g., Lamal & Greenspoon, 1992). Their behaviors are not necessarily shaped by possessing a current knowledge of the principles of human behavior that facilitate the implementation of effective public policy. The contingencies that shape the behaviors of AFDC recipients are more likely to be subsistence-oriented, where the meeting of basic need is paramount. We will first address principles of learning theory as applied to AFDC recipients.

In order to analyze examples of AFDC policy from a behavior analytic perspective, we must first review the four categories of consequences that may affect behavior. The two primary consequences that affect behavior are punishment and reinforcement. Simply stated, punishing consequences reduce the probability of specific future behavior, and reinforcing consequences increase the probability of specific future behavior. Each of these contingency operations can be dichotomized into positive and negative, thus we have positive or negative reinforcement and positive or negative punishment. A consequence is called "positive" (whether reinforcing or punishing) when it involves *presenting* something, and labeled "negative" when it involves *removing* something (Thyer, 1992).

Carefully examining each of the "rules" described below reveals that the ultimate result of the implemented policy is not to reinforce work behavior, but to punish receiving AFDC. Punishing the reception of AFDC is useless without shaping/reinforcing more adaptive or socially functional behavior to take its place. Here, behavior is like other natural laws in that it abhors a vacuum. As Nietzsche (1956) wrote, "What punishment is able to achieve, both for man and beast, is increase of fear, circumspection, control over the instincts. Thus man is tamed by punishment, but by no means improved; rather the opposite" (p. 216). The behaviors that are more likely to occur as a result of punished AFDC recipient behavior are those that are usually considered abuses of the system because no more functional behavior has replaced them. Skinner (1971) addressed this by explaining, "The trouble is that when we punish a person for behaving badly, we leave it up to him to discover how to behave well" (p. 62). To assert that work is its own reward or that work behavior should preempt AFDC reception is naive. The contingencies that shape productive employment are, for many people, such things as attaining or maintaining a standard of living, being protected by benefits such as insurance, recognition for accomplishments, and interaction with people with similar vocational interests. AFDC recipients are not likely to obtain work that provides such benefits.

This argument might reasonably be challenged on the basis that the behavior of adults is not considered to be contingency shaped, but is viewed as *rule-*

governed behavior. Rule-governed behavior is the more complex learning that takes place with the acquisition of verbal language. Behavior is then shaped through the reinforcing or punishing effects of rules rather than being contingency shaped. However, this does not weaken the position outlined above. If a person's most basic needs are met through predominantly one source (e.g., AFDC) then rule-following behavior (e.g., get a job), having not been reinforced, is less likely to occur.

Beyond this, though, is that AFDC eligibility workers speak of a "culture" among the long-term recipients of AFDC. They use this term to refer to those who have been recipients for so long or who have been involved in intergenerational poverty (and subsequent assistance) for so long that the receipt of AFDC is seen as a right and a way of life (Sanders, 1991). The client receiving AFDC sees the reduction or loss of benefits as punishment.

People tend to acclimate to their circumstances, and most will find reinforcing contingencies in some aspect of their existence, no matter how dire the situation, which is to say that people adapt to their environments. Even though a person receiving AFDC may be living on an entitlement that provides only minimal subsistence, many will adapt to their situation and, if not exactly flourish, find contentment as did the Apostle Paul when he said, "I know what it is to be in need, and I know what it is to have plenty. I have learned the secret of being content in any and every situation, whether well fed or hungry, whether living in plenty or in want" (Philippians 4:12). For those who have found contentment, or who have found reinforcing contingencies in their reception of AFDC (the issue of attaining employment and having work behavior subsequently strengthened by the reinforcing properties presumed to be inherent in working), there is the behavioral issue of a massive *extinction* process of all the reinforcing contingencies of their former lifestyle. Extinction occurs when the contingencies reinforcing a behavioral repertoire (e.g., remaining consistently employed) are removed, and the strength of that behavior subsequently declines. Just as a grieving spouse does not revel in the reinforcing possibilities of unfettered frivolity at the death of a partner, and just as a quitting smoker does not delight in the reinforcing consequence of a longer life, the AFDC recipient should not be expected to fall under the sway of the long-term consequences of regular and productive employment. Contingencies that are strongly reinforcing (incentives) would be more likely to facilitate the transition from behaviors conducive to AFDC receipt to behaviors conducive to self-supporting work. AFDC policy, as written in the state of Georgia, does not provide these contingencies. Below, we delineate specific examples of AFDC policy and discuss plausible results of these policies.

SOME ILLUSTRATIONS FROM THE GEORGIA AFDC PROGRAM

A family that receives AFDC does so because the children are deprived of the care and support of one or both parents. A child could be deprived if a parent is unemployed, disabled, or deceased. Commonly, deprivation is based on the absence of a parent—usually the father. A single mother who receives AFDC because the father is absent from the home risks losing her benefits if she marries a working man. The mother can have a live-in boyfriend whose income does not count in the AFDC case, but if they marry, a portion of his income would be calculated in her AFDC case, even if he is not the father of any of her children. As long as the couple simply live together without legal marriage, his income is not counted, regardless of the amount. This is a policy issue that is widely discussed, and the results are obvious, regardless of one's knowledge of behavioral principles—marriage is punished. The corollary is that single parenthood is likely to increase. Both these inadvertent consequences of AFDC policies were confirmed in Ozawa's (1988) analysis.

The next example is less widely known and is also more complex. In Georgia, an AFDC recipient who finds employment may continue to receive benefits, depending on the family's total income. When a recipient works, certain deductions are applied to the family's income—deductions that families whose only income is from unearned sources do not experience. If the working recipient's income is below the Gross Income Ceiling (GIC), a budget is calculated each month to determine the recipient's check amount. After all applicable deductions are calculated, the net income is subtracted from the Standard of Need (SON) to determine the check amount. If the net income exceeds the SON, the family is said to be ineligible for cash benefits, and the case type is changed to one of the AFDC-related Medicaid types. The SON and GIC are incremental, based on the number of people in the AFDC family.

All working recipients get a $90 standard work expense deduction. As long as the recipient works, the family will receive the standard work expense deduction each month. In addition, the recipient will receive the 30 1/3 deduction for the first four consecutive months of employment. To calculate the 30 1/3 deduction, subtract the $90 standard work expense deduction, subtract $30, divide the difference by 3, and then subtract the 1/3 from the difference.

Example:	family's total gross income	$420
	standard work expense	−90
		$330
		−30
		$300 × 1/3 = 100
		−100
		$200

In this example, $200 would be counted as the family's net income. After receiving the 30 1/3 deduction for four consecutive months, the 1/3 deduction stops. The family would continue to receive the $30 deduction for up to eight months, as long as the recipient continues to work. Using the above example, the net income for the family would be $300.

The 30 1/3 policy is intended to gradually reduce the AFDC check and has actually been referred to as *shaping*, which refers to gradually changing a response (e.g., obtaining paid work) by the reinforcement of successive approximations to a goal (reducing AFDC benefits to the point of elimination). Often, however, the recipient is no longer eligible once the 1/3 deduction is removed. A recipient working at minimum wage for only 30 hours a week, with a household of three persons, would become ineligible for cash benefits when the 1/3 deduction is terminated. The incremental refinement of the response needed for shaping is not accommodated by such a rapid requirement for behavioral change. Moreover, if the recipient quits the job before the end of the four months of the 1/3 deduction, then the next time she finds a job, the 1/3 deduction starts over for up to four consecutive months. Ultimately, this reinforces leaving old jobs for new ones and staying on the AFDC payroll. If this set of rules is confusing to the reader, imagine how it is experienced by AFDC recipients!

Obviously, in the example above, AFDC perpetuates unemployment or underemployment and continued enrollment. As with many other AFDC policies, it is far too complex for any recipients to understand (Moffitt, 1992). This exemplifies the failure of AFDC policies to adhere to the tenets of rule-governed behavior by being so intricate as to preclude understanding.

There are more blatant illustrations of AFDC policies which fail to shape self-supporting work behavior. An AFDC recipient who goes to work can receive assistance with child care services even if she is no longer eligible for an AFDC allotment. If the same recipient also wishes to attend school, her child care services are limited to the time she is at work—she must pay the full amount of child care during the period she is in school. If she quits her job and returns to the AFDC rolls, she can then receive child care services to attend school. However, a person with a baccalaureate degree, who can qualify to receive AFDC, cannot receive child care services to work or go to school.

Our final example points to a myth about AFDC recipients and childbearing behaviors. It is widely believed that it is a profitable affair for a woman receiving AFDC to have additional children in order to increase her monthly allotment. In order to address this problem, the state of Georgia instituted a family cap waiver that prevents AFDC recipients from receiving an increase in their monthly allotments due to giving birth to additional children—or so the issue was proposed to the body politic. Although not intended, AFDC policy continues to provide incentives for mothers to have additional children. Ironically, this incentive comes from one of the more politically popular proposals for AFDC recipients—Work First. Georgia has two work programs: Work First and PEACH. In both of these programs, the requirement to work is waived for women with children under three years of age. This is a classic example of good intentions—presumably keeping mothers home with young children—having disastrous social results—the facilitation of birth of additional children out of wedlock without sufficient means of support. Also, while the AFDC monthly allotment does not increase for new recipients, this contingency occurs after the recipient has been on AFDC for 24 continuous months. We are assured by eligibility workers that 24 months is ample time for a recipient to give birth to an additional two children, and that additional births are common during this 24-month period. Note, too, that this requirement is for continuous months—a break in receiving one monthly allotment starts the 24-month clock over. Again, this was indubitably intended by well-meaning policy makers as a transition period, but it has resulted in a reinforcing contingency to have additional children—quickly.

SOME CONSTRUCTIVE SUGGESTIONS

The current zeitgeist of the body politic of the United States appears to be one of attaching characterological blame to AFDC recipients for their position. This view is consistent with contemporary mentalistic explanations of human behavior, with the origin of comportment residing in some unseen metaphysical homomunculus within the individual's mind. These entities have been variously called "character," "traits," "morals," "dispositions," "intentions," and so forth. Although it is tempting to claim that human behavior is the result of internal mechanisms, such claims fail to explain where these traits themselves originate! And of course, it is through an analysis of how our environment and learning history shape up those behaviors we label as "diligence," "hard-workingness," "independence," and the like, that we will ultimately learn to predict and effectively promote such actions.

A further problem of dispositional and attributional accounts is that they usually involve the logical errors of reification and circular reasoning. If the only evidence for the existence of the character trait called "apathy" is the fact that an AFDC recipient does not do much to find employment, then labeling the lack of employment-seeking behavior as apathetic represents reification, wherein the only evidence for the existence of a mentalistic construct is the very behavior the construct/trait is said to cause. When reified traits are invoked as causal agents, then circular reasoning occurs. If Mrs. Jones does not do much except collect her AFDC checks, she might be called "apathetic" (privately) by her caseworker. If her inertia is then said to be *caused* by apathy, apparent (but not) real closure is achieved in explaining apathetic behavior. How do we know she is apathetic? She does not do much. Why doesn't she do much? She is apathetic. In such circular accounts, causes and effects are indistinquishable from one another, and end up really explaining nothing. Moreover, dispositional/cognitive accounts tend to discourage more productive enquiry into the contingencies of reinforcement and punishment, which cause *both* feeling apathetic toward obtaining employment *and* actively seeking work.

We need, as a society and as governmental policy, to move away from ascribing the effects of extinction and punishment to the "characters" of welfare recipients. Characters, unlike the goddess Athena, do not spring forth fully formed from the forehead of Zeus. Those behaviors which we consider evidence of character are the result of a lifelong interaction of one's genetic endowment, infant and childhood learning experiences, family and community culture, and larger system influences. Good character (i.e., behavior) comes from *somewhere*. Figuring out where and what that somewhere is is the task of behavior analysis.

Some steps are being taken in this direction. President Clinton reprised a famous line of his 1992 campaign when referring to the new welfare reform bill, that "a long time ago I concluded that the current welfare system undermines the basic values of work, responsibility, and family, trapping generation after generation in dependency" (cf. Church, 1996, p. 20). The new welfare reform effort includes four major changes in the AFDC program. The four major changes include: (1) the elimination of the individual's federally mandated legal entitlement to social benefits, (2) a change from formula to block grant funding, (3) the inclusion of time limits, and (4) work requirements (Summary of Provisions, 1996). Implicit in the programmatic changes is the notion that behavioral changes on the part of AFDC recipients are imminent, brought about by altering contingencies of reinforcement and punishment.

A behavior analytic perspective is needed to develop suggestions to improve the contingencies associated with AFDC. An important component to the behavior analytic perspective is adequate outcome research. Any proposed modifications of the AFDC program should be pilot tested in real life, small-scale experiments and evaluated for their behavioral outcomes, prior to being implemented at the national or state level. We recommend that pilot tests on policy implementations be rigorous, empirical studies conducted with strict adherence to methodological concerns. An AFDC eligibility worker in a rural Georgian Department of Family and Children Services explained to us that the family cap waiver discussed earlier was an experiment that was being conducted by the state. Eligibility workers were instructed to systematically sample AFDC applicants and fail to inform the control group that they would not receive an increase in their AFDC allotment if they bear additional children. However, due to overwhelming work demands on the eligibility workers, they report that the eligibility workers did not have time to participate appropriately. Instead, the eligibility workers routinely informed each applicant of the family cap waiver requirements, effectively rendering as useless any conclusions formed as a result of this experiment.

Another suggestion is that adherence to empirically derived methods of behavioral change be observed during AFDC policy construction and implementation. For example, we have demonstrated that the complexity of AFDC policy (e.g., benefit reduction rate) is often so great that the majority of recipients could not possibly understand it. If AFDC recipients are being asked to exchange work for welfare, then the principles of rule-governed behavior demand that recipients first be able to comprehend the rules. Otherwise, desired behavioral change is unlikely. An additional concern is that behavioral change on the part of AFDC recipients is a gradual process, and requiring drastic changes without appropriately incremental reinforcers is empirically and practically untenable. AFDC policy needs to incorporate immediately reinforcing contingencies that will facilitate shaping long-term goals such as self-supporting work. Without strong, incremental reinforcers, shaping cannot occur, and eliminating recipients' dependence on AFDC is unlikely to be achieved.

Next, the issues of education and training need to be addressed from a behavior analytic perspective. It has been shown that small, short-term training programs do not result in AFDC recipients obtaining employment that is meaningful to them or that such training enables them to engage in self-supporting work behavior. AFDC policy, as written, reinforces underemployment and remaining enrolled in assistance programs. If AFDC-receiving behavior is to be extinguished then education and training must help recipients to achieve a level of employment that will provide them with the same contingencies for work behavior that the majority of the American electorate receives from working—adequate food, housing, and health care for themselves and their families. It is important to remember that issues of basic subsistence such as food and housing result in direct contingency-shaped behavior, but we aspire to AFDC recipients being able to move into employment situations that provide contingencies that shape work-sustaining behavior such as collegial interaction, recognition for a job well done, and hope for the future.

In addition, exemptions to the rules of AFDC implementation must be scrutinized closely for possible adverse behavioral outcomes. We have shown that past exemptions written into AFDC policy may have provided incentives for increased childbearing on the part of AFDC mothers, contrary to the idealized outcomes. A summary of provisions provided by the Office of the Assistant Secretary for Planning and Evaluation of the Department of Health and Human Services for the new welfare reform act includes two noted exemptions. Single parents of children below the age of six who cannot find child care cannot be penalized for failure to meet work requirements. States may also exempt from the work requirement single parents with children under age one (Summary of Provisions, 1996). We suggest that, rather than allowing exemptions that preclude recipients engaging in the target behavior, AFDC policy make provisions that support engaging in the target behavior. For example, making sure that child care is available for single parents with young children will allow shaping and operant conditioning to occur.

These ideas are not particularly new (e.g., DiGiacomo, 1977; MacLean, 1977; Presthus, 1965; Thyer, 1996); however, they are not widely disseminated and have not been significantly adopted on any but the most casual, commonsense basis. Social work and psychology share a commitment toward undergirding interpersonal and societal interventions on a foundation of sound, empirical research. Almost 60 years ago it was claimed:

The new sciences afford us a better understanding of *causes and consequences* in human affairs. It remains only to continue our research and apply sensibly the knowledge we already have. (Kelso, 1928, p. 421, emphasis added)

Perhaps it is time to apply the science of behavior analysis more effectively to the design and evaluation of social welfare policies, toward the betterment of society.

REFERENCES

Berkowitz, E., & McQuaid, K. (1992). *Creating the welfare state: The political economy of twentieth-century reform* (rev. ed.). Lawrence, KS: University Press of Kansas.

Church, G. J. (1996, August 12). Ripping up welfare. *Time, 148 (8)*, 18–22.

DiGiacomo, R. (1977). Behavior modification: Toward the understanding and reform of welfare policy. *Corrective and Social Psychiatry 23*, 101–110.

DiNitto, D. M. (1995). *Social welfare: Politics and public policy* (4th ed.). Boston: Allyn & Bacon.

Ginsberg, L. (1996). *Understanding social problems, policies, and programs* (2nd ed.). Columbia: University of South Carolina Press.

Heffernan, W. J. (1992). *Social welfare policy*. New York: Longman.

Jencks, C., & Edin, K. (1995, Winter). Do poor women have a right to bear children? *American Prospect, 20*, 43–53.

Kelso, R. W. (1928). *The science of public welfare*. New York: Holt.

Lamal, P. A., & Greenspoon, J. (1992). Congressional metacontingencies. *Behavior and Social Issues, 2*, 71–81.

MacLean, M. E. (1977). Learning theory and chronic welfare dependency. *Behavior Therapy, 8*, 255–259.

Miller, D. C. (1983). AFDC: Mapping a strategy for tomorrow. *Social Service Review, 57*, 599–613.

Moffitt, R. (1992). Incentive effects of the U.S. welfare system: A review. *Journal of Economic Literature, 30*, 1–61.

Murray. C. (1984). *Losing ground: American social policy, 1950–1980*. New York: Basic Books.

———. (1994, June). Dethroning the welfare queen: The rhetoric of reform. *Harvard Law Review, 107*, 2013–2030.

Nietzsche, F. (1956). *The genealogy of morals*. New York: Doubleday.

Ozawa, M. N. (1988). Welfare policies and illegitimate birth rates among adolescents: Analysis of state by state data. *Social Work Research and Abstracts, 25 (1)*, 5–11.

———. (1994). Women, children, and welfare reform. *Affilia, 9*, 338–359.

Presthus, R. (1965). *Behavioral approaches to public administration*. University: University of Alabama Press.

Sanders, J. M. (1991). ''New'' structural poverty. *Sociological Quarterly, 32*, 179–199.

Skinner, B. F. (1971). *Beyond freedom and dignity*. New York: Vintage Books.

Summary of Provisions: Personal Responsibility and Work Opportunity Reconciliation Act of 1996 (H.R. 3734). (1996, September). Prepared by the Office of the Assistant Secretary for Planning & Evaluation. Washington, DC: GPO.

Thyer, B. A. (1992). A behavioral perspective on human development. In M. Bloom (Ed.), *Changing lives: Studies in human development and professional helping* (pp. 410–418). Columbia: University of South Carolina Press.

————. (1996). Behavior analysis and social welfare policy. In M. A. Mattaini & B. A. Thyer (Eds.), *Finding solutions to social problems: Behavioral strategies for change* (pp. 41–60). Washington, DC: American Psychological Association.

Trattner, W. I. (1994). *From poor law to welfare state* (5th ed.). New York: Free Press.

9

Improving Childrearing in America's Communities

ANTHONY BIGLAN, CAROL W. METZLER,
ROLLEN C. FOWLER, BARBARA GUNN,
TED K. TAYLOR, JULIE RUSBY, AND BLAIR IRVINE

As we come to the end of the twentieth century, we can see many ways in which the human condition has improved. Advances in medicine and technology have lengthened and enriched the lives of many. Life expectancy for a newborn in the United States has increased more than 25 years since the turn of the century (Johnson & Dailey, 1995). Transportation and communications have changed more in the last 100 years than in all of prior human history.

There have also been significant, though less widely known, advances in the behavioral sciences. In clinical psychology and psychiatry, beneficial treatments have been identified for most of the common difficulties of children and adults. In public health, we have seen the identification of the most significant behavioral risk factors for cancer and cardiovascular disease and substantial reductions in the prevalence of major risk factors. Previously, children with autism or Down's Syndrome often faced short lives in miserable institutions. Their prospects for productive and reinforcing lives in their communities have improved remarkably, thanks in part to research on how to intervene with children with these problems (e.g., Lovaas, 1987) and to significant advances in research on effective teaching (e.g., Becker, 1986). Advances in sociology have helped to pinpoint the major factors contributing to crime (e.g., Sampson & Groves, 1989). In anthropology, a plausible account has emerged of the factors influencing the evolution of cultural practices (Harris, 1989).

Yet despite spectacular scientific advances in the past century, few would express satisfaction with the social conditions of the United States. The rates of violent crime are higher than in most other industrialized countries (Interpol, 1988) and have increased over the past twenty years (United States Bureau of Investigation, 1994), even though the rate of incarceration nearly doubled between 1985 and 1995 ("Oregon, Idaho . . . ," 1996). The proportion of children living in poverty was 21.8% in 1994, 3.5% higher than it had been in 1980 (U.S. Census Bureau, 1995). According to the Department of Health and Human Services, the rate of child abuse in the United States increased by 107% between 1986 and 1993 (Child abuse, neglect rise sharply, 1996). Racism appears to be worse now than it was twenty years ago. Some would argue that science is simply not relevant to the solutions of these complex social problems. Certainly public discussion gives no greater attention to scientific approaches to these problems than to many other nonscientifically based belief systems (Sagan, 1995).

We suggest a more optimistic view. If, despite the scientific achievements of the twentieth century, we find ourselves confronted with substantial and distressing social problems, it may be because science has not yet been brought to bear on them. Although we have made enormous progress in understanding the factors that influence the behavior of individuals, we know much less about how to bring about widespread changes in behavior. We are, however, at a propitious moment. The accumulated knowledge about the behavior of individuals provides the basic building blocks for developing a science for bringing about beneficial changes in cultural practices.

This line of reasoning is particularly applicable to the problems we confront in childrearing. Science has identified many of the family, school, and neighborhood factors that contribute to children's successful development and researchers have developed programs that significantly improve the chances of success for at-risk children. However, we have not yet built upon this knowledge a science of how to improve the *prevalence* of successful children.

The present chapter focuses on how a science for improving childrearing in American communities might go forward. It is offered as an example of one direction the behavioral sciences might take, if behavioral scientists wish to ensure that our knowledge leads to widespread improvements in the human condition.

CHILDREARING AS A SET OF CULTURAL PRACTICES

If we want to increase the proportion of children who are successfully raised, we need a framework that will guide us toward effective action. One thing that behaviorism has taught us is to study the development of behavior in terms of ongoing interactions between organism and environment. The first step, then, would appear to be to enumerate the environments in which children develop and to characterize the optimal conditions in each of those environments. The key environments are families, schools, and peers.

The second step in determining how to increase the proportion of successful children involves ensuring optimal conditions in each of these environments. In other words, what variables influence these settings to be optimal? In this chapter, we will sketch factors that have been identified thus far as important influences on each of these environments.

Our task, however, is not simply to understand how a single child could be well raised, but rather to ensure that the maximum number of children are well raised. Thus, in the third step of our analysis we need to specify the variables that would affect the *prevalence* of beneficial environments for children. The behavioral sciences have made much less progress on this problem. Yet we have accumulated enough knowledge relevant to the first two questions above to make it appropriate to turn some of our resources to this problem. Indeed, increasing the prevalence of beneficial environments may be the next major advance in applied behavioral research on childrearing.

The following sections summarize what is known about problematic and beneficial family, school, and peer environments. Each section then discusses how we might build on existing knowledge in each of these areas in order to increase the prevalence of beneficial family, school, and peer environments. Ultimately, substantial increases in the prevalence of beneficial environments will require changes in the way communities are organized. Therefore, the final section focuses on how community organizations might be influenced to adopt and maintain practices that would benefit children and families.

THE FAMILY ENVIRONMENT

Problematic and Beneficial Practices of Families

Empirical research has identified a number of problematic and beneficial interactions between parent and child that have significant impact on the behavior of the child. First, coercive parent-child interactions have been shown to be a key contributor to the development of antisocial behavior in young children (Patterson, DeBaryshe, & Ramsey, 1989; Patterson, Reid, & Dishion, 1992). Coercion is defined as control of another person through aversive means. Coercive interactions lay the foundation for an escalating cycle of coercive interchanges. The child is positively reinforced for negative or coercive behavior, by getting what he/she wants or by getting attention, or is negatively reinforced, by getting the parent to stop doing something that is aversive. At the same time, the parent is negatively reinforced for his/her coercive behavior, because the crying, whining, or misbehavior temporarily stops (Patterson et al., 1992). Because both parties are reinforced in the exchange, the coercive pattern is maintained.

Patterson et al. (1992) have shown that such coercive interchanges are associated with harsh and inconsistent discipline. Parents who are caught in a coercive cycle with a child are more likely to fail to follow through with mild discipline for minor problem behaviors in order to avoid the child's coercive behavior. When the child's behavior becomes highly aversive, however, they tend to react with explosive and harsh punishment. This pattern of harsh and inconsistent punishment is especially likely to contribute to the development of antisocial behavior in the child, as rules and limits are only intermittently en-

forced. Indeed, there is evidence that children will misbehave in order to pro-
voke a negative but predictable reaction from the parent (Wahler & Dumas,
1986).

On the other hand, when parents respond to their children's misbehavior by
removing all opportunity for positive reinforcement for coercive behavior (by
ignoring whining or tantrums, for instance) and by consistently punishing misbehavior with time-out, removal of privileges, and other mild response-cost alternatives, children show much lower levels of aggression and other misbehavior
(Patterson & Narrett, 1990).

Second, the extent to which the parent and child are involved in prosocial
interactions has also been shown to be an important factor in children's development (Hawkins, Catalano, & Miller, 1992; Patterson et al., 1992). In particular, the degree to which the parent provides positive reinforcement for the
child's positive behavior is an important factor in a child's development of
prosocial skills (Webster-Stratton & Herbert, 1993).

Of particular importance is a parent's involvement in his/her child's intellectual and academic life. Children whose parents track, teach, and provide stimuli
and reinforcement for activities that promote language development, reading,
and numeracy in young children, and in older children, for homework and academic progress, are more likely to succeed in school (Mason & Allen, 1986).
Adams (1990) reported that primary grade children with high and low levels of
language and prereading skills showed marked differences in the average amount
of time per day that their parents spent with them on activities that promote
language development (30 minutes versus 1 minute, respectively).

A third class of parenting behaviors involves direct supervision and monitoring of the child's behavior when the child is away from the parent (Dishion,
1990; Richardson et al., 1989). Monitoring and supervision are a prerequisite
for a parent's ability to provide contingencies for positive and negative behavior. Monitoring allows the parent to provide consequences for the child's behavior when he or she is away from the parent. Research has shown that
children and adolescents who are inadequately monitored are more likely to associate with deviant peers and engage in problem behaviors (Ary et al., in
press; Dishion, 1990). This is especially problematic in early adolescence, as
children naturally come under decreasing control of their parents and increasing
control of peers.

In summary, prosocial involvement, coercive interactions, and monitoring are
three types of parent-child interaction that have an important influence on child
development.

The Context for Problematic and Beneficial Parent-Child Interactions

As critical family practices have been delineated, research has increasingly
turned to the study of the contextual conditions that influence family functioning.

One important contextual factor appears to be family structure. Divorce and single parenthood are harmful to children to the extent that they disrupt family stability and interfere with effective parenting. For example, Capaldi and Patterson (1991) reported that child behavior problems increase with the number of parental transitions (whether divorce or remarriage), suggesting that it is family stability, not simply the presence of two adults, that influences child behavior.

Another contextual factor is the degree of aversive stimulation that parents are receiving from outside the family. For example, mothers who have aversive interactions with people outside the family are more likely to have difficulties in their interactions with their children (Wahler & Dumas, 1987). Economic hardship appears to a particularly harmful form of aversive intrusion. Conger and his colleagues (Conger et al., 1991, Conger et al., 1992; Conger, Patterson, & Ge, 1995) found that family economic difficulties such as low income, unstable work, and indebtedness are associated with more problematic parent-child interactions which are, in turn, associated with child and adolescent behavior problems. On the other hand, social support appears to be an important protective factor for parents, affecting parents' behavior toward their children (Andresen and Telleen, 1992) and buffering the effects of stressful events (Cohen & Wills, 1985; Gottlieb, 1988; Kessler & McLeod, 1985).

Research on social disorganization in neighborhoods suggests that neighborhoods in which there are few formal or informal social connections among neighbors have higher rates of crime (Sampson & Groves, 1989). Socially disorganized neighborhoods may be less likely to have both adequate social support for families and effective supervision of young people.

In sum, optimal parenting practices appear to be more likely in the context of stable families and socially organized neighborhoods in which families receive social support and are exposed to little aversive intrusion from those outside the family, and in which economic hardship is minimized.

Affecting the Prevalence of Good Family Practices

The preceding analysis indicates that if we want to increase the prevalence of successful children, we should attempt to increase the prevalence of parents who are skilled and nurturing, and that skilled and nurturing parents are more likely in supportive contextual conditions. Given this focus, we are interested in *any* variables that would increase the prevalence of effective parenting and optimal family contexts. This approach is the essence of the public health perspective, in which one seeks to affect the incidence or prevalence of a disease or problematic behavior and to identify any ways in which incidence or prevalence can be affected. The public health approach contrasts with, though does not contradict, the usual emphasis on the individual and interventions delivered via clinical means.

It would seem that the first step in affecting the prevalence of nurturing families would be to ensure that effective parenting skills training programs are

widely available. Therefore, in this section, we first describe efficacious interventions targeting parenting skills. This is followed by a discussion of the obstacles to these programs being widely available and then by an analysis of how
we might affect the quality of family environments through nonclinical means.
We have presented a more detailed discussion of strengthening families from a
public health perspective elsewhere (Biglan & Metzler, 1996).

The Efficacy of Parenting Skills Training

Over the past 30 years, behavioral parent training has proven to be highly
effective at modifying parents' problematic parenting practices, as well as children's problematic behavior (Dumas, 1989; Kazdin, 1987; Webster-Stratton,
1990; Webster-Stratton, Hollinsworth, & Kolpacoff, 1989). Typically, such
programs offer guidance on how to play with young children in ways that stim-
ulate imagination and language development, how to be involved with older
children's activities, and how to monitor and supervise children of all ages.
These programs frequently emphasize the importance of catching children being
good, through use of praise and rewards for appropriate behavior. In addition,
such programs typically help parents reduce unnecessary commands and instructions, while at the same time giving effective directions and setting clear rules
and expectations concerning important behavior. Parents are taught to ignore
whining, tantrums, and other inappropriate, attention-seeking behavior, and to
use nonviolent discipline strategies such as time-out for deliberately defiant,
aggressive, or destructive behavior. Effective communication and problem-
solving strategies are another central component of most current programs.

Properly controlled research studies evaluating behavioral parent training have
demonstrated a range of positive effects. Parent training has been shown to be
effective at reducing conduct problems such as aggression and defiance (e.g.,
Kazdin et al., 1987a, 1987b; Patterson, Chamberlain, & Reid, 1982; Webster-
Stratton, 1984, 1989; Webster-Stratton, Hollinsworth, & Kolpacoff, 1989), as
well as symptoms of Attention Deficit Disorder with Hyperactivity (Pisterman
et al., 1989).

Behavioral parent training has also been shown to lead to changes in parents'
feelings and behavior. It has been shown to improve the manner in which parents
communicate with their children, to reduce parent reports of anger (Taylor,
Schmidt, & Hodgins, 1996), and to reduce the amount that parents rely on
physical punishment when disciplining their children (Webster-Stratton, Kolpacoff, & Hollinsworth, 1988). Given these findings, it is perhaps not surprising
that behavioral parent training has been shown to be an effective treatment for
parents who have abused their children (Azar & Twentyman, 1984; Reid, Taplin,
& Lorber, 1981; Szykula & Fleischman, 1985; Wolfe, Sandler, & Kaufman,
1981).

The Efficacy of Parenting Skills Training for Multiproblem Families. A number of studies have demonstrated that parents who have difficult children are

also more likely to be experiencing other problems, including depression, marital problems, or social isolation (Dumas & Wahler, 1985; Emery, 1982; Wahler, 1980). For such families, the evidence suggests that additional help in these areas often results in greater benefits for the child as well (e.g., Dadds, Schwartz, & Sanders, 1987; Griest et al., 1982; Pfiffner et al., 1990; Webster-Stratton, 1994; Wells, Griest, & Forehand, 1980).

Recruitment of At-Risk Families. One impediment to the widespread provision of effective parenting skills training is the fact that many of the parents who are in most need of such programs are also the most difficult to recruit and retain. Numerous clinic-based studies have reported that parents experiencing more severe problems with their children, as well as parents with other problems, including single-parent status, poverty, social isolation, depression, and marital conflict, are less likely to participate in such programs, and more likely to drop out prior to completion (Forehand & McMahon, 1981; Wahler, 1980; Webster-Stratton & Hammond, 1990).

There are, however, several examples of very high recruitment rates (above 65%) and retention rates (above 85%) among families in disadvantaged schools (Reid, 1993), families in Head Start (Webster-Stratton, 1995), and families seeking help from a children's mental health center (Taylor et al., 1996). Each of these studies included many participants who were experiencing multiple problems. A common element in them was an initial meeting with the parents to explain the program and to encourage them to participate. The meetings were held at the family's convenience, and typically in its home. Also common was that child care was offered, and the program was either offered close to the home (e.g., at the child's school) or rides were offered for those who needed them.

The Problem of Disseminating Effective Interventions. Finally, there is the problem of making validated parenting skills training and family intervention widely available. This is a matter for research on both provider and consumer behavior. How can we influence providers to use the best interventions? How can we influence consumers to seek such programs? How can we induce organizations in our communities to put resources into making parent and family interventions available to those who need them? The latter question is addressed below.

Influencing Family Practices through Nonclinical Means

We cannot expect to achieve large changes in the prevalence of effective parenting practices through clinical means alone (Biglan, Glasgow, & Singer, 1990; Biglan, Metzler, & Ary, 1994). Even if we are enormously successful in ensuring that validated family interventions are widely available and fully subscribed, it is unlikely that we can reach all at-risk families in this way alone or that we would have sufficient resources to provide needed services if we could. Moreover, clinical interventions can be expected to have only a limited impact on many of the problems that appear to be impediments to effective parenting, such as poverty. Thus, we need systematic research on nonclinical means of influencing parenting practices.

Smoking control research provides a model for how a health-related behavior might be influenced in a population (Biglan, 1995). In essence, the smoking control strategy has been to identify all of the channels through which smokers might be reached and to develop brief, persuasive interventions to prompt them to attempt quitting. In a similar fashion, we need to identify systematically ways to reach parents and to provide them with information and assistance in adopting and maintaining the most effective parenting practices.

Four channels through which parents might be reached with information, advice, and activities relevant to effective parenting can be readily identified. Perhaps the most important channel is mass media. A wealth of evidence indicates that media can affect other behaviors. Flay's (1987) review of the effects of media on smoking concluded that mass media can motivate people to change their behavior and, in conjunction with support, can assist them in quitting smoking. Barber, Bradshaw, and Walsh (1989) showed that alcohol consumption can be influenced via mass media, and evidence indicates that media campaigns have affected drunk driving (Niensted, 1990). Admittedly, it is difficult to do well-controlled studies of the effects of media, but their potential should not be overlooked. Experimental evaluations are needed of the use of systematic mass media campaigns to inform parents about available parenting programs (e.g., Hawkins et al., 1987) and to directly influence their practices.

Pediatricians and family practice physicians are a second channel for reaching parents. These health care professionals could be assisted in developing methods of brief screening for parents who need help and of providing brief counseling about ways of handling common problems. This brief counseling could be provided by doctors, nurses, multimedia kiosks in their offices, or by referrals to service agencies.

Churches are a third channel for influencing parents. Many churches already provide parenting skills programs of various sorts. Research is needed on the nature of existing programs, the ways in which churches might be assisted in adopting and maintaining the most effective programs, and the ways in which they might recruit the families most in need.

Finally, the schools are an important channel for reaching families. Schools might routinely screen for children's behavior problems and provide parenting skills training to parents of children who are at risk for these problems. In addition, it may be possible to influence parenting practices through homework assignments to students and other kinds of school-based activities. For example, in one study, we developed a parent-child interview about tobacco use that was designed to prompt parents to tell their children that they did not want them to use tobacco (Biglan et al., 1996).

It should also be noted that research is needed on how contextual conditions such as poverty, neighborhood organization, and social support might be altered and whether changes in such conditions lead to improvement in parent-child interactions, even in the absence of further family interventions.

THE PRACTICES OF SCHOOLS

Beneficial Teaching Practices

Empirical evidence suggests that if schools were more successful in educating young people, fewer adolescents would drift into antisocial activities and other problem behaviors (Biglan, 1995). Yet, a substantial proportion of students fail to attain an adequate level of basic skills. According to a recent U.S. Department of Education nationwide assessment of fourth-, eighth-, and twelfth-grade students, only a quarter to a third were readers who could handle challenging assignments at their grade level (U.S. Department of Education, 1993). This could be indicative of changing demography, of students' capacity to learn, or of their home life—factors that schools cannot directly control. The data also suggest, however, that students can learn despite these circumstances. The quality of resources we commit to the education of students, and the ways in which these resources are used in practice, can positively affect learning outcomes.

There are a number of teaching practices that are reasonably well established as best practices (e.g., Becker, 1986; Slavin, Karweit, & Madden, 1989). Becker (1986) has provided a summary of the key features of instructional approaches that result in successful education.

1. Objectives are specified.
2. Preskills are tested to ensure that placement is appropriate.
3. Procedures are developed to motivate and engage the student in active learning.
4. [Instruction is designed] that teaches the targeted objectives effectively and efficiently.
5. Differential time is allowed for different students to reach mastery.
6. Ungraded, frequent testing is provided to monitor progress.
7. Corrective-remedial procedures are provided if an approach fails.
8. Adequate practice to mastery of subskills is provided.
9. There is testing for longer-term mastery of objectives.

Unfortunately, it has proven difficult to achieve the widespread adoption of these practices.

Beneficial and Problematic Behavior Management Practices

In addition to effective instruction, it is essential that schools identify and remediate the social behavior problems of children. Children's disruptive behavior poses a critical problem for education for at least three reasons. First, many children who display inappropriate behaviors do so to escape aversive academic or social stimuli (Dunlap et al., 1993; Shores, Gunter, Denny, & Jack, 1993; Shores, Gunter, & Jack., 1993). Thus, failure to handle disruptive behavior effectively can contribute to academic failure. Second, teachers have low tolerance for problem behaviors related to classroom control, discipline, noncompliance, academic achievement, stealing, self-injury, physical aggression, and sexual misbehavior (Gersten, Walker, & Darch, 1988; Hersh & Walker, 1983; Kauffman, Lloyd, & McGee, 1989; Ritter, 1989; Safran & Safran, 1984; Walker & Rankin, 1983). Indeed, problems with disruptive behavior affect teachers' levels of stress and burnout (Dunham, 1981; Zabel, Boomer, & King, 1984). Third, children with disruptive behavior problems are at risk to develop increasingly serious behavior problems as they grow older (Walker, 1995).

Unfortunately, educational practitioners have seen an alarming rise in the numbers of students who display disruptive or challenging behaviors. The proportion of students who display such behaviors in public schools ranges anywhere from 2% to 30% (Walker & Bullis, 1990). Prevalence rates of children exhibiting problematic behaviors have been estimated to be between 2% and 6% of the school age population (Cullinan, Epstein, & Kauffman, 1984; Rubin & Balow, 1978).

There has been considerable research on how disruptive behavior is affected by teacher-student interactions (e.g., Landrum, 1992). For example, Wehby, Symons, and Shores' (1995) analysis of social interactions in classrooms for children with emotional and behavioral disorders revealed that teachers' social and instructional commands were among the top three antecedents that preceded children's aggressive behavior toward teachers. These negative interaction patterns are consistent with previous student-teacher interaction research in regular and special education classrooms (e.g., Gunter et al., 1993; Shores, Gunter et al., 1993; Shores, Jack et al., 1993; Shores et al., 1993), and complements Patterson's social interaction research with antisocial children in home settings (Patterson, 1982; Patterson et al., 1992).

Teacher-student interaction research also indicates that teachers typically (a) provide lean schedules of positive reinforcement for desirable behavior and correct academic responses, (b) do not individualize instruction for diverse learners, and (c) engage in trial-and-error teaching practices (e.g., Shores, Gunter et al., 1993; Strain et al., 1983; Thomas et al., 1978; White, 1975). Moreover, teachers' negative attitudes and interaction patterns with disruptive children may be linked to less frequent use of or training with effective instructional and behavior management strategies (Bender, Vail, & Scott, 1995; Shores, Gunter et al., 1993).

Clearly, if students with disruptive behaviors are to improve their academic and social skills, educational practitioners must be encouraged to adopt effective models of behavior management and academic instruction.

Such models are available, at least for children in elementary school. Walker (1995) provides a comprehensive review of programs that have been shown to remediate both peer-related and teacher-related social behavior problems. For example, the CLASS program (*C*ontingencies for *L*earning *A*cademic and *S*ocial *S*kills) provides a carefully arranged schedule of reinforcement for remaining on task in classroom settings. It has been shown to dramatically increase on-task behavior (Hops, Walker, & Greenwood, 1987). The RECESS program (*Re*programming *E*nvironmental *C*ontingencies for *E*ffective *S*ocial *S*kills) has been shown to bring about significant reductions in aggressive behavior directed toward peers (Walker, Hops, & Greenwood, 1981).

The Importance of High-Quality Preschool and Day Care Settings

There is a growing need for communities to provide quality child care opportunities for families. The trend for employment of mothers with young children is increasing. In the 1960s, 17% of married women with children under the age of six were employed; this number increased to 30% in the 1970s and to 54% by 1986 (Matthews & Rodin, 1989). Approximately 76% of working women are employed full-time. Additionally, one out of four children in America lives in a single-parent home (Carnegie Task Force, 1994). According to the Carnegie report, the United States does a poor job of providing paid parental leave and subsidized child care after the birth of a baby, compared to other industrialized countries.

Studies of the impact of child care on children's cognitive and social development indicate that the quality of care is a critical variable. Scarr, Phillips, and McCartney (1990) outlined the characteristics of high-quality child care: (a) a low child/caregiver ratio, (b) caregiver training, and (c) stability of child care settings and caregivers.

High-quality child care has been found to increase the cognitive and social development of young children raised in poor family environments (Ramey, Bryant, & Suarez, 1985). In a study of four-year-old children, the relationships observed with their child care teacher better predicted social competence with peers than did the children's attachment relationship with their mothers (Howes, Matheson, & Hamilton, 1994). Children who attended child care in center-based settings also received higher positive ratings of sociability from teachers and parents (Phillips, McCartney, & Scarr, 1987) and higher levels of observed compliance (Howes & Olenick, 1986).

High-quality child care has cascading effects on families and communities. Parents who were involved in Head Start came to value education more and had more sensitivity for their children's developmental level than did parents who had no involvement (Weld, 1973). In a review of studies regarding the impact of Head Start programs, Zigler and Freedman (1987) noted that families involved in Head Start programs had increased life satisfaction, improved life skills, better job training and employment opportunities, and participation as leaders in other community activities. Further, Calhoun and Collins (1981) indicate that the development of Head Start services in a community results in a further improvement of services for low-income and minority families within the community. In contrast, young children in low-quality care show lower levels of intelligence and achievement, less complex and more aimless play, and less cooperation and more hostility with peers (Clarke-Stewart, Gruber, & Fitzgerald, 1994).

In summary, the research clearly shows the importance of high-quality child care and preschools to supplement parents' care of young children in a nurturing, responsive environment and to promote cognitive and social development before entering school.

Increasing the Prevalence of Effective Schooling Practices

Widespread adoption of empirically based teaching and behavior management practices in schools and preschool settings could make a substantial contribution to reducing the prevalence of young people who are failing academically or socially. Despite the high volume of school reform activity in the United States, there is little evidence that empirically based teaching practices are being widely adopted. Research in education needs to shift from the identification of effective teaching practices to the problem of how to influence schools to adopt and maintain such practices.

At present we know relatively little about what influences the adoption and maintenance of schooling practices. Most research involves case studies or is anecdotal. Some of the most comprehensive studies (e.g., Huberman & Miles, 1984) provide descriptive accounts of how change was implemented and of the correlates associated with acceptance and maintenance of new practices, but they do not provide much information about how one might influence schools that have not sought to change.

There are a few studies that have described methods of bringing about improvement in teaching and/or behavior management practices. Mayer et al. (1983) have shown that a program of teacher training, in which a core cadre of teachers are taught how to establish a small number of clear rules and to greatly increase their positive attention to positive behavior, can significantly improve students' social behavior and reduce the level of vandalism in schools. Hawkins, Doueck, and Lishner (1988) reported beneficial effects of a program that included training teachers in proactive classroom management, the use of many of the teaching practices listed above, and the use of cooperative learning procedures. Gottfredson (1987) has described an organizational development approach to bringing about changes in discipline practices. The approach uses an ongoing evaluation process to assist schools in developing a specific plan for school change. Gottfredson (1987) reported that the process was associated with a reduction in disorderly behavior. Colvin, Kameenui, and Sugai (1993) have described a staff development model for assisting schools in adopting effective school-wide discipline procedures.

Further research on strategies for encouraging schools to adopt effective practices are needed; only one of the above-cited studies involved an experimental manipulation of the school change procedure. In addition to studies focusing on how a consultant or trainer might work with individual teachers or the school organization on change, we need to have a better understanding of the larger social context that influences school practices. In particular, studies are needed of the influence of parents, curriculum specialists, school boards, unions, textbook publishers, and businesses on schools' teaching and behavior management practices. Studies that document the role that each group plays in the determination of a school's teaching practices would be of value. Even more valuable, however, would be studies that test ways to mobilize one or more of these groups to influence schools to adopt effective instructional and behavior management practices.

PEER INFLUENCES

The Influence of Peers on Problem Behavior

One of the most well-established findings in the behavioral sciences is that adolescents are influenced to engage in problem behaviors through associations with peers who engage in these behaviors. This has been shown for tobacco use (Biglan et al., 1995), illicit drug use (Dishion & Loeber, 1985), high-risk sexual behavior (Biglan et al., 1990; Metzler et al., 1994), and antisocial behavior (Patterson et al., 1992). In recent studies, we have found that a construct defined by engagement in diverse problem behaviors is predicted by associations with deviant peers (Ary et al., in press).

Dishion et al. (1995) conducted a study that illustrates some of the contingencies that appear to be operative in relationships among deviant peers. They observed boys, ages thirteen or fourteen, talking with a friend. They found they could predict alcohol, tobacco, and marijuana use two years later from a measure of the degree to which the dyad laughed contingent on talk about rule-breaking. Thus, deviant peers appear to reinforce talk of rule-breaking, and presumably, actual rule-breaking.

Patterson, DeBaryshe, and Ramsey (1989) reviewed evidence that, at least for antisocial boys, difficulties with peer relationships may begin early. They argued that young boys who are aggressive are particularly likely to be rejected by peers, and that as they grow older, rejected peers tend to form friendships with each other. If we can prevent the formation of such deviant peer groups, we may prevent a great deal of problem behavior.

Interventions to Facilitate Positive Relationships with Prosocial Peers

Many of the school-based social behavior interventions we described above, such as the RECESS program (Walker et al., 1981), are designed to remediate social behavior that will lead to children being rejected. There is, as yet, insufficient data on whether these programs are powerful enough to significantly decrease the likelihood that young people will drift into deviant peer groups as they enter adolescence. Long-term studies of this question would be very valuable.

Another intervention that shows promise in preventing the formation of deviant peer groups is cooperative learning (Johnson & Johnson, 1975). Young people are taught to work cooperatively in small groups on academic assignments. Rewards such as grades and approval go to the group. Hawkins et al. (1988) showed that a program that included the implementation of a cooperative learning program was associated with improved school performance and decreased delinquency among boys.

A Public Health Perspective on Peer Relations

From a public health perspective, the goal is to reduce the prevalence of deviant peer groups. Interventions of the type just cited would likely contribute to this goal; so, too, may parenting and family interventions that increase the parents' monitoring of their children's friendships. However, if our target is the prevalence of such groups, other things might also be done to prevent the development of deviant peer groups.

The provision of supervised recreation might help in two ways. If supervised activities were organized to encourage the mixing of diverse children, they could function like cooperative learning programs to decrease the formation of deviant peer groups. In addition, they could ensure that at-risk young people are not spending unsupervised time with other at-risk youth, experimenting with behaviors that are problematic.

Some evidence suggests the value of supervised recreation. Jones and Offord (1989) found, in a quasi-experimental design, that the provision of supervised recreation that emphasized skill development led to a decrease in antisocial behavior among poor children living in a large, low-income housing project.

Chinman and Linney (1996) review evidence that community service activities may be beneficial in promoting prosocial behavior among young people. Part of the problem with deviant peer groups may be that there are too few prosocial activities to engage them. Increased availability of community service activities might be useful in that regard.

Practices that Contribute to Deviant Peer Groups. There is evidence to suggest that some of the things that our communities routinely do in the name of combating antisocial behavior actually contribute to it. In their review of the evidence, O'Donnell, Manos, and Chesney-Lind (1992) found that programs that bring at-risk youth into interactions with other at-risk youth increase the likelihood of subsequent arrests. For example, in one study, Fo and O'Donnell (1974) found that a buddy system that linked triads of at-risk youth with a nondelinquent buddy in the neighborhood led to youth without prior criminal records having significantly *greater* rates of arrest. Apparently, the system brought these youngsters into greater contact with peers who influenced them to engage in crime. Communities would do well to review their juvenile justice procedures to be sure that they do not congregate at-risk youth in ways that contribute to the further development of youth problem behavior.

COMMUNITY INTERVENTIONS TO IMPROVE CHILDREARING

An important strategy for increasing the prevalence of good childrearing practices involves community intervention research. There are both methodological and practical reasons for a focus on community interventions. One can assess the prevalence of parenting and teaching practices and children's behavior within a community at a reasonable cost. One can conduct group design and multiple baseline design experimental analyses of interventions to affect the prevalence of behaviors in communities (e.g., Biglan, 1995; Biglan et al., 1996; COMMIT Research Group, 1995a, 1995b). At the same time, communities are the social unit in which much of the influence on childrearing practices takes place; there is a potential to bring about large changes in the prevalence of successful children when working at the community level, since one can comprehensively intervene to affect families, schools, and peer groups through a variety of channels.

The evidence reviewed above suggests goals for community interventions. It implies that a community will have a greater proportion of its young people successful in school, work, and social relationships if it ensures that (a) its families are skilled in parenting, (b) its schools teach effectively and ensure the development of cooperative social behavior, and (c) its peer groups are places where appropriate social behavior is supported.

The fundamental problem for research on community interventions on childrearing, then, would seem to be determining how communities can be assisted in establishing these conditions. The remainder of the chapter will sketch an agenda for such research.

A brief comment on collaborative approaches to community intervention is in order, however. Community interventionists have tried carefully to articulate procedures for conducting community intervention research that involve active participation of community members in the formulation and conduct of research (Biglan, 1995; Fawcett, 1990, 1991; Kelly, 1988). There are at least two reasons for such a collaborative approach to community interventions. One is the realization that the communities with which we work may have different values and goals than the ones that an outsider might have. Without a collaborative approach, in which members of the community help to determine the goals and procedures of community change efforts, the efforts may fail to meet the needs of the community. Indeed, they may be an intrusion. This is, of course, a strategic as well as an ethical issue. Thus, a second reason for a collaborative approach to community interventions is that people are more likely to make a commitment to a change process if they participate in the setting of goals and the determination of procedures for achieving those goals.

Understanding the Influences on Community Organizations

We believe that a key step in assisting communities in increasing the prevalence of beneficial family, school, and peer environments involves working with community organizations to enhance what they are doing to affect these environments. Social service agencies may or may not be using the optimal family interventions. Schools may or may not be using the most effective instructional and behavior management approaches. Civic organizations may be supporting and advocating effective programs or they may be advancing programs and policies that are useless or even counterproductive. If communities are going to be assisted in achieving the best possible environments for children, a much better understanding of what influences the actions of organizations will be needed. Why does a community organization adopt a program or policy or join a coalition that might benefit families or youth? What influences it to maintain or abandon a program, policy, or coalition?

Research on what influences the actions of community organizations has been sparse. Speer et al. (1992) reported that no more than 4% of papers published in the *American Journal of Community Psychology* or the *Journal of Community Psychology* between 1973 and 1988 focused on any constructs having to do with organizations.

A contextual analysis (e.g., Biglan, 1995) would search for the determinants of organization actions in the environment of the organization. A promising, yet underexplored possibility is that the consequences of organization actions select and maintain those actions in a manner analogous to the effects of reinforcement on the behavior of individuals. Glenn (1988) has used the term *metacontingency* to describe this effect. The interconnected behavior of two or more people results in an outcome that may serve to maintain that pattern of interconnected activity. For example, a business organization maintains a marketing practice because it maintains an increased level of sales. As another example, a civic organization may provide recognition and rewards to its members for recruiting new members. The recognition and rewards to members presumably reinforce them for recruiting new members, but it is the flow of new members that presumably maintains the organization's reinforcing practices.

Funding. What types of consequences might function as outcomes that shape and maintain the actions of organizations? Funding would appear to be a key consequence. Certainly for business organizations, enough money must flow to the enterprise to pay for workers and resources. And, if profit doesn't accrue to the owners, they are likely to sell or abandon the business. The mechanisms for funding of service organizations are typically different from those for business organizations. Service agencies that are part of government typically receive an annual budget. Nongovernmental service agencies typically receive funds from government contracts, government and foundation grants, charitable contributions, and, increasingly, from profit-making activities. Voluntary civic organizations also require funding, though at a more modest level. Typically, they are funded by member dues and by fund-raising activities. An organization that fails to get members to pay their dues or to have a successful fund-raising program may cease to exist.

In one sense, the influence of funding on the actions of organizations is obvious and mundane. Yet the role of economic contingencies in community interventions is seldom mentioned and we are aware of no empirical analyses of how funding affects what organizations do about child well-being. If we are correct that funding influences what organizations do, then we will not have community organizations providing the kinds of validated programs and policies outlined above unless funding is contingent on their doing so.

Thus, we need a whole new line of research that examines the current structure of funding for childrearing programs and policies and that experimentally evaluates methods of bringing about secure funding for them. Such research would map the current system of funding for organizations that provide programs for children and families, including the schools. It would describe where funding comes from (e.g., tax money, foundations, fees, donations) and where it flows. It would describe the criteria and decision process involved in money being given to a particular organization; it would pay special attention to whether empirical evidence was used in this decision-making process. Ultimately, it would evaluate interventions that are designed to increase the flow of funding to organizations that implement programs and policies that are most likely to benefit children and families.

The Social-Verbal Context. This is not to say that economic contingencies are the only ones influencing the activities of organizations. Organizations exist in a social-verbal context (Biglan, 1995). The verbal analysis consists of written and stated descriptions of what is important for the organization and its members to do, why the described goals are important, and how the goals might be accomplished. The verbal analysis may be as formal as a written mission statement and a strategic plan, or it may be as informal as the things that organization members and those interacting with organization members say are "the way we do things around here."

In recent years, a cogent analysis of the way in which verbal framing affects the functions of stimuli has been developed (Hayes & Hayes, 1992). According to relational frames analysis, verbal behavior involves the framing of relationships among stimuli. For example, in a context in which it is believed, the statement "It is important for at-risk parents to receive parenting skills training" changes the value of parenting skills training for the listener. For verbal human beings, the positive and negative values of stimuli are a function of the way that verbal behavior links the stimuli to other stimuli that already have positive or negative function.

Thus, we conceive of organizational members as having a verbal analysis of what they and their organization are about. The analysis specifies what is of value and what is not. It specifies what they and others should be doing. To understand what an organization is likely to do, we must understand what its members say about it and its relationship to the world.

The other feature of the social-verbal context is the social contingencies. Social behavior is shaped and maintained by its social consequences. The immediate consequences of the behavior of organizational members are typically social. The efforts of members to recruit new members to a civic organization are publicly recognized and applauded. An innovation in a manufacturing process is approved and ultimately adopted by a company. A proposal for a new way of organizing work groups is criticized and therefore abandoned. A company's proposal to build a new plant in a community is dropped when citizen opposition in the form of harsh criticism of corporate leaders prompts them to withdraw the proposal.

There is, of course, a close link between the social contingencies influencing organizational practices and the verbal analysis. Indeed, the term "social-verbal" is hyphenated to connote that social reinforcement practices occur in the context of a verbal analysis and the verbal analysis is shaped and maintained by social contingencies.

Organizational members and those outside the organization are likely to praise and approve behavior that is consistent with their verbal analysis and to disapprove behavior that is inconsistent with it. Teachers in a school in which the whole language philosophy for teaching reading is widely held are likely to disagree with a consultant who recommends phonics instruction. Family counselors who have been trained in the Dreikursian philosophy are likely to criticize a new counselor who teaches parents to use praise and rewards.

Conversely, the verbal analysis is influenced by the social contingencies. The things that people say they believe about what an organization should do are influenced by the social consequences for expressing those views. Members of a team-oriented work organization may ignore or disapprove the divisive comments of a coworker. A Lion's Club president who states strong opposition to a school support measure may find that the membership is highly critical.

This view of organization functioning should not be taken to imply that the social-verbal context is unconnected to the economic contingencies for the organization. Indeed, the verbal analysis and social contingencies of organizational members must contribute to the organization's financial success or the analysis and contingencies must change.

If the verbal analysis is not accurate about aspects of the world that are critical to the organization's survival, the organization may not survive. If the leather company's analysis says, "Make buggy whips!" when horse-drawn carriages are on their way out, trouble may lie ahead. If the school board says, "Raise teacher's pay 15%!" when voters are already angry about their taxes, both the schools and the board members are put at risk.

The organization is similarly imperiled by social contingencies that do not support effective action. Criticism and divisiveness may generally be fatal to an organization if it punishes people for taking action that would contribute to the organization's well-being. Civic organizations that do not ensure that meetings are socially reinforcing for their members will dwindle in size.

In sum, we believe that the fundamental influences on the practices of organizations involve the financial consequences of their actions. The financial consequences shape a set of verbal and social practices that shape and maintain the day-to-day behavior of members of organizations and the actions that organizations take. If we want to influence the practices of community organizations, we must understand their financial contingencies and their verbal-social context.

Implications for Community Organizing and Advocacy

What then, are the implications of this analysis for what might be done to assist communities in improving the outcomes for children? In essence, we need to take three important steps: (1) identify the organizations that are likely to influence each of the three primary environments for children and adolescents; (2) clarify the contingencies that influence these organizations' actions; and (3) design a plan to influence the organizations to take actions that are likely, in turn, to influence families, schools, or peer groups.

To illustrate, let's consider how community organizations might be mobilized to influence family environments. The goals of such a mobilization are suggested by the analysis provided above. The clearest priority indicated by the empirical evidence is that the community should have validated family interventions that reach at-risk families. In addition, the community may benefit families by ensuring that media, schools, physicians, and churches have policies and programs that support and encourage effective parenting.

How then might community organizations be influenced to adopt and maintain the best family interventions? In a study we are currently conducting, we have adopted a strategy that involves four steps. First, we are identifying all of the organizations that currently provide programs for families, as well as organizations that might support or advocate for effective family interventions. Second, we are clarifying the nature of existing family programs in order to gauge how consistent they are with best practice as defined by the empirical evidence. These might seem like simple questions, but we have found that there are no systematic methods for identifying or assessing such organizations.

We began by identifying all of the organizations in each community that might have anything to do with children or families. The list of organizations was obtained from a review of all available program directories in the community and interviews with key informants. Then a representative of each organization was called in a screening call, to determine whether it, in fact, had programs or policies that might affect children or adolescents. Next, we interviewed a representative of each organization to find out what programs it was conducting. In addition to providing information that will guide the intervention, we are obtaining a baseline regarding what the community is already doing relevant to family interventions.

In the third step, we are analyzing the social, verbal, and financial context for each organization along the lines described in the preceding section. We are trying to understand what each organization's verbal analysis is of (a) the need for family interventions, (b) the types of programs that are most useful and why they are viewed as useful, and (c) what is needed to strengthen either the amount or quality of family intervention in the community. In addition, we are trying to understand the social contingencies involved in the community's system for providing family interventions. Do representatives of the various programs interact? Are they supportive (versus critical) of each others' actions? Are there support and recognition in the community for organization members who are working to provide family interventions? Finally, we are clarifying the funding arrangements that support these programs. We want to understand who funds family programs and what criteria they use for funding them.

Fourth, we are developing a plan of advocacy in light of our analysis of the social-verbal context for existing organization practices. That advocacy must link the provision of validated family interventions to things that are already important to the members of the organization. The "positives" to which such programs might be linked include good outcomes for children, further funding, and approval of important people in the community. Advocacy is also needed that increases support in relevant sectors of the community for the types of interventions we are advocating. It will do little good to persuade service agencies of the value of parenting skills training programs if support for such programs cannot be obtained from funding sources.

We believe that the fifth step in this process will be to ensure that any adoption or modification of existing practices leads to reinforcing consequences for organization members and outcomes for the organization as a whole that ensure its survival. New programs and program modifications must contribute to increased or more secure funding. Thus, we must understand how an advocated program may pose difficulties for an agency or organization. Will it cost more to deliver? Will it be opposed by a funding agency? Will it cost too much to buy the materials for it? It may be necessary to help the organization articulate the value of a newly adopted program to community leaders and funding agencies.

Finally, we must consider the contingencies for those who will deliver the program. Will the delivery of this program be more or less reinforcing than what they are currently doing? The effective implementation of a program in an organization will require training and consultation that make the advocated practices more reinforcing, by modeling them, by demonstrating their effects, by creating a collaborative and reinforcing setting in which to try them, by ensuring that providers are successful in helping families, and by ensuring that good outcomes for families are seen as an important outcome.

CONCLUSION

In 1953, Skinner described the promise of a science of human behavior for solving the most important problems that human populations face (Skinner, 1953). The progress that has been made on how to influence the behavior of individuals shows that much of the promise of that science has been realized. Yet, we remain far from a society in which traditional problems such as crime, poverty, and injustice have been eliminated.

We will realize the benefits of the behavioral sciences to society as a whole if we translate what is known about human behavior into changes in the incidence and prevalence of problematic and beneficial behaviors in populations. Doing this will also require an understanding of the variables that influence the actions of organizations.

A particularly important venue for this expansion of the scope of behavior science research involves the prevention of the diverse problem behaviors of youth that are so costly to young people and their communities. We know enough about effective parenting and programs to promote effective parenting that our research can now target affecting the prevalence of good parenting in small communities. We know enough about effective schooling practices that we can turn to research on how to disseminate and maintain those practices. We may also be able to reduce the incidence and prevalence of youth problem behaviors if we can assist communities in providing for the reinforcement of prosocial behavior in community settings.

Unfortunately, we know little about how communities can be assisted in bringing about optimal family, school, peer group, and community conditions. A more effective analysis of the contextual conditions influencing the actions of community organizations appears likely to contribute to our ability to do so.

REFERENCES

Adams, M. (1990). *Beginning to read: Thinking and learning about print*. Cambridge, MA: MIT Press.

Andresen, P. A., & Telleen, S. L. (1992). The relationship between social support and maternal behaviors and attitudes: A meta-analytic view. *American Journal of Community Psychology, 20*, 753.

Ary, D. V., Duncan, T. E., Biglan, A., Metzler, C. W., Noell, J. W., & Smolkowski, K. (in press). A developmental model of adolescent problem behavior. *Journal of Abnormal Child Psychology*.

Azar, S. T., & Twentyman, C. T. (1984). *An evaluation of the effectiveness of behavioral versus insight oriented group treatments with maltreating mothers* (unpublished).

Baker, J. M., & Zigmond, N. (1990). Are regular education classes equipped to accommodate students with learning disabilities? *Exceptional Children, 56*, 515–526.

Barber, J. G., Bradshaw, R., & Walsh, C. (1989). Reducing alcohol consumption through television advertising. *Journal of Consulting & Clinical Psychology, 57*, 613–618.

Becker, W. (1986). *Applied psychology for teachers*. Chicago: Science Research Associates.

Bender, W. N., Vail, C. O., & Scott, K. (1995). Teachers' attitudes toward increased mainstreaming: Implementing effective instruction for students with learning disabilities. *Journal of Learning Disabilities, 28*, 87–94.

Biglan, A. (1995). *Changing cultural practices: A contextualist framework for intervention research*. Reno, NV: Context Press.

Biglan, A., Ary, D. V., Yudelson, H., Duncan, T. E., Hood, D., James, L., Koehn, V., Wright, Z., Black, C., Levings, D., Smith, S., & Gaiser, E. (1996). Experimental evaluation of a modular approach to media campaigns for the prevention of adolescent tobacco use. *American Journal of Community Psychology, 24 (3)*, 311–339.

Biglan, A., Duncan, T. E., Ary, D. V., & Smolkowski, K. (1995). Peer and parental influences on adolescent tobacco use. *Journal of Behavioral Medicine, 18 (4)*, 315–330.

Biglan, A., Glasgow, R. E., & Singer, G. (1990). The need for a science of larger social units: A contextual approach. *Behavior Therapy, 21*, 195–215.

Biglan, A., & Metzler, C. W. (1996). *A public health perspective for research on family-focused interventions*. Washington, DC: National Institute on Drug Abuse.

Biglan, A., Metzler, C. W., & Ary, D. V. (1994). Increasing the prevalence of successful children: The case for community intervention research. *The Behavior Analyst, 17 (2)*, 335–351.

Biglan, A., Metzler, C. W., Wirt, R., Ary, D. V., Noell, J., Ochs, L., French, C., & Hood, D. (1990). Social and behavioral factors associated with high-risk sexual behavior among adolescents. *Journal of Behavioral Medicine, 13 (3)*, 245–261.

Calhoun, J. A., & Collins, R. C. (1981). From one decade to another: A positive view of early childhood programs. *Theory into Practice, 20*, 135–140.

Capaldi, D. M., & Patterson, G. R. (1989). *Psychometric properties of fourteen latent constructs from the Oregon youth study*. New York: Springer-Verlag.

———. (1991). Relation of parental transitions to boys' adjustment problems: A linear hypothesis. II. Mothers at risk for transitions and unskilled parenting. *Developmental Psychology, 27*, 489–504.

Carnegie Task Force. (1994). *Starting point: Meeting the needs of our youngest children. Report of the Carnegie Task Force*. Carnegie Corporation.

Child abuse, neglect rise sharply. (1996, September 19). *The Register-Guard*, Eugene, OR, p. 7A.

Children's Defense Fund. (1990). *A vision for America's future—an agenda for the 1990s: A children's defense budget*. Washington, DC: Author.

Chinman, M. J., & Linney, J. A. (1996). *Toward a model of adolescent empowerment: Theoretical and empirical evidence* (unpublished).

Clarke-Stewart, K. A., Gruber, C. P., & Fitzgerald, L. M. (1994). *Children at home and in day care*. Hillsdale, NJ: Lawrence Erlbaum.

Cohen, S., & Wills, T. A. (1985). Stress, social support, and the buffering hypothesis. *Psychological Bulletin, 98*, 310–357.

Colvin, G., Kameenui, E. J., & Sugai, G. (1993). Reconceptualizing behavior management and school-wide discipline in general education. *Education and Treatment of Children, 16*, 361–381.

COMMIT Research Group. (1995a). Community intervention trial for smoking cessation (COMMIT): I. Cohort results from a four-year community intervention. *American Journal of Public Health, 85 (2)*, 183–192.

———. (1995b). Community intervention trial for smoking cessation (COMMIT): II. Changes in adult cigarette smoking prevalence. *American Journal of Public Health, 85 (2)*, 193–200.

Conger, R. D., Conger, K. J., Elder, G. H. J., Lorenz, F. O., Simons, R. L., & Whitbeck, L. B. (1992). A family process model of economic hardship and adjustment of early adolescent boys. *Child Development, 63*, 526 541.

Conger, R. D., Lorenz, F. O., Elder, G. H., Melby, J. N., Simons, R. L., & Conger, K. J. (1991). A process model of family economic pressure and early adolescent alcohol use. *Journal of Early Adolescence, 11 (4)*, 430–449.

Conger, R. D., Patterson, G. R., & Ge, X. (1995). It takes two to replicate: A mediational model for the impact of parents' stress on adolescent adjustment. *Child Development, 66*, 80–97.

Cullinan, D., Epstein, M. H., & Kauffman, J. M. (1984). Teachers' ratings of students' behaviors: What constitutes behavior disorder in schools? *Behavioral Disorders, 10*, 9–19.

Dadds, M. R., Schwartz, S., & Sanders, M. R. (1987). Marital discord and treatment outcome in behavioral treatment of child conduct disorders. *Journal of Consulting and Clinical Psychology, 55*, 396–403.

Dishion, T. J. (1990). The family ecology of boy's peer relations in middle childhood. *Child Development, 61*, 874–892.

Dishion, T. J., Capaldi, D. M., Spracklen, K. M., & Li, F. (1995). Peer ecology of male adolescent drug use. *Development and Psychopathology, 7*, 803–824.

Dishion, T. J., & Loeber, R. (1985). Adolescent marijuana and alcohol use: The role of parents and peers revisited. *American Journal of Drug Abuse, 11 (1&2)*, 11–25.

Dumas, J. E. (1989). Treating antisocial behavior in children: Child and family approaches. *Clinical Psychology Review, 9*, 197–222.

Dumas, J. E., & Wahler, R. G. (1985). Indiscriminate mothering as a contextual factor in aggressive-oppositional child behavior: "Damned if you do, and damned if you don't." *Journal of Abnormal Child Psychology, 13*, 1–17.

Dunham, J. (1981). Disruptive pupils and teacher stress. *Educational Research, 23*, 205–213.

Dunlap, G., Kern, L., dePerczel, M., Clarke, S., Wilson, D., Childs, K. E., White, R., & Falk, G. D. (1993). Functional analysis of classroom variables for students with emotional and behavioral disorders. *Behavioral Disorders, 18*, 275–291.

Emery, R. E. (1982). Interparental conflict and the children of discord and divorce. *Psychological Bulletin, 92 (2)*, 310–330.

Fawcett, S. B. (1990). Some emerging standards for community research and action. In P. Tolan, C. Keys, F. Chertok, & L. Jason (Eds.), *Researching community psychology. Issues of theory and methods* (pp. 64–75). Washington, DC: American Psychological Association.

————. (1991). Some values guiding community research and action. *Journal of Applied Behavior Analysis, 24*, 621–636.

Flay, B. R. (1987). Mass media and smoking cessation: A critical review. *American Journal of Public Health, 77 (2)*, 153–160.

Fo, W. S. O., & O'Donnell, C. R. (1974). The buddy system: Relationship and contingency conditions in a community intervention program for youth with nonprofessionals as behavior change agents. *Journal of Consulting and Clinical Psychology, 42*, 163–169.

Forehand, R., & McMahon, R. J. (1981). *Helping the noncompliant child: A clinician's guide to parent training*. New York: Guilford Press.

Gersten, R., Walker, H., & Darch, C. (1988). Relationship between teachers' effectiveness and their tolerance for handicapped students. *Exceptional Children, 54*, 433–438.

Glenn, S. S. (1988). Contingencies and metacontingencies: Toward a synthesis of behavior analysis and cultural materialism. *The Behavior Analyst, 11*, 161–179.

Gottfredson, G. D. (1987). *Using organization development to improve school climate, Report No. 17*. Baltimore, MD: Center for Research on Elementary and Middle Schools.

Gottlieb, B. H. (1988). Marshaling social support: The state of the art in research and practice. In B. H. Gottlieb (Ed.), *Marshaling social support: Formats, processes, and effects* (pp. 11–52). Newbury Park, CA: Sage.

Griest, D. L., Forehand, R., Rogers, T., Breiner, J., Furey, W., & Williams, C. A. (1982). Effects of parent enhancement therapy on the treatment outcome and generalization of a parent training program. *Behavior Research and Therapy, 20*, 429–436.

Gunter, P. L., Denny, R. K., Jack, S. L., Shores, R. E., & Nelson, C. M. (1993). Aversive stimuli in academic interactions between students with serious emotional disturbance and their teachers. *Behavioral Disorders, 18*, 265–274.

Harris, M. (1989). *Our kind*. New York: Harper & Row.

Hawkins, J. D., Catalano, R. F., & Miller, J. Y. (1992). Risk and protective factors for alcohol and other drug problems in adolescence and early adulthood: Implications for substance abuse prevention. *Psychological Bulletin, 112 (1)*, 64–105.

Hawkins, J. D., Doueck, H. J., & Lishner, D. M. (1988). Changing teaching practices in mainstream classrooms to improve bonding and behavior of low achievers. *American Educational Research Journal, 25 (1)*, 31–50.

Hawkins, R. P., Gustafson, D. H., Chewning, B., Bosworth, K., & Day, P. M. (1987). Reaching hard-to-reach populations: Interactive computer programs as public information campaigns for adolescents. *Journal of Communication, 37 (2)*, 8–28.

Hayes, S. C., & Hayes, L. J. (1992). Verbal relations and the evolution of behavior analysis. *American Psychologist, 47*, 1383–1395.

Hersh, R., & Walker, H. M. (1983). Great expectations: Making schools effective for all students. *Policy Studies Review, 2*, 147–188.

Hops, H., Walker, H. M., & Greenwood, C. R. (1987). *CLASS (Contingencies for Learning Academic and Social Skills) program*. Del Ray Beach, FL: Educational Achievement Systems.

Howes, C. H., Matheson, C. C., & Hamilton, C. E. (1994). Maternal, teacher, and child care history correlates of children's relationship with peers. *Child Development, 65*, 264–273.

Howes, C. H., & Olenick, M. (1986). Child care and family influences on compliance. *Child Development, 57*, 202–216.

Huberman, A. M., & Miles, M. B. (1984). *Innovation up close: How school improvement works.* New York: Plenum.

Interpol. International Crime Rates, 1988. (1988). International Crime Statistics, International Criminal Police Organization.

Johnson, D. W., & Johnson, R. (1975). *Learning together and alone: Cooperation, competition, and individualization.* Englewood Cliffs, NJ: Prentice-Hall.

Johnson, O., & Dailey, V. (Eds.). (1995). *Information Please Almanac, Atlas and Yearbook, 1995* (48th ed.). New York: Houghton Mifflin Co.

Jones, M. B., & Offord, D. R. (1989). Reduction of antisocial behavior in poor children by nonschool skill-development. *Journal of Child Psychology & Psychiatry, 30 (5)*, 737–750.

Kauffman, J. M., Lloyd, J. W., & McGee, K. A. (1989). Adaptive and maladaptive behavior: Teachers' attitudes and their technical assistance needs. *Journal of Special Education, 23*, 185–200.

Kazdin, A. E. (1987). Treatment of antisocial behavior in children: Current status and future directions. *Psychological Bulletin, 102 (2)*, 187–203.

Kazdin, A. E., Esveldt-Dawson, K., French, N. H., & Unis, A. S. (1987a). Problem-solving skills training and relationship therapy in the treatment of antisocial child behavior. *Journal of Consulting & Clinical Psychology, 55 (1)*, 76–85.

———. (1987b). Effects of parent management training and problem-solving skills training combined in the treatment of antisocial child behavior. *American Academy of Child and Adolescent Psychiatry, 26 (3)*, 416–424.

Kelly, J. G. (1988). *A guide to conducting prevention research in the community: First steps.* New York: Haworth Press.

Kessler, R., & McLeod, J. (1985). Social support and mental health in community samples. In S. Cohen & S. Syme (Eds.), *Social support and health* (pp. 219–240). New York: Academic Press.

Landrum, T. J. (1992). Teachers as victims: An interactional analysis of teachers' roles in educating atypical learners. *Behavioral Disorders, 17*, 135–144.

Lovaas, O. I. (1987). Behavioral treatment and normal educational and intellectual functioning in young autistic children. *Journal of Consulting and Clinical Psychology, 55*, 3–9.

Mason, J., & Allen, J. B. (1986). A review of emergent literacy with implications for research and practice in reading. *Review of Research in Education, 13*, 3–47.

Matthews, K. A., & Rodin, J. (1989). Women's changing work roles: Impact on health, family, and public policy. *American Psychologist, 44*, 1389–1393.

Mayer, G. R., Butterworth, T., Nafpaktitis, M., & Sulzer-Azaroff, B. (1983). Preventing school vandalism and improving discipline: A three-year study. *Journal of Applied Behavior Analysis, 16*, 355–369.

Metzler, C. W., Noell, J., Biglan, A., Ary, D. V., & Smolkowski, K. (1994). The social context for risky sexual behavior among adolescents. *Journal of Behavioral Medicine, 17 (4)*, 419–438.

Niensted, B. (1990). The policy effects of a DWI law and a publicity campaign. In R.

Surette (Ed.), *The medical and criminal justice policy: Recent research and social effects* (pp. 193–203). Springfield, IL: Charles C. Thomas.

O'Donnell, C. R., Manos, M. J., & Chesney-Lind, M. (1992). Diversion and neighborhood delinquency programs in open settings. A social network interpretation. In J. McCord (Ed.), *Facts, frameworks and forecasts* (pp. 251–269). New Brunswick, NJ: Transaction Publishers.

Oregon, Idaho inmate numbers in top 10. (1996, August 19). *The Eugene Register Guard*, Eugene, OR, p. 3A.

Patterson, G. (1982). *Coercive family process*. Eugene, OR: Castalia Publishing.

Patterson, G., DeBaryshe, B., & Ramsey, E. (1989). A developmental perspective on antisocial behavior. *American Psychologist, 44*, 1–7.

Patterson, G. R., Chamberlain, P., & Reid, J. B. (1982). A comparative evaluation of a parent-training program. *Behavior Therapy, 13*, 638–650.

Patterson, G. R., & Narrett, C. M. (1990). The development of a reliable and valid treatment program for aggressive young children. *International Journal of Mental Health, 19 (3)*, 19–26.

Patterson, G. R., Reid, J. B., & Dishion, T. J. (1992). *Antisocial boys: A social interactional approach, Volume 4*. Eugene, OR: Castalia Publishing Company.

Pfiffner, L. J., Jouriles, E. N., Brown, M. M., Etscheidt, J. A., & Kelly, J. A. (1990). Effects of problem-solving therapy on outcomes of parent training for single-parent families. *Child and Family Behavior Therapy, 12 (1)*, 1–11.

Phillips, D., McCartney, K., & Scarr, S. (1987). Child-care quality and children's social development. *Developmental Psychology, 23*, 537–543.

Pisterman, S., McGrath, P., Firestone, P., Goodman, J. T., Webster, I., & Mallory, R. (1989). Outcome of parent-mediated treatment of preschoolers with attention deficit disorder with hyperactivity. *Journal of Consulting and Clinical Psychology, 57*, 628–635.

Ramey, C. T., Bryant, D. M., & Suarez, T. M. (1985). Preschool compensatory education and the modifiability of intelligence: A critical review. In D. Detterman (Ed.), *Current topics in human intelligence* (pp. 247–296). Norwood, NJ: Ablex.

Reid, J. (1993). Prevention of conduct disorder before and after school entry: Relating interventions to developmental findings. *Development and Psychopathology, 5*, 243–262.

Reid, J. B., Taplin, P. S., & Lorber, R. (1981). A social interaction approach to the treatment of abusive families. In R. Stuart (Ed.), *Social learning approaches to prediction, management, and treatment*. New York: Brunner/Mazel.

Richardson, J. L., Dwyer, K., McGuigan, K., Hansen, W. B., Dent, C., Johnson, C. A., Sussman, S. Y., Brannon, B., & Flay, B. (1989). Substance use among eighth-grade students who take care of themselves after school. *Pediatrics, 84 (3)*, 556–566.

Ritter, D. R. (1989). Teachers' perceptions of problem behavior in general and special education. *Exceptional Children, 55*, 559–564.

Rubin, R. A., & Balow, B. (1978). Prevalence of teacher identified behavior problems: A longitudinal study. *Exceptional Children, 45*, 102–113.

Safran, S. P., & Safran, J. S. (1984). Elementary teachers' tolerance of problem behaviors. *The Elementary School Journal, 85*, 237–243.

Sagan, C. (1995). *The demon haunted world*. New York: Random House.

Sampson, R. J., & Groves, W. B. (1989). Community structure and crime: Testing social-disorganization theory. *American Journal of Sociology, 94*, 774–802.

Scarr, S., Phillips, D., & McCartney, K. (1990). Facts, fantasies and the future of child care in the United States. *Psychological Science, 1*, 26–35.

Shores, R. E., Gunter, P. L., Denny, R. K., & Jack, S. L. (1993). Classroom influences on aggressive and disruptive behaviors of students with emotional and behavioral disorders. *Focus on Exceptional Children, 26 (2)*, 1–10.

Shores, R. E., Gunter, P. L., & Jack, S. L. (1993). Classroom management strategies: Are they setting events for coercion? *Behavioral Disorders, 18*, 92–102.

Shores, R. E., Jack, S. L., Gunter, P. L., Ellis, D. N., DeBriere, T., & Wehby, J. (1993). Classroom interactions of children with severe behavior disorders. *Journal of Emotional and Behavioral Disorders, 1*, 27–39.

Skinner, B. F. (1953). *Science and human behavior*. New York: Macmillan.

Slavin, R. E., Karweit, N. L., & Madden N. A. (1989). *Effective programs for students at risk*. Needham Heights, MA: Allyn and Bacon.

Speer, P., Dey, A., Griggs, P., Gibson, C., Lubin, B., & Hughey, J. (1992). In search of community: An analysis of community psychology research from 1984–1988. *American Journal of Community Psychology, 20 (2)*, 195–209.

Strain, P. S., Lambert, D. L., Kerr, M. M., Stagg, V., & Lenker, D. A. (1983). Naturalistic assessment of children's compliance to teacher's requests and consequences for compliance. *Journal of Applied Behavior Analysis, 16*, 243–249.

Szykula, S. A., & Fleischman, M. J. (1985). Reducing out-of-home placements of abused children: Two controlled field studies. *Child Abuse & Neglect, 9*, 277–283.

Taylor, T. K., Schmidt, F., & Hodgins, C. (1996). *A comparison of two treatments for young conduct problem children* (unpublished).

Thomas, J. D., Presland, I. E., Grant, M. D., & Glynn, T. L. (1978). Natural rates of teacher approval and disapproval in grade seven classrooms. *Journal of Applied Behavior Analysis, 11*, 91–94.

U.S. Bureau of Investigation. (1994). *Uniform crime reports of the United States*. Washington, DC: Author.

U.S. Census Bureau. (1995). *The census and you*. Washington, DC: U.S. Government Printing Office.

U.S. Department of Education. (Fall 1993). How literate are American adults? Office of Educational Research and Improvement Bulletin. Washington, DC: Office of Educational Research and Improvement.

Wahler, R. G. (1980). The insular mother: Her problems in parent-child treatment. *Journal of Applied Behavior Analysis, 13*, 207–219.

Wahler, R. G., & Dumas, J. E. (1986). Maintenance factors in coercive mother-child interactions: The compliance and predictability hypothesis. *Journal of Applied Behavior Analysis, 19*, 13–22.

———. (1987). Stimulus class determinants of mother-child coercive interchanges in multidistressed families: Assessment and intervention. In J. D. Burchard & S. N. Burchard (Eds.), *Prevention of delinquent behavior* (pp. 190–219). Beverly Hills, CA: Sage Publications.

Walker, H., Hops, H., & Greenwood, C. (1981). RECESS: Research and development of a behavior management package for remediating social aggression in the school setting. In P. Strain (Ed.), *The utilization of classroom peers as behavior change agents* (pp. 261–303). New York: Plenum.

Walker, H. M. (1995). *The acting-out child: Coping with classroom disruption.* Longmont, CO: Sopris West.

Walker, H. M., & Bullis, M. (1990). Behavior disorders and the social context of regular class integration: A conceptual dilemma? In J. W. Lloyd, N. N. Singh, & A. C. Repp (Eds.), *The regular education initiative: Alternative perspectives on concepts, issues, and models* (pp. 75–93). Sycamore, IL: Sycamore Press.

Walker, H. M., & Rankin, R. (1983). Assessing the behavioral expectations and demands of less restrictive settings. *School Psychology Review, 12,* 274–284.

Webster-Stratton, C. (1984). *The Parents and Children Videotape Series.* Eugene, OR: Castalia Publishing Co.

———. (1989). Systematic comparison of consumer satisfaction of the cost-effective parent training programs for conduct problem children. *Behavior Therapy, 20,* 103–115.

———. (1990). Long-term follow-up of families with young conduct problem children: From preschool to grade school. *Journal of Clinical Child Psychology, 19,* 144–149.

———. (1994). Advancing videotape parent training: A comparison study. *Journal of Consulting and Clinical Psychology, 62,* 583–593.

———. (1995). Parent training with low-income clients: Promoting parental engagement through a collaborative approach. Paper presented at Association for Advancement of Behavior Therapy, Washington, DC.

Webster-Stratton, C., & Hammond, M. (1990). Predictors of treatment outcome in parent training for families with conduct problem children. *Behavior Therapy, 21,* 319–337.

Webster-Stratton, C., & Herbert, M. (1993). ''What Really Happens in Parent Training?'' *Behavior Modification, 17 (4),* 407–456.

Webster-Stratton, C., Hollinsworth, T., & Kolpacoff, M. (1989). The long-term effectiveness and clinical significance of three cost-effective training programs for families with conduct-problem children. *Journal of Consulting & Clinical Psychology, 57,* 550–553.

Webster-Stratton, C., Kolpacoff, M., & Hollinsworth, T. (1988). Self-administered videotape therapy for families with conduct-problem children: Comparison with two cost-effective treatments and a control group. *Journal of Consulting & Clinical Psychology, 56,* 558–566.

Wehby, J. H., Symons, F. J., & Shores, R. E. (1995). A descriptive analysis of aggressive behavior in classrooms for children with emotional and behavioral disorders. *Behavioral Disorders, 20,* 87–105.

Weld, L. A. (1973). Family characteristics and profit from Head Start. *Dissertation Abstracts International, 34 (3-B),* 1172.

Wells, K. C., Griest, D. L., & Forehand, R. (1980). The use of a self-control package to enhance temporal generality of a parent training program. *Behaviour Research and Therapy, 18,* 347–358.

White, M. A. (1975). Natural rates of teacher approval and disapproval in the classroom. *Journal of Applied Behavior Analysis, 8,* 367–372.

Wolfe, D. A., Sandler, J., & Kaufman, K. (1981). A competency-based parent training program for child abusers. *Journal of Consulting and Clinical Psychology, 49*, 633–640.

Zabel, R. H., Boomer, L. W., & King, T. R. (1984). A model of stress and burnout among teachers of behaviorally disordered students. *Behavioral Disorders, 9*, 215–221.

Zigler, E. F., & Freedman, J. (1987). Head Start: A pioneer of family support. In S. L. Kagan, D. Powell, B. Weissbourd, & E. F. Zigler (Eds.), *America's family support programs: Perspectives and prospects* (pp. 57–75). New Haven, CT: Yale University Press.

10

The Formation and Survival of Experimental Communities

JOHN A. NEVIN

My interest in experimental communities began in 1959, when a friend loaned me a copy of B. F. Skinner's *Walden Two* (1948). I had never studied psychology, and Skinner's vision of a rational, planned community based on empirical analysis added to my growing interest in the science of behavior.

I read *Walden Two* again in 1968, when protests against the Vietnam War were coupled, for many people, with attempts to establish small, self-sufficient communities that would isolate their members from the violence and greed that seemed to permeate "the system." Communes were sprouting all over the United States, and I discussed experimental communities with several groups of young people. In that tumultuous time, my renewed encounter with Skinner's vision—which I then understood more deeply—stirred me to tears.

After Skinner's death in 1990, A. C. Catania organized a memorial symposium for the meetings of the Eastern Psychological Association in 1991, and asked me to talk on "B. F. Skinner, Utopian." I read *Walden Two* a third time, and was moved, as before, by Skinner's vision of a community based on behavioral principles where people could be productive, creative, and happy, and would have no occasion to consume a disproportionate share of the world's resources. If such a community could pass the ultimate selection criterion—survival—it might reproduce itself, multiply, and save the world.

Skinner's "Utopia as an Experimental Culture" (1969) suggests that utopian communities can be regarded as pilot experiments for society at large. Thus, *Walden Two* may be regarded as a pilot "thought experiment," designed to explore the feasibility of a good, enduring communal life through explicitly arranged contingencies of positive reinforcement. In his introduction to the second edition of *Walden Two* (1976), Skinner noted that he was familiar with the practices of real nineteenth-century experimental communities from his reading of *Freedom's Ferment* (1944) by Alice Tyler, and that Tyler's work had contributed to his writing of *Walden Two*. However, Skinner (1969) did not discuss the experiences of real experimental communities; and Frazier, Skinner's surrogate in *Walden Two*, argued that no lessons could be learned from them because they were set up, not as "real experiments, but to put certain principles into practice" (1976, p. 145).

Although none of the nineteenth-century experimental communities (to my knowledge) were "experimenting" communities in the sense of systematically varying and evaluating their own practices, there was a good deal of unplanned variation between communities, and it seemed to me that comparisons between communities could provide data bearing on the survival value of different cultural practices. Accordingly, I examined data on the longevity of a sample of 31 experimental communities formed in the United States between 1780 and 1860, and found that religious communities tended to survive, on average, at least ten times longer than secular communities. I described these results at the Skinner memorial symposium (1991), and speculated on the differences in cultural practices that might be responsible for this striking difference in longevity. When Peter Lamal invited me to prepare a chapter for this volume, I took the opportunity to explore this question further.

THE DATABASE

Experimental communities differed on many dimensions, and the question is how to identify those dimensions that can be helpful for analysis. Considering all such communities as an aggregate, there are two obvious dependent variables: the rate at which communities were formed, and the rate at which they disbanded. One might then try to find historical factors that influenced their formation, and once formed, the internal and external factors that influenced their longevity. The analysis is related, in spirit at least, to the study of acquisition of diverse operants in an individual, and the relative persistence of those operants once acquired. Clearly, reliable data are needed.

The first question is how to define an "experimental community." For example, what degree of property sharing, communality of work, and so forth, is necessary to distinguish an experimental community from a cooperative housing association? Rather than attempting a definition, I relied on secondary sources: any group that was listed by at least two books on intentional communities in the library of the University of New Hampshire, and that actually operated for some time in the United States, was included in the data set, provided that it had been founded early enough to estimate its longevity.

In the literature on experimental communities, there is occasional disagreement about founding dates and longevities. Therefore, I included only those communities for which at least two sources agreed, within two years, on the date of founding. For nearly all of these communities, information on the date of disbanding was also available from at least two sources. Requiring agreement between two or more secondary sources on identification as an experimental community, and on dates of founding and disbanding, is analogous to requiring interobserver agreement on the occurrence and timing of a subject's responses when strict mechanical definition is not possible.

There is also some uncertainty about how to define a community when it had multiple locations. When a single group established communities at different locations in a sequence (such as the Harmonists, who moved from Harmony in Butler County, Pennsylvania, to Harmony [later New Harmony] in Indiana, and finally to Economy in Beaver County, Pennsylvania), or when a single group had a number of concurrent locations under a single system of governance (such as Amana, which succeeded Ebenezer and comprised seven neighboring villages), I scored it as a single community.

The resulting list includes 248 communities. As a first cut at analysis, and following a number of scholars, I divided them into 111 religious communities and 137 secular communities, where "religious" implies that the community was founded on the basis of an otherworldly ideal and all members adhered to a single set of spiritual doctrines and practices of worship. By contrast, "secular" implies the absence of a central religious or spiritual ideal, or that the members gave their primary allegiance to some worldly political or economic ideals (which might include various spiritual doctrines and practices). In fact, "religious" and "secular" are probably better construed as broad and partially overlapping regions along a continuum that ranges from a religious sect requiring total conformity to the teachings of a divinely inspired leader at one extreme, to an atheistic, communist society committed to Marxist doctrines at the other. An anarchist collective with no doctrinal presciptions might not fit comfortably on such a continuum, but it would surely be classed as secular. I relied on Table 1 in Oved (1988) for classification when no other secondary sources provided relevant information. Because there is some arbitrariness in my decisions on how to categorize and count communities, the full data set is given in the Appendix, together with a list of the sources I used.

The list begins with Plockhoy's Commonwealth, a community of Dutch Mennonites founded on the banks of the Delaware River in 1663. It was plundered by the British in 1664, thus lasting less than two years. The list ends with Holy City, founded in central California in 1919 by a self-proclaimed priest and racist. Its founder was brought to court repeatedly on charges including sedition, and the community collapsed about 1958. I stopped at 1920 because very few communities founded after that year were listed in more than one of the secondary sources I consulted, and more recently founded communities (e.g., Twin Oaks) would have an arbitrary upper limit—the date of the most recently published source—on their longevity.

THE FORMATION OF RELIGIOUS AND SECULAR COMMUNITIES

The analysis of individual operant behavior has traditionally relied on cumulative records to portray changes in the rate of a repeatable response. Vari-

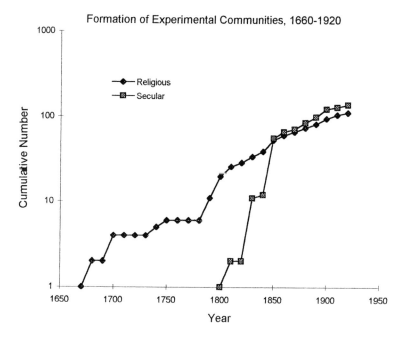

Figure 10.1. A cumulative record of the formation of religious and secular experimental communities in the United States from 1660 to 1920. Note that the y-axis is logarithmic, on which a straight, upward-sloping line implies a constant rate of increase.

ations in the vigor of the communal movement in the United States can be illustrated similarly. Figure 10.1 presents cumulative records of the formation of all religious and secular communities by date of founding, blocked in ten-year intervals. The y-axis is logarithmic, as in the standard celeration charts employed in Precision Teaching, to give a direct visual representation of rate of increase in the frequency with which experimental communities were formed. In a plot of this sort, a positively sloped straight line implies a constant rate of increase; for example, an increase from 20 to 30 communities (50%) over, say, 20 years is equivalent, in slope, to an increase from 60 to 90 communities (also 50%) over a subsequent 20-year period.

Inspection of Figure 10.1 suggests sporadic growth in the number of religious communities up to the late eighteenth century, at which point there is a rapid increase, attributable largely to the formation of a number of Shaker communities between 1787 and 1810. Thereafter, religious communities continue to be founded at a steadily increasing rate of about 15% per decade. Secular communities exhibit two growth spurts in the first half of the nineteenth century, one beginning in 1825, inspired by Robert Owen's proposal of communitarian alternatives to industrial capitalism, and the second in the 1840s, inspired by Albert Brisbane's promotion of the social theories of Charles Fourier. After

1850, secular communities continue to be founded at a steadily increasing rate which is similar to that of the religious communities.

THE LONGEVITY OF RELIGIOUS AND SECULAR COMMUNITIES

Figure 10.1 suggests that the year 1850 provides a natural break point for the analysis of the longevity of experimental communities. Accordingly, the longevities of religious and secular communities are displayed as survivorship graphs for the periods before and after 1850 in the two panels of Figure 10.2. The y-axis, which is logarithmic, shows the number of communities that survived for the number of years represented on the x-axis. Thus, of the 51 religious communities founded between 1663 and 1850, all 51 survived at least one year; 47 survived at least two years; 44 survived at least three years; and so forth, out to over 100 years, at which time 15 communities—all of them Shakers—were still functioning.

The slope of a logarithmic survivorship graph provides a way to evaluate the longevity of a group of communities: the shallower the slope, the greater the longevity. Between 1663 and 1850, the plot for religious communities is a shallow, roughly linear function, at least after the first ten years after founding. The slope of the major segment of the function is about −.03 log units per decade, which implies that about 7% of religious communities disbanded per decade after founding, at least after surviving their first ten years. This simply quantifies their widely recognized longevity (e.g., Bestor, 1970; Holloway, 1966; Noyes, 1870/1966).

The plot for secular communities founded between 1663 and 1850 is also tolerably linear, with one outlier at 30 years (Icaria). The slope (neglecting the outlier) is about −1.0 log unit/decade, which implies that 90% of secular communities disbanded per decade of their lifetimes since founding. The difference in survivorship for the early religious and secular communities is striking.

There is an equally striking difference between the periods before and after 1850. As shown in the lower panel of Figure 10.2, the survivorship plot for religious communities remains roughly linear over much of its range. However, its slope is about −.22 log units per decade, implying that 40% of religious communities disbanded per decade of their lifetimes since founding—a far more rapid rate of loss than for apparently comparable communities founded before 1850. The plot for secular communities has a slope of about −.44 log units/decade, which is double that for the religious communities founded after 1850, and implies a loss rate of 64% of the secular communities per decade since their founding. This is a substantially lower rate of loss than for the period before 1850. All in all, it appears that after 1850, the longevity of secular communities increased, whereas the longevity of religious communities decreased.

Something about religious communities, or the political and economic conditions of the society in which they lived, evidently changed dramatically around

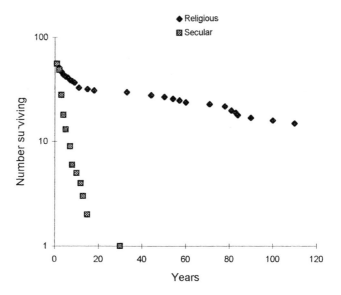

Communities founded between 1663 and 1850

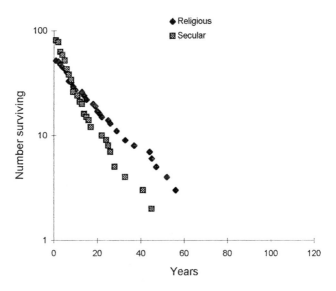

Communities founded between 1851 and 1920

Figure 10.2. Survivorship graphs for all religious and secular communities founded in the United States between 1663 and 1850 (upper panel) and between 1851 and 1920 (lower panel). Note that the y-axis is logarithmic; see text for explanation.

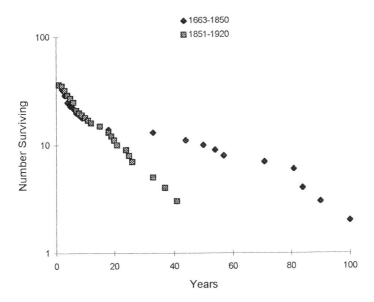

Figure 10.3. Survivorship graphs for all religious communities founded before 1850 except the Shakers, and for all religious communities founded after 1851 except the Hutterites. Note that the y-axis is logarithmic, as in Figure 10.2.

the middle of the nineteenth century. One obvious difference is that only two new Shaker communities were founded after 1850. Because the Shaker communities have been noteworthy for their longevity (e.g., Holloway, 1966; Oved, 1988), because they formed a large proportion of the religious communities founded before 1850, and because they had a communal federation and could therefore be viewed as a single community with multiple locations founded at different times, I repeated the pre-1850 analysis with the Shakers represented only once, at 100+ years. In a sense, the Shakers were replaced by the Hutterites in the period after 1850, when nineteen Hutterite communities were founded. As a group, the Hutterites have also been noteworthy for their longevity (Altus, 1990; Oved, 1988), so I repeated the post-1850 analysis with the Hutterites represented only once, at 100+ years. The resulting functions are compared in Figure 10.3. By inspection, they overlap during the initial curvilinear portions, but subsequently diverge, with the pre-1850 slope about −.11 log units per decade after the first ten years, and the post-1850 slope about −.25 per decade. Evidently, religious communities founded between 1663 and 1850 tended to be longer-lived than their post-1850 successors, even with the extraordinarily long-lived Shaker settlements removed. However, comparison of the slope of the function for post-1850 secular communities (Figure 10.2, lower panel) and post-

1850 religious communities (Figure 10.3) suggests that religious communities were generally longer-lived than their secular contemporaries, even with the Hutterites removed.

There is another feature of logarithmic survivorship functions that should be appreciated. To the extent that they are linear, they indicate that disbanding occurs randomly in time. Many communities experienced disastrous events such as epidemic disease or fire, which would occur randomly in time with respect to their founding and which often precipitated their demise. Assuming that disasters occurred equally often and with equal severity, on average, for religious and secular communities, the slopes of the survivorship curves in Figure 10.2 suggest that religious communities were more likely to carry on after a disaster than their secular counterparts. Much of this chapter is concerned with possible reasons for this difference.

FACTORS INFLUENCING FORMATION AND LONGEVITY

Although the difference in longevity between religious and secular communities diminished sharply after 1850, there is an enduring difference in the longevities of these broad classes of communities. There are three issues to be considered. First, what factors account for the decline in the longevity of religious communities founded after 1850? Second, what factors account for the improved longevity of secular communities after 1850? And third, what factors account for the persistent advantage of religious over secular communities?

There are two kinds of factors to consider: those that are external to the communities, such as changes in social and economic aspects of society in the United States and the world at large, and those that are internal to the communities, such as mode of property ownership and practices governing daily life and work. I'll begin with external factors. For example, at the beginning of the period from 1660 to 1920, the present United States was a sparsely populated British colony. After the American Revolution, there was an extended period of agricultural and industrial development in the East and Midwest, with occasional stagnation and economic depression, but an open frontier to the West provided an escape hatch for the poor and disaffected. As the nineteenth century ended, industrial development intensified, the labor movement grew, and the frontier was essentially closed, although cheap land remained available in the West. Some of these developments influenced the formation and survival of religious communities, which will be considered first.

Religious Communities

During the seventeenth and eighteenth centuries, several European religious sects that had suffered from political persecution and social ostracism emigrated to America as coherent groups. Fertile land was readily available and the political climate was tolerant, an ideal combination permitting these groups to establish communities that would isolate them from the outside world while they pursued their various paths to salvation and maintained their physical well-being through agriculture and crafts. Bestor (1970) characterized them as foreign-language sectarian communities, and noted that many of them were remarkably long-lived. Most such communities were founded before 1820, and none but the Hutterites was established after 1860. Therefore, the longevity of religious communities founded before 1850 may reflect their long and distinctive histories of church membership and group persecution in Europe, and their linguistic separation from the larger society in the United States. These external factors may be more important than their internal communal practices.

Although the early Shakers came to the United States in the late eighteenth century as a group from England, where they had moved from France because of persecution of Protestants during the Counter-Reformation, they were not isolated by language, and many people born in the United States joined their communities during their 100+ years of vigorous existence. If anthing, the Shakers were isolated by internal practices such as celibacy and unconventional worship. Because of the low population density during the post–Revolutionary War period, they were able to establish relatively secluded self-sufficient communities on fertile land, but they interacted with neighbors and had frequent visitors who were intrigued by their way of life and admired their success. Accordingly, internal factors such as shared work, common housing (which was divided according to sex), ritual, social life, and lifelong security were probably important for the rapid multiplication and longevity of the Shaker communities. By 1850, however, the growth of population and industry, and the increasing availability of a secure life within the society at large—without the drawbacks of celibacy—made Shakerism less appealing. The Shaker communities that were founded in the 1890s had relatively short life spans, suggesting that their distinctive set of internal practices did not suffice to ensure longevity.

The Hutterite communities, which were established in the United States two centuries after the first religious groups and a century after the Shakers, shared some of the special characteristics that made the earlier groups so long-lived. The Hutterites were narrowly sectarian, religious pacifists with a long history of communal living and a distinctive dialect. They emigrated en masse to the United States from Russia, where they were threatened with military conscription, and settled at Bon Homme on the plains of South Dakota. They did not practice celibacy, and their birth rate was (and remains) high. By 1917, they had expanded to nineteen communities. However, when the United States entered World War I, they were persecuted for their pacifism. All but one of their communities disbanded and their members moved to Canada. However, many Hutterites returned to the United States during the 1930s, and their communities continued to expand. As of 1990, there were 362 Hutterite communities with nearly 35,000 members in the United States and Canada (Altus, 1990). They learn English as a second language, they have adopted modern farming technology, and they have regular contact with modern society through agricultural markets and town visits, but they live simply and remain largely isolated by their customs and rural locations. Their success is probably attributable to this level of isolation and the resulting homogeneity within their communities, which is maintained by a strong program of education in Hutterite traditions (Oved, 1988).

With the exception of the Hutterites, the foreign-language sects of the sort that founded the early religious communities stopped forming communities after 1850, at least in the United States. At the same time, the Shakers stopped expanding. Thus, these traditionally long-lived communities were not replaced (again excepting the Hutterites, whose full longevity cannot be known). The remarkable longevity of religious groups founded before 1850, excluding the Shakers, probably reflects special external conditions that favored the arrival and separatism of the foreign-language sects rather than any specific internal factors or cultural practices that were distinctively associated with these groups.

Secular Communities

As noted above, there were two growth spurts in the founding of secular communities during the first half of the nineteenth century. The first was inspired by the writings and lectures of Robert Owen, an industrialist and social reformer who believed that the social ills associated with industrial capitalism could be avoided if workers owned the means of production and worked together in small communities to secure their material well-being. About a dozen Owenite experiments were initiated in 1825–26, and three more were attempted in the early 1840s (Bestor, 1970). Although the external conditions—workers' discontent with their lot in the increasingly industrialized United States, availability of cheap land to establish agriculture and manufacturing enterprises, and growing markets for produce and manufactured goods—were highly favorable, none of these communities survived for more than four years, and their median longevity was two years. Despite the enthusiasm that accompanied the founding of the first Owenite community at New Harmony, factions soon formed and acrimonious disputes led to secessions and eventual dissolution. Similar problems arose at Yellow Springs. Other Owenite communities such as Kendall, whose members had lived in the area and were familiar with local farming conditions (and each other), failed despite a year or two of steady and harmonious work, when the members concluded that they could achieve more material security for themselves and their families by working individually. Evidently, a combination of external and internal factors—relatively prosperous times and an open-admissions policy that permitted wide variation in ideology and commitment to communal living among the members—worked to bring these groups to an early end.

The second growth spurt, beginning in 1843, was inspired by the social theories of Charles Fourier. Many of Fourier's ideas for an orderly and harmonious society were fantastic, but his proposals for the division of labor into "Series" within a "Phalanx," where the most disagreeable work would receive the highest rate of pay and industrial effort would be made attractive through cooperation, seemed practical and timely. A depression had caused widespread unemployment, and many thoughtful people were debating alternative social systems. In Europe, talk of revolution was in the air, and in the United States, reform movements proliferated. When Albert Brisbane introduced Fourier's proposals to the United States, they were greeted with immediate enthusiasm. In the years from 1843 to 1845, about 25 experimental communities attempted to realize Fourier's program, but most of them failed within three years because of economic difficulties resulting from poor planning and internal disagreements resulting from a failure to screen new members.

The North American Phalanx in New Jersey—the longest-lived of the Fourier-inspired communities—avoided internal disagreements for several years by strict selection practices, including a one-year probationary period, and operated a profitable market garden that shipped its produce to New York. As a result, it achieved a high standard of cooperative living. About ten years after its founding in 1843, internal disputes arose and a number of its members seceded. In 1854, a fire destroyed its mills and food stores. Other groups—especially the religious communities—have endured such calamities, but once the harmonious life of the Phalanx had been disrupted by disputes, the members seized the opportunity to return to their private lives (Oved, 1988). Thus, even careful selection and economic success were not sufficient to sustain the Fourierist communities.

It is probably fair to say that the rapid rate of founding of the Owenite and Fourierist communities resulted from social and intellectual movements that were sparked by external circumstances, and that their rapid collapse resulted from the general lack of selection and preparation of the membership for communal life. Other secular communities founded within the same period, such as the Christian-inspired reformist Hopedale and the anarchist Utopia, fared somewhat better, but as a group the secular communities were short-lived.

Internal Factors and Longevity

The foregoing discussion has treated religious and secular communities as distinct categories, despite their overlaps. Now, I ask whether there are any internal factors or practices, other than the centrality of religious doctrine and worship, that are associated with longevity when religious and secular communities are considered together.

A similar approach was taken by Kanter (1972), who concentrated on a sample of communities founded between 1780 and 1860. She identified a variety of commitment mechanisms, that is, "concrete social practices that helped generate and sustain the commitment of their members" (p. 75) that might be correlated with longevity, such as personal abstinence (e.g., celibacy), irreversible financial investment in the community, communal labor, and mortification (e.g., confession and mutual criticism). She found that the nine communities in her sample that survived more than 25 years were consistently more likely to have commitment mechanisms as a central part of their communal life than the 21 communities that disbanded within 25 years. However, these commitment mechanisms were highly correlated with religious beliefs and practices: as listed in the Appendix, all nine of her longer-lived groups were religious communities, whereas only five of the 21 shorter-lived groups were religious.

My analysis complements Kanter's, but differs in that I have not tried to identify, a priori, any practices that might be expected to enhance commitment or longevity. I examined the secondary sources listed in the Appendix for information on the practices of all communities founded after 1850, excluding the Hutterites because of their similarities to the pre-1850 sectarian and Shaker groups. More specifically, I searched for information on practices such as governance, property sharing, work and housing arrangements, meals, child care, and personal abstinence, which would affect the character of daily life. I also noted membership selection requirements such as fees and screening, and the degree to which the community interacted with the outside world. I did not score for religious practices, which have been considered at length above.

In order to arrive at a reasonable sample size, it was necessary to combine information across sources because most gave only partial information for some communities and none at all for others. Thus, there is almost certainly a lot of variation attributable to the authors' differing criteria for describing a particular practice as a central feature of the group, or even mentioning its presence. Also, the sources rarely noted the specific absence of a practice such as membership screening or personal abstinence. Finally, some communities altered some of their practices during their lifetimes: for example, governance might initially have been autocratic under an inspired founder, and then changed to a board of managers when the founder died. When this happened, I listed both.

The practices of 44 communities were described in one or more of the secondary sources. Not surprisingly, there was more information on longer-lived groups. To evaluate the relations between communal practices and longevity, I divided the total sample into those communities that survived more than ten years (n = 18), and those that survived ten years or less (n = 26). The total number of scorable community practices was about the same in these two subsets. However, the resulting tabulation is at best a tentative summary; a more complete and less biased characterization requires a program of careful examination, by several independent scholars, of historical archives and original sources such as diaries and letters of community members.

The numbers of communities in the longer- and shorter-lived subsets that were described as engaging in various practices are listed in Table 10.1, which shows a striking similarity between the longer- and shorter-lived subsets. For example, in both, there was a roughly even distribution across three ways of handling property: all property held in common, a mixed model that distinguished between communal property (such as land or farm equipment) and personal possessions, and all property held by individuals. Also in both, communities

Table 10.1
Summary of Communal Practices in Experimental Communities Founded in the United States between 1850 and 1920, Separated According to Whether They Lasted More or Less than Ten Years

Practice		Longevity > 10	Longevity ≤ 10
Governance --	Autocratic	5	7
	Board of Managers	6	3
	Elected Officers	2	3
	General Meeting	2	2
	No formal gov't	3	
Property --	Communal	4	3
	Mixed	4	5
	Individual	4	3
Work --	Communal	10	11
	Mixed	2	2
	Individual	3	1
Housing --	Communal	2	2
	Mixed	5	3
	Individual/family	6	6
Meals --	Communal	6	3
	Mixed	1	1
	Individual/family	6	3
Child care --	Communal	7	5
	Family	3	3
Mutual criticism practiced		2	2
Personal abstinence required		6	5
Admission Fees/screening	Yes	7	8
	No	2	2
Interaction with outside --	Lots	5	4
	Little	4	4

that arranged communal work were far more numerous than those that relied on individual work, or mixtures of communal and individual work, to sustain them. One cannot prove a null hypothesis by a statistical test, but a chi-squared test of association between longevity and the frequency of various practices listed in Table 10.1 would strongly suggest that there were no overall differences in the practices of longer- and shorter-lived communities.

The possibility remains that some special, interacting combination of practices might enhance longevity; this would have to be evaluated by a close study of case histories, which is quite different from the aggregative approach taken here. In view of the general lack of relation between communal practices and longevity as aggregated in Table 10.1, the centrality of a religious belief and its associated practices appears to be the only factor that has consistently contributed to communal survival.

RELIGION AND COMMUNAL SURVIVAL

This chapter has come full circle. My initial analysis of the difference between religious and secular communal survival (Nevin, 1991) was based on a sample of communities established between 1780 and 1860. On the basis of this sample, I suggested that the longevity of the religious communities might have been enhanced by the fact that their members had belonged to the same church or related group before entering the communal life. This would have the effect of establishing patterns of social interaction during shared work on church projects, caring for elderly members, and the like, that could carry over naturally to communal life. This precommunal repertoire of cooperative behavior and its accompanying social reinforcement would probably be conducive to persistent cooperative action in a community, even in the face of adversity.

I also noted, following Kanter (1972), that mortification practices such as mutual criticism or confession were relatively common in the early religious communities. These practices exposed individual deviations from communal norms and provided occasions for public sanctions for deviation, as well as opportunities for public social reinforcement of cooperative behavior. This would not only promote homogeneity of behavior within the community, but also reduce the sense of individual self-determination and freedom that might obstruct cooperative action.

The summary in Table 10–1 of post-1850 communal practices suggests that the latter—mutual criticism in some form—is probably not important for longevity. The former—a shared history of interaction and social reinforcement before joining the community—may be an important factor for communal longevity, but it is not sufficient to ensure survival in the face of internal dissension or adversity. For example, the Russian Jewish immigrants who formed the New Odessa community had shared expenses and worked through disagreements in Odessa before coming to New York together; and in New York, they lived and worked communally for about a year before moving as a group to Oregon (Fogarty, 1990; Oved, 1988). Nevertheless, their community collapsed within five years, despite considerable economic success, as a result of internal disputes and a fire that destroyed their communal hall. They shared several of the characteristics of the successful foreign-language religious sects: persecution in their homeland, collaborative work before forming a community, and subsequent cultural isolation. However, most of the members were intellectual radicals who did not have a set of religious principles in common. I am left with the uncomfortable conclusion that religious communities survive longer than their secular counterparts for reasons that remain obscure.

One way of expressing the difference between religious and secular groups is that religious groups achieved a "We-spirit" in contrast to the "I-spirit" of secular communities (French & French, 1975, pp. 71–73). French and French point out some specific practices of the early religious communities that would contribute to the "We-spirit," such as providing equal benefits for all, regardless of their work. In the language of molar reinforcement contingencies, individual benefits were independent of immediate individual work effort, and instead depended directly on communal well-being, which in turn depended, over the long run, on individual work in collaboration with others. Thus, the usual ratio-like contingency between individual work effort and individual consequences—the harder you work, the more you get—was mediated by the community, leading to delayed and distributed consequences. Such contingencies should shift control from immediate individual benefits to deferred communal well-being, leading to behavior summarized as the "We-spirit." However, such contingencies were arranged in many short-lived secular communities that were committed to strict Communism (e.g., New Odessa) as well as long-lived religious communities, and thus cannot be the sole determiners of longevity.

Religious and secular communities also differed in their stated or implicit goals. Religious communities were founded to help their individual members achieve salvation or prepare for the Second Coming by perfecting their lives and observing the precepts of their faith, usually as promulgated by an inspired leader. By contrast, many secular communities were founded to demonstrate the feasibility of cooperative living and collective security from the harsh exploitative practices of industrial capitalism, along lines suggested by social, economic, and political theories. At the risk of overgeneralizing, I suggest that religious communities had individualistic goals, but their members generally behaved communally, whereas secular communities had communal goals that encompassed the society at large, but their members often argued and behaved selfishly.

In the first scholarly survey of experimental communities, Noyes (1870/1966) laid the blame on human nature: "we discover a remarkable similarity in the symptoms that manifested themselves in the transitory Communities, and almost entire unanimity in the witnesses who testify as to the causes of their failure. GENERAL DEPRAVITY, all say, is the villain of the whole story" (p. 646, capitals in original). As a preacher of Christian perfectionism, Noyes quite naturally placed the blame on the lack of a firm religious foundation in the short-lived communities; and as an empiricist, he used the historical record of success of the religious communities founded before 1850 to support his argument. He concluded his book by challenging secular approaches (which he called "Paganism, infidelity, or nothingarianism") to prove him wrong.

Concerning the role of religion, Noyes (1870/1966) remarked that "Earnest men of one faith are more likely to be respectful to organized authority and one another, than men of no religion or men of many religions held in indifference and mutual counteraction'' (p. 656). A Hutterite quoted by French and French (1975) said it more succinctly: ''Without religion sharing doesn't work'' (p. 77). Evidently, there is something about a strong, otherworldly faith, held in common, that makes people who share space, income, work, and social life especially likely to act on behalf of one another, thereby prolonging communal life.

Throughout this chapter, I have taken longevity as an implicit criterion for communal success, in common with a number of others (e.g., Kanter, 1972). An alternative criterion was expressed by Henry Demarest Lloyd in an address to the Ruskin community in 1897:

Only within these communities have there been seen in the wide borders of the United States a social life where hunger and cold, prostitution, intemperance, poverty, crime, premature old age and unnecessary mortality, panic and industrial terror have been abolished. If they had done this for a year, they would have deserved to be called the only successful ''society'' on this continent. (quoted in Fogarty, 1990, p. 134)

I cannot disagree with Lloyd's moving statement. However, sheer longevity is at least a crude index of success. French and French (1975) suggest that ''to the extent that it is successful, so that its members need not turn to the discontented society outside to meet their needs, the group is likely to last'' (p. 76). The Skinnerian, selectionist criterion of survival also argues for longevity as a fundamental measure of success. However, the strongest test of success is the extent to which a cultural variant replicates itself and spreads throughout its host society. The quantitative analyses above suggest that the growth rate of 15% per decade in the formation of new communities between 1850 and 1920 was insufficient to achieve a net increase in the number of active communities because, in the aggregate, they were relatively short-lived. The communal movement remains alive and well, but if experimental communities are to play a significant role in the culture as alternatives to current patterns of living, it is essential that we understand the determiners of their longevity.

In the conclusion to his preface to the second edition of *Walden Two* (1976), Skinner said:

It is now widely recognized that great changes must be made in the American way of life. Not only can we not face the rest of the world while consuming and polluting as we do, we cannot for long face ourselves while acknowledging the violence and chaos in which we live. The choice is clear: either we do nothing and allow a miserable and probably catastrophic future to overtake us, or we use our knowledge about human behavior to create a social environment in which we shall live productive and creative lives and do so without jeopardizing the chances that those who follow us will be able to do the same. Something like a Walden Two would not be a bad start. (p. xvi)

Since Skinner wrote that passage, the disparity between rich and poor has grown, and the adverse environmental consequences of the individualistic, high-consumption lifestyle now prevalent in the postindustrial nations have become more evident. The need for communal sharing of resources is greater than ever. If the factors that make for the longevity of experimental communities can be identified, that knowledge can be put to use on behalf of the human future. An analysis of the ways in which cooperative social behavior is enhanced by a commitment to religion, broadly construed as reverence for a power that transcends the worldly life of individual humans, would not be a bad start.

APPENDIX

Experimental communities that are listed in at least two secondary sources with reasonable agreement (+/−2 yrs) on founding date and, separately, on longevity. Multiple communal locations are scored as a single community if it was continuous through several successive locations (e.g., Harmony) or if several groups with centralized leadership existed simultaneously at different locations (e.g., Amana, Oneida-Wallingford). However, they are scored as separate communities when independent groups split off from an originator (e.g., Icaria). The sources are: Bestor (1970); Calverton (1941); Fogarty (1980); Fogarty (1990); French and French (1975); Hinds (1961); Holloway (1966); Kanter (1972); Kesten (1993); Noyes (1870/1966); Oved (1988); and Spann (1989). Communities denoted (Sh) are Shaker, and those denoted (Hut) are Hutterite.

Note: Longevity is the number of years, or parts of years, between founding and disbanding (e.g., longevity for a community founded in 1873 and disbanded in 1875 is scored as three years). When two sources disagree, the smaller is used. When three or more sources disagree, the median is used.

Year	**Religious**		**Secular**	
	Name	*Longevity*	*Name*	*Longevity*
1663	Plockhoy	2		
1683	Bohemia Manor	44		
1694	Woman in Wilderness	54		
1696	Irenia			
1732	Ephrata	81		
1744	Moravian			
1787	Mt. Lebanon (Sh)	100+		
1788	Jerusalem	33		
	Watervliet NY (Sh)	100+		
1790	Enfield (Sh)	100+		
	Hancock (Sh)	100+		
1791	Harvard (Sh)	100+		
1792	Canterbury (Sh)	100+		
	Tyringham (Sh)	84		
1793	Alfred (Sh)	100+		
	Enfield (Sh)	100+		
	Shirley (Sh)	100+		

Year	Religious		Secular	
	Name	*Longevity*	*Name*	*Longevity*
1794	Gorham (Sh)	100+		
	Sabbathday Lk (Sh)	100+		
1798			Dorrilites	2
1800	Snow Hill	71		
1804			The Union	7
1805	Harmony Society	100		
	Union Village (Sh)	100+		
1806	Watervliet OH (Sh)	100+		
1809	Pleasant Hill (Sh)	100+		
	South Union (Sh)	100+		
1810	West Union (Sh)	18		
1817	Pilgrims	2		
	Savoy (Sh)	9		
	Zoar	81		
1822	North Union (Sh)	78		
1825	Coal Creek	8	Goshen	2
	Whitewater (Sh)	83	New Harmony	3
			Yellow Springs	2
1826	Sodus Bay (Sh)	11	Blue Springs	2
			Franklin	1
			Forestville	2
			Kendal	4
			Nashoba	4
			Valley Forge	1
1827	Teutonia (OH)	5		
1830	Kirtland	9		
1831	Enoch	4		
1832	N. Phil/Gr. Enc/Gtn	50		
1833	Oberlin	9	Equity	3
1836	Berea	2		
	Sonyea (Sh)	60		
1841			Brook Farm	7
			Hopedale	15
1842	Teutonia (PA)	3	Marlborough Assoc.	5
			Social Reform Unity	2
			Northampton Assoc.	5
1843	Abram Brook's Exp	3	Bureau County	2
	Ebenezer (Amana)	90	Fruitlands	2
	Peace Union	3	Goose Pond	2
	Putney	6	Hunt's Colony	4
			Jefferson County	2
			Morehouse Union	2
			North American Ph.	13
			Skaneateles	4
			Soc. One Mentian	2
			Sylvania	3
1844	Bethel-Aurora	57	Alphadelphia Phalanx	5
			Clarkson Assoc.	2
			Clermont Phalanx	3
			Iowa Pioneer Ph.	2
			LaGrange Phalanx	3

Year	Religious Name	Longevity	Secular Name	Longevity
			Leraysville Phalanx	1
			Mixville Assoc.	2
			Ohio Phalanx	2
			Ontario Phalanx	2
			Prairie Home	1
			Sodus Bay Phalanx	3
			Trumbull Phalanx	5
			Union Home	3
			Wisconsin Phalanx	7
1845	Voree	6	Canton Phalanx	1
			Columbian Phalanx	1
			Fruit Hills	8
			Grand Prairie	3
			Integral Phalanx	2
			Kristeen	2
			Phila. Industrial	3
			Utilitarian	4
1846	Bishop Hill	15	Pigeon River	2
			Spring Farm Phalanx	3
1847	Brotherhood	2	Bettina	2
	Zodiac	7	Communia	10
			Utopia	12
1848	Kingdom St. James	9	Icaria-Nvoo-Corning	30
	Oneida	33		
1849	Ephraim (Tanktown)	4		
1851	Harmonia	11	Modern Times	13
	Jasper	3		
	Mountain Cove	3		
1853	Ephraim (Door Co.)	12	Grand Prairie Inst.	2
	Preparation	6	Raritan Bay	6
			Rising Star	5
1854	St. Nazianz	21	Berlin Heights	5
1855			Reunion (TX)	5
1856	Germania Co.	24	Memnonia	2
1858			Cheltenham (Icaria)	13
1860			Harmonial Vegetarian	5
			Point Hope	2
1861	Adonai Shomo	37		
1862	Ora Labora	7		
1863	Celesta	2		
	Amenia	5		
1865			Berlin	2
1867	Brocton	15		
	Walla Walla	15		
1868			Reunion (MO)	3
1869			Union Colony	4
1870			German Company	2
			Silkville	15
1871	Western Colony	3	Chicago Colorado	3
			Progressive	8
1872			Friendship	6

Year	Religious		Secular	
	Name	*Longevity*	*Name*	*Longevity*
1873			Bennett	5
1874	Bon Homme (Hut)	100+	Cawn Valcour	2
	Orderville	10	Social Freedom	7
	Women's Commonwealth	33		
1875	Wolf Creek (Hut)	56	Cedarvale	3
			Investigating Comm.	1
1876	Fountain Grove	25		
1877			Esperanza	2
			Modjeska	2
1878	Elmspring (Hut)	52		
1879	Tripp (Hut)	6	Jeune Icaria	8
			New Icaria	17
1880			Rugby	8
			Thompson	
1881			Icaria-Speranza	6
			Sicily Island	2
			Washington Colony	4
1882			Alliance	25
			Beersheba	4
			Bethlehem Yehuda	4
			Cremieux	8
			Painted Woods	6
			Rosenhayn	8
1883			Mutual Aid	5
			New Odessa	5
1884	Joyful	1		
	Shalam	18		
	Tidioute (Hut)	3		
1885			Kahweah	8
1886	Jamesville (Hut)	33	Nehalem	7
	Miltown (Hut)	22		
1887			Puget Sound Coop	4
1888	Koreshan	100+		
1889	Lord's Farm	19		
1890	Kutter Colony (Hut)	29		
1891	Rockport (Hut)	44	Union Mill	7
1893			Hiawatha Assoc.	4
			Winter Island Coop	6
1894	Narcoosee (Sh)	19	Altruria	2
			Colorado Coop	17
			Glennis	3
			Home Employment	13
			Ruskin	8
1895	New House of Israel	26	Fairhope	14
			Willard Coop	2
1896	Christian Comwealth	5	Magnolia	1
	Christian Corp.	2		
1897			Freedom	9
			Equality	11
1898	White Oak (Sh)	5	American Settlers	2
			Burley	11
			Home Colony	24
			Point Loma	45

Year	Religious		Secular	
	Name	*Longevity*	*Name*	*Longevity*
1899	Christian Social	6	Niksur	1
	Comwealth of Israel	4		
	Friedheim	2		
	Lystra	4		
	Spirit Fruit	9		
	Straight Edge	20		
1900	Maxwell (Hut)	19	Apalachicola	5
			Arden	90+
			Freeland	7
			Kinder Lou	2
			Roycrofters	16
1901	Rosedale (Hut)	18		
	Zion City	6		
1903	House of David	26	Temple Home	11
1905	Spink Colony (Hut)	14		
	Beadle Colony (Hut)	14		
1906	Huron Colony (Hut)	13	Helicon Hall	2
	Richards Colony (Hut)	13		
1907	Buffalo Colony (Hut)	8	Fellowship Farm	12
1909			Little Landers	8
			Tahanto	26
1910	Milford (Hut)	9	Free Acres Assoc.	41
			Order of Theocracy	22
1911			Fruit Crest	2
			Halidon	28
1912	Spring Creek (Hut)	9	Fellowship Frm (LA)	16
			Krotona	13
			Lopez	9
1913	Burning Bush	6	Bohemian Coop Farm	4
	James Valley (Hut)	6		
	Warren Range (Hut)	6		
1914	Pisgah Grande	8	Army of Industry	5
			Llano/New Llano	26
1915			Ferrer	32
1919	Holy City	40		

REFERENCES

Altus, D. (1990). *The Hutterites: A lesson in cultural survival.* Paper presented at the meeting of the Association for Behavior Analysis, Nashville, TN, May.

Bestor, A. (1970). *Backwoods utopias* (2nd ed.). Philadelphia: University of Pennsylvania Press.

Calverton, V. F. (1941). *Where angels dared to tread.* New York: Bobbs-Merrill.

Fogarty, R. S. (1980). *Dictionary of American communal and utopian history.* Westport, CT: Greenwood.

———. (1990). *All things new.* Chicago: University of Chicago Press.

French, D., & French, E. (1975). *Working communally.* New York: Russell Sage Foundation.

Hinds, W. A. (1961). *American communities.* New York: Corinth Books.

Holloway, M. (1966). *Heavens on earth* (rev. ed.). New York: Dover.

Kanter, R. M. (1972). *Commitment and community*. Cambridge, MA: Harvard University Press.

Kesten, S. R. (1993). *Utopian episodes*. Syracuse: Syracuse University Press.

Nevin, J. A. (1991). *B. F. Skinner, Utopian*. Paper presented at the memorial symposium for B. F. Skinner at the meeting of the Eastern Psychological Association, New York, April.

Noyes, J. H. (1966). *History of American socialisms*. New York: Dover (original work published in 1870).

Oved, Y. (1988). *Two hundred years of American communes*. New Brunswick, NJ: Transaction.

Skinner, B. F. (1948; 2nd ed. 1976) *Walden Two*. New York: Macmillan.

———. (1969) Utopia as an experimental culture. In *Contingencies of reinforcement* (pp. 29–49). New York: Appleton-Century-Crofts.

Spann, E. K. (1989). *Brotherly tomorrows*. New York: Columbia University Press.

Tyler, A. F. (1944) *Freedom's ferment*. Minneapolis: University of Minnesota Press.

11

Corporate Control of Media and Propaganda: A Behavior Analysis

RICHARD E. LAITINEN
AND RICHARD F. RAKOS

The intellectual heart of behavior analysis assumes that all human behavior—overt and covert—is environmentally determined (e.g., Skinner, 1971). While behavior analysts have devoted a great deal of empirical and theoretical effort toward assessing the impact of various physical, social, interpersonal, and cultural stimuli on people's responses, the control of behavior by the mass media has been virtually ignored (Rakos, 1993, 1995).

Modern media systems and information technologies are now capable of transmitting information rapidly and without regard for artificial political borders or ideological restrictions. The collapse of socialism in Eastern Europe in 1989 exemplifies how high-tech information transfer can shatter the psychological isolation of a citizenry and lead to significant social upheaval (Rakos, 1991). In contemporary democracies, the absence of oppressive government control of information is typically considered a fundamental characteristic of a "free society." However, the lack of aversive control does not mean that information is "free" of controlling functions. On the contrary, current mechanisms of influence, through direct economic and indirect political contingencies, pose an even greater threat to behavioral diversity than do historically tyrannical forms. Information control today is more systematic, continuous, consistent, unobtrusive, and ultimately powerful (cf. Rakos, 1992).

The control of behavior by media manipulation is the essence of propaganda. It is curious that behavior analysts have shown scant interest in a form of stimulus control that influences political, consumer, lifestyle, and popular culture choices. The traditional view of propaganda masks its behavior control ideology behind cognitive-sounding definitions, such as "any organized or concerted group, effort, or movement to spread particular doctrines, information" (*Webster's New Collegiate Dictionary*, 1961). However, communication scholars have not been oblivious to the true meaning and potential of propaganda. Qualter (1985) suggested that the term denotes "the deliberate attempt by the few to influence the attitudes and behaviour of the many by the manipulation of symbolic communication" (p. 124). Similarly—and in terms even more comfortable for behaviorists—Jowett and O'Donnell (1992) assert, "Propaganda is the deliberate and systematic attempt to shape perceptions, manipulate cognitions, and direct behavior to achieve a response that furthers the desired intent of the propagandist" (p. 4). The use of familiar language, however, does not mean that communication scholars utilize behavioral concepts in their analyses. On the contrary, of perhaps a dozen recent books on the subject, only one introduced a brief discussion of "the behaviorist tradition"—and that mention was used only to justify a quantitative content analysis of the consequences of a message (Shoemaker & Reese, 1991). So the phenomenon that is "the most powerful means of modern social learning" (Combs & Nimmo, 1993, p. 19) is bereft of the analytic tools most powerful in understanding and countering it.

It is clear that propaganda control may promote outcomes that are at times socially desired (Farquhar, 1991; Flay, 1987a, 1987b). Nevertheless, it has become just as clear that the control exerted by the postmodern, information- and media-driven environment is systematic, extensive, and generally in the interest of the controller. Three factors that contribute to this outcome are discussed below.

First, the nature of propaganda has changed. Pre–twentieth-century propaganda recognized that the message had to convince an audience that might initially be inclined to reject the thesis being presented. Such propaganda was characterized by speakers producing logical and reasoned messages directed toward an elite audience composed of interested, informed, knowledgeable persons (Combs & Nimmo, 1993). In other words, the recipients of the message were presumed to possess countercontrol skills, necessitating that the message address and then neutralize its own aversive elements.

Today the elite audience for propaganda has been supplanted by one that is enmeshed and engulfed in a harried lifestyle, less well-informed, and less politically involved. An integral feature of the chaotic lifestyle is broad exposure to media messages that are tailored to influence the mass audience by presenting conclusions rather than reasons, simple slogans rather than complex analyses, visual images rather than verbal ideas, facts presented as a single reality rather than observations about which one could argue, and attractive messengers rather than sophisticated experts. In fact, what little actual content is left in these messages is palaver or "talk" that is beguiling and charming but also confusing and circular (Combs & Nimmo, 1993). The modern consumer of propaganda lacks the skills to resist or even recognize the palaver. A striking example of this phenomenon occurred during the Persian Gulf War: the more television an American watched during the 1990–91 crisis, the more likely he or she was to support the U.S. position, but the less he or she knew about the background issues and context of the war (Morgan, Lewis, & Jhally, 1992).

A second factor involves the use of sophisticated polling and survey procedures, whose results are used by the propagandists to increase their influence. As examples, polling was used incessantly during the buildup to and the conduct of the Persian Gulf War, and computerized tracking of sales is regularly employed by retailers to target consumers with additional offers and new catalogs that are likely to be attractive and effective prompts for further purchasing behavior.

Finally, the incorporation of media companies into megaconglomerates significantly expands the behavior-control potential of information. The globalization of industrial society is a natural consequence of a world dominated by democratic capitalism. The corporate dedication to growth and maximization of profits through mass production and consumption seizes the opportunities presented by both government support and noninterference and by continuous technological advances in transportation and communication. Countless multinational megaconglomerates have formed in recent years, but few have been as dramatic as those in the media industry. Bagdikian (1992) observed that the

concentration of control over our mass media has intensified. Ownership of most of the major media has been consolidated in fewer and fewer corporate hands, from fifty national and multinational corporations at the time of the first edition [1983] to twenty with this fourth edition [1992]. Although there are sometimes hundreds or thousands of small firms sharing the market that remains, the power of these scattered firms is negligible. They operate in a world shaped by the giants. For example, there are more than 3,000 publishers of books, but five produce most of the revenue. (p. ix)

And while the United States has 1,800 daily newspapers, fourteen companies have control over half the daily newspaper business (Bagdikian, 1992).

The conglomeration of media giants into ever larger units continues to the present day, as Bagdikian predicted. Time Warner announced plans to purchase Turner Broadcasting System in September 1995. Disney has purchased Capital Cities (the parent corporation of ABC). Westinghouse Electric Corporation (comprised of financial service, industrial construction, community development, and commercial and defense electronic companies) bought CBS Inc. for $5.4 billion in November 1995. Westinghouse then added to its media holdings with the $4.9 billion purchase in June 1996 of Infinity Broadcasting Corp., which united the nation's two largest radio companies and gave the conglomerate dominance in the country's top ten markets. In June 1996, Conrad Black's Hollinger Inc. purchased twenty Canadian dailies, giving Black control of 58 of Canada's 104 daily newspapers and 40% of the national circulation. Hollinger is now the Western world's third largest newspaper chain, with 110 American dailies, papers in London, Jerusalem, and Sydney, the leading papers in numerous Canadian cities, and all the dailies in three Canadian provinces. ''There's absolutely no printed voice in my region that doesn't trace back to Conrad Black,'' noted an Ontario politician where Hollinger owns the daily and four weeklies (''Some Canadians Question Dominance of Major Publisher,'' 1996).

Despite the immersion of media companies within huge multinational corporations, the illusion of a "free press" is maintained. The major dailies and authoritative television news shows present the appearance of independence; as Schiller (1996) points out, "the foundation of American press freedom, a *privately owned* press, or radio, or TV station, is sacrosanct terrain" (p. 14). But the reality now is that the independence is only from direct and aversive government control.

Before information became an electronic commodity, the media were comprised primarily of print and secondarily of television/radio. There was greater competition among, and more impact from, print outlets in a given geographic region compared to today and compared to over-the-air sources then. Any corporate empire was limited to one medium that influenced at most one continent (Auletta, 1995). In effect, stimulus diversity existed and the media were unable to exert systematic control over citizen behavior.

In contrast, the media today are characterized by multiple types of outlets (many fewer print, many more broadcast, cable, electronic, etc.) that are part of global conglomerates that integrate content and distribution within one organization. For example, Rupert Murdoch's holdings include movies, television shows, and publishing houses (content) and television networks, cable networks, and television satellite systems (distribution). The empire spans six continents through nine media sources: newspapers (32), magazines (25, including the largest circulation *TV Guide*), books (two publishing houses), broadcast outlets (Fox Network, 12 television stations), satellite television, cable networks, a movie studio (20th Century Fox), home video (Fox), and on-line internet (Delphi) (Auletta, 1995). The scope and integration of the Time Warner and Disney empires is similar. In effect, the corporate structure of the media conglomerate offers only the illusion of many independent outlets.

Diversity in the media is compromised further by a homogeneous pool of journalists—those individuals who choose, interpret, and communicate information. Journalists are selected by economic contingencies that (a) favor wealth, (b) operate throughout the social and educational systems, and (c) culminate in journalism schools that earn prestige by employing "former influential journalists who have connections to secure good jobs for their students" (Schiller, 1996, p. 13). These journalists are then additionally socialized by powerful economic, cultural, and professional demands, resulting in de facto behavioral conformity. Thus, a minor ado erupted when a reporter for the *Wall Street Journal* and later the *Los Angeles Times* admitted he was an avowed socialist (Schiller, 1996). Similarly, both *Nightline* and the *McNeil/Lehrer NewsHour* present guests who overwhelmingly represent the establishment value system (white, male, elite, center-right; Hoynes & Croteau, 1989, 1990). Not surprisingly, when the Persian Gulf crisis emerged, these shows failed to serve the interests of true public debate. In the first month after Iraq invaded Kuwait, when the American public expressed reservations about a military response, both shows limited discussion to center–far right versions of reality ("Who Spoke on the Gulf?" 1990). As essentially identical messages are transmitted from seemingly diverse sources, the conditioning effect is one of repeated trials in which similar stimuli prompt similar responses with similar consequences. Concurrent and multiple schedules of reinforcement that define consumer choice are eliminated, resulting in highly refined and narrow response repertoires and the extinction of behavioral variants. Consent is manufactured (Herman & Chomsky, 1988), as when the Gulf crisis evolved and the whole country learned "to stop worrying and love the war" (Combs & Nimmo, 1993, p. 113).

CULTURAL ANALYSIS OF POSTMODERN MEDIA SYSTEMS

The growth of media conglomerates necessitates an analysis that extends beyond the contingencies that shape and maintain the actions of individuals and the impact of the industry's product (influential verbal stimuli) on individual and mass behavior. The next level of analysis must account for those variables and processes that have given rise to and maintain the industry as a viable cultural entity. Harris's (1964, 1977, 1979) cultural materialism offers behaviorists an analytic tool appropriate for this task.

Harris (1977, 1979) argues that cultural practices are ultimately selected because they contribute to the survival of the group, and that every cultural practice includes three interacting levels of social activity: infrastructural, structural, and superstructural. The infrastructural level supports those practices that both regulate population and produce the goods needed to sustain it. Structural practices encompass those actions that maintain secure and orderly relations among a society's constituent groups, including differing social classes, political organizations, and education and socialization practices. Superstructural practices comprise those cultural practices that promote a society's beliefs, ideals, and standards of truth, art, and beauty. Only those structural and superstructural practices that support or maintain necessary infrastructural practices will be strengthened by selective contingencies.

Harris (1964) also identified several molecular cultural units. *Actones* name those behaviors or actions in which individuals engage in contexts of daily living. The contexts themselves are *scenes*, with a *nomoclone* specifying a set of individuals who take part in one or more specific scenes. Nomoclones specify the first level of interlocking social contingencies of individuals acting within and across scenes. The identity of a nomoclone varies with the strength of its defining contingencies and parameters of social interaction (i.e., daily rates and duration of same person contacts, interdependency of actions, etc.). A fourth molecular unit, the *permaclone*, identifies those cultural practices that promote the continued maintenance of fundamental behavioral scenes and nomoclones across people and generations. Such corporate practices as mission and vision statements, organizational structure, procedural guidelines, and written statements of individual job duties and responsibilities support the permaclonic structure of an organized social unit. Thus, nomoclones and permaclones describe social, physical, and institutional structures that shape and constrain the behavior of individuals. Finally, Harris conceptualized *permaclonic systems* as those cultural entities comprised of two or more interlocked permaclones, which include those social, physical, and institutional structures that shape and constrain individual permaclones and subordinate nomoclones. Contemporary media outlets and information producers, as part of a permaclonic corporate structure, are typically directed by the parent company to disseminate information that supports rather than harms the revenue streams generated by the other companies that make up the permaclone. For example, General Electric Corp., which owns NBC, is a major defense contractor that also owns Federal Home Life Insurance Company and GE Nuclear Energy Corporation. NBC is highly unlikely to broadcast critiques of these companies or their products. Even independent media outlets and news producers are made members of the permaclonic system through advertising subsidies (for commercial outlets) and foundation grants and corporate sponsorships (for public broadcasting outlets), because the financial support is likely to come from several interlocked sources.

METACONTINGENCIES THAT CONTROL MEDIA CONGLOMERATES

As a collective business enterprise consisting of diversified companies, a conglomerate is dependent upon the technologies and practices employed by its constituent companies for expanding or maintaining their individual modes of production and, as a result, contributions to the total corporate income. Affiliated companies are typically responsible for developing technologies and cultural practices that produce a targeted income stream for the corporate parent. If the "profit stream" is insufficient, the parent company may either divest the company, or it may escalate its support by working to increase the subsidiary's productive capacity and market share while decreasing its cost of production. A conglomerate, then, represents a permaclonic system of interlocking metacontingencies. A *metacontingency* describes a cultural practice in all its variations and the aggregate outcome of the practice (Glenn, 1991). The smallest cultural unit that can be influenced by a metacontingency is the nomoclone. The metacontingency selects the interlocking contingencies of reinforcement that make up a cultural practice, and the contingencies then select the behavior of individuals performing actones within scenes. In effect, the metacontingencies operating on a conglomerate act to shape and maintain the collective cultural practices carried out within subordinate permaclones (companies) and nomoclones (departments and offices). In regard to media conglomerates, three interrelated metacontingencies will be examined: corporate size and ownership, advertising revenue, and sourcing of news.

Corporate Size and Ownership of the Mass Media

The costs involved in establishing and running a profitable media outlet have risen in the past 150 years to such levels that, today, only the most wealthy individuals, families, or corporations can afford their ownership (Curran & Seaton, 1985). Two factors responsible for this change in the cost of media ownership are technological improvements and revenue growth based on reaching large audiences (Herman & Chomsky, 1988). Consequently, as described above, media outlets are becoming subsumed within megaconglomerate entities. These outlets become part of the interlocking metacontingencies that drive the conglomerate's technological and cultural practices, including those imposed by (a) the profit orientation of the conglomerate's board of directors and shareholders, and (b) the interests of aligned corporations, banks, and government entities.

The extraordinary range of affiliations and shared interests among conglomerates can be identified through an analysis of the makeup of the board of directors of both parent and affiliated companies. For example, D. Wayne Calloway, a member of the board of General Electric Corporation (GE), whose subsidiaries include NBC, is chairman of the board of PepsiCo. Inc., whose subsidiaries include Frito Lay, Kentucky Fried Chicken, Pizza Hut, and Taco Bell. A second GE board member, Douglas A. Warner III, not only sits on the board of directors of Bechtel Group, Inc. and Anheuser-Busch Co., Inc., but is chairman, president, and CEO of J. P. Morgan & Co., Inc.—a major financial services company with subsidiaries in twenty countries that provide strategic advice and capital-raising services to a broad range of government and nongovernment financial institutions (Directory of Corporate Affiliations, 1996). The cumulative assets of the companies that these two men represent amount to more than $400 billion.

The interests of the media conglomerates clearly influence the ''selection of topics, distribution of concerns, framing of issues, filtering of information, emphasis of tone, and [the] keeping [of] debate within the bounds of acceptable premises'' (Herman & Chomsky, 1988, p. 298). While some control is subtle, occasionally a glaring example of conglomerate control is evident, such as when the top two editors of *Premiere*, a magazine devoted to movies, resigned as a consequence of repeated efforts by the owners of the magazine to control editorial decisions. The final straw for the editors occurred when they were instructed to kill a story on an actor's financial involvement in a restaurant chain with which the magazine owner was about to enter into a joint venture. In justifying the owner's demand, the company's CEO said, ''There are hard-hitting journalistic pieces that have hurt the magazine, because I do not see an increase in readership. I've seen a decrease in advertising. I don't see the risk-profit relationship at all'' (''Top Editors Quit Movie Magazine,'' 1996). This candid statement also identifies a second metacontingency controlling the media—advertising.

Corporate Influence through Advertising Revenue and Corporate Sponsorships

The May 1934 passage of the Federal Communications Act ushered in the Federal Communications Commission (FCC) and established the rules by which corporations are allowed to dominate communications airwaves through commercial ownership, sponsorship, and "underwriting." Even then "The network-dominated, advertising-supported basis of U.S. broadcasting was anything but the product of an informed public debate" (McChesney, 1993, p. 257). With media companies now pumping millions of dollars into congressional coffers ("Newt and the Dirty Dozen," 1996), government remains unwilling to question the private interest control of a limited natural resource that John Dewey (1934) proclaimed "the most powerful instrument of social education the world has ever seen. It can be used to distort facts and to mislead the public mind" (p. 309).

Aggressive corporations have long been aware of their potential to influence programming through financial support of commercial and noncommercial media outlets. Recently, however, corporate sponsors have become more brazen. For example, Arts & Entertainment's History Channel almost agreed to develop a series called "The Spirit of Enterprise," which was to feature corporate profiles paid for and approved by the target companies (e.g., AT&T, DuPont, General Motors) ("History Channel," 1996). CNBC, however, still plans to air *Scan*, a series on technology in daily life to be sponsored exclusively by IBM. And although the network insists "the editorial control rests here at CNBC, not at IBM," the latter's director of media strategy avers otherwise: "If we see something that we really don't want aired, of course we have final veto" (Goetz, 1996a, p. 9). Newspaper reports of the deal support the IBM perspective: "The deal gives the computer giant final approval on content" ("History Channel Kills Business Series," 1996, p. 2D).

The importance of advertising and sponsorship revenues should not be underestimated. They allow media outlets to market their products at below their true production costs (Curran, 1978; Curran & Seaton, 1985). In effect, advertisers act as de facto licensing authorities whose backing significantly improves an outlet's ability to reduce costs, increase sales, and invest in marketing research and development programs. Unsubsidized outlets must operate without these advantages and will tend to be marginalized or eliminated. Consequently, the effect of advertising revenue on the survivability and prosperity of media outlets is a stronger influence than the outlet's "market" share. McManus (1994) noted that the journalistic

effort undertaken to satisfy the audience, whether in broadcast or print, is not democracy of the one-person-one-vote variety. Market journalism values the attention of the wealthy and young over the poor and old because news selection must satisfy advertisers' preferences. In fact, rational market journalism must serve the market for investors, advertisers, and powerful sources before—and often at the expense of—the public market for readers and viewers. To think of [market-driven journalism] as truly reader- or viewer-driven is naive. (p. 197)

In this context, the demise in the early 1960s of Britain's *Daily Herald*, a social-democratic newspaper with an enormous average daily readership of 9.3 million, is understandable. The *Daily Herald*'s ruin was largely due to inadequate advertising revenue that was a function of the paper's readership: working-class people whose cumulative discretionary income made them a less attractive "marketing segment" to advertisers seeking maximal return on investment. As noted by Turow (1984), "producers presenting patrons [advertisers] with the greatest opportunities to make a profit through the publics will receive support while those that cannot compete on this core will not survive" (p. 52).

Sourcing the Mass-Media News

The media's capacity to influence cultural practices and citizen behavior is further enhanced by the structure of, and control over, the sources of information that produce the media content. This is accomplished in postmodern societies through the use of government and corporate offices and services that distribute ostensibly credible and acceptable information. Operating on a leviathan scale, the aggregate financial resources available to government and corporate information services for public relations and lobbying activities exceeds many billions of dollars a year (Biglan, 1995; Herman & Chomsky, 1988).

Government and corporate information services make it easy and convenient for media sources to gather the news needed to meet deadlines and satisfy an audience. The status of the data sources allows the media to maintain its persona of objectivity in "reporting the news," though the verification of the information is rarely pursued. Often, the only criteria for the acceptability of such reports is that they "make sense" and reinforce peoples' beliefs and attitudes.

Information sourcing outlets are convenient permaclones in which the roles and actions of the participants are fixed and predictable. Fact sheets and summary pages are handed out, reporters ask appropriate questions, and "experts" and press agents respond or expound. The scheduling of these events is often orchestrated to meet established deadlines. As a result, an interlocking system of economic and interpersonal contingencies is engineered and maintained to the advantage of the sponsoring entities. For instance, the cost of news production is reduced and favored "old boy" networks ensure that expectations are met—such as who gets to ask the first question at a press conference.

Through the systematic control of these contingencies, government and corporate information services can wield powerful influence over opposing, "unofficial" viewpoints and reports. For example, by systematically flooding the media with stories and information that "foist a particular line and *frame* [italics added]" (Herman & Chomsky, 1988, p. 23), the voices of critics or distracters are likely to be drowned. In addition, these entities have used their monies to establish a network of co-opted "experts" (Owen & Braeutigam, 1978) who dispense information and analyses to fit official and preferred views. The media's inbreeding reduces claims that diversity flourishes to palaver, at best, if not to outright mockery. For example, the May 28, 1996 *Charlie Rose Show*, broadcast by the allegedly liberal Public Broadcasting System, focused on Whitewater with guest host Morton Zuckerman, owner of the right-leaning *U.S. News and World Report* and avowed Republican Party supporter. The conservative view was represented by a *Wall Street Journal* reporter, while the "left" was represented by a reporter for *U.S. News and World Report*! As Goetz (1996b) reported, "you couldn't ask for a better illustration of the way today's media actually works: No matter what [the *US News and World Report* reporter] actually believes or wants to say, does anybody expect him to cross his boss on national TV?" (p. 9). The end result is that consumers are denied access to respectable, but "unofficial" sources of authoritative dissent. Herman & Chomsky (1988) succinctly summarize the essence of this strategy:

This process of creating the needed body of experts has been carried out on a deliberate basis and a massive scale. Back in 1972, Judge Lewis Powell (later elevated to the Supreme Court) wrote a memo to the U.S. Chamber of Commerce urging business "to buy the top academic reputations in the country to add credibility to corporate studies and give business a stronger voice on the campuses." One buys them, and assures that— in the words of Dr. Edwin Feulner, of the Heritage Foundation (a decidedly right-wing think tank)—the public-policy area "is awash with in-depth academic studies" that have the proper conclusions. Using the analogy of Procter & Gamble selling toothpaste, Feulner explained that "They sell it and resell it every day by keeping the product fresh in the consumer's mind." By the sales effort, including the dissemination of the correct idea to "thousands of newspapers," it is possible to keep debate "within its proper perspective." (pp. 23–24)

And, of course, the homogeneity that is characteristic of media reporters, as described earlier, significantly decreases the likelihood that these superficially credible sources will be challenged. The reporters themselves become part of the process, resulting in newspapers and television news shows that present opinion within the very narrow right-center band of the political spectrum.

CASE EXAMPLE: THE GULF WAR

The acute national crisis and elevated stakes endemic to armed conflict have prompted governments to wage systematic propaganda campaigns as part of the war effort. Indeed, the scientific analysis of propaganda began with Lasswell's (1927) seminal study *Propaganda Technique in the World War*. The Iraqi invasion of Kuwait on August 2, 1990, and the subsequent buildup of tensions and outbreak of war in January 1991 provide an excellent example of the behavioral processes involved in modern nationalistic propaganda. In the discussion that follows, we will identify the media-government stimulus control that shaped and then maintained popular support for the emission of aggressive behaviors. As the analysis is developed, it will be important to bear in mind that this cultural outcome was a function of the metacontingencies that control the media permaclonic system—size and ownership of the media, advertising revenue, and sourcing of news. These metacontingencies produced the uniformity in news content that then shaped "war fever" behaviors by citizens.

Media-Government Collaboration to Shape Popular Support for Confrontation: Antecedent Stimulus Control

The six and a half months between the Iraqi invasion of Kuwait and the U.S.-led attack on Iraq were characterized by a classic government-orchestrated and media-produced propaganda campaign (Rakos, 1993). Although the Bush administration saw the invasion as an opportunity for the United States to gain political and economic hegemony in the region (Chomsky, 1992; Clark, 1992), the administration's public posture asserted only that the invasion was a grave threat to legitimate American interests, particularly economic ones pertaining to the supply of oil. On August 15, 1990, President Bush asserted that "our freedom and the freedom of friendly countries around the world would all suffer if all the world's great oil reserves fell into the hands of that one man, Saddam Hussein" (*Extra*, 1991). Bush, therefore, insisted that an immediate and forceful response to Iraq was essential.

However, most Americans viewed the Iraqi invasion as a relatively benign stimulus that lacked the motivational attributes that would prompt citizens to forcefully oppose Iraq and vigorously defend Kuwait. Its weakness derived from informed Americans' understanding of the broader context of geopolitics: Iraq was to some extent a U.S. ally (stemming from the Iran-Iraq war of the 1980s) and Kuwait was justly perceived as an unfriendly, undemocratic, and sexist nation (MacArthur, 1992). Thus, the Bush administration needed to embark upon a propaganda campaign: "In August 1990, the Bush administration's task was to sell two images—an ugly one of Hussein and a handsome one of Kuwait—to the American media. Then, God willing, the media would help sell it to the American people" (MacArthur, 1992, p. 43).

The Bush administration was fortunate, indeed, to have the willing media accomplice: the mainstream press primarily reported pro-administration perspectives and ignored opposition critics (MacArthur, 1992; Parenti, 1993). Further, the media simply did not present the historical, political, and economic context within which the Persian Gulf crisis evolved (Mowlana, 1992). "Lacking critical information and argument to the contrary, the public rallied around the troops and treated the war as a just undertaking" (Parenti, 1993, p. 71).

The administration accomplished its objective of engineering public support for war by utilizing the traditional wartime deception strategies of restricting information, slanting information, and spreading disinformation (Combs & Nimmo, 1993; Jowett & O'Donnell, 1992; Qualter, 1985; Parenti, 1993). A behavior analysis of this manufacturing and manipulation of information identifies four categories of antecedent stimulus control and their impact on behavior.

The first type of stimulus control is the *discriminative stimulus* (S^D) which is a learned cue that evokes a response because that response has been reinforced in the presence, but not the absence, of that stimulus (Michael, 1980); stated differently, the operation of a specific behavioral contingency is more probable in the presence of an S^D (Malott, 1989). The second type is an *establishing operation* (EO), which alters an organism's motivation and thereby changes the effectiveness of reinforcing and discriminative stimuli in controlling behavior (Malott, Whaley, & Malott, 1993; Michael, 1982, 1993). The third kind, a *rule*, is a verbal stimulus that specifies or describes a behavioral contingency (Malott et al., 1993; Schlinger, 1993). The impact of rules on behavior is somewhat controversial: some contend that they are basically discriminative stimuli (Cerutti, 1989) while others assert that rules are function-altering stimuli (Schlinger, 1993) or possibly EOs (Malott et al., 1993). Finally, a *symbol* is a stimulus formed through operations such as stimulus equivalence (Sidman, 1994), in which responses come under the control of stimuli that have not been directly associated with reinforcement. In a typical equivalence procedure, three or more arbitrary stimuli are conditionally related as in "if A, pick B" and "if B, pick C." Research has shown that such pairings typically result in the formation of "untaught" symmetrical, transitive, and equivalence relations among the involved stimuli. In symmetrical relations, the trained discrimination "given A, pick B" leads to the derived discrimination "given B, pick A." Training "given A, pick B" and "given B, pick C" leads to the derived transitive relation "given A, pick C" and the derived equivalence relation "given C, pick A."

Rakos (1993) analyzed these four stimulus operations as propaganda tools by employing a heuristic model centered on the "U.S. citizen" (see Figure 11.1), conducting a content analysis of the media presentation of Bush administration contentions, and identifying the temporal relationship between the media messages and relevant citizen responses. His study surveyed every *New York Times* between August 2, 1990, and the outbreak of war on January 16, 1991. Rakos identified six EOs that the Bush administration employed to arouse citizen opposition to Iraq's action. One involved the deliberate use of stimulus equivalence operations to develop symbols: through repeated transitive stimulus equivalence operations, Hussein ("A") was equated with Hitler ("B"), and hence with unspeakable and irrational evil ("C"). In addition, through information restriction, disinformation, and various information slanting techniques, Iraq was portrayed as an unstable aggressor: its army was described as huge (the world's fourth largest); it was alleged to possess and be willing to use unconventional chemical, biological, and nuclear weapons; it had taken hostages (prompting an anxiety response that generalized from Iran's taking of U.S. hostages a decade

$$\text{EO (Establishing Operation)} \longrightarrow \text{Rule Cues} \longrightarrow R^1 \longrightarrow S^{R1} (S^{D1}) \longrightarrow R^2 \longrightarrow S^{R2} (S^{D2}) \longrightarrow R^3 \longrightarrow S^{R3}$$

EO: IRAQ IS VERY BAD AND A DANGER TO OUR WAY OF LIFE

RULE CUES: UNPROVOKED AGGRESSION MUST BE STOPPED BY THE RIGHTEOUS U.S.

R^1: VERBAL AGREEMENT BY U.S. CITIZENS AND CONGRESS TO "DO SOMETHING": "*PATRIOTIC SOLIDARITY*"

S^{R1}: SOCIAL REINFORCEMENT AMONG PEERS; VERBAL SELF-STATEMENTS ACKNOWLEDGING THAT "ACCEPTABLE THINGS" ARE BEING DONE

ACCEPTABLE THINGS (S^{R^+})	UNACCEPTABLE THINGS (S^{R^-})
* DIPLOMATIC EFFORTS	* TROOP DEPLOYMENT
* PROMPTING U.N. ACTION	* MILITARY FIGHTING
* COALITION FORMATION	
* SANCTIONS/BOYCOTT/EMBARGO	

S^{D1}: (AVERSIVE): TROOP DEPLOYMENT AND MILITARY ACTION

* PRESENTED WITHIN GRADED STIMULUS HIERARCHY (INITIALLY BELOW THRESHOLD LEVEL NECESSARY TO PROMPT AVOIDANCE OR NONCOMPLIANT RESPONSE)
* PRESENTED WITH POSITIVE STIMULI
* OPERATION: *COUNTERCONDITIONING* HABITUATION TO INCREASINGLY AVERSIVE STIMULI; NO AVOIDANCE (APPROACH MAINTAINED); S^{D1} BECOMES NEUTRAL OR POSITIVE

R^2: COGNITIVE, VERBAL, AND OVERT BEHAVIORS THAT "ACCEPT" INCREASED MILITARY ACTIONS: "*PATRIOTIC STOICISM*"

S^{R2}: SOCIAL REINFORCEMENT; SELF-REINFORCEMENT VIA SELF STATEMENTS

S^{D2}: SOCIAL AND VERBAL STIMULI THAT CONFIRM THAT MILITARY ACTION AGAINST IRAQ IS NECESSARY **PLUS** TELEVISION PRESENTATION OF COMBAT AND COMMENTARY

R^3: HIGH FREQUENCY TV VIEWING; VERBAL SUPPORT FOR MILITARY ACTION: "*PATRIOTIC ENTHUSIASM*"

S^{R3}: CRUSADE AND ENTERTAINMENT

Figure 11.1. The behavior chain of the "U.S. citizen" in response to U.S. propaganda after Iraq's invasion of Kuwait.

EO (Establishing Operation) $\longrightarrow$ Rule Cues $\longrightarrow$ R^1 $\longrightarrow$ S^{R1}

(S^{D1}) $\longrightarrow$ R^2 $\longrightarrow$ S^{R2}

(S^{D2}) $\longrightarrow$ R^3 $\longrightarrow$ S^{R3}

EO: IRAQ IS VERY BAD AND A DANGER TO OUR WAY OF LIFE

RULE CUES: UNPROVOKED AGGRESSION MUST BE STOPPED BY THE RIGHTEOUS U.S.

R^1: VERBAL AGREEMENT BY U.S. CITIZENS AND CONGRESS TO "DO SOMETHING": *"PATRIOTIC SOLIDARITY"*

S^{R1}: SOCIAL REINFORCEMENT AMONG PEERS; VERBAL SELF-STATEMENTS ACKNOWLEDGING THAT

"ACCEPTABLE THINGS" ARE BEING DONE

ACCEPTABLE THINGS (S^{R+})	UNACCEPTABLE THINGS (S^{R-})
* DIPLOMATIC EFFORTS	* TROOP DEPLOYMENT

250

* PROMPTING U.N. ACTION   * MILITARY FIGHTING

* COALITION FORMATION

* SANCTIONS/BOYCOTT/EMBARGO

S^{D1}: (AVERSIVE): TROOP DEPLOYMENT AND MILITARY ACTION

* PRESENTED WITHIN GRADED STIMULUS HIERARCHY (INITIALLY BELOW THRESHOLD LEVEL NECESSARY TO PROMPT AVOIDANCE OR NONCOMPLIANT RESPONSE)

* PRESENTED WITH POSITIVE STIMULI

* OPERATION: *COUNTERCONDITIONING*

  HABITUATION TO INCREASINGLY AVERSIVE STIMULI; NO AVOIDANCE (APPROACH MAINTAINED); S^{D1} BECOMES NEUTRAL OR POSITIVE

R^2: COGNITIVE, VERBAL, AND OVERT BEHAVIORS THAT "ACCEPT" INCREASED MILITARY ACTIONS: *"PATRIOTIC STOICISM"*

S^{R2}: SOCIAL REINFORCEMENT; SELF-REINFORCEMENT VIA SELF STATEMENTS

S^{D2}: SOCIAL AND VERBAL STIMULI THAT CONFIRM THAT MILITARY ACTION AGAINST IRAQ IS NECESSARY **PLUS** TELEVISION PRESENTATION OF COMBAT AND COMMENTARY

R^3: HIGH FREQUENCY TV VIEWING; VERBAL SUPPORT FOR MILITARY ACTION: *"PATRIOTIC ENTHUSIASM"*

S^{R3}: CRUSADE AND ENTERTAINMENT

Figure 11.1. (continued)

earlier); it was arrogant in threatening other countries and predicting victory in war; it perpetrated human rights violations (though not nearly of the magnitude portrayed by the Bush administration); and it was seen to be treacherous and untrustworthy. The media reinforced the administration's perspective by saturating its outlets with opinion and editorial content that demonized Hussein and dehumanized Iraqis (Clark, 1992).

The EO of Iraq and Hussein as barbaric and intolerable violators of decency and human rights was forcefully developed by the famous baby incubator story. This is a particularly vivid example of *disinformation*, a technique that has a long and noble history in warfare, particularly in relation to atrocities. An early example was a British newsreel showing a Red Cross tent under fire from Boers while valiant British medical personnel treated the wounded. In actuality, the film was staged with actors on London's Hampstead Heath (Qualter, 1985). In World War I, atrocity disinformation emerged as the major form of propaganda, though in World War II such a strategy was infrequently employed. However, in the Gulf War, disinformation achieved new levels when its use incorporated the scientific strategies of modern public relations firms. The story is long and involved, but the highlights follow.

Media outlets uncritically reported the allegation that marauding Iraqi invaders rampaged through a Kuwaiti hospital and disconnected 312 incubators, leaving helpless and ill infants to die in a cold and heartless manner. This story began on October 10, 1990, with the tearful exposé of a fifteen-year-old Kuwaiti girl who claimed to witness such action in regard to fifteen babies. Later it was revealed that this girl, whose identity was kept secret allegedly to protect her family in Kuwait, was really the daughter of the Kuwaiti ambassador to the United States. But even more telling was that "Citizens for a Free Kuwait," a U.S.-based but Kuwaiti-government funded advocacy group formed within days of the Iraqi invasion, hired on August 10, 1990, a U.S. public relations firm with close ties to the U.S. government to promote the Kuwaiti cause. As part of its multimillion dollar contract, the public relations firm conducted focus groups to determine what would best mobilize public support for Kuwait. The firm concluded that a horrific atrocity was necessary, as Americans' sentiments are more easily aroused in support of an underdog. So the atrocity story began, was uncritically repeated in the media, grew to 312 babies wrenched from their life support, and was employed repeatedly by Bush in speeches before the public and Congress (Jowett & O'Donnell, 1992; MacArthur, 1992). After the war ended, the story was thoroughly discredited by human rights groups such as Middle East Watch. It appears that some babies were indeed hastily removed from incubators—but by their panicking Kuwaiti parents. What is striking in this scenario is the demonstrated potential for scientific refinement of establishing operations.

EOs were also manufactured through *information restriction*. For example, in early February 1991, 81% of television viewers knew the name of the missile used by the United States against Iraq (Patriot), but only 13% knew that the

U.S. Ambassador to Iraq directly and unambiguously informed Hussein on July 25, 1990, that the United States was neutral in regard to Iraq's dispute with Kuwait. Even fewer knew the specifics of the dispute—only 2% knew that Kuwait unilaterally lowered oil prices, thus undermining Iraq's war-torn economy, or that Kuwait was slant-drilling across the border into Iraqi oil reserves. Such knowledge would have undermined the establishing operations maintaining or building war fever (Hussein as irrational and Hitlerian, the Iraqi invasion as "unprovoked aggression"). Thus, it is not surprising that the more people knew the less likely they were to support the war (Morgan et al., 1992).

The general EO, therefore, developed by the Bush administration and disseminated uncritically through the mainstream media was: "Iraq and Hussein are irrational and very, very bad *and* a threat to our way of life." As the aversive quality of Iraq as a stimulus was established, the administration asserted rules that specified the alleged contingencies—learned well in other contexts and generalized to the present one: "Unprovoked aggression by the malevolent must be stopped" and "taking hostages will not be tolerated" combined into the rule "illegitimate aggression must be punished by the righteous or it will be rewarded and encouraged." A corollary rule, pervasive in guiding the response of Americans in numerous military, economic, and cultural conflicts, is "the U.S. is good and righteous and must prevail" (see Figure 11.1).

The EOs and rules were designed to evoke specific verbal responses by the "U.S. citizen" that "something" had to be done to stop Hussein. These verbal behaviors (R^1 in Figure 11.1) are termed "patriotic solidarity" and were reinforced (S^{R1} in Figure 11.1) by peer social approval and by verbal self-statements that recognized that "acceptable things were being done" by the administration. Acceptable "things" (positive reinforcers) included diplomatic efforts, the prompting of United Nations action, coalition formation, and various penalties (e.g., sanctions, boycotts, embargoes).[1]

On the other hand, "patriotic solidarity" verbalizations did not undergo response generalization—verbalizations that endorsed actual fighting. Throughout the first months of the Iraqi occupation of Kuwait, the American public was reluctant to approve of massive troop deployment and hasty military action, suggesting that these outcomes were "unacceptable actions" (aversive stimuli or negative reinforcers). As S^Ds in the chain, these latter noxious options were problematic from the Bush point of view: they prompted verbal behavior from the "U.S. citizen" that was incompatible with administration efforts to marshal popular support for active military intervention. In fact, they disrupted the chain and prevented emission of R^2—verbalizations that accepted the necessity of military action ("patriotic stoicism").

Therefore, in the five months after the Iraqi invasion, these aversive S^Ds (i.e., troop deployment, military action) were presented to the public through the mainstream media *within a graded stimulus hierarchy*. Initially, the aversive stimuli were introduced in a very weakened form—below the threshold necessary to prompt the emission of avoidance or noncompliant responses. Concurrently, the weakened aversive stimuli were paired with positive ones such as sanctions and embargoes, diplomatic initiatives, and alliance building. This procedure progressed by pairing increasingly aversive stimuli with the positive ones as habituation to the previous level of aversiveness was achieved. Under these conditions, avoidance and noncompliant responses (at R^2 in Figure 11.1) were virtually nonexistent and approach responses were maintained by the American public and Congress even when full offensive combat was initiated. In effect, the aversive S^Ds became neutral or even positively valanced as *counterconditioning* proceeded (see Table 11.1). Throughout this process, approach behavior was maintained by a verbal community that initially agreed the Iraqi threat was being contained and later concurred it was about to be removed through necessary military action. In effect, war fever was inculcated as the newly conditioned S^Ds eventually prompted cognitive, verbal, and motoric behaviors that "accepted" increased military actions (R^2 in Figure 11.1), and "patriotic stoicism" replaced the "patriotic solidarity" previously established. S^{R2} was positive social reinforcement and self-reinforcement, setting the stage for overt military action on January 16, 1991.

The analysis presented above suggests that two distinct conditioning processes were experienced by the "U.S. citizen." First, aversive EOs and rules were introduced to mobilize public support for warlike behaviors and the verbal reinforcement for support focused on the containment of the Iraqi threat. This corresponds to negative reinforcement: the citizen behavior that supported government policy resulted in the escape from—or at least reduction of—the Iraqi threat. Second, counterconditioning of the military option into a positive stimulus altered the behavior chain from one maintained by negative reinforcement into one maintained by positive reinforcement. No longer was containment of Hussein the main reinforcer—with military action now a positive S^D, the idea of military conquest became a potent positive reinforcer (Rakos, 1995). And as soon as actual fighting began, the combat itself became a powerful positive reinforcer. In effect, citizen behavior that endorsed or supported military combat was positively reinforced by the fighting as both *"crusade"* and as *"entertainment."* We shall examine these phenomena next.

Media-Government Collaboration to Maintain Popular Support for Offensive Military Action

By mid-January 1991, citizen behavior was under the influence of social and verbal statements that confirmed that military action against Iraq was necessary. That reinforcer (S^{R2}) functioned as the discriminative stimulus ("social agreement that military action is necessary; S^{D2}) for the next response in the behavior chain. However, S^{D2} was a compound stimulus that added visual and verbal stimuli from television and presented war with palaver instead of casualties. The citizen response (R^3) was to view sanitized combat on television with "crusade and entertainment" as the reinforcing stimuli (S^{R3}). The high-tech, bloodless,

Table 11.1
Graded Stimulus Hierarchy for Counterconditioning of Aversive Stimuli

	Administration Media Reports		Citizen Responses
Aug. 4	"Military intervention of some kind" possible		
Aug. 9	U.S. may send 50,000 troops	Aug. 9	"Cautious support" 76% support embargo 66% support troops
Aug. 11	Troop estimate 100,000		
Aug. 14	Possible call-up of reserves, but not 200,000		
Aug. 18	Reserve call-up approved, administration reluctant to disclose extent of deployment		
		Aug. 21	Few protest Bush's big stick — expect defensive and short
Aug. 22	40,000 reservists called up; may not be the limit	Aug. 22	Bush popularity soars 77% support troops to Saudi Arabia
Sept. 1	Force is defensive, offensive discussion only "hypothetical"		
Sept. 6	U.S. "will review all options" including force		
Sept. 7	Offensive action possible by Oct. 15		
Sept. 12	Bush hints at use of force		
Sept. 16	Additional troop build-up to provide "additional military options"		
Sept. 20	U.S. "continues to review all options"		
		Sept. 27	Overwhelming majority support defensive action
Sept. 29	Call-up of 27,000 more reservists considered		
Oct. 16	U.S. in Gulf for "long haul," build-up to provide "additional military options"		
Oct. 20	400–500 tanks sent, Bush to "consider all options"		
Oct. 21	Need "to make the military threat more credible"		

Table 11.1 (continued)

	Administration Media Reports		Citizen Responses
Oct. 24	U.S. considers increasing force beyond 240,000		
Oct. 26	U.S. to add up to 100,000		
Nov. 1	"Get people ready for any eventuality"		
Nov. 2	Schwarzkopf: War "anytime" but not soon		
Nov. 5	U.S. to activate combat reserves		
Nov. 8	U.S. to add 100,000 troops (350,000 total)		
Nov. 9	U.S. to add 150,000 troops (380,000 total)		
Nov. 11	"Offensive military intervention now possible"		
		Nov. 15	Americans "uneasy and fearful"
		Nov. 20	Bush support drops to 50% due to "bellicosity"
Dec. 4	Military intervention necessary; reserve call-up limit raised from 125,000 to 188,000		
		Dec. 14	48% delay offensive past 1/15; 40% start on 1/15
Dec. 22	Force necessary "to get [Hussein] out"		
Dec. 29	Bush will not heed Army desire for delay of military action		
		Jan. 9	50% support offensive action on 1/15
		Jan. 14	55%: Bush did everything to avoid war
Jan. 16	U.S. weighs timing for attack		
Jan. 17	Opening of air war on Iraq reported		
		Late Jan.	Bush receives 75% approval rating

victorious war game provided its reinforcement on a rich variable ratio schedule, and—as would be expected on such a reinforcement schedule—rapidly established consistent high-frequency television viewing behavior. Clearly, in terms of reinforcers, the performance of missiles supplanted the punishing of Hussein, and citizens were now emitting behaviors that encompassed "patriotic enthusiasm."

The Bush administration achieved this outcome by again employing information restriction as a key element in developing reinforcers that maintained popular support for the war. In fact, information restriction as a propaganda strategy was redefined during the Gulf War by the close monitoring, and the limited access to military sites and information, of rotating pools of accredited reporters (Parenti, 1993). (More primitive versions of media restriction in the modern age were enacted in the 1980s by the British in the Falklands War and by the United States in its invasions of Grenada and Panama (Clark, 1992; MacArthur, 1992; Ottosen, 1992)). The strict media rules in the Gulf conflict were accepted without protest by the mainstream media (Parenti, 1993; Schiller, 1992), as the metacontingencies described earlier exerted their impact.

This information and access restriction plan was developed at the beginning of the conflict. Dubbed "Annex Foxtrot," the intent was to manage information in a manner that facilitated the current political goals and avoided the propaganda errors of Vietnam. In fact, the Bush administration maintained an obsessional belief that the press was responsible for the erosion of popular support for the Vietnam War (Jowett & O'Donnell, 1992). As MacArthur (1992) described it "[i]n the Fall of 1990 [as the Pentagon's public relations men] refined their plans for controlling media coverage of the coming conflict, they were said to be propelled by the notion that an uncensored American press had 'lost' the Vietnam War by demoralizing the public with *unpleasant news*" (p. 112, emphasis added).

The lesson learned from Vietnam by the Bush administration was that the press was hostile to government and could not be trusted to support military action. Therefore, the Pentagon's cardinal rule from the outset was that reporters would be "escorted at all times. Repeat, at all times" (reported in MacArthur, 1992, p. 7). This strategy proved highly successful, as a survey taken several weeks into the armed conflict indicated 84% supported Bush's decision to use military force (Morgan et al., 1992). Bush, in a moment of candor, chortled to Ted Koppel on ABC's *Nightline* (October 28, 1992), "we shaped public opinion."

As a consequence of the masterful management of information, the mass media, primarily via television, presented a distorted and antiseptic view of the war. There was little, if any, "unpleasant news" of the sort that allegedly undermined the effectiveness of the Vietnam policy. Information restriction, combined with the palaver to be noted shortly, resulted in a smug, eager, but ignorant populace: as noted earlier, the correlations between amount of television watching and extent of knowledge were generally negative. Even global perceptions were affected by the duration of television viewing. Light television watchers gave a mean estimate of 9,848 Iraqi deaths as of February 4, 1991, while heavy viewers provided a mean figure of 789—only 8% of the light viewers' guess (Morgan et al., 1992). However, the shockingly low absolute value of the light viewers' estimate suggests that even casual observers learned the desired response to the palaver-propaganda that "smart" bombs were surgically striking (unoccupied?) buildings but not people, as they heard reporters like ABC's Peter Jennings gush about "the brilliance of laser-guided bombs" and lament the use of an Iraqi missile, which he described as "a horrifying killer" (Parenti, 1993, p 167) In fact, the media constantly extolled the alleged efficiency and precision of high-tech weapons directed toward military targets and consistently omitted reference to or discussion of Iraqi casualties at the hands of incessant bombing and eventual strafing of retreating soldiers (Clark, 1992; Schiller, 1992). Yet the CIA estimated between 100,000 and 250,000 Iraqi dead, numbers seemingly in the ballpark, as French military intelligence estimated 200,000 and Greenpeace more than 150,000 (Frank, 1992). The bombing also resulted in at least 100,000 Iraqi deaths from disease and malnutrition, and the virtual destruction of the Iraqi economic infrastructure (Clark, 1992). But the enemy wasn't the only participant whose human costs were invisible. The Pentagon's control of the media prevented any photographs of corpses, body bags, or coffins of dead American soldiers (Combs & Nimmo, 1993).

Thus, the media—primarily television—presented a sanitized "Nintendo" war, embedded within palaver such as "surgical strikes" and "precision bombing" and virtually no human casualties on either side (MacArthur, 1992; Parenti, 1993). In fact, missiles and bombs that hit targets were replayed on television, but those that missed were not (Parenti, 1993). *In other words, no aversive stimuli were produced by intense military combat (war)!* This removes any mystery as to why heavy television viewers estimated that Iraqi casualties totaled less than 800. Despite the fact that over 90% of the bombs were traditional "low-tech," free-falling gravity bombs, whose impact could not be pinpointed and whose combined explosive power equaled seven Hiroshima atomic bombs and exceeded the total tonnage dropped in World War II, headlines such as *Newsweek*'s on February 18, 1991, screamed the ultimate palaver: "The New Science of War, High-tech Hardware: How Many Lives Can It Save?" And so, John Chancellor noted on NBC that "the most important thing to be said (about the war is that) there were very few casualties" (Parenti, 1993, p. 168).

A war without casualties is a moral war, a good war (Aksoy & Robins, 1992). The Pentagon's behavior management techniques worked so well and provided so much positive reinforcement that the media learned self-regulation, that is, to produce propaganda without direct Pentagon oversight. When CNN showed the destruction and hundreds of deaths from the U.S. bombing of a civilian bomb shelter, the media blamed the victim. On NBC, Tom Brokaw intoned that "We must point out again and again that it is Saddam Hussein who put these innocents in harm's way." On CBS, Ron Allen asserted that "Iraq is trying to gain sympathy,'' a sentiment echoed on the *MacNeil/Lehrer Newshour* as ''heavy-handed manipulation.'' Self-righteousness dripped from another CBS report: ''Hussein promised a bloody war, and here [is] the blood'' (all quotes from Parenti, 1993, p. 168). Further, news services themselves destroyed photographs of dead bodies and refused to use material that showed heavy casualties or was critical of the war. The few reporters who deviated from unqualified support for the administration's position were terminated, suspended, or sent on ''vacation'' by television networks and major newspapers (Clark, 1992; Parenti, 1993). The power of the metacontingencies to select group outcomes is clearly evident in the suppression of dissent.

The media reporting of the war constituted only theatrics and palaver. In effect, bloodless, high-tech battles and the enthusiastic media cheerleading provided powerful high-quality positive reinforcement that was likely made even more potent by a *positive contrast effect*. During the buildup to military action, popular support for the administration was reinforced by social and self-reinforcement. The previous experience with this relatively modest reinforcer probably enhanced the potency of the ''clean'' military action as a positive reinforcer. Similarly, for those who previously learned from Vietnam and World War II the noxious qualities that accompany complex war stimuli, the positive valence of the present version was increased dramatically.

Summary

The Bush administration's propaganda campaign altered control of the citizens' behavior chain from negative reinforcement to positive reinforcement. The EOs developed the conditions that made Iraq and Hussein into aversive stimuli and the rules introduced aversive contingencies: unprovoked aggression must be countered to preserve freedom and righteousness. This prompted a consensual verbal agreement to ''do something''—''patriotic solidarity'' that was reinforced by recognition that nonmilitary options were enacted to contain (i.e., escape from) the threat. However, concurrently, the aversive stimulus of troop deployment was also introduced, albeit initially in such weak form that it failed to prompt avoidance or noncompliant responses. Troop deployment and military posturing were then presented in increasingly intense forms, always accompanied by the more positive stimuli of diplomatic efforts, coalition formation, boycotts, and UN action. The process became one of counterconditioning, as the public habituated to increasingly intense military stimuli—''patriotic stoicism.'' By the time the war began, military action was a positive stimulus and the war could be fought for positive reinforcement rather than for negative reinforcement. And positive reinforcement was ensured by removing the aversive consequences of war and presenting only technical achievements and successful conquests. Military propaganda, promulgated via the mass media, transformed the Gulf War from a defensive battle to prime-time entertainment— the citizen response became one of ''patriotic enthusiasm.'' We had, indeed, learned a lesson well from the Vietnam experience: to gain and maintain support for war in the age of mass communication, stimulus control must be pervasive and exacting and positive reinforcement easily obtainable and on a lavish schedule of reinforcement. The lesson, of course, was enacted through the interlocking metacontingencies operating on the media conglomerates.

RESEARCH ON BEHAVIORAL AND CULTURAL PRACTICES

As a natural science, behavior analytic research focuses on the prediction and influence of individual behaviors and group practices by describing and manipulating environmental variables that have a relationship with the behavior or practice of interest. In fulfilling this agenda, both the incidence (or occurrence of a behavior or practice within a given population over a given time) and the prevalence (or proportion of individuals or organizations within a population engaged in a given behavior or action over a given time) of a behavior or group action need to be defined and measured. These data provide the information needed to identify correlational relationships among environmental and behavioral variables, which can then be used to direct research to identify the functional relations that determine the incidence, prevalence, probability, and frequency of important behaviors or actions. Therefore, the comprehensive empirical investigation of propaganda will require the use of both group-based statistical and individual-based functional analytic procedures and methods. Several possibilities are outlined below.

Research on the Actions of Permaclonic Systems: Education

The current analysis suggests that the general population does not understand the consequences of media monopolization. One strategy that addresses this skill deficit is to focus intervention on the younger generations in various levels of the education system. For example, the extent to which public control over the airwaves is debated in consumer science classes is unknown but predicted to be small. Data on the incidence and prevalence of curricular materials and instructional activities aimed at teaching our children about the inherent conflicts of interest that influence our modern media system would provide important contextual information regarding the need for public awareness and information campaigns on the topic. Another strategy would employ supplementary review of the archival records of school district boards-of-directors and administration plans, to identify the extent to which formal efforts are made at this level of our educational system to address media monopolization as a significant negative trend within our society. In addition, reports and records of national teaching councils can be reviewed to identify incidence and prevalence of concern and awareness of this issue within professional organizations that are ostensibly committed to the promotion of democratic ideals through factual and effective curriculum materials. After baseline data are acquired on the practices within the education "permaclonic system," programming to effect change can be developed and evaluated.

Research on the Product of Permaclonic Systems: Media Content

Content analyses can yield valuable insights into the functioning of the media, as the analysis of the Gulf War propaganda demonstrated. One strategy would identify the characteristics of "scientific" or "consumer" data that are initially reported in professional journals and are then disseminated widely through the mass media. Drug studies and healthy lifestyle research that provide economic benefits to the pharmacology and insurance industries, respectively, are reproduced regularly in the mass media. How does such coverage compare to that afforded, say, to the *Consumer Reports* data concerning the use of mental health services by consumers (Seligman, 1995)? Longer therapy, consumer choice of therapist, and the absence of insurance limitations on therapy were all significantly associated with greater improvement and satisfaction. However, these conclusions are inconsistent with the managed care emphasis on cost containment, and managed care companies are big media advertisers. To what extent do these economic factors affect media coverage (space, prominence, editorials, etc.)?

A second approach would assess the central features or attributes of broad "social policies" that are characterized as failures in the media versus those that are described as continuous struggles. Busing, welfare, and affirmative action are current "failures" yet the "war on drugs" is not. What are the criteria by which these declarations are made (economic, political, moral) and whose interests are served by the designations? The media presentation of these social issues might illuminate the controlling variables for the societal conclusions.

Research on Actones, Scenes, and Nomoclones: The Behavior of Individuals

There are many behavior analytic–based research possibilities at this level of analysis. Earlier we described how stimulus equivalence concepts (Sidman, 1994) can illuminate an important stimulus control property of effective propaganda. Recent developments in Relational Frame Theory (RFT) (S. C. Hayes, 1994) may provide further understanding of the behavior control properties of broad classes of propaganda techniques.

RFT and Understanding How Propaganda Tactics Effect Behavior. RFT attempts to account for how humans come under the influence of arbitrarily applicable stimulus relations (e.g., opposite of, different than, better than, etc.), and how such relations can be applied toward an empirical analysis of important behavioral phenomena such as emotion, metaphor, values, beliefs (S. C. Hayes,

1996), and, in general, "listening with understanding and speaking with meaning" (L. J. Hayes, 1996, p. 282). Arbitrarily applicable stimulus relations represent an important subset of stimulus control relations that are derived, learned, and controlled by context. An example of a derived relation under contextual control would be that entailed between A and C if the relations "A = B, and B > C" were established through direct training procedures. Emergence of the untaught A/C relation "A > C" would indicate the formation of a generative relational frame. Whereas equivalence relations coordinate arbitrarily related stimuli, relational frames allow for an infinite variety of arbitrary relations, even physically impossible ones, to gain control over human verbal and nonverbal behavior.

The application of RFT to an analysis of propaganda suggests that the two most important characteristics of "framing" behavior are (a) the merging of the emotional and affective content associated with one member of a stimulus set with the emotional and affective content associated with the other members of the set, and (b) the emergence of a consonance/dissonance function entailed by the framing itself. That is, once established, relational frames acquire automatic reinforcement and punishment functions (Sundberg et al., 1996). This aspect of framing behavior becomes of interest when one considers that much of propaganda is devoted to the shaping and extension of "beliefs" and "attitudes" that are thought to determine overt responding (Ajzen, 1988; Fishbein & Ajzen, 1975). As extensive verbal frames, beliefs and attitudes are often attributed to self-actualizing and self-determining qualities that are likely due to and maintained by automatic reinforcement.

Propagandists employ framing behavior to justify an act. For example, the bombing of Iraq following Bush's visit to Kuwait was legitimized through verbal frames such as "an investigation produced compelling evidence of an Iraqi plot that required a firm and commensurate response to protect our sovereignty." The key relational words and phrases within this statement are "investigation," which implies a detailed and systematic inquiry; "evidence," which implies the collection of data upon which a conclusion or judgment may be based; and "protect our sovereignty," which implies that our independence and self-rule are at risk. As pointed out by Delwiche (1995), "propagandists love short-cuts, particularly those which short-circuit rational thought. They encourage this by agitating emotions, by exploiting insecurities, by capitalizing on the ambiguity of language, and by bending the rules of logic" (p. 4). Behavior analytic investigation of the derived relations inherent in these "shortcuts" would identify important psychological processes that establish the functional nature of propaganda techniques.

CONCLUSION

We have argued that sophisticated methods and techniques of popular persuasion (propaganda) are being employed to benefit the exploitative agenda of an elite power group whose main reinforcement is the centralization and control of political and economic power. Nevertheless, many of these practices also result in significant short-term benefit for much of the population. For example, intensification of the use of public forest and mining lands subsidizes the daily cost of living for much of the population by containing housing and commercial fuel costs. As a result, any effort to establish a countercontrolling influence over such practices is surely to be met with resistance. In other words, societal stability may be evident in the short run.

Harris (1977) has clearly illustrated that "stationary," oligarchic societies, where the popular standard of living rests slightly above or below the threshold of subsistence, can endure for thousands of years. The dynasties and supporting bureaucracies of ancient China, India, Mesopotamia, and Egypt stand as grim examples that "there is nothing inherent in human affairs to ensure material and moral progress" (p. 235). Contemporary capitalism is fast creating a worldwide oligarchy of a similar nature. The general standard of living may end up being somewhat above that of the ancient empires, but the static or stationary nature of these systems is much more real and much more widespread than popular media portray. It is apparent from current trends that the world is indeed heading toward a period of "intensification"—the increased investment of both material and human resources per unit of time or area—to deflect current threats against living standards. Net income has stagnated in the past 25 years (Deibel, 1996), yet living standards are increasingly defined only through the accumulation of private wealth and material reinforcement (Rakos, 1992). Consequently, households must have more wage earners working longer hours, increase their reliance on credit and loans, and tolerate expansive and deep cuts in public and social services. Simultaneously, environmentally harmful practices are intensifying as new housing and business developments level forests, shrink natural habitats, and accelerate our consumption and pollution of potable water.

As the abuse of the natural environment continues and living standards decline further, people will experience more and more "problems" (Malagodi & Jackson, 1989). In response, the corporate-controlled media will trumpet explanatory fictions such as: a "breakdown of individual character and resolve," and prescribe more work, sacrifice, and commitment on the part of individuals as the means for resolving the "issue" (Malagodi & Jackson, 1989). These fictions will be accepted because they will "make sense" as an extension of our Western-European moral and ethical system, and also because there will be no diversity of perspective offered through the media conglomerates. The actions and practices of government and business entities will remain unchecked until an imminent catastrophe exposes their accountability. As noted by Biglan (1995), "We may never control the variables that would make governments and organizations willing to propagate [preventive] practices, but we must be prepared for sudden enlightenment or major catastrophe to motivate them" (p. 399).

On the other (more optimistic) hand, a refined behavior analytic understanding of the pervasive controlling functions of postmodern media propaganda may provide the basis upon which destructive cultural practices *can* be changed. The challenge, of course, is great, but when the issue is stimulus control, behavior analysts possess the analytic tools that can best meet the challenge.

NOTES

The authors wish to express special thanks to Chris Bedosky for his helpful suggestions in editing this manuscript and preparing it for publication.

1. However, at least two of these positive reinforcers were presented by the media only in a distorted form that preserved their desired function in the behavior chain: neither the several serious proposals by Iraq for a negotiated settlement nor the consistent violation of the UN charter by the United States received meaningful media coverage (Chomsky, 1992).

REFERENCES

Ajzen, I. (1988). *Attitudes, behavior and personality.* Chicago: Dorsey Press.

Aksoy, A., & Robins, K. (1992). Exterminating angels: Mortality, violence and technology in the Gulf War. In H. Mowlana, G. Gerbner, & H. I. Schiller (Eds.), *Triumph of the image: The media's war in the Persian Gulf—a global perspective* (pp. 202–212). Boulder, CO: Westview Press.

Auletta, K. (1995, November 13). The pirate. *The New Yorker, 71 (36),* 80–94.

Bagdikian, B. H. (1992). *The media monopoly* (4th ed.). Boston: Beacon Press.

Biglan, A. (1995). *Changing cultural practices: A contextualist framework for intervention research.* Reno, NV: Context Press.

Cerutti, D. T. (1989). Discrimination theory of rule-governed behavior. *Journal of the Experimental Analysis of Behavior, 51,* 259–276.

Chomsky, N. (1992). The media and the war: What war? In H. Mowlana, G. Gerbner, & H. I. Schiller (Eds.), *Triumph of the image: The media's war in the Persian Gulf—a global perspective* (pp. 51–63). Boulder, CO: Westview Press.

Clark, R. (1992). *The fire this time: U.S. war crimes in the Gulf.* Emeryville, CA: Publishers Group West.

Combs, J. E., & Nimmo, D. (1993). *The new propaganda: The dictatorship of palaver in contemporary politics.* New York: Longman.

Curran, J. (1978). *The British press: A manifesto.* London: Macmillan.

Curran, J., & Seaton, J. (1985). *Power without responsibility: The press and broadcasting in Britain* (2nd ed.). London: Methuen.

Deibel, M. (1996, September 13). Wage-earners see no headway, economists say. *The Commercial Appeal,* p. B7.

Delwiche, A. (1995). *Propaganda analysis home page.* [On-line]. Available: http://carmen.artsci.washington.edu/propaganda/home.htm

Dewey, J. (1934). Radio's influence on the mind. In J. A. Goydston (Ed.), *The later works, 1925–1954, Volume 9: 1935–1937.* Carbondale: Southern Illinois University Press.

Directory of corporate affiliations, 1996. (1996). New Providence, NJ: National Register Publication Co.

Extra (1991, May). p. 9 [quoted public statement of August 15, 1990].

Farquhar, J. (1991). The Stanford cardiovascular disease prevention program. *Annals of the New York Academy of Science, 623*, 327–331.

Fishbein, M., & Ajzen, I. (1975). *Belief, attitude, intention, and behavior: An introduction to theory and research.* Reading, MA: Addison-Wesley.

Flay, B. R. (1987a). Mass media and smoking cessation: A critical review. *American Journal of Public Health, 77*, 153–160.

———.(1987b). *Selling the smokeless society; 56 evaluated mass media programs and campaigns worldwide.* Washington, DC: American Public Health Association.

Frank, A. G. (1992). A third world war: A political economy of the Persian Gulf War and the new world order. In H. Mowlana, G. Gerbner, & H. I. Schiller (Eds.), *Triumph of the image: The media's war in the Persian Gulf—a global perspective* (pp. 3–21). Boulder, CO: Westview Press.

Glenn, S. S. (1991). Contingencies and metacontingencies: Relations among behavioral, cultural, and biological evolution. In P. A. Lamal (Ed.), *Behavioral analysis of societies and cultural practices* (pp. 39–73). New York: Hemisphere.

Goetz, T. (1996a, July 8). And now the documercial. *In These Times, 20 (17)*, 9.

———. (1996b, June 24). Squeaky wheels. *In These Times, 20 (16)*, 9.

Harris, M. (1964). *The nature of cultural things.* New York: Random House.

———. (1977). *Cannibals and Kings: The origins of cultures.* New York: Random House.

———. (1979). *Cultural materialism: The struggle for a science of culture.* New York: Simon & Schuster.

Hayes, L. J. (1996). Listening with understanding and speaking with meaning. *Journal of the Experimental Analysis of Behavior, 65*, 282–283.

Hayes, S. C. (1994). Relational frame theory: A functional approach to verbal events. In S. C. Hayes & L. J. Hayes (Eds.), *Behavior analysis of language and cognition* (pp. 9–29). Reno, NV: Context Press.

———. (1996). Developing a theory of derived stimulus relations. *Journal of the Experimental Analysis of Behavior, 65*, 309–311.

Herman, E. S., & Chomsky, N. (1988). *Manufacturing consent: The political economy of the mass media.* New York: Pantheon Books.

History Channel kills business series. (1996, June 8). *The Charlotte Observer*, p. 2D.

Hoynes, W., & Croteau, D. (1989, January/February). "Are You on the *Nightline* Guest List?" *Extra, 2 (1)*, p. 1.

———. (1990, Winter). All the Usual Suspects: *McNeil/Lehrer* and *Nightline. Extra, 3 (4)*, p. 1.

Jowett, G. S., & O'Donnell, V. (1992). *Propaganda and persuasion* (2nd ed.). Newbury Park, CA: Sage.

Lasswell, H. D. (1927). *Propaganda technique in the world war.* New York: Peter Smith.

MacArthur, J. R. (1992). *Second front: Censorship and propaganda in the Gulf War.* New York: Hill and Wang.

Malagodi, E. F., & Jackson, K. (1989). Behavior analysis and cultural analysis: Troubles and issues. *The Behavior Analyst, 12*, 17–33.

Malott, R. W. (1989). The achievement of evasive goals: Control by rules describing contingencies that are not direct acting. In S. C. Hayes (Ed.), *Rule-governed behavior: Cognition, contingencies, and instructional control* (pp. 269–322). New York: Plenum.

Malott, R. W., Whaley, D. L., & Malott, M. E. (1993). *Elementary principles of behavior* (2nd ed.). Englewood Cliffs, NJ: Prentice-Hall.

McChesney, R. M. (1993). *Telecommunications, mass media, and democracy: The battle for control of U.S. broadcasting.* New York: Oxford University Press.

McManus, J. H. (1994). *Market-driven journalism.* Thousand Oaks, CA: Sage.

Michael, J. (1980). The discriminative stimulus or S^D. *The Behavior Analyst, 3*, 47–49.

———. (1982). Distinguishing between discriminative and motivational functions of stimuli. *Journal of the Experimental Analysis of Behavior, 37*, 149–155.

———. (1993). Establishing operations. *The Behavior Analyst, 16*, 191–206.

Morgan, M., Lewis, J., & Jhally, S. (1992). More viewing, less knowledge. In H. Mowlana, G. Gerbner, & H. I. Schiller (Eds.). *Triumph of the image: The media's war in the Persian Gulf—a global perspective* (pp. 216–235). Boulder, CO: Westview Press.

Mowlana, H. (1992). Roots of war: The long road of intervention. In H. Mowlana, G. Gerbner, & H. I. Schiller (Eds.). *Triumph of the image: The media's war in the Persian Gulf—a global perspective* (pp. 30–49). Boulder, CO: Westview Press.

Newt and the dirty dozen. (1996, September/October). *Mother Jones, 21 (5),* 38.

Ottosen, R. (1992). Truth: The first victim of war? In H. Mowlana, G. Gerbner, & H. I. Schiller (Eds.), *Triumph of the image: The media's war in the Persian Gulf—a global perspective* (pp. 137–144). Boulder, CO: Westview Press.

Owen, B., & Braeutigam, R. (1978). *The regulation game: Strategic use of the administrative process.* Cambridge, MA: Ballinger.

Parenti, M. (1993). *Inventing reality: The politics of news media.* (2nd ed.). New York: St. Martin's Press.

Qualter, T. H. (1985). *Opinion control in the democracies,* New York: St. Martin's Press.

Rakos, R. F. (1991). Behavior analysis of socialism in Eastern Europe: A framework for understanding the revolutions of 1989. In P. A. Lamal (Ed.), *Behavioral analysis of societies and cultural practices* (pp. 87–105). New York: Hemisphere.

———. (1992). Achieving the just society in the 21st century: What can Skinner contribute? *American Psychologist, 47*, 1499–1506.

———. (1993). Propaganda as stimulus control: The case of the Iraqi invasion of Kuwait. *Behavior and Social Issues, 3*, 35–62.

———. (1995, May). Marshaling popular support for war: A behavior analysis of media manipulation. In P. A. Lamal (Chair), *Why are some swords sharpened while others are beaten into plowshares?* Symposium conducted at the meeting of the Association for Behavior Analysis, Washington, DC.

Schiller, H. I. (1992). Manipulating hearts and minds. In H. Mowlana, G. Gerbner, & H. I. Schiller (Eds.), *Triumph of the image: The media's war in the Persian Gulf—a global perspective* (pp. 22–29). Boulder, CO: Westview Press.

———. (1996). *Information inequality: The deepening social crisis in America.* New York: Routledge.

Schlinger, H. D. (1993). Separating discriminative and function-altering effects of verbal stimuli. *The Behavior Analyst, 16*, 9–23.

Seligman, M. E. (1995). The effectiveness of psychotherapies: The *Consumer Reports* study. *American Psychologist, 50*, 965–974.

Shoemaker, P. J., & Reese, S. D. (1991). *Mediating the message: Theories of influences on mass media content.* New York: Longman.

Sidman, M. (1994). *Equivalence relations and behavior: A research story*. Boston: Authors Inc. Publishers.

Skinner, B. F. (1971). *Beyond freedom and dignity*. New York: Knopf.

Some Canadians question dominance of major publisher. (1996, June 25). *Cleveland Plain Dealer*, p. 4C.

Sundberg, M., Michael, J., Partington, J. W., & Sundberg, C. A. (1996). The role of automatic reinforcement in early language acquisition. *The Analysis of Verbal Behavior, 13*, 21–37.

Top editors quit movie magazine. (1996, May 13). *Cleveland Plain Dealer*, p. 8D.

Turow, J. (1984). *Media industries: The production of news and entertainment*. New York: Longman

Webster's New Collegiate Dictionary (1961). Springfield, MA: G. & C. Merriam Co.

Who Spoke on the Gulf? (1990, November/December). *Extra,* p. 4.

12

A Behavioral View of the Visual Arts

P. A. LAMAL

In the more than quarter-century since B. F. Skinner's 1970 lecture on "Creating the Creative Artist," behavior analysts have had very little to say about the visual arts.[1] I would like to partially remedy that oversight. I will be attempting to accomplish two goals. First, I will attempt to subvert the widely and strongly held view that there is such a thing as universally good art. In the culture of the visual arts before the current postmodern era, it was often said that some person or other "has a good eye." If that means, as it invariably did, that having a good eye enabled one to discriminate good art from bad and mediocre art, the question arises as to what is good art. An important related question is whether good art is universally good or whether determinations about the value of artworks are relative to time and place.

My second goal is to apply some principles of behavior analysis to the behaviors of those persons involved in various ways in the visual arts. As is true with other arenas of human behavior, the activities of those who produce, evaluate, collect, and deal in artworks have been predominantly described in nonbehavioral terms. But an attempt at a behavioral approach to these practices is warranted and long overdue.

SOCIETIES AND VISUAL ARTS

The visual arts are often a matter of great concern to many members of societies. The Nazis, for example, devised a category of what they called "degenerate art," which they vilified and destroyed or sent out of Germany (Sauerlander, 1994). The rulers of the former Soviet Union and of China denigrated artworks that did not conform to what is known as the "socialist realist" school of art.

In the United States, the National Endowment for the Arts (NEA) has come under attack a number of times for supporting the work of certain artists. Some politicians periodically attack the NEA with the obvious expectation that the consequences of such behavior will be favorable for them. According to the group, People for the American Way, local attacks on artistic freedom are proliferating across the United States ("Challenges to Artistic Expression Growing on Local Level, Group Says," 1994): "in 60% of the cases, challengers enjoyed at least some successes in removing or restricting the funding of works they considered blasphemous, obscene, or politically incorrect" (p. 3A). Interestingly, nearly one-fourth of the complaints about artwork originated in those free marketplaces of ideas, college campuses.

How can one decide what kinds of art should be promoted, which artists should be positively reinforced for producing art, and what kinds of art should be discouraged, which artists should be punished, or at least not positively reinforced? If you were able to design a culture, on what grounds would you make such decisions? Are Norman Rockwell and Wassily Kandinsky of equal value? Why or why not? An art museum in Denmark exhibited six beheaded pigs left to rot in glass coffins. Is that good or bad art?

Perhaps you have a "good eye" and can reliably discriminate between good art and art that is only mediocre or that is unarguably bad. Or perhaps you know others who have a good eye and you can rely upon their recommendations about what art to promote and what art to discourage.

But the notion of a "good eye" is not without problems. A question that immediately presents itself is the origin of a good eye. Are some fortunate few born with a good eye, do they learn to have a good eye, or are both learning and genetic endowment responsible for a good eye?

There are lines of evidence and argument that militate against the very notion of a good eye and the related notion of good art. (Remember, a good eye is able to discriminate between good art and art that is not good.) One of these approaches stems from postmodernism and "cultural studies," which also reject the notion of a good eye. These programs share the behavior analytic view that art and its evaluation are culturally determined. But this agreement should not be read as meaning that behavior analysis, on the one hand, and postmodernism and cultural studies, on the other, necessarily have much in common. But a consideration of those questions is beyond the scope of this chapter.

Now, a usually unspoken corollary of the notions of good eye and good art is that a good eye picks out art that is *universally* good. That is, an exemplar of good art is assumed to be always and everywhere good. Its value as a good piece of art is unchanging.

The history of art, however, calls into serious question the concept of good art as being universally good. And, if there is no such thing as universally good art to be picked out, the concept of the good eye is seriously undermined.

Any number of art historians and critics have pointed out that the reputations of various artists and the value placed on their work have fluctuated over time.

The eminent art historian Haskell (1976), for example, wonders why collectors admired certain types of paintings "which had been of little interest a hundred years earlier, or neglected others which were to be passionately loved a hundred years later" (p. 3).

Haskell goes on to say that "there would be few lovers of the arts today who would deny that Piero Della Francesca or Caravaggio or Vermeer or Watteau painted 'excellent' pictures, though their very names were certainly unfamiliar or distasteful to" (p. 4) art lovers during part of the nineteenth century. Where were the good eyes during that part of the nineteenth century? According to Haskell (1976):

The nineteenth century . . . witnessed . . . a startling series of revaluations of the art of the past that have radically affected our appreciation and understanding to this day: whole schools such as the early Flemish and Italian, seventeenth-century Spanish and eigh-teenth-century French were, at different times, in different places, and in the eyes of different publics, restored to favor; while others, such as the Italian Baroque and the Italianate Dutch, were rejected as valueless and even pernicious, and individual artists were elevated to dizzy heights or degraded to the lowest abyss. (p. 21)

Also in nineteenth-century Europe, an extraordinary number of artists who are now considered great, including Constable and Turner, Delacroix, Millet, and Courbet, Monet and the Impressionists, Gauguin, and Van Gogh, met "with a degree of incomprehension and often savage hatred that to us is astonishing" (Haskell, 1987, p. 208). The denigration of these painters is astonishing because they could rarely be associated with any of the political, religious, social, or moral issues of their times.

The great changes in the esteem in which an artist might be held could occur in one's lifetime. For example, Haskell (1976) says that "It would just have been possible to have been brought up believing that an Annibale Carracci was a great artist, to live for many years dismissing him as a sterile eclectic, and to enjoy a ripe old age admiring his pictures once more" (p. 22). The now much-admired Lucian Freud was previously dismissed (Blackwood, 1993; Richardson, 1993).

Let me describe three contemporary examples of how quickly the value of artworks can change. The first involves prints. Prints by contemporary and modern artists have plummeted in value since the end of the 1980s' extremely bullish market for art. Some works are reported to have lost up to 80% of their former value (Tully, 1993).

The second example involves a dispute over the value of the estate left by Andy Warhol. A person with a claim on a percent of the estate has asserted that the estate is worth $827 million. The chief beneficiary of the estate, however, argued that the estate is worth only $220 million—because Warhol's popularity may soon wane. An eminent art dealer, testifying on behalf of the Warhol ben-eficiary (i.e., for the lesser value) had this to say:

If we go back in history, we come to artists who in their time were as fashionable and acclaimed as Warhol was in his time but who subsequently went through periods of total oblivion. . . . These are all artists who in their time were the most fashionable, the most popular artists, who within the span of a decade or so went into oblivion, to be rescued perhaps a decade or a few decades down the line. ("Andy Warhol: Fourteen Minutes and Counting," 1994, p. 24)

I would add that some formerly popular artists were never rescued from oblivion. In the Warhol case, the art dealer went on to say that it is always difficult to predict what our children will think of the art *we* like. "But we know that what they think will be different from what we think today ("Andy Warhol: Fourteen Minutes and Counting," 1994, p. 25).

My third example involves a postal clerk and a librarian, both now retired. Herbert and Dorothy Vogel lived on her librarian's salary and spent his postal clerk wages while amassing a collection of more than 2,000 pieces of minimalist and conceptual artwork by some of today's best-known artists. How in the world could the Vogels do this on their modest income? The answer is that the artists whose work they collected were not always well-known and their work was not always highly valued. The Vogels bought these art works "when the artists were young, their work sold cheap and everyone else was saying it wasn't art" (Lewis, 1994).[2] Now, with a few exceptions, this artwork is highly acclaimed and worth a great deal of money.

So, the concepts of a good eye and good art are refuted by evidence of the relativity of taste. Rather than good eyes picking out art that will be always and everywhere considered good (at least by connoisseurs), we find that context, the time and place in which art is evaluated, is paramount.

NONUNIVERSALLY GOOD ART

In lieu of the *strong position*, that is, of good eyes picking out universally good art, one might fall back on a *weak position*. According to this weak position, there is such a category as good art, but no claim is made that good art is *universally* good, that is, that it will be considered good always and everywhere. The good eyes, then, pick out that nonuniversally good art.

This weak position seems to me to be a more defensible position. But I am still bothered by the notion of a good eye. It is clear that in at least many cultures, including ours, there is decided disagreement about what may even count as *art*, much less count as good art. Rather, what we have is a collection of subcultures, each of which uses different sets of defining characteristics of art and good art. The behaviors of individuals belonging to different subcultures with respect to art and good art are shaped and maintained by different sets of contingencies and rules. The production of one kind of art may be positively reinforced in one subculture, but extinguished in another subculture. Thus it is not surprising to find that some people consider Elvis on black velvet to be good art, while others consider it a bad joke.

It is even less surprising, then, to discover that what is considered good art varies across cultures and within cultures as they evolve. Taste changes within cultures over time.

And what of the construct of "art"? What *is* art? To ask "what is art?" is to commit the essentialist fallacy of believing that there are one or more defining attributes that all artworks share. On the contrary, art is an open concept (Kennick, 1958). There are no ultimate canons to which one can justifiably appeal when deciding whether something is a piece of art or whether an artwork is or is not good.

One source of the essentialist fallacy is classical philosophy of language with its assumption of (1) correspondence between words and entities, and (2) essences. These assumptions lead, as Weitz (1964) puts it, to "the perennial quest for 'theories' in philosophy and the arts: for true, real definitions of different kinds of essence" (p. 222). For example, the true essence of visual artworks has been claimed by some to be expression, by others it has been claimed to be good form.

In a series of lectures, the famous art historian Kenneth Clark addressed the question "What Is a Masterpiece?" Clark (1979) took it that there *are* artworks that *are masterpieces*. He recognized that there were, and perhaps still are, people who maintain that the word "masterpiece" is merely the expression of a personal opinion. But to Clark, this view seems "to undermine the whole fabric of human greatness" (p. 5). Why the questioning of the construct of a masterpiece should have such a pernicious effect is not, however, made clear by Clark. According to Clark, a clear example of a masterpiece is Donatello's *Annunciation. Anyone*, Clark asserts, "who has looked for long at this sublime work will have experienced a series of deep and complex emotions" (p. 9). Absolutely no evidence is adduced in support of this claim.

It is helpful here to consider Weitz's (1964) useful distinction among three approaches to any artwork: description, explanation, and evaluation. Only description has truth-value. For example, if someone asserts that a certain painting includes certain colors, this can be determined to be either true or false. But it is a mistake to believe that all questions in art criticism are questions to which true or false answers can be given. That is, many questions in art criticism do not have truth-value.

Unlike descriptions of artworks, *explanations* (i.e., interpretations) can be challenged. The ideal interpretation (explanation) of an artwork can never be attained. As Weitz (1964) points out: "both *what* is to be explained and *how* it is to be explained are constant sources of dispute" (p. 258). For example, what is primary, central, or most important in an artwork?

Evaluation of artworks involves the application of criteria of artistic merit, the clarification of those criteria, and the justification of those criteria. So this is an attempt to establish rule-governed behavior. The principle is that if an artwork has certain properties, that is, it meets certain criteria, it should be responded to with approbation. To the extent that the artwork lacks those properties (fails to meet the criteria), we should not respond with approval.

Let us return to Kenneth Clark, addressing the question ''What Is a Master-piece?'' Clark says that masterpieces share certain properties. One property of a masterpiece, according to Clark, is that a masterpiece involves ''a confluence of memories and emotions forming a single idea'' (p. 10). A second character-istic of a masterpiece is said by Clark to be ''a power of recreating traditional forms so that they become expressive of the artist's own epoch and yet keep a relationship with the past'' (pp. 10–11). On Clark's view, there are masterpieces and there are *masterpieces*, because he goes on to assert that ''the *highest mas-terpieces are illustrations of great themes*'' (p. 20). This, presumably, is not a property of lesser masterpieces.

But the problem with evaluation is how to *justify* the criteria, how to justify the rules. On Weitz's (1962, 1964) view, *no* property has been shown on *any* ground, empirical, conceptual, or metaphysical, to be a necessary or sufficient property of artistic greatness. In the same vein, a recent writer (Ferry, 1993) asserts that ''One of the central problems of the philosophy of art is that of the criteria which permit us to assert or not that a thing is beautiful'' (p. 19). So even if we defer to the experts, the persons of taste, the problem is not solved. If the persons of taste disagree, who is to decide, and in the name of what, about the value of artworks? There is no universally agreed-upon standard or set of standards (i.e., rules) that is external to the experts' judgments. Hauser (1974/1982, chap. 4) also acknowledged this state of affairs.

Now, from time to time a consensus among experts in their evaluation of some works of art may be reached. But there is no guarantee that such a con-sensus will, or does, hold universally. Such a consensus is, however, important. Functioning as a rule, it can exert strong control over the behavior of artists, collectors, museum curators, and dealers. A well-known example involves so-called ''primitive'' or tribal art. After African tribal objects were displayed in the studios of such artists as Matisse and Picasso, such objects were sought after by some of the influential rich. Only after that did the objects begin to be displayed as art in museums (Halle, 1993). This example probably illustrates the importance of imitation as much as it does rule-governed behavior.

Thus, the evaluation of art has no set of defining properties of good art upon which it can rely. All a critic can do when his or her criteria of value (his or her rules) are challenged is to justify them by further reasons, which cannot be probative (Abrams, 1989). The upshot is that there is very little, if any, role for rules to play in controlling the behavior of art critics, artists, collectors, dealers, and viewers of art.

The designer of a culture will thus build in positive reinforcement for variation in the visual arts. Individuals will differ greatly in what they select as good art from this variation, and what may count as a good eye in one culture or sub-culture at one time may be considered a terrible eye in another culture or sub-culture at the same or other times. Good art is that which is selected from the variety available in any culture or subculture.

CONTINGENCIES AND THE VISUAL ARTS

What are the contingencies that are typically operative in the world of the visual arts? We can consider contingencies in effect for individuals belonging to different groups. These groups include: (a) artists, (b) viewers, (c) collectors, and (d) art dealers (and gallery owners). Let us consider the relevant contingencies in turn.

What are the contingencies of reinforcement with which artists are involved? One powerful reinforcer for most, if not all, artists seems to be the production of artworks. That is, artists seem to be positively reinforced by the fact that they simply *produce* artworks. The *process* of producing something in many cases seems sufficiently reinforcing to keep the artist behaving as an artist. Then the end product may or may not be more or less reinforcing to the artist.

Skinner (1957, chap. 16) maintained that in the world of literature a low level of self-editing by writers is encouraged. He described literary behavior as being characterized by license. "It is rich in verbal magic, trivial controlling variables, and multiple effects. . . . It is also rich in metaphor" (Skinner, 1957, p. 396). The same can be said of the visual arts. But reference to the low level of self-editing on the part of writers and artists should not be misunderstood. Just as many writers edit and revise their work very carefully, so too, many artists revise and discard during the process of creating artworks. What Skinner meant by a low level of self-editing was the freedom of the fiction writer from having to accurately describe the world. The same freedom is enjoyed by the visual artist. So the artist is not punished, and may be positively reinforced, for descriptions of the world that may be totally at variance with our knowledge of it.

Another potential source of positive reinforcement for the artist may be the responses of others to the artist's work. The responses of other artists, gallery owners, curators, and others knowledgeable about art to the artist's work may be highly reinforcing to the artist. Of course the converse is also true. The responses of others to his or her work may be punishing to the artist. Thus the artist may be much less likely to show his or her work to others. There is also another possible result. The artist may change his or her art in important ways as a result of punishing contingencies. The artist may self-edit analogously to self-edited verbal behavior (Skinner, 1957) by, for example, scraping a canvas.

An important audience for many artists is actual and potential viewers of their artwork. Many, but not all, artists are strongly reinforced by the favorable verbal responses of viewers. Many artists are also strongly reinforced when viewers buy their work. The positively reinforcing effect can be so strong that an artist whose work has sold well may continue to produce artwork that is very similar to the work that has sold. The writer was once told that a particular artist "has been painting the same picture for 20 years." Paintings by the artist in question had initially sold well, and he continued to produce paintings very similar to those. Conversely, artists whose work does not sell may change their work in significant ways, including producing work that others may denigrate as "commercial." It is also not unknown for artists to imitate the styles of other artists who have been critically and/or commercially successful.

According to Fitzgerald (1995), artists have usually been studied in isolation from the marketplace of which they were a part. But in Fitzgerald's view, this is a mistaken omission because many avant-garde artists of the latter nineteenth century as well as the twentieth century were actively involved in the business of the art marketplace. Renoir and Monet, for instance, worked to develop the market for their art. Van Gogh and Gauguin are often thought of as turning their backs on the potential reinforcers available in the art marketplace, but Fitzgerald maintains that "their attitude toward the marketplace was both considerably more complex and much less dismissive than might be assumed" (p. 8). Commercial contingencies were critical to the avant-garde artists. Unless dealers foresaw a chance to sell their work, the exhibitions of such artists as Matisse and Picasso would not occur. And there could be no favorable critical reception and publicizing of their work if it was not exhibited. So these artists were dependent upon galleries as important sources of positive reinforcement.

From his arrival in France, Picasso cultivated those who could develop his reputation and help to make him rich. He said early on that he had always wanted to be rich (Fitzgerald, 1995). In one of his first shows, in 1901, Picasso included portraits of the three backers of the exhibition. In Fitzgerald's view this was an attempt to curry the backers' favor. He also gave two other of his works to critics who wrote complimentary reviews of his show. This certainly appears to be a case of mutual positive reinforcement, and apparently was not uncommon among the avant-garde artists of the time. Artists' cultivation of influential individuals can be critical to the advancement of their careers. The society arbitress Eugenia Errazuriz, for example, counseled Picasso on his dress and behavior and paid many of his expenses during the very weak art market caused by World War I. "In thanks, Picasso seems to have given her two of his finest paintings from that period" (Fitzgerald, 1995, p. 70). He also cultivated patrons whom Errazuriz introduced to him in 1918 at her villa. Picasso flattered them by sketching pencil portraits of several of the women and gave Errazuriz a sketchbook in return for her hospitality. According to Fitzgerald, the extremely influential dealers Paul Rosenberg and Georges Wildenstein gave Picasso's work serious attention because they believed that their clients, influenced by such tastemakers as Errazuriz, would make him a success (and them money and prestige).

What we can thus discern in the careers of many, if not all, of the avant-garde artists is the operation of contingencies of reinforcement that importantly affected the behaviors of the artists, critics, dealers, and collectors. The details of the contingencies affecting the contemporary players in the culture of the visual arts may differ from those of an earlier time, but we can nevertheless be confident that contingencies are still operating.

Some artists have been concerned with making statements about the socio-political scene of their time. Francisco Goya is a well-known example of an artist who attempted (successfully) to portray the viciousness and stupidity of his time. Reitlinger (1961) noted the high value placed on "misery pictures" (e.g., by Millet) in the nineteenth century (p. 156). Robert Hughes (1993) has outlined his objections to the politicization of contemporary American arts. Clearly, some artists are reinforced by "making statements" about the dismal and unjust features of their societies. Often, the more shocking the statement, the better, in the sense that more shocking work is often more likely to receive more attention than less shocking work, and for many artists attention is doubt-less highly reinforcing. Again, this is not unique to contemporary American artists. Moulin (1967/1987) has pointed out that "the works of genius of the late nineteenth and early twentieth century regularly caused scandals. Since then there has been a great temptation to take anything that causes a scandal for a work of genius" (p. 24).

Artists now are often shown for what they represent rather than for what they have produced. "Victim art" has recently been fashionable and whatever is fashionable is the product at least in part of behaviors that have been reinforced. Museums are eager to exhibit victim art, dealers deal in it, some collectors presumably buy it, and viewers flock to galleries and museums to look at it. Also, under the influence of contemporary critical theory and the slow art market of the 1990s, ideas, rather than artworks, are salable. Much contemporary art (e.g., much installation art) is based on theory (rules), whereas theory was pre-viously often based on art. "If you can't sell pictures, you can still sell ideas" (R. Kirschbaum, personal communication, December 6, 1995). But yesterday's avant-garde artist is today's member of art tradition. The avant-garde of any particular time die out because they become banal. "The break with traditon itself becomes tradition" (Ferry, 1993, p. 196). But this occurs across genera-tions of artists.

I have not placed money in the forefront of artists' reinforcers for the reason that many artists are demonstrably *not* highly reinforced for doing art by the consequence of money. We all know the names of the superstars of the world of the visual arts, but of course the superstars constitute only a tiny percentage of artists. Some other artists do make a living solely on their production of artwork, but most do not. Most artists must support themselves in other ways, teaching being perhaps the most common.

So money is not a reinforcer controlling the behavior of most artists most of the time.

What about viewers? What contingencies are operative for those who look at art relatively frequently? Skinner's (1957) discussion of the literary audience is relevant.

Many readers may be reinforced by the emotional effects that accompany their reading. Such emotional effects may also be reinforcing to viewers of art. With the necessary changes, Skinner's (1957) interpretation concerning the reader may also apply to the viewer of art:

A text [artwork] is a world in which one behaves with a minimum of effort, not only because of the promptings and probings . . . or because the "right" book [artwork] for a given reader [viewer] strengthens just that behavior which is strong, but because the behavior can usually be emitted without editing. . . . The book [artwork] itself and the act of reading [viewing] constitute a tolerant situation in which verbal behavior is freely emitted. (p. 398)

Often, perhaps all we can say is that the viewer is simply reinforced by looking at an artwork—that is it. With other viewers we may find a preference, sometimes very strong, for certain kinds of art. One big divide among viewers is between those who prefer representational art and those who prefer abstract art.[3] Individuals' preferences for different styles of art have long been speculated about by those of a psychodynamic orientation (e.g., Kris, 1952; Machotka, 1976). In another approach, a number of studies have reported correlations between preferences for various styles of art and responses to personality scales (e.g., Juhasz & Paxon, 1978; Kloss & Dreger, 1971; Tobacyk, Myers, & Bailey, 1981). From a behavior analytic viewpoint, these are reports of response—response relationships. As Heinrichs and Cupchik (1985) noted, such personality measures rarely account for more than a small amount of the variance in preferences for various kinds of paintings.[4] Rather than being concerned with the effect of supposed personality traits or other constructs on individuals' art preferences, behavior analysts would assume that individuals' histories would be the predominant factor accounting for differences in such preferences. And there are groups of individuals who share important life experiences, such as formal education in art appreciation and art history. Even within this group, differentiations can be made among those with varying degrees of such education. And of course, most people have no formal postsecondary arts education. Thus in contemporary American society there are a number of taste cultures, the most common formulation being highbrow, middlebrow, and lowbrow. Finer distinctions can, however, be made. For example, Gans (1975) identified five American taste cultures, each with its own art. Taste cultures are distinguished by certain behaviors of their members; for example, by what they watch on television, by the frequency with which they visit various kinds of museums and attend various kinds of concerts, and by what they read. But members of a particular taste culture occasionally behave in ways characteristic of the behavior of members of a higher or lower taste culture. For example, some members of a lower culture may visit an art museum. This is not to say, however, that they will change their evaluations concerning what is good art. The major difference among taste cultures is the socioeconomic level of their members. And education is the most important variable of the set (income, occupation, education) determining socioeconomic level, that in turn is highly positively correlated with those behaviors defining taste.

An important discrimination can be made between experienced (informed) and naive viewers of art. There is a qualitative difference between the behaviors of informed and naive viewers (Cupchick & Gebotys, 1988; Winston, 1992). The latter prefer representational art, which may elicit pleasant associations (Martindale, 1984). Informed viewers, in contrast, respond to such sensory properties of pictures as color, texture, and the composition of the work. At the same time, however, it can be misleading to generalize about the preferences of groups of people. The pitfalls of group designs are well-known to behavior analysts. Halle's (1993) caveat is well taken: "many seemingly clear examples of differences in 'taste' between social classes turn out, on examination, to be elusive and hard to pin down" (p. 55). Halle, for example, found that landscapes were the most popular pictures among all the social classes he studied. Also, perhaps many viewers are reinforced by looking at art with which they are familiar, or about which they have some prior information. ("I remember reading about *Guernica* in my art appreciation class, and here I am actually seeing it!")

Collectors are probably reinforced for the same reasons that other viewers are. Unlike run-of-the-mill viewers, however, collectors may be more *strongly* reinforced by looking at certain artworks. Avid collectors seem to experience strongly reinforcing effects when obtaining sought-after artworks (Price, 1989). They are also willing and able to undergo the cost entailed in collecting artwork.

One class of collectors is more reinforced by the possible monetary consequences of collecting artworks. These collectors are really more accurately described as investors than the kind of collectors just referred to. Many of these collectors are institutions or businesses. The monetary considerations can be considerable, as illustrated by the go-go atmosphere of the 1980s. Three examples of paintings sold at auction during the period 1987–1990 are illustrative.

During this period, van Gogh's *Self-Portrait* sold for $26,400,000. But that ain't nothing; that piece was the *least* expensive of the ten most expensive paintings sold during that period. Renoir's *Au Moulin de la Galette* sold for $78,100,000. The top price was paid for van Gogh's *Portrait of Dr. Gachet*— $82,500,000 (Watson, 1992). So there was a good deal of that generalized reinforcer, money, changing hands.

And some of the hands into which that money was going belonged to art dealers and gallery owners. Obviously, art dealers and gallery owners are reinforced for selling art. But at least in some cases they are also reinforced for helping to create a market for certain kinds of art—art they have for sale.

Some gallery owners and art dealers have been known to buy the work of artists whose work they have for sale, in an attempt to increase the value of that work. Established gallery owners also, of course, advertise the work of the artists they represent. Because there is an overabundance of the supply of artwork, there is a continuing filtering-out process, and gallery owners function as gatekeepers, discriminating between those artworks that will come to the attention of collectors, critics, and the wider public, and those that will not.

It would be misleading, however, to leave the impression that all gallery owners are reinforced solely by the sale of art. The case can be made that there are two kinds of galleries, "those which conceive of themselves as primarily cultural institutions and those which conceive of themselves primarily as businesses" (Bystryn, 1989, p. 179). The first kind tends to provide its artists with social reinforcement, while the second provides more monetary reinforcement. The first kind of gallery may serve a gatekeeping function for the second kind, by giving artists their first show and providing for their first media coverage. The second kind of gallery then selects from this group, based to a large extent on the gallery owners' judgment of the artists' marketability. The selected artists are then heavily promoted. Also, contra the notion of artists as solitary geniuses, they are, with rare exceptions, actively engaged in the promotion of their art (Ridgeway, 1989). This has perhaps accelerated during the weak 1990s art market (e.g., Tomkins, 1995).

CONCLUSION

I have tried to illustrate that a behavioral approach to the visual arts is possible. In particular, I have tried to show that a behavioral approach brings into serious question the idea of universally good art. I have also considered some relevant reinforcement contingencies controlling certain behaviors of the members of the culture of the visual arts.

NOTES

I thank Robert Kirschbaum, Pauline Dove Lamal, and Dorothy and Herbert Vogel for helpful comments on an earlier draft of this chapter.

1. The behavior analytic studies concerned with training creativity and involving mostly children (Winston & Baker, 1985) fall outside the scope of this chapter.

2. The Vogels use the term "inexpensive," rather than "cheap." Also, according to them, many people, not "everyone else" were saying it was not art (D. Vogel, personal communication, October 21, 1995).

3. See Avital (1992) for a questioning of the very notion of abstract art.

4. See Arnheim (1992) for a denigration of preference studies.

REFERENCES

Abrams, M. H. (1989). *Doing things with texts: Essays in criticism and critical theory.* New York: Norton.

Andy Warhol: Fourteen minutes and counting. (1994, April). *Harper's Magazine*, pp. 24–25.

Arnheim, R. (1992). But is it science? In G. C. Cupchik & J. Laszlo (Eds.), *Emerging visions of the aesthetic process* (pp. 27–36). New York: Cambridge University Press.

Avital, T. (1992). The complementarity of art and design. In G. C. Cupchik & J. Laszlo (Eds.), *Emerging visions of the aesthetic process* (pp. 64–82). New York: Cambridge University Press.

Blackwood, C. (1993, December). Portraits by Freud. *The New York Review of Books*, 18–19.

Bystryn, M. (1989). Art galleries as gatekeepers: The case of the abstract expressionists. In A. W. Foster & J. R. Blau (Eds.), *Art and society; Readings in the sociology of the arts* (pp. 177–189). Albany: State University of New York Press.

Challenges to artistic expression growing on local level, group says. (1994, March). *The Charlotte Observer*, p. 3A.

Clark, K. (1979). *What is a masterpiece?* New York: Thames and Hudson.

Cupchik, G. C., & Gebotys, R. J. (1988). The search for meaning in art: Interpretive styles and judgments. *Visual Arts Research, 14*, 38–50.

Ferry, Luc (1993). *Homoaestheticus: The invention of taste in the democratic age.* Chicago: University of Chicago Press.

Fitzgerald, M. C. (1995). *Making modernism; Picasso and the creation of the market for twentieth century art.* New York: Farrar, Straus, and Giroux.

Gans, H. J. (1975). *Popular culture and high culture.* New York: Basic Books.

Halle, D. (1993). *Inside culture: Art and class in the American home.* Chicago: University of Chicago Press.

Haskell, F. (1976). *Rediscoveries in art.* Ithaca, NY: Cornell University Press.

———. (1987). *Past and present in art and taste.* New Haven: Yale University Press.

Hauser, A. (1982). *The sociology of art* (K. J. Northcott, Trans.). Chicago: University of Chicago Press (original work published 1974).

Heinrichs, R. W., & Cupchik, G. C. (1985). Individual differences as predictors of preference in visual art. *Journal of Personality, 53*, 502–515.

Hughes, R. (1993). *Culture of complaint.* New York: Oxford University Press.

Juhasz, J. B., & Paxon, L. (1978). Personality and preference for painting style. *Perceptual and Motor Skills, 46*, 347–349.

Kennick, W.E. (1958). Does traditional aesthetics rest on a mistake? *Mind, 67*, 317–334.

Kloss, M. G., & Dreger, R. M. (1971). Abstract art preferences and temperament traits: A study in the psychology of aesthetics. *Journal of Personality Assessment, 35*, 375–378.

Kris, E. (1952). *Psychoanalytic explorations in art.* New York: International Universities Press.

Lewis, J. A. (1994, June 5). A prescient present. *The Washington Post*, pp. G1, G6, G7.

Machotka, P. (1976). The functions of taste: Toward a workable theory. *Scientific Aesthetics, 1*, 107–119.

Martindale, C. (1984). The pleasures of thought: A theory of cognitive hedonics. *Journal of Mind and Behavior, 5*, 49–80.

Moulin, R. (1987). *The French art market: A sociological view.* (A. Goldhammer, Trans.) New Brunswick, NJ: Rutgers University Press (original work published 1967).

Price, S. (1989). *Primitive art in civilized places.* Chicago: University of Chicago Press.

Reitlinger, G. (1961). *The economics of taste: The rise and fall of picture prices 1760–1960* (Vol. 1). London: Barrie & Rockeliff.

Richardson, J. (1993, December 13). Paint becomes flesh. *The New Yorker*, 135–137, 139–143.

Ridgeway, S. (1989). Artistic groups: Patrons and gatekeepers. In A. W. Foster & J. R. Blau (Eds.), *Art and society: Readings in the sociology of the arts* (pp. 205–220). Albany: State University of New York Press.

Sauerlander, W. (1994, April). Un-German activities. *The New York Review of Books*, pp. 9–13.

Skinner, B. F. (1957). *Verbal behavior.* New York: Appleton-Century-Crofts.

———. (1970). Creating the creative artist. In *On the future of art* (pp. 61–75). New York: Viking.

Tobacyk, J., Myers, H., & Bailey, L. (1981). Field dependence, sensation-seeking, and preferences for paintings. *Journal of Personality Assessment, 45,* 270–277.

Tomkins, C. (1995, December 11). London calling. *The New Yorker*, 115–117.

Tully, J. (1993, September). *Art News*, pp. 39–40.

Watson, P. (1992). *From Manet to Manhattan.* New York: Random House.

Weitz, M. (1962). Reasons in criticism. *Journal of Aesthetics and Art Criticism, 20,* 429–437.

———. (1964). *Hamlet and the philosophy of literary criticism.* Chicago: University of Chicago Press.

Winston, A. S. (1992). Sweetness and light: Psychological aesthetics and sentimental art. In G. C. Cupchik & J. Laszlo (Eds.), *Emerging visions of the aesthetic process* (pp. 118–136). New York: Cambridge University Press.

Winston, A. S., & Baker, J. E. (1985). Behavior analytic studies of creativity: A critical review. *The Behavior Analyst, 8,* 191–205.

Index

About the Contributors

DONALD M. BAER is the Roy A. Roberts Distinguished Professor at the Department of Human Development at the University of Kansas. He has served often on many research-review panels and journal editorial boards. He has received awards from the Burlington Northern Foundation, the Northern California Association for Behavior Analysis, the Florida Association for Behavior Analysis, Divisions 25 and 33 of the American Psychological Association, and the Association for Behavior Analysis.

JANNETTE Y. BERKLEY is pursuing her Ph.D. in Developmental and Child Psychology in the Department of Human Development at the University of Kansas in Lawrence. She is a Research Associate of the Work Group on Health Promotion and Community Development of the Schiefelbusch Institute for Life Span Studies. Her research interests include community psychology, adolescent health issues, and promotion of academic and personal success of African-American adolescents.

ANTHONY BIGLAN is a research scientist at Oregon Research Institute. He was trained as a clinical and social psychologist. For the past fifteen years he has been doing research on the prevention of adolescent smoking and other problem behavior. He recently published a book entitled *Changing Cultural Practices: A Contextualist Framework for Intervention Research*. His most recent work has involved experimental evaluations of community interventions to reduce youth problem behavior.

W. FRANK EPLING is Professor of Psychology at the University of Alberta, Edmonton, Alberta, Canada. He is co-author with W. David Pierce of *Activity*

Anorexia: Theory, Research, and Application, Conditioning and Learning, and *Solving the Anorexia Puzzle: A Scientific Approach.* He is the author of numerous articles and book chapters on behavior analytic topics.

STEPHEN B. FAWCETT holds an endowed professorship at the University of Kansas where he is Kansas Health Foundation Professor of Community Leadership and University Distinguished Professor of Human Development. He is also Director of the Work Group on Health Promotion and Community Development of the Schiefelbusch Institute for Life Span Studies. A former VISTA volunteer, he worked as a community organizer in public housing and low income neighborhoods. Dr. Fawcett has been honored as a Fellow in both Division 27 (Community Psychology) and Division 25 (Experimental Analysis of Behavior) of the American Psychological Association. He is co-author of nearly 100 articles and book chapters and several books in the areas of health promotion, community development, empowerment, self-help, independent living, and public policy. Dr. Fawcett has been a consultant to a number of private foundations, community partnerships, and national organizations, including the MacArthur Foundation, the U.S. Commission on National and Community Service, the Institute of Medicine of the National Academy of Sciences, and the U.S. Centers for Disease Control and Prevention.

ROLLEN C. FOWLER is a Research Assistant at Oregon Research Institute. He was trained as a school psychologist and is a Ph.D. candidate in special education at the University of Oregon. Rollen's professional and research interests include the application of instructional and curricular design principles to teaching social skills, school-wide behavioral support, applied behavior analysis, and proactive instructional strategies to reduce classroom misbehavior.

VINCENT T. FRANCISCO is Associate Director of the Work Group on Health Promotion and Community Development, and Courtesy Assistant Professor with the Department of Human Development, University of Kansas. He is co-author of several research articles in prevention of substance abuse and cardiovascular disease. He is also a co-author on several manuals for community development in the areas of strategic planning and evaluation of prevention initiatives. Dr. Francisco has been a consultant for a variety of organizations including private foundations, community coalitions and advocacy organizations, and governmental agencies.

JOEL GREENSPOON is Visiting Research Professor in the Department of Behavior Analysis at the University of North Texas. He is the author of numerous articles and book chapters dealing with a variety of behavior analytic topics, and is a Fellow of the Division of the Experimental Analysis of Behavior of the American Psychological Association.

BARBARA GUNN is a Research Associate at both Oregon Research Institute in Eugene, Oregon, and the National Center to Improve the Tools of Educators (NCITE). She has published on approaches to teaching phonological awareness to first-grade students and the effects on word recognition and applications of instructional design to teaching phonological awareness to beginning readers. She is a co-author of "Emergent literacy: Curricular and instructional implications for diverse learners," in E. J. Kameenui and D. Carnine (Eds.), *What Reading Research Tells Us about Children with Diverse Learning Needs: The Bases and the Basics.*

MELBOURNE F. HOVELL is a Professor in the Graduate School of Public Health at San Diego State University (SDSU). He is also the Director of the Center for Behavioral Epidemiology and Community Heatlth at SDSU. He has published in the areas of behavioral medicine and public heath, including the prevention of tobacco use, secondhand smoke exposure, HIV and STDs, violence, and in the promotion of exercise and other healthy lifestyle practices.

BLAIR IRVINE has training in health education, exercise physiology, and biology. He is an Adjunct Research Scientist at Oregon Research Institute, a Research Scientist at the Oregon Center for Applied Science in Eugene, and is President of the Dolphin Biology Research Institute in Sarasota, Florida. His research in the last decade has focused on implementation of programs for at-risk families to improve parenting skills in nonclinical sites, on the use of multimedia technology to facilitate changes in health behaviors, and on studies of the behavioral ecology of a dolphin herd.

CATHERINE KRULL is an Assistant Professor of Demography in the Department of Sociology at the University of Nebraska at Omaha. She has published articles and book chapters on demographic issues related to the province of Quebec, Canada. A recent publication on suicide in Quebec appeared in *Social Forces* (1994). Dr. Krull is currently writing a book on demographic change and the survival of French Canadian culture in Quebec for the Canadian Population Studies Series, Oxford University Press.

RICHARD E. LAITINEN is Assistant Professor of Special Education at the University of Memphis. He has published both basic and applied research articles, book chapters, and educational materials in the area of moderate and severe disabilities. His current interests include investigating ways in which the media can be used to promote broader social awareness, acceptance, and participation of persons with disabilities.

P. A. LAMAL holds a Ph.D. from the University of Wisconsin-Madison. He has taught at SUNY College at Potsdam and at the University of North Carolina at Charlotte, and is the author of numerous articles and book chapters. He is also the editor of *Behavioral Analysis of Societies and Cultural Practices*, a member of the editorial board of three journals, a Fellow of the American Psychological Association (Division of Experimental Analysis of Behavior), and Emeritus member of the University of North Carolina at Charlotte Psychology Department.

CHRISTINE M. LOPEZ is a doctoral student in the Department of Human Development at the University of Kansas. She is also a research associate for the Work Group on Health Promotion and Community Development of the Schiefelbusch Institute for Life Span Studies at the University of Kansas. She provides technical assistance to community initiatives that address issues of health promotion, such as reducing adolescent substance abuse. Ms. Lopez's major interest is community-based research in the areas of substance abuse, youth violence, and health promotion in rural settings.

JENNIFER L. MAGNABOSCO is a doctoral candidate in Social Policy and Administration in the Columbia University School of Social Work.

MARK A. MATTAINI is an Associate Professor at Columbia University School of Social Work, Chair of the Walden Fellowship, Inc., and Director of the Musher Seminar Series on Science and Human Behavior. He is the author/editor of *More Than a Thousand Words: Graphics for Clinical Practice, The Foundations of Social Work Practice: A Graduate Text* (with Carol H. Meyer), *Finding Solutions to Social Problems: Behavioral Strategies for Change* (with Bruce A. Thyer), *Clinical Practice with Individuals*, and related articles and chapters. Current research involves constructing alternatives to social coercion through cultural design.

CAROL W. METZLER received a Ph.D. in Clinical Psychology from the University of Oregon in 1990. She is now a Research Scientist at the Center for Community Interventions on Childrearing at Oregon Research Institute. Dr. Metzler has authored and co-authored papers on the social context for high-risk sexual behavior and other problem behaviors in adolescents, and on the ways in which existing knowledge about the effectiveness of family and school interventions to reduce conduct problems may be utilized to reduce the prevalence of problem behavior in whole communities.

LARRY NACKERUD received a Ph.D. in Human Service Studies from Cornell University in 1991. He is an Assistant Professor of Social Work with the University of Georgia. The implications of social welfare and immigration policy is his primary area of research. He currently teaches at all three levels of the curriculum, B.S.W., M.S.W., and Ph.D.

JOHN A. NEVIN received a Ph.D. in Experimental Psychology from Columbia

University in 1963, and taught at Swarthmore College until 1968. He then returned to Columbia, where he was Professor and Department Chair. He was
Professor of Psychology at the University of New Hampshire, serving as Department Chair and as editor of the *Journal of the Experimental Analysis of
Behavior*. He is now Professor Emeritus of Psychology. He has published over
80 articles and book chapters on reinforcement processes, stimulus control, and
signal detection. He has also published several articles on behavioral interpretations of war making. His current work focuses on the momentum of rewarded
behavior and the implications of behavioral momentum for clinical, educational,
economic, and social issues.

W. DAVID PIERCE is Professor of Behavior Analysis in the Department of
Sociology, Director of the Centre for Experimental Sociology and Adjunct Professor of Neuroscience, Faculty of Medicine, at the University of Alberta. His
research has emphasized the experimental analysis of choice and preference and
a biobehavioral model of activity anorexia. Dr. Pierce has published more than
sixty articles in behavioral, physiological, and social psychological journals and
books. He is co-author with W. Frank Epling of the textbook *Behavior Analysis
and Learning* and the edited volume *Activity Anorexia: Theory, Research, and
Treatment*.

RICHARD F. RAKOS is Chair and Professor of Psychology at Cleveland State
University. He has published extensively in the areas of assertive behavior, behavioral self-management, law and psychology, and behavior analysis of societal
phenomena. Professor Rakos is the author of *Assertive Behavior: Theory, Research, and Training* and numerous book chapters and articles in professional
journals. He is a behavioral therapist who maintains an active private practice.

JULIE RUSBY is currently a school intervention specialist for the Community
Action for Successful Youth (CASY) Project at the Oregon Research Institute.
She also is a doctoral candidate in the school psychology program at the University of Oregon. Her recent work includes the development of training mod-
ules for the management and prevention of behavioral problems in the preschool
setting. Ms. Rusby has co-authored several coding systems for observing children's and adolescents' social interactions.

STERGIOS RUSSOS is a doctoral student in the Department of Human Development and a Research Associate of the Work Group on Health Promotion
and Community Development of the Schiefelbusch Institute for Life Span Studies at the University of Kansas. He completed the M.P.H. degree in Health
Promotion at the Graduate School of Public Health at San Diego State University. His research is focused on clinical and community-based preventive
medicine, tobacco control, youth development, and cardiovascular disease prevention.

TED K. TAYLOR is an Adjunct Research Scientist at the Oregon Research Institute. He has recently completed a randomized outcome study comparing traditional treatment in children's mental health with the Parents and Children Series program, an empirically validated, group-based parenting program.

MIYAKO TAZAKI received a Ph.D. from the University of Kansas, and is an Assistant Professor at the Science University of Tokyo. Her work for the World Health Organization (WHO) has resulted in a number of publications.

BRUCE A. THYER is Professor of Social Work and Adjunct Professor of Psychology at the University of Georgia, and an Associate Clinical Professor of Psychiatry and Health Behavior at the Medical College of Georgia.

DENNIS R. WAHLGREN is a Senior Research Associate at the Center for Behavioral Epidemiology and Community Health at San Diego State University, and also at the Pain Research Program at the San Diego VA Healthcare System. He has published in the areas of behavioral medicine and public health, including the prevention of tobacco use, secondhand smoke exposure, HIV and STDs, and also in the areas of asthma and chronic back pain.

KATHERINE WALLER graduated from Georgia College in 1992 with a B.M.E. degree. She was previously employed as a senior caseworker with the Department of Family and Children's Services in Walton County, Georgia.

R. JEFFERSON WALLER is a doctoral student at the University of Georgia School of Social Work, where he completed his M.S.W. in 1993. He is presently employed as a house parent with Families First, a family social service agency serving the Atlanta area.

ISBN 0-275-95776-4

9 780275 957766

HARDCOVER BAR CODE